# Coming to Terms

Published in cooperation with the
*Bulletin of Concerned Asian Scholars*

# COMING TO TERMS

## Indochina, the United States, and the War

EDITED BY

## Douglas Allen
## and Ngô Vĩnh Long
University of Maine

## WESTVIEW PRESS
Boulder • San Francisco • Oxford

Cover photo by Ngo Vinh Long

Published in 1991 in the United States of America by Westview Press, Inc., 5500 Central Avenue, Boulder, Colorado 80301, and in the United Kingdom by Westview Press, 36 Lonsdale Road, Summertown, Oxford OX2 7EW

A CIP catalog record for this book is available from the Library of Congress.
ISBN 0-8133-1222-1
ISBN 0-8133-1249-3 (pbk.)

Printed and bound in the United States of America

The paper used in this publication meets the requirements of the American National Standard for Permanence of Paper for Printed Library Materials Z39.48-1984.

10    9    8    7    6    5    4    3    2    1

# Contents

**PART THREE**
**Films and Scholarly Literature on Vietnam**

# Preface

This book had its roots in a special project for the *Bulletin of Concerned Asian Scholars*. When the editorial board of the *Bulletin* sought a theme for its twentieth anniversary issue, we proposed a comprehensive and widely accessible overview of Indochina, the United States, and the war. This was published as a triple-sized issue of the *Bulletin* in December 1989.

*Coming to Terms* is significantly different from the special issue of the *Bulletin of Concerned Asian Scholars*, however. This book has been designed as a text, to be used by a much broader and more varied readership than the general readers and area specialists who read the *Bulletin*. As a result, most of the original articles have been revised, and entirely new articles on postwar Vietnam and U.S. veterans have been added as well as chronologies and a selected bibliography. Not included are the anniversary issue's material about *BCAS*, interview with Daniel Ellsberg, course syllabi, and article on how to teach about the war.

We appreciate the efforts of our authors, most of whom had to be more flexible and more understanding and had to devote much more time and effort than they anticipated when they agreed to do a chapter for this volume. Rather than soliciting manuscripts from Indochina scholars in terms of their current research interests, we usually asked authors to formulate entirely new manuscripts consistent with the rationale of this book as formulated in our Introduction. Individual authors, both because of their own concerns and their commitment to this project, devoted a tremendous amount of time and energy to their manuscripts.

Special thanks must be given to Bill Doub, Nancy Doub, and Jay Dillon, without whose dedication the *Bulletin of Concerned Asian Scholars* could not survive, much less flourish. They worked tirelessly with us on the anniversary issue of the *Bulletin* and have provided invaluable assistance in working on this book. We are indebted to John Spragens and others who donated their photographs for this book. We also thank other editors of the *Bulletin* and other colleagues and friends, too many to name, who have encouraged us and have given us valuable input while we worked on the book project. Finally, we deeply appreciate the contributions of editor Susan McEachern at Westview

Press. Her conscientious review of material, constructive and insightful suggestions, and cooperative attitude in working with us have formed what for us has been an ideal authors-editor relationship.

*Douglas Allen*
*Ngô Vĩnh Long*

# Abbreviations

| | |
|---|---|
| AAS | Association for Asian Studies |
| ARVN | Army of the Republic of Vietnam |
| ASEAN | Association of Southeast Asian Nations |
| CCAS | Committee of Concerned Asian Scholars |
| CIA | Central Intelligence Agency |
| CMEA | Council for Mutual Economic Assistance (USSR) |
| COINTELPRO | (a U.S. program of infiltration and subversion of antiwar movement organizations by FBI agents and informants) |
| Comecon | (see CMEA) |
| CPK | Communist Party of Kampuchea (Khmer Rouge) |
| CPV | Communist Party of Vietnam |
| DK | Democratic Kampuchea |
| DMZ | demarcation zone |
| DRV | Democratic Republic of Vietnam |
| EC | European Community |
| FBI | Federal Bureau of Investigation |
| GDP | gross domestic product |
| GNP | gross national product |
| GVN | Government of Vietnam |
| ICP | Indochinese Communist Party |
| IDA | Institute for Defense Analysis (U.S.) |
| IRC | Indochina Resource Center |
| IVS | International Voluntary Services (U.S.) |
| KPNLF | Khmer People's National Liberation Front |
| KPRP | Khmer People's Revolutionary Party |
| LPDR | Lao People's Democratic Republic |
| LPF | Lao Patriotic Front (Neo Lao Hak Sat) |
| LPLA | Lao People's Liberation Army |
| LPP | Lao People's Party |
| LPRP | Lao People's Revolutionary Party |
| MACV | Military Assistance Command, Vietnam (U.S.) |
| MIA | missing in action |
| MIT | Massachusetts Institute of Technology |
| MSUGV | Michigan State University Group in Vietnam |
| NEZs | New Economic Zones |

| | |
|---|---|
| NLF | National Liberation Front for the Liberation of South Vietnam (Viet Cong) |
| NLHS | Neo Lao Hak Sat (Lao Patriotic Front [LPF]) |
| NPCC | National Political Consultative Council (Laos) |
| NSA | National Student Association |
| NSC | National Security Council (U.S.) |
| OSS | Office of Strategic Services (U.S.) |
| PAVN | People's Army of Vietnam (North Vietnam) |
| PDPE | Party Department of Propaganda and Education (Vietnam) |
| PGNU | Provisional Government of National Union (Laos) |
| PL | Pathet Lao |
| POW | prisoner of war |
| PRC | People's Republic of China |
| PRG | Provisional Revolutionary Government of South Vietnam |
| PRK | People's Republic of Kampuchea |
| PTSD | post-traumatic stress disorder |
| RLG | Royal Lao Government |
| RVN | Republic of Vietnam |
| SANE | Committee for a SANE Nuclear Policy (U.S.) |
| SDS | Students for a Democratic Society (U.S.) |
| SEATO | Southeast Asia Treaty Organization |
| SIU | Southern Illinois University |
| SNCC | Student Nonviolent Coordinating Committee (U.S.) |
| SPU | Student Peace Union (U.S.) |
| SRC | Southeast Asia Resource Center (U.S.) |
| SRV | Socialist Republic of Vietnam |
| UN | United Nations |
| USAID | U.S. Agency for International Development |
| USOM | U.S. Operations Mission (in Laos, Vietnam, and Cambodia) |
| VA | Veterans Administration (U.S.) |
| VBI | Vietnamese Bureau of Investigation |
| VC | Viet Cong (Vietnamese Communists or NLF) |
| VVAW | Vietnam Veterans Against the War (U.S.) |

Douglas
Allen
&
Ngô Vĩnh
Long | # Introduction

Sixteen years after the end of the Indochina War, the longest and costliest war in U.S. history, there remains a need to come to terms with that historically decisive experience. For those of us in the United States, there has been a tendency to avoid learning the invaluable, but politically, culturally, and psychologically difficult lessons of the war. The Indochina War is either ignored or distorted and mythologized.

Most of our students and other Americans of their generation are uninformed about Vietnam and Indochina, their limited images often gained from a Rambo rewriting of history or more recent Hollywood movies focusing on the suffering and victimization of U.S. soldiers. The few persons they may see on television discussing the lessons of the war tend to be the Nixons and Kissingers, repeating the same falsehoods and self-justifications that contributed to the U.S. disgrace in Indochina in the 1960s and early 1970s.

In many different ways, it has been equally difficult for the peoples of Indochina to confront the consequences of the war. One can speak of the tremendous economic, social, and psychological consequences of the war for the United States. But these pale in comparison with the economic, ecological, social, psychological, medical, and cultural devastation inflicted on the Indochinese peoples as well as the political factionalism, wars, economic embargos, and other hardships largely the aftermath of the Indochina War.

It is our view that in order to grasp the meaning and significance of the Indochina War—how the region was radically transformed by that experience, and how we live in a very different post–Indochina War world—we must gain some general perspective, some historical and cultural overview of that war. Such a comprehensive understanding is now rare. This book tries to provide such an overview.

In this regard, many of us have repeatedly noticed a serious void when examining publications on Indochina, the United States, and the war. A student, uninformed but curious about U.S. policy during the Indochina War

1

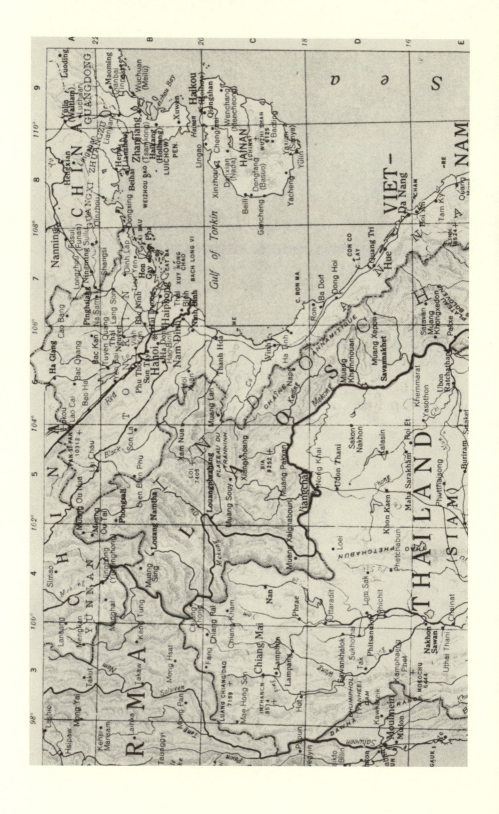

*Map of Kampuchea (Cambodia), Laos, Vietnam, Thailand, and Malaysia. Source: from the* Cosmopolitan World Atlas, *copyright © 1991 by Rand McNally. R.L. 91-S-23. Reprinted with permission.*

or U.S. relations toward Indochina since 1975, may ask us to recommend one good survey article with background information on the history, lessons, and present situation. Another student, confused about the ongoing fighting and other contemporary developments in Cambodia, asks for a reading that presents the general background and analysis necessary for gaining some understanding of Norodom Sihanouk, the Khmer Rouge, and U.S. policy. A teacher, offering a course on the literature of the Vietnam War or an Asian studies course in which one or two weeks are devoted to Indochina, asks for a few articles that will provide students with a broad historical and cultural foundation. We usually reply that we know of no such publications.

There are, of course, some excellent publications on the war. Gabriel Kolko's *Anatomy of a War*, for example, is a brilliant scholarly work, and George McT. Kahin's *Intervention* provides invaluable analysis and detail on how the United States became involved in Vietnam. Nayan Chanda's *Brother Enemy* is a well-written insightful study tracing the origins of the relations and conflicts between Vietnam, Cambodia, China, and the United States in the postwar period of 1975 until 1979. But most students and general readers have neither the time nor motivation to read such demanding or lengthy studies. And most other highly specialized books, of course, do not include the desired comprehensive overview.

One of the consequences of this absence of progressive, widely accessible, scholarly literature on the United States and Indochina has been to make it easier for the U.S. government and the mass media, sometimes working with scholars who have a long history of complicity in U.S. governmental, military, and corporate policies, to rewrite the history of the Indochina War and to undo the valuable lessons learned through many years of painful struggle.

In this book, we avoid narrow and technical studies directed primarily to a readership of specialized scholars and instead include a general introduction, a comprehensive overview, and a summary of the lessons of the Indochina War and its aftermath that are accessible not only to Asia specialists but also to students and general interested readers. Our aim is to present the most significant background information, systematic formulations, and penetrating interpretations about Vietnam, Cambodia, and Laos, the relation of U.S. Indochina policy to U.S. policy at home and throughout the world, the antiwar movement, veterans, the literature, and movies on Vietnam.

In Part 1 we focus on all of Indochina and its struggle for independence and avoid a common Western exclusive focus on "the Vietnam War." Through separate articles, chronologies, and bibliographies, we show that Vietnam, Cambodia, and Laos each have their own histories, cultures, problems, and struggles for independence. At the same time, readers will realize that these societies and states cannot be understood in isolation. They have had common problems, histories, and complex interactions as part of an Indochina significantly shaped by the shared experiences of French colonialism, Japanese occupation, and U.S. intervention.

We also placed Indochina first because of our concern with a typical Western exclusivism, provincialism, and ethnocentrism, often reflecting racist and imperialist attitudes toward the rest of the world. Westerners rarely attempt to look at the war from the perspectives of the Indochinese people or to examine the devastating consequences of the war on postwar Indochina. Instead, when the Indochina War is not totally evaded in Western literature and discussion, there is usually a total U.S. focus: whether or not Washington was justified in its policies and actions, the effects of the war on the United States, the need for the United States to overcome "the Vietnam syndrome," concern for the plight of U.S. veterans, and so forth.

The authors of this book provide more balance so that many Indochinese voices can be heard. We consider the first four chapters, under the Indochina heading, along with the fifth chapter (by Noam Chomsky), to be the indispensable foundation of our book in presenting a comprehensive overview of Indochina, the United States, and the war. The first two chapters on Vietnam are by Vietnamese; the chapters on Cambodia and Laos are by Americans who have lived for many years in Cambodia and Laos, empathize with Indochinese perspectives, and are very critical of Western ethnocentrism and imperialism.

Ngo Vinh Long, Vietnamese historian and leading antiwar critic, formulates what may be the only comprehensive essay on Vietnam that exists. He documents and analyzes the Vietnamese struggles for independence from the earliest stages of French colonialism in the 1850s, through U.S. interventionism beginning in 1946, and through the postwar years from 1975 up to the present.

Ngo Vinh Hai, an economic journalist in Vietnam during the war and postwar period, analyzes different stages of economic development and problems in Vietnam from 1975 to the present, providing us with insights largely absent from the official Vietnamese press and Western writings.

Michael Vickery, author of two books on contemporary Cambodia, offers a broad and inclusive overview of Cambodia's historical development. His chapter sheds considerable light on the origins of contradictions within Cambodia and the outside forces that perpetuate the tragedy that has befallen the Cambodian people.

Randall and Carol Ireson, who first worked in Laos from 1967 to 1969 and returned in the 1980s, present a general picture of early Laotian history continuing through the colonial and postwar struggles for independence. They conclude by focusing on contemporary issues and problems, especially those that affect village life.

Part 2 includes four chapters on the United States and the Indochina War. Noam Chomsky, the world's most influential linguist and a leading critic of U.S. foreign policy, contributes a bold and penetrating interpretation of U.S. policy in Indochina and argues that it was far from an aberration. He traces the roots of U.S. actions in Indochina to earlier domestic and foreign policies and shows the consistency of the Indochina experience with postwar U.S. policies throughout the world.

George Vickers, sociologist and a leader in the antiwar movement, debunks many of the contemporary myths about the U.S. antiwar movement, formulates a comprehensive history of its origins and development, and concludes by delineating some of the major "lessons" of the Indochina War for the United States.

Douglas Allen, professor of philosophy and antiwar activist, explores many of the relations between scholars of Asia and the Indochina War. He shows how Asia scholars were both an integral part of and active opponents of the U.S. war effort and how the war affected the lives and careers of those scholars, many of whom now do research and teach courses on the Indochina War.

Kevin Bowen, a Vietnam War veteran and codirector of the Joiner Center for the Study of War and Social Consequences, provides both a personal and historical account of the experience of the war from the perspective of U.S. veterans. He also presents the postwar history of changing images, personal struggles, and attempts at healing and reconciliation by U.S. veterans.

Part 3, "Films and Scholarly Literature on Vietnam," shows that the Hollywood films and most of the books are not so much about Indochina as about the United States and the U.S. experience of Indochina. Indochinese voices are rarely heard.

Jenefer Shute, professor of modern literature and film, analyzes recent so-called antiwar films. She shows that these tremendously popular films focus our attention on the victimization of U.S. soldiers; they present complex and subtle messages, hardly antiwar, and obscure the basic issues and lessons of the Indochina War.

Gaylyn Studlar and David Desser, professors of film studies, focus on the more right-wing Rambo phenomenon, providing much-needed psychological, cultural, and historical analysis of its incredible popularity. They show how the Rambo-type symbolic and mythic rewriting of history fulfills deep psychological needs and contributes to the evasion of the lessons of the war.

Marvin Gettleman, historian and editor of probably the best-selling book on Vietnam during the war, formulates a broad essay on three generations of English-language Vietnam literature from the 1950s to the present. In a creative rewording of "Cartesianism," he directs our attention to the past historical truth of "I invade you, therefore you exist" and the need to overcome such a limited and distorted imperialist perspective.

It is our hope that this book will serve as a catalyst for our students and others to think more critically than most of our generation did when the United States was first getting into and then escalating its involvement in the Indochina War; that the book will burst open some of the closed parameters of debate and reflection that prevent us from exploring the meaning and lessons of the Indochina War; and that it will move the peoples of the United States and Indochina toward finally coming to terms with the war in ways that allow for greater understanding, healing, and reconciliation and for more equitable and just relations.

# PART ONE

# Indochina and Its Struggle for Independence

# 1

## Ngô Vĩnh Long | Vietnam

Vietnam is a country of about 128,000 square miles (332,000 square kilometers) stretching more than 1,200 miles (1,930 km) from the southern boundary of China along the eastern coast of the Indochinese Peninsula and curving into the Gulf of Siam between the eighth and ninth parallels. About 80 percent of the country is mountainous, and about 90 percent of its population has been living in the lowland areas for a long time. In fact, the bulk of Vietnam's population—which increased from an estimated 10 million at the time the Vietnamese court surrendered all of Vietnam to the French in 1884 to about 21 million by the beginning of World War II, then to close to 53 million by the time of the last census in 1980 and to more than 65 million in 1989—has been crowded into the two proverbial rice baskets of the Red River Delta in the north and the Mekong River Delta in the south.

The central part of the country, traditionally referred to by the Vietnamese as the shoulder pole for carrying the two rice baskets, is a narrow strip of land that extends from near the nineteenth to the twelfth parallel. It has such poor soil and an unfavorable climate that many of the people there must make a living from the rock quarries and the salt fields. In this region dogs are said to eat stones and chickens rock salts (*cho an da ga an muoi*). Worse still, on this narrow strip of land from 1965 until the end of 1972 the United States dropped more than 2 million tons of bombs—about equal to the total amount of bombs dropped on all fronts during World War II—and delivered about 3 million tons of high explosives through artillery strikes as well as hundreds of thousands of tons of chemicals. The resulting destruction has kept population density there much lower than that in the northern and southern regions.

In the country as a whole, however, the result of the unprecedented destruction by the bombings (close to 5 million tons) and the artillery strikes (about 7 million tons) is that there is now only about one acre of cultivated

This chapter is a revised version of Ngo Vinh Long, "Vietnam: The Real Enemy," *Bulletin of Concerned Asian Scholars* 21, nos. 2–4 (April–Dec. 1989), pp. 6–34. Reprinted with permission.

surface for every six to seven Vietnamese. Although about 3 million acres of land have been reclaimed since 1975 at great cost in both financial and human terms, millions of tons of unexploded mines and ammunition still lie buried. In the southern half of the country where the United States declared that it came to "nation-build," U.S. bombing—which amounted to over 1,000 pounds of explosives for each man, woman, and child—was heavily responsible for over 10 million refugees and up to 2 million deaths out of a total estimated population of 19 million by 1972.[1]

What seems quite fantastic to most observers of Vietnam is how such a tiny nation, which is so stretched out geographically and economically, could have stood up to the U.S. military onslaught. What made the population there fight on in spite of such tremendous destruction and dislocation? The explanation by U.S. policymakers and mainstream scholars has been that the South Vietnamese had been coerced and terrorized by the North Vietnamese Communists and their henchmen in the South, the Vietcong. The North Vietnamese, in turn, were egged on by the Red Chinese. U.S. President Lyndon B. Johnson, for example, explained on 7 April 1965, "Over this war—and all Asia—is another reality: the deepening shadow of Communist China. The rulers in Hanoi are urged on by Peking."[2]

It has been convenient for U.S. policymakers and mainstream historians to refuse to acknowledge the real enemy in order to justify the U.S. war effort as well as the failure of that effort, but many serious students of Vietnamese history have realized over the years that the total disregard of the realities of Vietnam had doomed the U.S. intervention from the start. Joseph Buttinger, a noted Vietnam historian and an early mentor of President Ngo Dinh Diem of the so-called Republic of Vietnam ("South Vietnam," as U.S. policymakers have called it since 1954, although no Vietnamese anywhere ever used the term themselves), wrote in 1977:

> It is bad enough not to take into consideration that the Vietnamese people had struggled for over two thousand years against being absorbed by China, and had for almost one hundred years fought against colonial rule in order to regain independence. Much worse still was not to know, or knowingly to disregard, the fact that as a result of French colonial policies in Indochina the whole of Vietnam had become Communist by the end of World War II.
>
> I say the whole of Vietnam, not only the North—something which, in spite of thirty years of French and American propaganda, remains an undeniable historical fact.[3]

**FRENCH CONQUEST AND CONSEQUENCES: 1850–1945**

Although a number of books have detailed the long struggle of the Vietnamese against the French that finally led to the triumph of the revolutionary forces in 1945,[4] it is necessary to summarize a few pertinent facts here in order to give the reader a background for a better understanding of developments since the end of World War II.

On 31 August 1850 a French naval squadron came to the central part of Vietnam and attacked the port city of Da Nang, partly because it was accessible by sea and partly because it was only about thirty-five miles (fifty-six km) south of the imperial city of Hue. This started a war of colonial conquest that, aided by the policy of appeasement by the Vietnamese court, resulted in the takeover of the country in stages until its total annexation by the French in 1884. There were at least three reasons for the appeasement policy. First, the Nguyen court at the time was so unpopular that there was an average of 400–600 revolts and peasant uprisings against it per year. Hence the court wanted to reserve all its resources and energy for putting down these uprisings, which it perceived as the main threats to its survival. Second, the court did not fully understand the intentions of the French, thinking that since they came from so far away they would be interested only in obtaining certain trade advantages rather than conquering the country and occupying it by force. Third, the imperial forces, which marched in tight formations into battles, were no match for the long-range French rifles and cannons, and so the court thought it should avoid casualties for its own troops as well as buy time by making compromises with the French. But appeasement only whetted the appetite of the French, and as a result they kept on forcing the court to make one territorial concession after another, starting with the southern provinces of the Mekong Delta.

The people and the scholars continued to fight back, however, using guerrilla tactics to frustrate the French, in spite of the fact that the court, under treaty obligations to the French, ordered all popular resistance groups to withdraw from the conceded provinces. The quality of the popular resistance can be seen in the following account of a French historian and eyewitness in 1861, at the beginning of the intense armed struggle in the Saigon–Bien Hoa area, foreshadowing the experiences that U.S. troops were to encounter more than 100 years later:

One would like to put the finger on the main cause for the appearance of these bands which, during the rainy season, seemed to circulate freely around our columns, behind them when they advanced, ahead of them when they returned to their point of departure. They seemed to come up out of the ground. We imagined that there must be some central point from which they fanned out, some point where they had food and other supplies. That is why we concentrate on Bien Hoa. After Bien Hoa—Vinh Long. The fact is that the center of resistance was everywhere, subdivided *ad infinitum*, almost as many times as there were Annamites. It would be more exact to consider each peasant fastening a sheaf of rice as a resistance center. The trouble with fighting on a terrain where the enemy can live and hide is that the war becomes personal; it changes its aim and name—and becomes repression.[5]

From 1861 to 1897 popular armed struggles organized by various scholars and local leaders raged on in spite of a combination of repression by the French and the court. But since the court had betrayed the people and robbed them of the only possibility for unified actions on a nationwide scale, almost all popular armed struggles were suppressed by 1897. From then until the beginning of World War I the French were able to firmly establish their colonial structures for the political domination and economic exploitation of the country.[6]

Administratively the French divided Vietnam into three regions, or "countries" (*pays*) as they called them (see Map). The southern region, which extends from the southernmost tip of the peninsula to the twelfth parallel and which was now called Cochin China, became a direct French colony and was ruled by a French governor. The central region and northern region, renamed Annam and Tonkin, respectively, became "protectorates"—in other words, the French "residents" in Hue and Hanoi were now supposedly ruling these regions through the Vietnamese court and the traditional elites. In fact, however, they had stripped the court of almost all of its power, including all residual rights over the land.

## LANDGRABBING AND LANDLESSNESS

In the century before the French arrived, the distribution of wealth in the country was not as equitable as the names of the Nguyen land policy suggested: "equal-field land system" or "personal share land system." Nevertheless, every family had land to till that it could call its own. As soon as the French occupied a certain area after fierce struggles with the local populace, they confiscated the land belonging to the locals and gave this land to themselves and their Vietnamese "collaborators." Tens of thousands of acres of peasants' lands changed hands this way. Many of the French owned from 3,000 to 70,000 acres of land. But even after several decades of expropriation and usurpation by the French and their Vietnamese collaborators, most peasants still owned their own land.

After the turn of the century, however, the French and the collaborators increased their theft of peasants' land. Rice exporting was the biggest and most profitable way of making money for the French and the Vietnamese ruling class. By the 1920s and 1930s over half of the peasants in Tonkin and Annam were completely landless, and about 90 percent of those who owned any land owned next to nothing. In Cochin China about 75 percent of the peasant population was landless, and the majority of the current landowners (who were nearly 80 percent of all landowners) now owned almost nothing. According to official French statistics, at least 44 percent of the land in Tonkin, 39 percent of the land in Annam, and 88 percent of the land in Cochin China was owned by landlords.

Because most Vietnamese peasants became landless or nearly so, they had to work as agricultural laborers and as tenant farmers and sharecroppers. Agricultural workers were paid wages. Most of them owned no land and were unable to become tenants or sharecroppers. Most of the small landlords used agricultural workers, and many medium and all big landlords used tenant farmers and sharecroppers. By the late 1920s and early 1930s tenant farmers and sharecroppers worked about half of the cultivated surface in Tonkin and Annam. French estimates showed that in Cochin China some 80 percent of

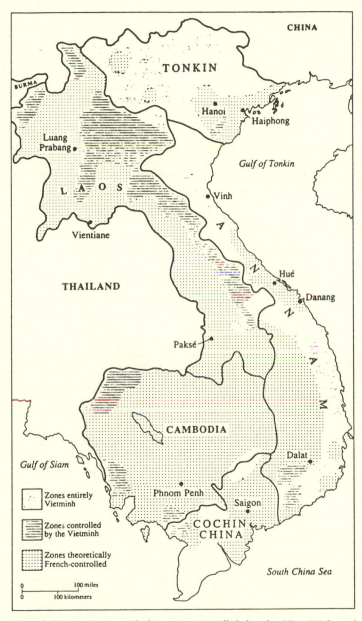

CHINA

TONKIN

Hanoi

Haiphong

Gulf of Tonkin

Luang
Prabang

BURMA

L A O S

Vinh

Vientiane

THAILAND

Hué

Danang

Paksé

A   N   N   A   M

CAMBODIA

Dalat

Gulf of Siam

Phnom Penh

Saigon

COCHIN
CHINA

South China Sea

Zones entirely
Vietminh

Zones controlled
by the Vietminh

Zones theoretically
French-controlled

0        100 miles
0      100 kilometers

*General Navarre's map of the areas controlled by the Viet Minh and theoretically controlled by the French in 1953. The map also shows the three divisions of Vietnam established by the French in the nineteenth century. (Map courtesy of Ngo Vinh Long.)*

the paddies were worked by tenants and sharecroppers. A large portion of the remainder was worked by wage laborers.

In Tonkin, and generally in Annam, tenant farmers had to give the landlords approximately half their gross income (in cash or in kind, depending on the terms) and had to pay for all the expenses of cultivation. The sharecropper, meanwhile, had to pay from 50 to 70 percent of his crops, besides all production costs. In addition, there were expensive gifts and services to landlords. Tenant farmers and sharecroppers who did not bring gifts or provide services frequently fell out of favor.

In Cochin China, the terms of tenancy were as bad as in the other regions. There was relatively little sharecropping; tenancy was the ubiquitous fact of life. Rents typically ranged from 50 to 70 percent of the tenants' crops and yet, as Le Thi Huynh Lan, a woman reporter for *Phu Nu Tan Van* [New literature on women] wrote in 1929, that was not enough:

> But this is not all, since the landlords do not let the tenants go freely tilling the land and gathering the paddies to pay the rent. They force the tenants to work for a whole month without any compensation. They force them to borrow 50 piasters which is to be paid by 100 *gia* [forty liters each, or 300 piasters at the current price] of paddy rice at harvest time [that is, six months later]. They force them to present white rice for offerings during holidays in the fifth months. . . .
>
> When the harvest comes, the landlords send their thugs to guard the threshing grounds. As soon as the rice is threshed, the thugs clean up everything. What is left for the tenants are the piles of hay. All they can do is hold their brooms and rakes and look on with tears in their eyes. . . . Any tenant who lacks good manners [that is, those who protest] would immediately have his house pulled down and would be evicted from the estate. . . . What I have just told you is only one-tenth of what actually happens. There are many more things piling up on the tenants' heads. . . .[7]

The situation in Annam and Tonkin was summarized by Truong Chinh and Vo Nguyen Giap, who later became the secretary general of the Vietnamese Communist Party and defense minister of the Democratic Republic of Vietnam, respectively, in their detailed account of the working and living conditions of the Vietnamese peasants:

> Every year the agricultural worker must go hungry for seven or eight months, the poor peasants for five or six months, and a number of middle peasants are short of food for three or four months. During these months they eat just one meal a day, sometimes one meal every two days. They eat . . . anything they can find to fill their stomachs. In the countryside near harvest time we see emaciated, pale faces with glassy eyes, foam-specked lips. These are the faces of hunger; the poor with bloodless faces carry a sickle looking for work.[8]

## REASONS FOR HUNGER

One reason for this sorry state of affairs was that there were few employment opportunities outside of the agricultural sector. Another reason was the horrible pay and working conditions in the mines, plantations, and industrial and commercial enterprises. In 1929, the peak year for employment during the colonial period, French official sources listed 52,000 workers in all Indochinese mines, 81,000 workers in the agricultural plantations, and 86,500 workers in all other industrial and commercial enterprises throughout Indochina.[9] There were actually many more workers than the official statistics showed because the French records counted only card-holding employees, while in fact two or three employees sometimes held one card. This was because each worker was responsible for about seventeen hours of work a day.[10] No one worker could maintain this pace. Family members, relatives, and friends had to substitute at least twice a week.[11] But even if the number of workers was two or three times larger than the official French estimate, this was still too small to make a difference in terms of absorbing the unemployed rural laborers. Besides, as colonial statistics testify, even a very "active" card-holding worker (in other words, several persons working one job) received an annual income of only 44 piasters in Tonkin, 47 piasters in Annam, and 55 piasters in Cochin China during the late 1920s, which was barely enough for the rice consumption of a single person.[12] Even a dog belonging to a colonial household cost 150 piasters a year to feed.[13]

Besides underemployment, there was chiseling. The workers explained this situation in a letter to the editor published in the 5 December 1936 issue of *Dong Phap* (Eastern France):

Each male worker gets a little more than two dimes [20 cents] to three dimes a day and a woman or girl worker gets only 18 cents. Even so, when the time comes for us to receive our pay we seldom get the full amount. The larger parts of our wages are taken by the supervisors and foremen . . . [and] our salaries are already too low. How can we survive with all these fines and cuts? Moreover, food prices increase every day and we have become hungrier and hungrier.

A number of Vietnamese studies have shown that 37 to 50 percent of some workers' earnings were taken.[14]

Even without the cuts, fines, and various types of "squeeze" by the supervisors and foremen, Vietnamese workers never actually received their full daily wages. Colonial capitalists did not pay wholly in cash. A large part of wages came in goods like rotten rice, decaying fish, and spoiling vegetables and greens at prices far above market rates. The price of these goods was automatically deducted from wages. Workers who did not go to the company stores to pick them up would lose their money.[15]

In the mines and plantations, workers also had to pay for living in shacks built by the companies. The usual charge was at least a month's pay. Workers also paid for all their tools—hoes, hammers, baskets—and paid for damages. In the mines and rubbber plantations workers were also frequently severely punished for even the slightest "infractions" and hence they called these places "hell on earth." Few escaped from that hell. The usual punishment for workers who ran away was death by torture, hanging, stabbing, or some other means that made examples of the "criminals." Because of this—and overwork, inadequate food, and terrible housing—the mortality rate was about 30 percent according to the rubber companies' own records. By the end of World War II the workers stopped calling the plantations "hell on earth" and substituted the name "slaughterhouses." The mining areas also became known as "death valleys" by those who worked there. French and Vietnamese descriptions generally indicate that the workers there suffered more deprivation and poverty than their counterparts in the plantations. Usually peasants did their best to stay away from the mines and plantations altogether, even though they had to subject themselves to unemployment and hunger as already described above.[16]

In 1945, in an article entitled "The Starvation Crisis of the People," a famous Vietnamese agronomist wrote:

> All through the sixty years of French colonization our people have always been hungry [original italics]. They were not hungry to the degree that they had to starve in such manners that their corpses were thrown up in piles as they are now. But they have always been hungry, so hungry that their bodies were scrawny and stunted; so hungry that no sooner than they finished with one meal than they started worrying about the next; and so hungry that the whole population had not a moment of free time to think of anything besides the problem of survival.[17]

**REVOLUTIONARY STRUGGLES: THE FIRST THIRTY YEARS**

In spite of the overwhelming social and economic difficulties described above, by the mid-1920s several revolutionary groups began to organize peasants, workers, and intellectuals in the struggle against the colonial regime and its collaborators. On 3 February 1930, at a unification meeting in Kowloon (China), the three Communist parties of Vietnam merged into a single party under the name of the Vietnam Communist Party (Dang Cong San Viet Nam). The meeting had been convened on 6 January by Nguyen Ai Quoc (later President Ho Chi Minh). The meeting adopted a political program, strategy, and shortened rules as well as regulations and strategy for the development of mass organizations such as workers' associations, peasants' associations, Communist Youth League, Women's Association for Liberation, the Red Relief Society, the Self-Defense Militia, and the Anti-Imperialist Alliance. In its political program, the Party stated that anticolonialism and antifeudalism (in other words, struggle against the landowning Vietnamese ruling class) were the principal and inseparable tasks of the revolution.[18] The Party subsequently changed its name to Indochinese Communist Party (ICP) and soon emerged as the undisputed leader of the Vietnamese revolution. From 1930 to 1931, under the banner of independence and democracy, the ICP organized and coordinated massive peasant demonstrations and workers' strikes in most parts of the country. In the southern part peasant struggles broke out in fourteen out of a total of twenty-one provinces and, in spite of brutal French repression, lasted for over a year. In the central part, as a result of the firm worker-peasant alliance brought about by the ICP, struggles against the French not only broke out in many provinces but seizure of administrative power also occurred in the two provinces of Nghe An and Ha Tinh. It took the French colonial administration over a year, with the deployment of divisions of soldiers and airplanes and with the use of "pacification methods" such as crop destruction, relocations, and starvation, to be able to reoccupy the two provinces.[19]

As a result of the arrest and imprisonment of some 16,000 persons, most of whom were Communist cadres, and the death of thousands of village inhabitants, the revolutionary movement in Vietnam under the leadership of the ICP suffered a period of setbacks during the Depression years of 1932–1934. Beginning in 1935, the Party began to rebuild its organizations and infrastructures and began a new period of struggles called the "1936–1939 democratic campaign." During this period the Party trained millions of people in the struggle against the French colonial administration, fascism, and war, and for democratic liberties, the improvement of the people's living conditions, and the maintenance of world peace. Whereas the Communist Party exerted its leadership mainly over the workers and peasants during the 1930–1931 period, it was now extending its leadership to other strata of the urban and rural population. As a result, a broad democratic front was created and a nationwide movement of unprecedented political struggles was achieved. Tactically, a combination of illegal, semilegal, and legal activities were employed. Thousands of party cells were formed all over the country, hundreds of organizations of all types were set up, and an average of five hundred demonstrations and strikes were staged every year. As a result, by the time World War II was about to begin, the revolutionary movement in Vietnam was already well prepared politically and organizationally, both in the towns and in the countryside.[20]

## LOOMING WAR AND WORSENING OPPRESSION

The danger of war and of Japanese aggression had become evident to the ICP in 1938. Right after the Munich Conference of September 1938, for example, the Regional Executive Committee of the ICP in the northern region of Vietnam decided to send many of its cadres into the countryside to carry out underground work and to set up bases in anticipation of enemy repression that would come mainly in the towns. In October 1938, the ICP, in a public manifesto, denounced France and Great Britain for their policy of capitulation to fascist pressures, called attention to the danger of Japanese aggression, and exhorted all groups and social strata, including the democratic French, to join the ICP-sponsored Indochinese Democratic Front in order to fight for freedom, peace, improvement of the people's living conditions, and the defense of Indochina. Effective defense of Indochina, the ICP maintained, could only be achieved with increased democratic liberties and decreased exactions by big colonial interests.

The French colonial administration, however, was at this time largely interested in the defense of the mother country, France itself. In 1938 it forced the Vietnamese population to buy 40 million piasters worth of bonds in order to buy war materiel for France. Early in 1939, 10 million piasters of new taxes were levied to build air bases and finance other war preparations. Paris also decided that Indochina should supply France with 1.5 million soldiers and workers, or fifteen times as many as the number required during World War I. It was also early in 1939 that the Japanese occupied Hainan Island, about 150 miles from the Vietnamese port of Haiphong, and advanced their troops in mainland China southward, close to the Vietnamese border. The bankrupt policy of the French, therefore, only served to rally more and more people into the ranks of the ICP.

On 1 September 1939, fascist Germany attacked Poland. On 3 September, France and Great Britain declared war on Germany. As World War II started, democratic and progressive movements in the colonies were subject to swift and merciless repression. In Indochina, the French colonialists immediately issued a series of decrees dissolving all democratic organizations and closing down all progressive newspapers. Since the ICP was the only party that had developed a comprehensive program as well as solidly built bases, it became the focal point of French terrorism and repression. On 4 January 1940, in a speech before the Indochinese Government Council, Governor General Georges Catroux explained the reason for the attack on the ICP: "We have launched a total and swift attack against the communist organizations; in this struggle, it is necessary to annihilate the communists so that Indochina may live in peace and remain loyal to France. We have no right not to win. The state of war forces us to act without mercy."[21]

To ensure that Indochina remained loyal to France, the French colonial administration increased the Indochinese armed forces to 100,000 and doubled the number of police and security service agents. Scores of so-called "camps of special laborers" were also quickly set up to detain thousands of political prisoners and "communist suspects." As soon as the war started, Paris ordered Indochina to supply France with 3.5 million metric tons of foodstuffs, 800,000 tons of tea, coffee, and sugar, 600,000 tons of rubber, and 300,000 tons of cable. Existing taxes were increased, and new taxes and duties were imposed. The budget of Indochina almost doubled, from 80 million piasters for 1938 to 134 million for 1940. Workers' wages were reduced drastically; working hours were increased to 72 hours a week and strictly enforced as a result of the 10 April 1939 decree by the governor general of Indochina. In the countryside, peasants were subjected to ever-worsening exploitation and oppression. Rents, interest rates, and taxes were increased; peasants' lands were expropriated; peasant males were rounded up to serve in the military and perform corvée (unpaid, forced) labor; paddy, boats, carts, and horses were requisitioned; and rice and maize crops were uprooted so that the land could be used for planting jute and castor-oil plants. By the end of 1939, tens of thousands of Vietnamese soldiers and workers had been sent to France. In the first eight months of 1940 another 80,000 Vietnamese youths were shipped to France to become cannon fodder.[22]

## DOUBLE COLONIZATION AND LIBERATION

On 10 May 1940 Hitler attacked France. A month later the French ruling class capitulated to the German fascists, declaring Paris an "open city." Two million

French soldiers were disarmed and a puppet government headed by Marshal Philippe Pétain was set up at Vichy. The French defeat caused great confusion among the colonialists in Vietnam. Any attempt whatsoever to resist Japanese aggression fizzled out, and the colonial administration readily yielded to all Japanese demands. On 22 September 1940, the Japanese attacked Lang Son (about 15 miles [24 km] south of the Vietnam-China border) and landed 6,000 troops at Do Son (near Haiphong). After some minor engagements with the Japanese near the Vietnam-China border, Governor General Jean Decoux surrendered Indochina to the Japanese.

Faced with these great changes in the internal and international situation, on 8 February 1941 Ho Chi Minh returned to Vietnam to assume direct leadership of the Vietnamese revolution. Ho made Pac Bo (Cao Bang Province) his base of operation. In May 1941 he convened the eighth plenary session of the IPC's Central Committee in Pac Bo, which decided that the most urgent task at the time was to liberate the country from Franco-Japanese domination. To this end, Ho Chi Minh proposed to change the name of the National Front Against the French and Japanese Fascists into Vietnam Independence League (Viet Nam Doc Lap Dong Minh or Viet Minh for short) to rally all social classes and political and religious groups. For the next four years, until May 1945, the IPC and its Viet Minh Front (adopting as its emblem the gold-starred red flag that had first appeared in the Mekong Delta in 1930) concentrated their efforts in setting up ever-increasing numbers of guerrilla bases and in expanding their infrastructure among the population to include even the landlords and bourgeoisie to fight against the French and the Japanese.

The struggle against the French and the Japanese from 1941 until 1945 required extremely patient organizing because these foreigners would not stop at any means to try to destroy the revolutionary movement. An example was the policy of rice collection, the purpose of which, as resident Jean Chauvet of Tonkin expressed it, was to cause hunger and starvation among the population in order to dampen their revolutionary spirit as well as to bring in the necessary food supplies for the French themselves and the Japanese. The result of this policy was an unprecedented famine that killed 2 million persons out of a total population of about 8 million in the northern region alone.[23] The famine conditions in Tonkin were described in the 28 April 1945 issue of *Viet Nam Tan Bao*, a Hanoi newspaper, as follows:

When we entered the villages we saw the peasants miserably dressed. Many of them had only a piece of mat to cover their bodies. They wandered about aimlessly in the streets like skeletons with skin, without any strength left, without any thoughts, and totally resigned to the ghosts of starvation and disease. Their rice had all been taken away from them by the government. They did not have any potatoes or corn. They were forced to eat everything, whether poisonous or not, they did not care. They had eaten up all the vegetation around them. . . . When a dog or a rat died, it was the occasion for the whole village to come around to prepare it and parcel it out among themselves.

In spite of such odds, the Viet Minh managed to organize the population to fight back and to attack French and Japanese granaries and rice transport systems to obtain the necessary food to feed the hungry population. We cannot go into the details here. We can only summarize the last stage of the struggle during this period that began on 13 August 1945 when the Viet Minh's Insurrection Committee issued an order to the armed forces and the people to immediately launch a general insurrection by attacking and taking over all urban areas and enemy strongholds. As soon as the order for general insurrection was issued, people's organizations and guerrilla and self-defense units everywhere moved into action. From 14 to 18 August the administrative centers of almost every village, district, and province of twenty-seven provinces were attacked and taken over, and revolutionary power was established in many of them almost immediately.

The administrations of the three major cities of Hanoi, Hue, and Saigon held out a few days longer, but the victory of the Viet Minh was swift and bloodless. Within a period of only twelve days, from 14 to 25 August, fifty-nine provinces were completely liberated, ending almost a century of colonial domination and hundreds of years of monarchic rule. For the first time in the long history of Vietnam, the administration of the entire country was in the hands of the people. This August Revolution, as the Vietnamese called it, was capped by two events of significant symbolic importance. On the afternoon of 30 August before tens of thousands of people assembled at the southern gate of the Imperial Palace, the yellow flag with three red stripes was lowered, and the yellow-starred red flag was hoisted. Emperor Bao Dai, the last ruling monarch of the Nguyen dynasty, read the abdication act, which said in part: "I prefer to be a citizen of an independent nation rather than to be the king of an enslaved country." He then handed over to Tran Huy Lieu, representative of the revolutionary provisional government, the gold seal and sword (the symbols of royal power) and formally declared the abolition of the monarchy in Vietnam.[24]

Two days later, on 2 September, before a crowd of over half a million assembled at the Ba Dinh square in Hanoi, President Ho Chi Minh introduced the Provisional Government of the Democratic Republic of Vietnam (DRV) and read the Declaration of Independence, which states in part:

> The French have fled, the Japanese have capitulated, Emperor Bao Dai has abdicated. Our people have broken the chains which for nearly a century have fettered us and have won independence for the Fatherland. . . .
>
> The whole Vietnamese people, animated by a common purpose, are determined to fight to the bitter end against any attempt by the French colonialists to reconquer our country.
>
> We are convinced that the Allied nations which at Tehran and San Francisco have acknowledged the principles of self-determination and equality of nations, will not refuse to acknowledge the independence of Vietnam. . . .
>
> . . . The entire Vietnamese people are determined to mobilize all their physical and mental strength, to sacrifice their lives and property, in order to safeguard their independence and freedom.[25]

As stated in the Vietnamese Declaration of Independence, the new leaders of Vietnam were concerned not only about the prospect of a French reconquest of Vietnam but also about intervention by certain Allied nations. These countries were understood to be the United States and Great Britain, although their names were not specifically mentioned in the Declaration of Independence because the Vietnamese were still hoping that they could be persuaded otherwise. According to the Vietnamese analysis at the time, Vietnam was the first colonial country to become independent after World War II under the leadership of a Communist party and was also becoming a socialist and anti-imperialist country; therefore it was only logical that colonial and imperial powers would try to destroy it.[26]

However, in his massively researched book on the origins of the U.S. intervention, George McT. Kahin concludes that

> the American policies that so heavily shaped the course of Vietnamese history for three full decades after World War II were never intrinsically Vietnamese in orientation: they were always primarily directed by considerations transcending that country. For at least the first three years after the war, because of France's position as the keystone of U.S. European policies, American priorities in Europe—not Asia—brought U.S. power indirectly, but nevertheless heavily, to bear in Vietnam. Insofar as communism was then an issue, it was primarily its potential in *France* that shaped American policy toward Vietnam.[27]

While the Vietnamese leaders were wrong about the real reasons for a possible U.S. intervention in Vietnam, they were certainly right in their fear that the United States and other Allied nations would support the French in their colonial reconquest of Vietnam. Again, according to Kahin,

> a badly ravaged postwar France possessed neither the military equipment nor the financial resources to mount a major military effort in Indochina. It was thanks to the United States that she was able to marshal the crucial elements of power which she began to apply there within a few months of the war's end. . . . Moreover, within two months of Japan's surrender, American ships in large numbers were carrying French forces to Vietnam, and Washington provided Paris with credits to help it purchase seventy-five U.S. troop transports. Thereafter the United States supplied Paris with a large quantity of modern weaponry—ostensibly for the defense of France and Western Europe, but with the understanding that a substantial part could be used for the military campaign in Indochina.[28]

### FRENCH COLONIAL RECONQUEST

Armed with U.S. weapons and supported by British troops, the French began an all-out attack on Saigon on the evening of 22 September 1945. A war of colonial reconquest thus began, as Joseph Buttinger sums it up: "The aim of the French, who at this time had not yet begun to talk about stopping Communism, was made clear by General Jean Leclerc, who, on September

30, 1945, stated in Saigon: 'I did not come back to Indochina to give it back to the Indochinese.' "[29]

For the next fourteen months, because of the need to solve the problem of famine as well as a host of other problems, such as the withdrawal of 200,000 of Chiang Kai-shek's Chinese troops that had entered the northern part of the country ostensibly to disarm Japanese troops under the Allied plan, the new Vietnamese government tried to avoid going to war with France by making every effort to accommodate the French through negotiations in Vietnam and Paris. But French troops multiplied their provocations throughout the country, and French reinforcements kept coming as the French government actively prepared for the reconquest of Indochina. The rest of this episode is summarized by Joseph Buttinger as follows:

> But not until November 1946 did the French feel strong enough—behind a screen of lies about events in the port-city of Haiphong—to start military action against the North. An incident over customs control, which the French tried to take away from the Hanoi government, served as a pretext for extending the war to the North. On November 23, 1946, the French killed, according to their own admission, over six thousand civilians in Haiphong. . . .
>
> Less than four weeks later, the French were ready to take decisive action in Hanoi as well. On December 19 they issued an ultimatum demanding that the Viet Minh government dissolve its para-military and police forces and let the French army assume control of the capital. Recognizing this as a declaration of war which left him only the choice of resistance or capitulation, Ho Chi Minh acted more as a nationalist than a Communist when he called on his people to defend Vietnamese national independence. . . .[30]

According to French propaganda, the Vietnamese decision to resist unprovoked French military intervention was the beginning of the First Indochina War. This resistance was soon denounced in the West as "Communist aggression."[31] As Joseph Buttinger has pointed out, this was a lie invented to justify the U.S. support for the French colonial war because without that support "the First Indochina War would then have never taken place, and without the First there would certainly never have been a Second Indochina War. But long before the United States financed 78 percent of the cost of the French Indochina war in 1953/54, their war had to some extent also become America's war."[32] The compilers of the *Pentagon Papers*, the official secret study of the U.S. involvement in Vietnam that was disclosed in mid-1971, concluded that because the United States backed the French from the very beginning, it ignored repeated appeals from Ho Chi Minh (eight messages from Ho between October 1945 and February 1946 received no reply). The United States also regarded as irrelevant the consistent and repeated reports by its own intelligence and other sources that reached the highest levels of government in Washington that Ho Chi Minh was first and foremost a nationalist, that there was great mass support for his government, that there was no alternative to this government and no hope of crushing the determination of Vietnamese people to safeguard their independence. By April 1946 the United States acknowledged French control of Indochina and "thereafter, the problems of

U.S. policy toward Vietnam were dealt with in the context of the U.S. relationship with France."[33]

## FOUR PHASES OF THE FIRST INDOCHINA WAR

The First Indochina War, or as the Vietnamese called it, the Nine-Year National Resistance, has been treated in detail elsewhere. What should be added here is that the war could be divided into four phases, each of which ended with ever-worsening French military defeats and ever-increasing U.S. intervention. The first phase began with the armed struggle that spread throughout the country in response to the calls of the government of the DRV and ended in the winter of 1947 after the greatest military offensive of the French up to that time, the "Lea" operation, resulted in almost complete disaster.

The second phase of the war lasted for about two-and-a-half years, from the spring of 1948 to the fall of 1950. Compelled to wage a protracted war, the French put into effect a "pacification" program and a "Vietnamization" program. This called for the setting up of a puppet administration and a "national army" composed of Vietnamese draftees. With increased U.S. aid, which totaled about $1.5 billion by the end of 1949, the puppet army was supposedly to be built up to about 100,000 men and entrusted with the task of "pacifying the occupied regions." From these occupied regions the French launched "mopping-up operations" (comparable to the later U.S. "search-and-destroy" missions) into the countryside, especially in the southern half of the country.

The United States also twisted the arms of the French to install a puppet regime in Saigon headed by the former monarch Bao Dai. As summarized by Kahin:

> A full year before the French Parliament finally, in February 1950, agreed to ratify the Élysée Agreement that was to be the charter of Bao Dai's rule, the United States had taken steps toward recognition of his yet-to-be-formed government. . . .
>
> On June 21, 1949—still some seven months before action was to be taken by the French legislature—the State Department publicly endorsed Bao Dai's "new unified States of Vietnam," announcing that its emergence "should serve to hasten . . . the attainment of Vietnam's rightful place in the family of nations," with Bao Dai's efforts to unite "all truly nationalistic elements" providing "the basis for the progressive realization of the legitimate aspirations of the Vietnamese people." It was thereby made very clear that the United States saw Bao Dai's putative regime as the legitimate representative of the Vietnamese people. . . . Ho Chi Minh's actually functioning government, it should be noted, had as yet received no similar promise of recognition from either Moscow or Peking.[34]

In spite of all the U.S. efforts, political and military initiative had passed into the hands of the Viet Minh by 1949. In the occupied areas the French met not only with increasingly intense guerrilla war but also with strong popular opposition. In the countryside, self-defense forces were organized. "Resistance villages" (comparable to "combat villages" during the 1960s and

1970s) were built everywhere. French storage depots, strategic and economic centers, and communication lines were under constant attacks. The war was even brought to the hearts of big cities such as Hanoi, Saigon, Hue, and Haiphong, where the French had thought they were secure. Hand in hand with the guerrilla force, during the 1949–1950 period the People's Army launched a series of campaigns over the entire country, destroying more than 200 fortified positions, killing more than 10,000 colonial troops, and liberating large territories.[35]

All this and the victory of the Chinese revolution caused great concern to France and the United States. In order to prevent Chinese military assistance, which the French asserted for the first time in April 1950 was forthcoming as a result of an alleged agreement between the Viet Minh and the Chinese Communists, the French tried to seal off the Sino-Vietnamese border as well as to encircle the Viet Bac region where the central organs of the Vietnamese Resistance were located. On the evening of 16 September 1950 the Vietnamese attacked the French positions. After six weeks of fierce fighting, all the strongly defended French garrisons in the region fell. According to the French military historian Bernard Fall: "When the smoke cleared, the French had suffered their greatest colonial defeat since Montcalm had died at Quebec. They had lost 6,000 troops, 13 artillery pieces and 125 mortars, 450 trucks and three armored platoons, 940 machine guns and more than 8,000 rifles. Their abandoned stocks alone suffice for the equipment of a whole additional Viet Minh division."[36]

The great victory of the Vietnamese in the fall of 1950 created disarray among the French. Martial law was proclaimed in Hanoi, and French nationals received orders to prepare for evacuation from Vietnam. In Paris some political parties called for the abandonment of Indochina in order to reinforce the defense of North Africa and other colonies, while others called for more troop reinforcements and more direct U.S. intervention in Indochina.

The third stage of the war began in December 1950 when Jean de Lattre de Tassigny, one of the most capable French generals, was sent to Indochina as high commissioner and commander-in-chief to try to turn the tide. According to the *Pentagon Papers*, "De Lattre electrified the discouraged French forces like General Ridgway later enheartened U.S. forces in Korea. . . . He calculated that he could win a decisive victory within fifteen months in Vietnam, and 'save it from Peking and Moscow.' . . . Moreover, De Lattre was convinced that the Vietnamese had to be brought into the fight."[37]

Basically, the de Lattre strategy was to obtain more U.S. military aid (especially aircraft), increase reinforcements from France, reorganize the "national army" and make them intensify the mopping-up operations, strengthen the defense of the Red River Delta by creating a "white belt" around it in which all dwellings were destroyed, and extend the pacification program over the entire country. In other words, escalate the war on all fronts. Thanks to the fantastic amounts of U.S. aid that came pouring in, air raids of the liberated areas became more frequent and destructive. Irrigation works and dikes were intentionally destroyed in order to create famine in the liberated areas.

"Sweep-and-clean" operations by re-equipped mobile units were launched more often, causing widespread devastation and deaths to the civilian population.[38]

In spite of all these efforts, de Lattre met with one military defeat after another and was replaced by General Raoul Salan in the spring of 1952. Salan immediately declared a "total war" against the Vietnamese, ordering mopping-up operations that involved 15 to 18 battalions in each operation and were supported by massive air strikes. But counterattacks by the Vietnamese guerrillas and regional forces in coordination with the regular army inflicted heavy losses on the French and liberated large areas in all regions of the country. Citing French official sources, Kahin concludes:

> Maintaining the military initiative in most areas, the Vietminh had, by the spring of 1953, extended their authority over more than two-thirds of the area of Tonkin. . . . In central and southern areas, the Vietminh held most of the coastal regions all the way down to the outskirts of Saigon, apart from the enclaves around Hue, Danang, and a few other towns; and about half of the Mekong Delta was firmly in Vietminh hands.[39]

### WORSE FRENCH DEFEATS, DEEPER U.S. INTERVENTION

In the summer of 1953 the war entered its final stage. In May 1953 General Henri Navarre replaced Salan as commander-in-chief of the French armed forces in Indochina and proposed a so-called "Navarre Plan" which—worked out in conformity with U.S. instructions—aimed at annihilating the Vietnamese forces and completely pacifying the country in eighteen months in three stages. At this time the Republican administration in Washington was fully committed to the defense of Indochina against "communist imperialism." John Foster Dulles, according to the *Pentagon Papers*, spoke of Korea and Indochina as two flanks, with the principal enemy—Red China—in the center. A special study mission headed by Representative Walter Judd, a recognized Republican spokesman on Asia, surveyed the Far East and reported on the mission's view of the high stakes involved: "The area of Indochina is immensely wealthy in rice, rubber, coal, and iron ore. Its position makes it a strategic key to the rest of Southeast Asia. If Indochina should fall, Thailand and Burma would be in extreme danger, Malaya, Singapore and even Indonesia would become more vulnerable to the Communist drive. . . . The Communists must be prevented from achieving their objectives in Indochina."[40]

Because of the tremendous importance that was now attached to Indochina, the United States stepped up its military supplies to the French and pressured them to attempt a military victory. The French government was under mounting public pressure to bring an end to the war, and hence it was ready to go to the negotiating table with the Viet Minh. The United States, however, consistently steered the French away from it. In the words of the *Pentagon Papers*, "In general, the U.S. sought to convince the French that military victory was the only guarantee of diplomatic success."[41] The Navarre Plan was thus adopted, and the United States became heavily involved in the conduct of the war. U.S. aid accounted for close to 80 percent of the French war expenditure for the 1953–1954 period, and airlifts were organized from France, the Philippines, and Japan for supplies to the French. Besides that, U.S. military advisers arrived on the scene, two aircraft carriers of the Seventh Fleet were dispatched to the Gulf of Tonkin, and 250 U.S. pilots took direct part in the fighting. In spite of this aid and in spite of the fact that General Navarre now had over half a million troops under his command, victory was still elusive. In Kahin's words:

> At the end of 1953, when it had become clear to Navarre that his central objective of recovering the initiative in Tonkin's Red River Delta was failing, he decided to put his chips on pinning down the Vietminh to do battle in surroundings where he believed his superior fire power and control of the air would ensure success. For this confrontation he chose the village of Dienbienphu, in a valley of northwestern Tonkin astride a major route into Laos, taking the "calculated risk" of garrisoning it with his "best units and reserves in the Tonkin Delta." Initially he had broad support for this tactic from Americans, including [President Dwight D.] Eisenhower, who was now taking a direct interest in French military efforts.[42]

In February 1954 Admiral Arthur W. Radford told the U.S. House of Representatives Foreign Affairs Subcommittee that the Navarre Plan was "a broad strategic concept which within a few months should insure a favorable turn in the course of the war."[43] The French government, however, already saw the writing on the wall and desired to seek a negotiated settlement to end the war. At the quadripartite foreign ministers' meeting in February 1954 in Berlin, the French used whatever leverage they had to have the Indochina problem placed on the agenda for the Geneva Conference that had been called to work out a political settlement for the Korean War. Although the United States had to agree to this demand partly as a result of the French threat to withdraw from the European Defense Community, the National Security Council ordered that "the U.S. should employ every feasible means to influence the French Government against concluding the struggle on terms inconsistent with the basic U.S. objectives. . . . *A nominally non-communist coalition regime would eventually turn the country over to Ho Chi Minh with no opportunity for the replacement of the French by the United States or the United Kingdom*" [emphasis added].[44]

It was in the same month that the Viet Minh forces started to surround Dien Bien Phu (correct Vietnamese spelling) and on 16 March launched their attack against the French garrison. Although most French mobile units had been defending the Red River Delta, this attack forced the French to move them to Dien Bien Phu and other fronts. In April, President Eisenhower wrote to Winston Churchill saying that France must grant "unequivocal independence" to Bao Dai's Vietnam "so that U.S. entry into Indochina would not have the taint of colonialism." Eisenhower said that the Western allies, particularly Great Britain, should indicate their willingness to become militar-

*President Ho Chi Minh (center) and General Vo Nguyen Giap (extreme right) briefed other members of the Viet Minh on the plan to attack Dien Bien Phu (1953). (Photo taken by Viet Minh. Collection of Ngo Vinh Long.)*

ily involved along with the United States in its direct intervention because this "would lend real moral standing to a venture that otherwise would be made to appear as a brutal example of imperialism."[45] Hand in hand with pressures on its allies, the United States also made actual preparations for direct armed intervention.[46] On 7 May 1954, after fifty-five days of fierce fighting, General Christian M. F. de la Croix de Castries, the field commander at Dien Bien Phu, surrendered with his remaining 16,200 men. At the same time, French military forces throughout the country were severely routed by the various revolutionary forces. Thus, in spite of last-minute maneuvers Washington was faced with a fait accompli: the First Indochina War was over.

**THE "DIEM SOLUTION" AND THE RISE OF THE NATIONAL FRONT FOR LIBERATION**

On 8 May 1954, one day after the fall of Dien Bien Phu, the Indochina phase of the Geneva Conference began to officially register France's defeat and to provide France with a face-saving means of disengagement. France did not want anything more than a graceful way out. On the first day of the conference, France immediately put forward a number of proposals for an armistice. But President Eisenhower and the Joint

*10 October 1954—Hanoi completely liberated. The regiment of the capital city returned in an atmosphere of victory and celebration. Banner reads: "Welcome the people's army into a liberated Hanoi." (Photo from Vietnam News Agency. Collection of Ngo Vinh Long.)*

Chiefs "agreed that the Government could not back the French proposal with its call for a supervised cease-fire."[47] Therefore, for the next two months the United States tried to do everything to sabotage the negotiations and to create the opportunity for direct intervention in Vietnam. This latter objective included forcing the French government to agree to a new "united action" in May 1954, to the installment of Ngo Dinh Diem as Bao Dai's premier in June, and to a position paper in July that would allow the United States to intervene in case of no settlement and to "see, with other interested nations, a collective defense association design to preserve, against direct and indirect aggression, the integrity of the non-Communist areas of Southeast Asia."[48]

Principally because of U.S. intransigence and U.S. public threats, the DRV delegation was pressured by both China and the Soviet Union to make significant concessions that finally allowed the Agreement on the Cessation of Hostilities in Vietnam to be signed by the French and the DRV governments on 20 July. The following day the multilateral Final Declaration of the Geneva Conference was endorsed by all participants except the United States. The United States, however, did make a "unilateral declaration" promising to abide by all the provisos of both agreements, especially the provision of free elections to reunify the country.

Because the agreement and the declaration—which were later known collectively as the Geneva Agreements—were important for the return of peace and political reconciliation in Vietnam, and because the United States immediately broke its promise and went about violating every provision of the agreements, it is necessary to summarize some of the most essential features contained therein. The "Agreement on the Cessation of Hostilities in Vietnam" provided the prerequisite foundation upon which the multilateral Final Declaration rests, so we should consider it first. This agreement incorporated the following essential features. First, there was to be established a "provisional military demarcation line" (fixed at the seventeenth parallel) "on either side of which the forces of the two parties shall be regrouped after their withdrawal, the forces of the People's Army of Vietnam to the north of the line and the forces of the French Union to the south" (Article 1). Civil administration in the regroupment zone to the north of the seventeenth parallel was to be in the hands of the Viet Minh, and the administration of the area to the south of the parallel was to be in the hands of the French (Article 8). Article 14 detailed the provisions for political and administrative control in the two regrouping zones pending the general elections. Paragraph (a) states in full: "Pending the general elections which will bring about the unification of Vietnam, the conduct of civil administration in each regrouping zone shall be in the hands of the party whose forces are to be regrouped there in virtue of the present Agreement." Paragraph (b) of Article 14 specified that following the evacuation of the Viet Minh troops from south of the parallel, the French would assume responsibility of the administration there until after the elections.

A group of four articles—16–19—provided for the insulation of Vietnam from the international pressures of the cold war by banning the introduction

*In violation of the Geneva Accords, the United States installed Ngo Dinh Diem as the prime minister of "South Vietnam" in 1954 and then backed a coup nine years later that killed him and his brother after they had shown some independence and contacted both the NLF and DRV to seek a negotiated settlement. Ngo Dinh Diem is shown here with his immediate family. His brother and chief adviser, Ngo Dinh Nhu, stands behind him; his powerful sister-in-law, Madame Nhu, is in the center; and his very influential oldest brother, Archbishop Thuc, is in the back on the right. (Photo courtesy of University Archives and Historical Collections, Michigan State University.)*

of all troops and military personnel, of all types of arms and war materiel, and of military bases and aggressive policy from the outside. Article 29 and most of the subsequent articles provided for the establishment of an International Commission for Supervision and Control, which was to be "responsible for supervising the proper execution by the parties of the provisions of the agreements" (Article 36).

The Final Declaration of the Conference endorsed the preceding armistice agreement and sanctioned, in even further details, the political and administrative arrangements outlined in the armistice agreement. One of the most important paragraphs, Paragraph 7, had a definite bearing on the Viet Minh's expectations concerning Vietnam's political future and hence deserves quotation in full:

> The Conference declares that, so far as Vietnam is concerned, the settlement of political problems, effected on the basis of respect for the principles of independence, unity and territorial integrity, shall permit the Vietnamese people to enjoy the fundamental freedoms, guaranteed by democratic institutions established as a result of free general elections by secret ballot. In order to ensure that sufficient progress in the restoration of peace has been made, that all the necessary conditions obtained for free expression of the national will, general elections shall be held in July 1956, under the supervision of an international commission composed of representatives of the Member States of the International Supervisory Commission, referred to in the agreement on the cessation of hostilities. Consultations will be held on this subject between the competent representative authorities of the two zones from July 20, 1955, onwards.

This was the most important reason for the many significant concessions made by the DRV at the conference. In Kahin's words:

> The major *quid pro quo* won by the Vietminh was the assurance that the struggle for control of Vietnam would be transferred from the military to the political level, a realm in which the Vietminh leaders knew their superiority over the French and their Vietnamese collaborators was even greater than it was militarily. Thus, in exchange for regrouping their military forces to the north of the seventeenth parallel into a territory considerably smaller than the total area they actually controlled, they had the assurance that in two years they would have the opportunity of winning control over the whole country through a nationwide election that they were, with good reason, confident of winning. For the Vietminh this was the heart of the Geneva Agreements. As [British Prime Minister Sir Anthony] Eden has categorically stated, without the firm and explicit assurance of national elections aimed at unifying the country, the Vietminh would never have agreed to the armistice. In that judgement, he has been unequivocally supported by Tran Van Do, Bao Dai's principal representative at Geneva.
>
> Ho's government had ample basis for believing those elections would indeed be held. Not only were they clearly promised for a definite date in Geneva's Final Declaration, but the bilateral armistice agreement with France also stipulated that the conduct of the civil administration south of the seventeenth parallel

was to be the responsibility of France, "[p]ending the general elections which will bring about the unification of Vietnam."

There was no doubt in Paris as to France's obligation to ensure "observance and enforcement" of the provisions of the Geneva Agreements in her southern area of responsibility, as stipulated in her armistice with the Vietminh. Although it was generally expected that France would stay on until national reunification elections were held, in case she did not both the armistice agreement and her treaty of June 4, 1954, with Bao Dai's regime provided that any Vietnamese administration succeeding hers was legally bound to assume her obligations.[49]

Although the United States was able to exact many concessions by throwing its weight around during the conference, the fact that the Agreements met the essential political objectives of the DRV was a bitter pill for the U.S. government to swallow. According to the *Pentagon Papers*, "When, in August, papers were drawn up for the National Security Council, the Geneva Conference was evaluated as a major defeat for United States diplomacy and a potential disaster for United States security interest in the Far East."[50] As a result, according to General James Gavin, "Admiral Radford was emphatically in favor of landing a force in the Haiphong-Hanoi area even if it meant risking war with China. In this he was fully supported by the Chief of Staff of the Air Force and the Chief of Naval operations." Secretary of State Dulles and the Central Intelligence Agency (CIA) generally agreed. It was assumed that the "expeditionary force" would be "eight combat divisions, supported by thirty-five engineer battalions, and all the artillery and logistical support such a mammoth undertaking requires."[51] Dulles was quoted as saying that a U.S. intervention had become possible because "we have a clean base there [in Indochina] now without a taint of colonialism. Dien Bien Phu was a blessing in disguise."[52] Extreme military pressure, however, was rejected by Eisenhower; and a "compromise" that involved the setting up of a "stable, independent government" was reached.[53] This was what later came to be known as the "Diem Solution," a flagrant violation of the Geneva Agreements and a decision that would bring about the grim consequences of later years. But the problem confronting the United States at the time was how to install a puppet regime in the southern part of Vietnam. As expressed by Leo Cherne, one of the original promoters of the "Diem Solution," in the 29 January 1955, issue of *Look* magazine: "If elections were held today, the overwhelming majority of Vietnamese would vote Communist. . . . No more than 18 months remain for us to complete the job of winning over the Vietnamese before they vote. What can we do?"

## DIEM AND REPRESSION

The first thing to do was to have Diem announce that his regime would refuse to participate in the scheduled conferences for elections stipulated in the Geneva Agreements or in the free and internationally supervised elections called for in 1956 as well as to get rid of the French, who were the guarantors of the Geneva Accords and of elections. On 28 April 1956, French troops were finally evacuated completely from Vietnam under U.S. pressure. The second thing that the United States and Diem did was to try to eliminate the revolutionary movement in the southern part of Vietnam by stepping up repression and pacification of the rural areas. With regard to repression, Kahin wrote:

> The Diem regime moved, publicly as well as covertly, to eliminate or stifle all opposition. Despite the Geneva Agreements' prohibition against political reprisal, it quickly targeted the most visible of large numbers of Vietminh sympathizers in the South. . . .
>
> In mid-1955, soon after the last Vietminh army units had been regrouped to the North, Diem launched an anticommunist denunciation campaign in which his administration dragooned the population into mass meetings to inform against Vietminh members and sympathizers. . . . In May 1956, after only ten months of the campaign, its head announced that more than 94,000 former Vietminh cadres had "rallied to the government," with an additional 5,613 having surrendered. Full figures were never released on the considerable number who were executed, jailed, or sent to concentration camps, euphemistically called "re-education camps." . . . More indicative of the actual scale of the problem and its exploitation was the February 1959 report that, in a single province of An Xuyen, a five-week campaign had resulted in the surrender of 8,125 communist agents and the denunciation of 9,806 other agents and 29,978 sympathizers. . . .
>
> The high tide in the campaign of repression began with Diem's promulgation of Law 10/59 on May 6, 1959. . . . Under the new law, within three days of a charge special military courts were to sentence to death—usually through guillotining—with no right of appeal, "whoever commits or attempts to commit . . . crimes of sabotage, or of infringing upon the security of the State" as well as "whoever belongs to an organization designed to help or to perpetrate [these] crimes." The scope for retribution was every bit as broad in the economic field. Here the death sentence was to be meted out to anyone "who intentionally proclaims or spreads by any means unauthorized news about prices, or rumors contrary to truths, or distorts the truth concerning the present or future situation of markets in the country or abroad, susceptible of provoking economic or financial perturbations in the country."[54]

## PACIFICATION AND REACTIONS

As far as pacification of the countryside was concerned, besides regular raiding operations with his regular army, Diem also carried out a so-called land reform program that in effect sent landlords back into the countryside to reclaim lands the revolution had parcelled out to the peasants during the resistance war and to collect land rents for as many years back as the landlords could lay claim to. In the best four-sided study of the war (that is, analysis from the perspectives of the DRV, the NLF, the Saigon regime, and the United States) published to date, Gabriel Kolko wrote:

> Diem's so-called land reform which began in early 1955 and was consolidated in October 1956 was an extremely complex effort to reestablish control of the Viet Minh regions in the Delta only, where it was applied most rigorously. . . .
> For the substantial portion of the peasantry that had benefited from the Viet Minh's reforms, Diem measures represented a counterrevolution, and its fear of

losing valuable gains and returning to the traditional peasant-landlord structure created a crisis in the rural areas. For it was Diem's land program, not the Party, which led inevitably to renewed conflict in South Vietnam. The moment he abolished the legal standing of the Viet Minh's land reforms, he unleashed social discontent and created actual and potential enemies.[55]

The fierce struggles by the peasants to defend their land rights led *Cach Mang Quoc Gia* (Nationalist Revolution), the veritable official organ of the Diem regime, to make the following complaint in the 23 February 1959 issue: "At present, in the countryside the landowners can no longer collect their land rents because they dare not return to their villages." This unrest in the countryside was of course blamed on the "Vietcong," or literally, "Vietnamese Communists." So in the same month, with the help of U.S. and British experts, a pacification program involving wholesale resettlement of the resident population was forcefully carried out in order to separate so-called loyal from disloyal groups. Because people were taken from their plots of land—on which their houses, paddy fields, ancestral tombs, and so on, were located—and moved to totally unsuitable areas, and since it often happened that many "loyal" families were grouped together with "suspect" families for no reason other than the fact that they might have relatives who had fought with the Viet Minh against the French, this resettlement technique brought protests even from the ranks of senior Saigon government officials.[56] In April 1959, more "sophisticated" relocation sites with barbed wire fences and spiked moats around them were constructed with forced labor and at enormous costs to the peasants and were euphemistically called "agrovilles." In many cases, when the houses and fields of those who had been relocated were considered too distant from the newly constructed agrovilles, they were simply burnt down.[57] On 14 July 1959, *Cach Mang Quoc Gia* declared: "We must let the peasants know that to give shelter to a communist or follow his advice makes them liable to the death penalty. We must behead them and shoot them as people kill mad dogs."

## BIRTH OF THE NATIONAL LIBERATION FRONT

Coupled with Law 10/59 this meant that any peasant who protested the relocation program, defended himself or herself against land grabbing, or asked for a rent or a tax reduction could be legally executed. This left the peasants with few choices except to resort to armed struggle to defend themselves. Throughout the latter half of 1959 armed engagements with the Diem army and police broke out in remote villages in many areas. In January 1960, insurrection broke out in Ben Tre Province—thirty-five miles (56 km) south of Saigon—under the leadership of former Viet Minh cadres. This brought about a chain reaction that helped liberate about half of the villages in all of southern Vietnam. Side by side with the peasant uprisings there were massive struggles by workers, students, ethnic groups, and various religious and political groups. On 20 December twenty of those organizations and groups born of the opposition and resistance to the United States and the

*This December 1960 photo shows the NLF leadership being sworn in. The man at the microphone is Nguyen Huu Tho, then chairman of the NLF and in 1990 vice-chairman of the Council of State of the Socialist Republic of Vietnam. (Photo from Vietnam News Agency. Collection of Ngo Vinh Long.)*

Diem regime merged into the National Front for Liberation—called National Liberation Front, or NLF, in the West—whose program called for the overthrow of the Diem administration, the liquidation of all foreign interference, the establishment of a national coalition government, a foreign policy of peace and neutrality, and a gradual advance toward the peaceful reunification of the country. Early in 1961, the People's Liberation Army came into being. From that time on the NLF dealt the Diem regime repeated military and pacification setbacks that convinced the United States that Diem was no longer equal to his task.

## COUPS AND MUSICAL CHAIRS

In January 1963, confronted with pressures from all sides and with the advice from his brother and chief political confidant, Ngo Dinh Nhu, Diem established contact with both the NLF and the DRV to seek a negotiated settlement. According to Kahin, "Nhu's flirtation with the Vietnamese Communists, serious or not, caused American officials enough concern so they listened to even the most radical arguments for ousting him and Diem. . . . Aware of American fears of a Nhu-Diem accommodation with the enemy, Saigon's generals concluded that Washington was all the more likely to support a move to oust them."[58] Ellen J. Hammer's recent book, *A Death in November*, has vividly documented the details of the U.S.-backed coup that resulted in the murder of Diem and his brother Nhu on 1 November 1963.[59] And Kahin was correct in his conclusion that "the President [John Kennedy] had certainly wanted to see Diem and Nhu removed from power, and he ordered full support to the generals who had overthrown them. [Henry Cabot] Lodge [U.S. ambassador in Saigon] and [Dean] Rusk [U.S. secretary of state] promptly established a close working relationship with the new government, headed by General Duong Van Minh."[60] The United States increased its military supplies and aid to Saigon, and in 1964 Secretary of Defense Robert McNamara came to Saigon to work out new pacification plans. But the deeply shaken Saigon regime and army were plunged into an endless crisis: within twenty months since the fall of Diem, thirteen coups, nine cabinets, and four charters followed one after another. The various U.S. services tried in vain to find a formula of government likely to allow the war to be conducted in an efficient way: military junta, associated military-civilian government, dictatorship under one general, rule by veterans or by "young Turks."

While the United States was playing musical chairs in Saigon, the NLF armed forces and the population went on the offensive. The strategic hamlets that had succeeded the agrovilles and had contained 85 percent of the rural population before the fall of Diem were, according to official U.S. estimates, completely destroyed.[61] Again, according to U.S. estimates, by the beginning of 1964 about half of the villages in South Vietnam were already under solid NLF control, and by the beginning of 1965 the NLF liberated zone covered nearly four-fifths of the territory and two-thirds of the population. Once again, Washington was confronted with the situation of either making peace or escalating the war. Throughout 1964, the NLF made repeated efforts to arrange a negotiated settlement based on the Laos model, with a neutralist coalition government. But the United States consistently rejected any such "premature negotiations" as incompatible with its goal of maintaining a non-Communist South Vietnam under U.S. control. And after a period of agonizing that has been documented and discussed in detail by George Kahin, President Johnson decided to side with those advisers who argued that "bombing the north will save the south." But as pointed out by Kahin, "It was soon evident that bombing the North was ineffective. There were none of the positive consequences in the South—either political or military—that Lyndon Johnson's advisers had confidently predicted. . . . As the political and military fabric of the southern regime continued to unravel even more rapidly than before, almost all of his advisers pressed for a second dimension of escalation—the introduction of U.S. ground forces."[62]

In other words, the United States was prepared to escalate the war because Saigon was about to fall to the southern NLF forces and not because of any threat—real or imagined—from the North. As we will see in the next section of this chapter, a small northern unit was identified by U.S. intelligence in the South for the first time only about seven weeks after U.S. troops had landed in Vietnam in large numbers.

**THE FULL-SCALE U.S. WAR, 1965–1975**

In January 1965, while the United States was preparing the pretexts for sending its troops into South Vietnam in great numbers, the Saigon regime was clever enough to see that it should respond to the NLF's call for a negotiated end to the war. General Nguyen Khanh, who was the head of the Armed Forces Council that ruled Saigon at the time, later confirmed that he was close to a political settlement with the NLF and an alliance with the Buddhists. When the Americans found this out, however, Khanh was removed and sent into exile in France. This helped foreclose any possibility for a peace settlement and propelled the United States toward a full-scale war in Vietnam.[63] On 6 March U.S. combat units landed in Da Nang, ostensibly to contain "North Vietnamese aggression." But, wrote Kahin, "on April 21, the day American intelligence confirmed the existence of what later emerged as a single battalion of PAVN [People's Army of Vietnam] troops in the South, many times more American combat units were already there. Indeed, at that time even the number of South Korean soldiers in South Vietnam (2,000) was greater than this North Vietnamese unit."[64]

The introduction of U.S. troops and "allied forces" started a full-scale U.S. war against Vietnam that was later called the "Vietnam War," or the "Second Indochina War." The conduct of the war by the United States and its allies has been described in vivid detail in many books and reports written in English.[65] Except for a handful of studies, the revolutionary side of the war has as yet to be adequately described and analyzed.[66] Because of space limitations in this chapter we will summarize only a few developments of the three main phases of this war: the period of massive escalation from 1965 to 1968, Nixon's "Vietnamization" period from 1969 to 1972, and the post–Paris Agreement period of 1973 to 1975.

About two weeks after the first introduction of U.S. ground forces to Vietnam, the National Liberation Front issued its "Five-Point Statement" that included an offer for a peaceful settlement of the war. On 8 April 1965 Prime Minister Pham Van Dong of the DRV also spelled out clearly in the "Four-Point Position" the desire of his government to seek a political settlement that was basically a return to the Geneva Agreements. But, as pointed out in the *Pentagon Papers*, the United States ruled out any compromise, and the "negotiating terms that the US proposed were . . . more akin to a 'cease and desist' order that, from the DRV/VC point of view, was tantamount to a demand for their surrender."[67] This marked the pattern that was to last until the end of 1967: The United States responded to every peace offer from the DRV and the NLF by further escalation with the hope that it could destroy the Vietnamese resistance through pacification and military destruction. But this only increased the popularity and support for the NLF, which in turn created problems for the U.S.-Saigon side. The French daily *Le Figaro* reported on 15 February 1967 that Pentagon generals were obliged to admit that the pacification program had become a complete failure and that by the end of 1966 the number of Saigon troop "desertions had reached a monthly figure of 500 per regiment." A report of the U.S. Senate Armed Forces Committee also maintained in early 1967 that "by the end of the dry season, the Viet Cong still controlled 80 percent of South Vietnam territory."[68] And on 1 March 1967 *Reuters* news service quoted Major Sam Wilson, the senior U.S.

adviser in Long An Province, which was a "priority pacification province" immediately south of Saigon, as saying: "For every hectare to pacify, we have devoted to this province more men, more dollars and other means than any other province of South Vietnam. Yet the results of these efforts are meager. . . . In reality, we can control only a very small area, according to the required norms. I would say that we control only 4 per cent in the daytime and only one per cent during the night."

But instead of responding to repeated peace-talk offers from the NLF and the calls from the DRV for "an unconditional cessation of U.S. bombing and all other acts of war against the DRV" so that peace negotiations could begin, the United States doubled and then tripled attack sorties against the North, demanding "reciprocity" in exchange for the bombing halt. On 29 December 1967, DRV Foreign Minister Nguyen Duy Trinh repeated the peace-talk offer, and President Lyndon B. Johnson again demanded reciprocity. Since Hanoi was not bombing the United States, the Vietnamese revolutionary leaders interpreted this demand as an attempt by the United States to get Hanoi to call off the struggle in the South. Therefore, the DRV and the NLF decided to carry out the Spring 1968 Offensive—later called the "Tet Offensive" in the United States—to force the U.S. government to deescalate the war against the North and to go to the negotiating table.

## TET: THE GREAT TURNING POINT

The 1968 Tet Offensive was the greatest turning point of the Vietnam war because of a combination of far-reaching political, military, psychological, and diplomatic impacts that can be fully understood only in the whole context of the Vietnam War and the nature of the revolutionary struggle in Vietnam. I and several other authors have dealt with this offensive in great detail elsewhere.[69] For our purpose here it is sufficient to point out that this offensive had three phases. The first phase began on 31 January when commando units and local forces attacked almost simultaneously all the major cities, 36 of the 44 provincial capitals, and 64 of the 242 district towns. "The enemy's Tet offensive," the author of the *Pentagon Papers* wrote shortly after it occurred, "although it had been predicted, took the U.S. command and the U.S. public by surprise, and its strength, length and intensity prolonged this shock."[70] The CIA on 10 February estimated that the offensive had already accomplished its main psychological, political, and military objectives. The Communists, it said, were now gaining control over vast new rural areas, smashing Saigon's military, economic, and political system and having more direct influence on the urban sector.[71] And, after a study tour to Saigon, General Earle Wheeler, head of the Joint Chiefs of Staff, had to admit in a report of 17 February to President Johnson that Tet was "a very near thing." He wrote that had it not been for the "timely reaction of the United States forces," the attacks would have succeeded in numerous places.[72] This very timely reaction included massive U.S. artillery and air strikes that leveled from 30 to 80 percent of many cities. But what was perhaps most difficult for the Americans to understand was how this "very near thing" could have been pulled off with such small numbers of attackers. In Saigon, for example, only 1,000 local NLF forces and sappers managed to hold off over 11,000 U.S. and Saigon troops and police for three weeks. Regular troops waited nearby but were not employed except in Hue where one thousand regular DRV troops captured the Citadel and occupied it until 24 February while U.S. firepower destroyed about 80 percent of the city.[73] Among other things, the offensive further proved to many people that the United States would never be able to win the war in Vietnam, first, because of the evident popularity of the NLF, and second, because, in its bombing destruction of the cities, the United States reconfirmed the fact that it had all along regarded the Vietnamese people themselves as the real enemy in Vietnam.

Because of mounting pressures from all fronts as a result of the Tet Offensive, on 31 March—the day that the United States considered the Tet Offensive ended—President Johnson made a major speech, announcing his decision to withdraw from the upcoming presidential election and to limit the bombing of the North to the panhandle area and saying that "the United States is ready to send its representatives to any forum at any time, to discuss the means of bringing this war to an end." It was a cunning maneuver designed to placate U.S. public opinion. The U.S. Air Force, seriously crippled by losses sustained over North Vietnam as well as in the South during the ground attacks, could no longer afford to scatter bombing raids over too vast a teritory. By limiting their strikes to the panhandle where 20 percent of the North Vietnamese population lived and which was an extremely valuable food-producing area, the United States could destroy more with the same tonnage. In fact, after 31 March the number of air sorties against the DRV and air and artillery strikes against South Vietnamese villages, especially in the Mekong Delta, increased to unprecedented levels and Johnson was able to increase the number of U.S. troops in Vietnam. He asked an additional $39 billion from Congress for his war expenditures. Under these conditions, Johnson hoped that the Vietnamese would refuse his offer. But he was taken by surprise on 3 April 1968, when the DRV declared itself ready to meet with the United States. It turned out that Johnson's "any forum at any time" did not include Phnom Penh, Warsaw, and Paris; and Washington immediately put up absurd conditions for the selection of a meeting place.

### TET: THE SECOND AND THIRD PHASE

On the night of 4 May the second phase of the Tet Offensive began when 119 bases, towns, and cities were attacked by NLF forces. The main objective was to get the United States to deescalate the war against the North and go to the negotiating table as well as to disrupt the Saigon military and political system. Again the allied forces had to rely heavily on helicopter gunships and napalm strikes in populated areas in the attempt to drive out the infiltrators. As a result, for example, some 8,000 homes in Saigon's eighth district were destroyed in five days. U.S. officers strongly defended this tactic although it brought about new devastation on Saigon. "There is no clean way of fighting a city war," argued one U.S. general. "If you try to fight with gloves on, the casualty rate is going to be so high that you can't stomach it, and you don't get the enemy out anyway." This was the kind of logic that forced one Saigon officer to complain bitterly, "We cannot go on destroying entire blocks every time a Vietcong steps into a house."[74] Again, these attacks exposed the nature of the U.S. involvement and thereby scored some important political points for the NLF in the long run. In the short run, however, both the United States and the Saigon regime were forced to join the Paris Peace Talks on Vietnam, which began on 13 May 1968. But President Johnson was still very much committed to sustaining the struggle, and so he refused to stop the bombing over the North and deescalate the war in the South.

The third and last phase of the offensive began on 17 August with the shelling by NLF forces of U.S. installations and a series of coordinated assaults throughout South Vietnam. For the next six weeks mortars, rockets, and small local units were largely employed by U.S. forces to minimize the loss of manpower. To forestall a ground assault against Saigon, U.S. B-52 bombers poured close to 1 million pounds of bombs a day on the surrounding areas and the suspected infiltration routes. This third phase proved to be the most costly for the NLF. Regular NLF troops were trapped in the environs of Saigon and other cities and towns, isolated from their rural base of support, and killed in large numbers. As a result, that rural base of support was vulnerable to savage repression. But during the first weeks of renewed fighting more than 700 Americans died in action, the highest rate in three months. This showed the American people that the war was not winding down, a relevant point to drive home during the final weeks of the presidential election. On 31 October, in a last-ditch effort to save Hubert Humphrey's presidential bid, Johnson had to order the unconditional cessation of the bombing of North Vietnam and announce that a four-party conference with NLF and Saigon representatives participating would start on 6 November. But the American people had lost confidence in Johnson and his party, whom they held responsible for the continuing war. With his promises of bringing about peace, Richard Nixon got himself elected president of the United States.

### NIXON'S "PEACE PLAN": VIETNAMIZATION

Just like Johnson before him, Nixon talked peace in order to make war. Ambassador Averell Harriman, who was still the chief U.S. negotiator in Paris in the period between November and Nixon's inauguration on 20 January, later wrote that during that time Nixon manipulated the Nguyen Van Thieu regime to deliberately destroy the chances for a negotiated peace and that, after Nixon took over, Henry Cabot Lodge (who replaced Harriman) succeeded in destroying almost everything that had been achieved. Instead of talking peace, Nixon put into effect his "Vietnamization" program, which he called his "peace plan." Harriman denounced Nixon's "peace plan" in language about as strong as could be expected from a man in his position: "The Administration's program of Vietnamization of the war is not in my opinion a program for peace, but it is a program for the continuation of the war. . . .

Furthermore, the Vietnamization of the war is dependent on an unpopular and repressive government. . . ."[75]

The Vietnamization program involved the massive build-up of the Saigon forces in an attempt to get Vietnamese to kill other Vietnamese. The Nixon administration was able to carry this out thanks to the heavy U.S. bombing of Indochina and such programs as the Accelerated Pacification Program and the Phoenix Program. The United States dropped 5 million tons of bombs on Indochina, the great bulk of them on the countryside of South Vietnam in 1969 and 1970. This is more than twice the tonnage dropped on all fronts during World War II! The Accelerated Pacification Program increased massive relocation and destruction in the rural areas. The Phoenix Program was a wholesale assassination plan that was responsible for the deaths of 20,000 NLF cadres and the "neutralization" of about 80,000 more, making it almost impossible for the Vietnamese people to survive in the countryside. In these circumstances the Nixon administration was able to increase the regular forces of the Saigon army (the Army of the Republic of Vietnam—ARVN) to over 1.1 million men and the local forces to over 4 million out of a total population of about 18 million.

All this was being done not simply to save American lives but also to save American dollars. It cost the United States $38,000 to send an American to Vietnam to fight for one year. But it cost an average of only $400 to support an Asian mercenary—Koreans and Thais included—to fight for a year. Saving American lives and dollars served to persuade the American public that the war was winding down so that the American people would be more patient with Nixon's conduct of the war. The pressganging of Vietnamese youth into the army also served to deny the NLF fresh supplies of troops. Moreover, Trinh Pho, a Vietnamese officer in the Political Warfare Section of the Saigon army, explained in a long article entitled "The Mobilization of Soldiers in a New Sweep" in the Saigon magazine *Quan Chung* (5 September 1969) that the main reason for drafting so many people into the army was to keep them under government control.

While under military control, these people were forced to go out on some 300 mopping-up operations in South Vietnam every day in 1969 and 1970 to draw enemy fire so that U.S. tactical air support and artillery strikes—which accounted for over a million tons of high explosives a year on the southern part of Vietnam—could destroy them. Such mopping-up operations were also designed to pacify the countryside. As a result, according to hundreds of Vietnamese in the southern provinces whom I have interviewed since 1979, the darkest years for the southern revolutionaries and their supporters were 1969 and 1970. Thousands of NLF fighters were either killed or forced to desert during this period. The losses of the NLF forces and cadres also contributed to increasing PAVN casualties in the South because the former had provided the political structure and hence the necessary logistical support for the main PAVN forces. By the fall of 1969 some PAVN forces in the South had to become guerrillas, divided into company-sized bodies, which in turn were partially broken down into sapper units, in order to survive. Others had to move to the Cambodian border areas.

*After having destroyed most of the so-called "military targets" such as bridges many times over, U.S. bombers attacked civilian targets. Churches, pagodas, hospitals, schools, and residential areas were bombed consistently under the Nixon administration. This photo shows the quarter*

## INVASION OF CAMBODIA AND NLF RECOVERY

In May 1970, over 50,000 U.S. and Saigon troops invaded Cambodia to "clean up the sanctuaries" and dismantle the "Vietcong Pentagon." This invasion was preceded by the most massive air bombardments since the start of the Vietnam war, including for the first time B-52 bomber raids against towns, wiping out half a dozen frontier towns in as many minutes. The full story of this bloody act by Nixon in his "search for peace," which ended in complete disaster, has been documented elsewhere.[76] What should be mentioned here is that this was a mistake that gave the revolutionary movement in the southern provinces, especially the Mekong Delta, the space and time to reorganize itself and fight back. The recovery of the southern revolutionary forces helped the other areas in the country tremendously, especially in military terms. This was because the Mekong Delta forces pinned down more Saigon forces than all other areas combined and hence allowed the other areas the time and space to develop their forces and recover. By the end of 1970 and the beginning of 1971, the NLF recovered almost completely. This contributed to a series of disastrous military defeats for Saigon that, in turn, led to massive anti-Saigon and anti-U.S. demonstrations in the urban areas in South Vietnam.

Because of its weak political and military situation, throughout 1971 the United States rejected all offers by the DRV and PRG (Provisional Revolutionary Government, a coalition of the NLF and other forces set up in June 1969) for a cease-fire and a tripartite coalition government in exchange for the United States setting a date for withdrawal of its forces from Vietnam. In

*of the housing project in the Thuong Ly section of Haiphong that was razed on 16 April 1972. (Photo from Vietnam News Agency. Collection of Ngo Vinh Long.)*

February 1972, while suspending the Paris Peace Talks and stepping up the bombings in Vietnam, Nixon and Kissinger went to China to get Chinese leaders to put pressure on Vietnam to end the war on U.S. terms. In Hanoi the official newspaper *Nhan Dan* reacted strongly by saying: "The time when the great powers could decide the fate of small nations is past and gone."[77] In the south the Spring 1972 Offensive began in March with the attacks and routing of Saigon main forces in several provinces. Although the attacks were largely carried out by southern revolutionary forces, with PAVN regular forces participating only in Quang Tri Province (south of the Demilitarized Zone), Nixon retaliated with the most massive bombing of northern towns and cities and its dams and dikes up to that time. All ports of the DRV were also mined so as to cut off supplies from the outside. But the bombing had no effect on the battlefields in the south. The U.S. and Saigon forces had completely lost any initiative and were reduced to defensive reactions wherever the PRG-DRV forces chose to strike.[78]

This time the United States had nowhere to go but back to the negotiating table. Finally, it was announced in Hanoi on 26 October that full agreement had been reached; this was confirmed by Secretary of State Henry Kissinger at a Washington press conference later on the same day. The agreement was to be signed "exactly on the 31st" of October. But at this press conference, while saying that "peace is at hand," Kissinger tried to back away from what had been negotiated by pretending that there were some "minor linguistic difficulties" that would have to be solved in another negotiating session. The

*The signing of the Paris Peace Agreement on 31 January 1973. The PRG delegation is on the left, the DRV delegation on the right, the Saigon delegation faces the camera, and the U.S. delegation is in the forefront. (Photo from Vietnam News Agency and NLF News Agency. Collection of Ngo Vinh Long.)*

Vietnamese maintained that the agreement had been reviewed by the two sides sentence by sentence, word by word, until there was total agreement on the texts. Nixon and Kissinger, however, put up all kinds of excuses for delaying the signing. The talks did not resume again until 20 November, two weeks after Nixon had used the agreement to defeat George McGovern. And for the next fourteen negotiating sessions Kissinger demanded 126 substantive changes in all, affecting all nine sections of the agreement. The Vietnamese refused to comply.

Late on the evening of 18 December, Premier Pham Van Dong received a communication from Nixon demanding that either he consent to changes Kissinger had proposed in the agreement or Hanoi would be heavily bombed. Within minutes waves of B-52s conducted their carpet bombing of Hanoi and later Haiphong. Between 18 and 30 December, over 40,000 tons of bombs were dropped on Hanoi and 15,000 tons on Haiphong by B-52 attacks alone. But the Nixon-Kissinger team bombed themselves back to the negotiating table in Paris, and on 17 January 1973 signed the Paris Agreement—an agreement that was virtually unchanged from its October 1972 version.[79]

### SAIGON'S PEACE VIOLATIONS AND COLLAPSE

But both the United States and the Thieu regime believed that carrying out the Paris Agreement to the letter would lead to an eventual political takeover by the Vietnamese revolutionaries. Therefore, in spite of the fact that the Paris Agreement established two parallel and equal parties in South Vietnam—the Saigon regime and the Provisional Revolutionary Government—and that the two parties were supposed to reach a political settlement under conditions of full democratic rights without U.S. interference (Articles 1, 4, 9, and 11), the

United States and Thieu consistently denied the PRG any political role in South Vietnam. Article 12 of the Paris Agreement also stipulates that a National Council of National Reconciliation and Concord would be created with three equal segments. The third segment was supposed to be composed of nonaligned "neutralists" or "third force," as it was then known. But as soon as the Paris Agreement was signed Thieu reiterated, with U.S. acquiescence if not outright support, his Four No's Policy: no recognition of the enemy, no coalition government, no neutralization of the southern region of Vietnam, and no concession of territory. Later on, in an interview published in the 15 July 1973 issue of *Vietnam Report*, an English-language publication of the Saigon Council on Foreign Relations, Thieu stated: "The Vietcong are presently trying to turn areas under their control into a state endowed with a government, which they could claim to be the second such institution in the South. . . . In the first place, we have to do our best so that the NLF cannot build itself into a state, a second state within the South." In the same interview Thieu also ruled out any role for the third segment, branding all third-force people as pro-PRG.

Thieu's bellicose stance was certainly encouraged by the fantastic amounts of military aid given to him by the United States. After the signing of the Paris Agreement the United States supplied the Thieu regime with so many arms that, as Maj. Gen. Peter Olenchuck testified before the Senate Armed Services Committee on 8 May 1973, "We shortchanged ourselves within our overall inventories. We also shortchanged the reserve units in terms of prime assets. In certain instances, we also diverted equipment that would have gone to Europe."[80] In fiscal year 1974, Congress gave Saigon $1 billion more in military aid. Saigon expended as much ammunition as it could—$700 million worth. This left a stockpile of at least $300 million, a violation of the Paris Agreement, which had stipulated that equipment only be replaced on a one-to-one basis. For fiscal year 1975, Congress again authorized $1 billion in military aid, but appropriated $700 million—about what was actually spent in 1974.

Meanwhile, according to the report entitled "Vietnam—A Changing Crucible," issued by the House Committee on Foreign Affairs on 15 July 1974, "Hanoi faces uncertainty over the level of Soviet and Chinese support. . . . There is no evidence that Hanoi's allies are prepared to mount a 'massive' resupply operation to the extent believed necessary for an all-out attack. In recent briefings to troops and cadres in the south, the Communist high command . . . has accused Moscow and Peking of having cut back aid and of having opposed certain North Vietnamese objectives." This cut of military aid from the Soviet Union and China might have influenced the cautious attitude of the Vietnamese policymakers, resulting in their defensive posture during the postagreement period.

In any case, the fantastic amount of U.S. military aid, plus an explicit oral guarantee given to Thieu by Nixon that the United States would reenter the war, at least with air power to bail him out if worse came to worst, encouraged Thieu to sabotage the agreement by carrying out the so-called "military operations to saturate the national territory" through indiscriminate bombings and shellings as well as ground assaults on PRG-controlled areas. The 16 February 1974 issue of the *Washington Post* quoted Pentagon officials as saying that the Thieu armed forces were "firing blindly into free zones [that is, PRG-controlled areas] because they knew full well they would get all the replacement supplies they needed from the United States." A study by the U.S. Defense Attaché Office in conjunction with the Saigon Joint General Staff and the U.S. Pacific Command revealed that "the countryside ratio of the number of rounds fired by South Vietnamese forces [since the signing of the Paris Agreement] to that fired by Communist forces was about 16 to 1. In Military Regions II and III, where South Vietnamese commanders have consistently been the most aggressive and where some U.S. officials said that random 'harassment and interdiction' fire against Communist-controlled areas was still common, the ratio was on the order of 50 to 1."[81] In addition to the shellings, on the average about 15,000 bombs were dropped and 10,000 different military operations were conducted in the countryside every month.

According to "Vietnam—A Changing Crucible," this military aggressiveness actually enthralled many congressional supporters of the war because "the GVN has fared well during the post-ceasefire maneuvering: Since January 1973 it has added 770 hamlets to the list of those over which it has dominant control, and it has reportedly reduced the number of disputed hamlets by well over a third. . . . In fact, our Embassy estimates that the GVN has maintained 'dominant access' to roughly 93–94 percent of the population since the ceasefire. . . ." But the Saigon regime's military aggressiveness also inflicted untold death and suffering on the civilian population as well as exposing Saigon's own armed forces to danger and death. As early as 30 August 1973 the respected French newspaper *Le Monde* reported that the Saigon high command had stated that about 41,000 of its troops had been killed and 4,000 were missing since the signing of the Paris Agreement. Saigon was never known for inflating its own casualty statistics. The suffering and death caused by Thieu's sabotage of the Paris Agreement made his regime increasingly unpopular among the general population.

Worse still, because of the increase in economic aid to the Thieu regime in 1973 and 1974 the regime felt confident enough to carry out an "economic blockade" designed to inflict hunger and starvation on the PRG areas.[82] This blockade, which was also known as the "rice war" in the U.S. press at the time, included prohibitions on the transport of rice from one village to another, on rice milling by anyone except the government, on storage of rice in homes, and on the sale of rice outside the village to any except government-authorized buyers. The blockade caused widespread hunger and starvation. According to reports by Saigon deputies and Catholic priests, up to 60 percent of the population of the central provinces were reduced to eating bark, cacti, banana roots, and the bulbs of wild grass. Children and the aged were the first victims. In some central Vietnam villages deaths from starvation reached 1 to 2 percent of the total population each month.[83] And in the once rice-rich Mekong Delta, acute rice shortages became commonplace in many provinces.[84]

As for the economy, Thieu's policies precipitated a major depression. On 25 February 1974 *Hoa Binh* ("Peace," a conservative Catholic daily newspaper in Saigon) quoted Deputy Premier Phan Quang Dan as complaining that there were from three to four million unemployed persons in the Saigon-controlled areas alone. Throughout Thieu's Vietnam, firms were firing workers in droves. The owners frequently mistreated and insulted their workers to force them to quit. Even foreign companies, which enjoyed many special privileges such as exemption from all income taxes, had to cut back their work force by 30 percent.[85]

Hunger and unemployment increased crimes, suicide, and demonstrations throughout the areas under Saigon's control. Demonstrations demanding jobs and food occurred almost daily. Here are a few random examples taken from a single Saigon daily to illustrate the intensity of the urban struggles by August and September of 1974. The 30 August 1974 issue of *Dien Tin* reported that 1,000 disabled veterans and other inhabitants of Do Hoa village in Thua Thien Province blockaded the streets with barbed wire, demanding that the government provide them with food and jobs. Later, on 19 September, 116 trade unions in Saigon and Cholon met to demand food and clothes and an end to mistreatment and unwarranted layoffs (*Dien Tin*, 20 September 1974). Two days later, the whole work force of Saigon, Cholon, and Gia-dinh demonstrated for food, clothes, and temporary relief (*Dien Tin*, 22 September 1974). While this was going on, huge numbers of workers in Da Nang, the second largest city in South Vietnam, marched in the streets and then went on a mass hunger strike (*Dien Tin*, 22 and 24 September 1974).

The death and suffering caused by Thieu's military attacks and economic blockade not only intensified the general population's hatred of the Thieu regime, they also forced the PRG to fight back. In the summer of 1974, the PRG's counterattack forced Thieu's armed forces to make one tactical withdrawal after another. Even in the heavily defended delta provinces, Saigon was forced to abandon 800 fire bases and forts in order to "increase mobility and defense."[86] Gabriel Kolko is certainly correct in drawing the following conclusion:

> The RVN (Republic of Vietnam [Saigon regime]) was by mid-1974 politically and economically brittle. The volume of aid in no way explains its political weaknesses; its real economic dilemma was intrinsic in the countless structural distortions the United States had built into the RVN system over a decade. Its military fragility was the consequence of a collapsing army, underpaid and without morale, which traumatized the peasants, who increasingly turned against the RVN and toward the Revolution. Given also the other American dilemmas, it was certain that the balance of forces in Vietnam by the summer of 1974 had tilted overwhelmingly against the RVN, and it would not take much more to shatter its institutional layers and create fatal political traumas and economic upheavals.[87]

But instead of drawing some lessons from the whole experience and responding to the repeated calls of the PRG and the general population of

Vietnam to return to the Paris Agreement, both the Thieu regime and the Ford administration tried their own tricks to obtain more aid from Congress to shore up the already hopeless situation. For its part, the Ford administration tried to set in motion a plan they had long held in reserve. This was the replacement of Thieu by a right-wing coalition capable of winning more aid from the Congress and keeping some control of the country. High CIA agents were sent in droves to South Vietnam in September and October 1974.[88] The U.S. embassy in Saigon publicly encouraged a coalition of conservative forces within the Catholic, Buddhist, Cao Dai, and Hoa Hao churches to give the appearance of widespread popular backing for Thieu's successor regime.[89] The whole rightist Catholic opposition to Thieu was based on the narrow accusation against Thieu on six specific charges of corruption and called itself the Anti-Corruption Campaign. Father Tran Huu Thanh, the campaign's chairman, was quoted by the *Washington Post* as saying that the reasons for the Catholic actions were that "South Vietnam also needs a clean government so our allies will trust us and will send foreign aid and investment."[90]

On 19 November 1974 Colonel Vo Dong Giang, PRG spokesman at the two-party Military Commission in Saigon, held a press conference in which he criticized Father Thanh and his campaign for trying to maintain the Thieu regime, for following U.S. policy, and for refusing to move towards peace as called for by the Paris Peace Agreement and the Vietnamese people. The colonel warned that unless the United States heeded the aspirations of the Vietnamese people and returned to the Paris Agreement, there would soon be an uprising by the Vietnamese people. But even the so-called "liberal" U.S. press did not take the Vietnamese revolutionaries seriously; the *New York Times*, which reported this press conference the next day, chided the colonel for bragging and for being arrogant.

Perhaps impressed by the show in Saigon and by the Ford administration's promise that there would soon be a regime worth supporting, the Congress on 17 and 18 December authorized $450 million in economic aid to Saigon for FY 1975, which represented a $100 million increase over the amount authorized for FY 1974. The PRG evidently interpreted this action by Congress as a renewed commitment to the Saigon regime. In answer, they increased their counterattacks against Thieu's aggressive military stance, and by early January 1975, eight districts and a province fell into PRG hands. But the Ford administration and Saigon used this opportunity to accuse Congress of having weakened South Vietnam militarily by its reduction of aid requests, and these administrations clamored for supplemental appropriations. But it was already clear to most Saigon observers that aid was not the real problem. Huynh Trung Chanh, a deputy in the Saigon Lower House, for example, wrote the following in an editorial in the 17 January 1975 issue of *Dien Tin*:

> The leaders of the Republic of Vietnam are now spreading the view that the present deteriorating situation is due to the lack of aid. But the reality of the situation is that the difficulty is not because of a lack of aid but because of *lack of support of the people* [original emphasis]. In previous years, aid was overly abundant and yet what was ever solved? Now, if there were supplemental aid in

order to meet this military situation, then the difficult period will only be prolonged and in the end nothing will be solved.

Even Father Nguyen Quang Lam, an ultraconservative Catholic priest, was compelled to write the following in the 9 February issue of *Dai Dan Toc*:

> Yesterday I wrote that whether there is an additional $300 million or $3,000 million in aid, South Vietnam will still not be able to avoid collapse. . . . In the afternoon a reader called me up and said that I should have put it more strongly. I must say that the more the aid, the quicker the collapse of South Vietnam. All I had to do was to take a look at our society. . . . Come to think of it, the reader has a point there. The American dollars have really changed our way of thinking. People compete with each other to become prostitutes, that is to say, to get rich in the quickest and most exploitative manner. . . . No wonder whenever our soldiers see the enemy they run for their lives, even though they might have a basement full of ammunition which they could presumably fire till kingdom come.

It was already perfectly clear to even the most conservative Vietnamese that Saigon was ready to fall even though at that time it had 1.1 million men in its regular army and the world's third largest air force and eighth largest navy. There was no longer any will for any kind of military confrontation. But neither the Saigon nor the Ford administrations would take any hint, and they clamored for the supplemental aid requested. Meanwhile, perhaps in an effort to mislead Congress in order to obtain the supplemental aid, CIA agents were sent to Capitol Hill in mid-January to brief many in the Senate about a "Heartland" policy. They maintained that the Saigon army had high morale, was well trained and fully equipped, but was overextended. They recommended abandonment of some central highland provinces and withdrawal to the coastal areas to preserve the strength of the Saigon troops. This would also help provide tighter control of populated areas, making it possible to conduct and manage the upcoming elections so as to create the impression that a future Saigon regime indeed had overwhelming popular support. Therefore, when the PRG and the DRV were forced to mount an offensive in early March to try to get the United States and Saigon to come back to the Paris Agreement, Thieu withdrew his forces from the central highlands and caused a stampede as one province after another fell with hardly a fight. Thieu has often been blamed for the hasty withdrawal, but it seems that Thieu might have listened too well to his U.S. advisers. The *Far Eastern Economic Review* reported on 25 April 1975 that "the United States knew in advance of Saigon's plans to withdraw its troops from part of the north of the country, according to a report from Tokyo. Japanese financial leaders were reportedly told by sources close to the U.S. secretary of state, Henry Kissinger, in early February that the Americans were prepared to condone a South Vietnamese military 'redeployment' from the north in order to form a new, stronger defense perimeter near Saigon." On 26 March, General Frederick C. Weyland, army chief of staff, was sent to Saigon to assess the situation as well as to help Saigon set up a last defense anchor thirty-five miles (56 km) north of the city. Frantic diplomatic and political maneuvers were also employed with the hope of stopping, or at least delaying, the offensive. This included getting China and the Soviet Union to put pressure on the DRV as well as installing the former General Duong Van "Big" Minh, with the connivance and support of the French government, as the new president of South Vietnam. This last act of the charade is described by Gabriel Kolko as follows.

> On the afternoon of April 28, during a thunderstorm, Minh in his inaugural speech called for a negotiated peace but also asked the Revolution immediately to cease hostilities. His own troops he urged "to defend the territory which is left and to defend peace," adding, "Keep your spirit high, your ranks intact, and your positions firm. . . ." He drew up plans not only to continue resisting but also to counterattack the Communist forces.
>
> . . . Minh's utopian message reinforced definitely the Party's natural reluctance to continue the charade with another puppet. . . . On the morning of April 29, the offensive against Saigon began, quickly cutting off the city on all sides. [American Ambassador Graham] Martin ordered the final evacuation by helicopter, and the last Americans left by 5 A.M. on April 30. By that hour all of the key approaches to the city were in PAVN hands, while local forces, sympathizers, and sappers fanned throughout the city itself.
>
> . . . South of Saigon, in the Mekong Delta, the remnants of the RVN's armies were surrendering and disintegrating to local NLF units, sometimes several guerillas capturing hundreds of superbly equipped soldiers. At 10:15 Minh broadcast a cease-fire to his own forces, urging them also to remain in their positions and asking the Communists to do the same until there was a discussion of the orderly transfer of power. It was a surrender, but scarcely an unconditional one which acknowledged the reality of the battlefield.[91]

Consequently, less than an hour later a group of three PAVN tanks went straight to the Saigon presidential palace and crashed through the huge iron gate. At about 11:30 A.M. the NLF flag was raised on a flagpole at the palace, and Minh was taken to the radio station to announce his unconditional surrender. Finally, the Vietnam War had ended—with a bang and a whimper.

**POSTWAR CONFLICT AND ECONOMIC PERFORMANCE, 1975-1990**

Even before the Vietnam War had ended, conflict with the Communist Party of Kampuchea (CPK, also variously known as the Khmer Rouge or Pol Pot group) and China had begun. The root reasons for this conflict have been documented in detail by Nayan Chanda, the veteran reporter for the *Far Eastern Economic Review*, in his universally acclaimed book on the subject.[92] Chanda reported that the ultranationalistic Khmer Rouge had become extremely wary of the Vietnamese precisely because the latter had provided what Prince Norodom Sihanouk called the "indisputably effective and heroic shield" to help the Khmer resistance forces grow in strength. Chanda continued: "The very success of the resistance meant the beginning of the end of CPK-Hanoi alliance. . . . According to a CIA report in September 1970, Khmer

*A guerrilla fighter guiding a tank unit toward the Saigon Presidential Palace on 30 April 1975. (Photo from Vietnam News Agency. Collection of Ngo Vinh Long.)*

troops fired on Vietnamese Communist forces from behind while the latter were attacking a Lon Nol [Phnom Penh regime] unit in Kompong Thom."[93] From then on, the situation got worse:

> The simmering tension between the Vietnamese and the Khmer Rouge reached a crisis in late 1972 when, during the final stage of U.S.-Vietnamese peace talks in Paris, an attempt was made to bring the Khmer Rouge into negotiation with Lon Nol. U.S. negotiator Henry Kissinger's demand to this effect was passed on to the Khmer Rouge leadership in several clandestine meetings in late 1972 and, for the last time, in a January 24–26, 1973, encounter between Vietnamese Politburo member Pham Hung and Pol Pot. The idea was rejected scornfully. Pol Pot saw that the military situation could produce a quick victory, since the isolated and discredited Lon Nol regime was on its last legs. The Vietnamese warning to the Khmer Rouge that their refusal would bring heavy punishment from the United States was seen as a blackmail attempt. . . .
>
> But the Vietnamese were right about the punishment. Free from duty in the rest of the Indochinese theater, American bombers dropped 257,465 tons of bombs on Cambodia between February and August 1973—50 percent more than the total tonnage dropped on Japan during World War II. There were a great number of civilian casualties. Four years later, sitting in the bunkerlike Democratic Kampuchean embassy in Hanoi, In Sivouth bitterly recalled "the Vietnamese betrayal" in signing a separate peace with the enemy, enabling the Americans to direct their full fury at Cambodia. This accusation is a classic example of how racial prejudice and feelings of historical enmity led the Pol Pot group to blame all their woes on the Vietnamese. . . . Ironically enough, if the peace agreement

*The people of Saigon waved or flew revolutionary flags to greet the liberation army as it entered Saigon on 30 August 1975. This woman and her family certainly look totally delighted with the liberation of Saigon and Vietnam. (Photo by Van Bao/ Vietnam News Agency. Collection of John Spragens, Jr.)*

with the Vietnamese freed American hands in Cambodia, tacit support for the bombing, according to Kissinger, came from Zhou [Prime Minister of China] who "needed our military actions in Cambodia for the effectiveness of his policy almost as much as we did." The U.S. bombing, according to him, was a bargaining chip for getting China's Khmer Rouge allies to accept a negotiated settlement with Sihanouk as the leader. . . .

The Paris Agreement in 1973 also marked the beginning of Khmer Rouge attacks on Vietnamese arms depots, hospitals, and base camps inside Cambodia—attacks that were explained away by the Pol Pot group as stemming from misunderstanding and unruly conduct by lower-level soldiers. . . . In February 1975 an entire NLF cultural troupe from My Tho died in an ambush while passing through Cambodian territory to visit liberated areas of Tay Ninh Province. . . . Hanoi's principal task was to liberate the South, not to exacerbate a conflict with wayward allies. Thus, despite growing tension between the two, the Vietnamese played along. In response to a Khmer Rouge request, they sent sapper and artillery units that helped to finally strangle Phnom Penh.[94]

But the Khmer Rouge immediately turned their guns on the Vietnamese, producing many deaths and forcing at least 150,000 Vietnamese to flee from Cambodia to Vietnam during the first five months after the fall of Phnom Penh. The Vietnamese reaction was one of restraint because, in Chanda's words,

Vietnam's need for caution toward Cambodia was underlined by the fact that Phnom Penh had a powerful friend. . . . On June 21 [1975] Pol Pot got a hero's welcome from his ideological mentor, Mao. . . .

The friendship between Mao's China and Democratic Kampuchea was based on ideology and, more importantly, on identity of national interest. . . . As opposition to the Vietnamese domination of the Indochinese peninsula became the primary concern of the Pol Pot group, they naturally turned out to be China's key ally in its traditional strategy of preventing the emergence of a strong power on its southern border.

Not surprisingly, in August 1975, as a bedridden Zhou was explaining China's inability to help Vietnam to the top Vietnamese planner, Le Thanh Nghi, Peking was giving a grand welcome to the Cambodian deputy premiers Khieu Samphan and Ieng Sary and promising them $1 billion in aid over a five-year period. . . .

While Samphan and Sary's triumphant visit, and the pledge of economic assistance, was a public demonstration of China's total support for Cambodia, secret negotiations on Chinese arms aid had begun in June—when Pol Pot made his unpublicized trip to China. In August and October, teams of experts from China's defense ministry conducted an extensive survey in Cambodia to assess defense needs, and, on October 12, submitted a draft aid plan to Phnom Penh for its approval.[95]

Another reason for the Vietnamese restraint was the huge and urgent task of stemming hunger in the southern cities and of restoring production in the countryside. Before the war ended, even with all the U.S. economic aid, the South Vietnamese economy was already a mess. Nguyen Van Hao, Saigon's deputy prime minister in charge of economic affairs, was quoted in the 16 October 1973 issue of *Dai Dan Toc* as saying that between one and one-half million people (about a fifth of the adult work force) were unemployed. To this one must add the several million Saigon soldiers and the 300,000–500,000 prostitutes who suddenly found themselves out of work. Also, hundreds of thousands of war invalids and 800,000 orphans had to be fed. The immediate objective of the Vietnamese government at that time, therefore, was to restore economic and hence social and political stability in the South. The slogan in the North at that time was: "All for the brotherly South; all for the building of socialism." From the beginning of May to the end of the year the North sent several hundred thousand tons of food, tens of thousands of tons of chemical fertilizers, thousands of tons of fuel oil, several hundred thousand head of cattle and buffalo, several hundred thousand fertilized eggs, and tens of thousands of tons of cotton and other supplies to the South. Hundreds of agronomists, engineers, and specialists in other fields were also dispatched quickly to the South.[96]

## FOREMOST VIETNAMESE PRIORITY: POSTWAR RECONSTRUCTION

The foremost Vietnamese priority during the first couple of years was postwar reconstruction and economic recovery. This can be seen in the adoption in early 1977 of the Second Five-Year Plan of 1976–1980, which was made with full expectation that massive amounts of foreign aid from Western capitalist countries and from socialist countries, including China, would be forthcoming. Hence, Vietnam did not want to do anything that would jeopardize this aid, which was absolutely essential for realizing the ambitious targets set in the plan. For example, food production (rice and subsidiary crops converted into rice at a rate of three to one, that is, three tons of potatoes was equal to one ton of rice) was supposed to be increased from 12 million metric tons in 1976 to 21 million metric tons by 1980, and industrial output, labor productivity, and national income were to be raised by 16 to 18, 7.5 to 8.0, and 13 to 14 percent, respectively, per year.

However, by 1977 China had cut almost all aid to Vietnam while its increased military aid to the Khmer Rouge, including hundreds of Chinese military advisers in Cambodia, encouraged the Khmer Rouge to step up attacks on Vietnamese border provinces. The result was that from 1977 to December 1978 tens of thousands of Vietnamese civilians (in Vietnam) were made homeless and thousands of others massacred in the most sadistic manner. In an interview given to Agence France Press at the Tan Son Nhut airport in Ho Chi Minh City (Saigon) on 30 June 1988, Lieutenant General Le Khai Phieu, the deputy commander of the Vietnamese forces in Cambodia, disclosed that 30,000 Vietnamese soldiers were killed in just two years (1977 and 1978) defending the border provinces against Pol Pot forces, as compared to the 25,000 killed on the battlefields in Cambodia since December 1978 when Vietnam counterattacked in the attempt to get rid of Pol Pot. The general added that during the first two years in Cambodia 15,000 Vietnamese soldiers were killed and from 1982 to June 1988 another 10,000 died in battle. The total number of Vietnamese soldiers killed in the conflict with Pol Pot until

June 1988 is therefore equal to the number of U.S. combatants killed in the entire Vietnam War. The human costs of Pol Pot's attacks against Vietnam in 1977 and 1978 explain in part why Vietnam finally lost its self-restraint and went into Cambodia in late December 1978. Another reason was that Pol Pot had already murdered, according to estimates, about 1 million Cambodians, many of whom were suspected of sympathy for Vietnam.[97] A third reason was that China had already massed about 300,000 to 500,000 troops along the northern border since May 1978 and attacked Vietnam almost daily. It was about this time that, in Nayan Chanda's words,

> unknown to the Vietnamese, Peking had decided to "teach Vietnam a lesson" and had intensified its effort to establish full diplomatic relations with the United States before undertaking that adventure. The Chinese design meshed well with that of Jimmy Carter and his national security adviser, seeking China's partnership in a global anti-Soviet alliance. They decided to shelve normalization with Vietnam and secretly push for establishing ties with Peking. Three decades after going to war in Vietnam to fight "Chinese expansionism," the United States became a silent partner in Peking's war against Vietnam.[98]

On 11 October 1978 the United States said that it was not going to normalize relations with Vietnam although both sides had already agreed to this, down to the details as to where each other's embassies would be placed and how many staff members were to be in each. On 15 December the United States announced that it would recognize China and would invite Deng Xiaoping, China's "paramount leader," to visit the United States to finalize things. Vietnam realized that a pincer attack was coming from the north as well as the southwest and decided to break the military encirclement by moving against Pol Pot on 25 December. The Khmer Rouge were driven out of Phnom Penh by 7 January 1979, only to find sanctuary along the Thai-Cambodian border. In mid-January representatives of China and Thailand met to formalize their common support of a guerrilla war against Vietnam. On 28 January Deng arrived in Washington and immediately informed President Carter of his planned invasion of Vietnam. On 17 February China launched an invasion against Vietnam. The very next day an editorial in the *Washington Post* disclosed that the White House had encouraged Deng in his decision to attack Vietnam for a number of reasons, one of which was to help cement China's new relationship with the Western world by making it burn the bridge to other socialist countries behind it. Millions of dollars of U.S. military aid were also subsequently channeled through Thailand in the guerrilla effort against Vietnamese and Cambodian troops.

**THE NEGATIVE IMPACT OF CONFLICT ON DEVELOPMENT**
The negative impact of conflict with China and the Khmer Rouge on Vietnamese economic development was enormous. First, the six northern provinces were physically destroyed by the Chinese invaders. Second, labor was diverted from development to the military: Half a million men were sent to the northern border to protect it against further Chinese attacks, and about 160,000 men

were kept in Cambodia to prevent the return of Pol Pot. Third, the population was displaced: For example, from 1978 to 1979 300,000 Vietnamese and ethnic Chinese fled Vietnam and thereby deprived the country of much needed skill and labor for reconstruction and economic development. In addition, as a reaction to Vietnam's invasion of Cambodia and under very strong U.S. pressures, almost all aid from capitalist countries to Vietnam was cut. In June 1978 China had terminated all trade with Vietnam, which amounted to 75 percent of all of Vietnam's foreign trade; the United States had already imposed a strict trade embargo on Vietnam. Therefore, the tremendous outlays for defense and economic aid to Cambodia as well as the huge food and other subsidies provided to the gigantic urban population—close to 5 million in Ho Chi Minh City alone—and the burgeoning bureaucracy created an ever-worsening budgetary deficit that in turn created rampant inflation and diffi-culties in almost every economic sector. The impacts of these and other factors, which we cannot go into here for reason of space, on the overall economic performance of Vietnam during this period is summarized by a Vietnamese economist, Vo Nhan Tri, as follows:

> By the end of the Second Five-Year Plan in 1980, Vietnam's total food production was 14.4 million tons, compared to the target of 21 million. Between 1976 and 1980 food production increased only 6.45 percent, while the population grew by 9.27 percent. Per capita food production thus decreased from 274 kg to 268 kg, forcing Vietnam to import 8–9 million tons of food during 1976–1980. Even so, malnutrition was widely evident, especially among young children.
> . . .
> Overall, industrial output (including handicrafts, which accounted for approx-imately half of the total) increased from 1976 to 1978, and then fell during the years 1979 and 1980 as a consequence of socialist transformation and other factors, such as poor management, lack of capital, and shortages of energy and raw materials. Over the full 1976–1980 period industrial production increased a mere 0.1 percent. . . . Labor productivity decreased in the state sector, and many enterprises operated at only 30–50 percent of capacity.[99]

## REFORMS AND READJUSTMENTS

This situation called for a series of economic reforms beginning in the fall of 1979 that quickly brought about good results. From 1980 to 1984 food production increased by an average of about 6 percent per year, and industrial output rose by about 9 percent per year. Two Western economists correctly observed:

> During the early 1980s the Vietnamese economy started to evolve rather rapidly. Grass-roots changes interacted with policy concessions and periodic drives to clamp down on selected targets such as the free market. . . . The overall effect was to show the scope for sharply improved short-term resource utilisation in some areas, where output increased without significant additional inputs. An important factor here was the effect of higher incomes upon labour inputs, especially in agriculture. However, the effects of such liberalizations were pri-marily short-term, and could not have sustained long-term results if the deep

structural problems of the economy remained unsolved. Official policy failed to deal with this problem.[100]

As a result of this policy failure, production plateaued in 1985 while population continued to grow at an estimated rate of 2.5 percent a year. This plus the increasing government budget deficit caused by the continuing war (with Pol Pot along the Thai-Cambodian border and China along the northern Vietnamese border) and rampant subsidies, inappropriate wage and price policies, and mismanagement created a hyperinflation, which in turn affected production in almost all sectors. Food production decreased from 1986 on, and by early 1988, when inflation reached about 30 percent a month, widespread food shortages and hunger occurred.

All this forced the government to institute yet another series of reforms in 1988, which were quite fundamental and far-reaching. These reforms included allowing farmers in the cooperatives to keep at least 50 percent of the crop yields after all taxes and production costs; and reduction of government deficit, subsidies, and credit, The program has brought about some intended results. By the beginning of 1989 inflation was reduced to about 6 percent a month and then to about 3.5 percent by May. Agricultural production reversed its downhill slide to achieve a 4.1 percent growth rate in 1988 as opposed to 1.3 percent in 1987. Overall, economic growth attained a reasonable rate of 5.8 percent in 1988 as opposed to only 2.2 percent in 1987. By the end of 1989 and the beginning of 1990 inflation was reduced to 1 to 2 percent a month. In 1989 grain production totaled 21 million metric tons, as compared to 18 million metric tons in 1988. There was a significant rice surplus and so Vietnam was able to export 1.5 million metric tons of milled rice, but at extremely low prices because of lack of markets due to the U.S.-imposed trade embargo that is still honored by many of its allies.

The Vietnamese leaders realized, therefore, that steady economic, social, and political stability in Vietnam required a solution to the Cambodian situation and the conflict with China as well as access to the international markets and foreign aid, which are all closely related. Confident that it had already helped Cambodia back on its feet, in early July 1988 Vietnam pulled its entire military command and half of its remaining troops out of Cambodia, placing the rest under Phnom Penh's command, and stated that it would bring all of its troops home by the end of 1989 or much earlier if there were a political settlement. Subsequently, because there was little movement in the direction of a political settlement and because of continuing hostility on the part of the United States and China, Vietnam announced many times that it would definitely bring all of its troops home from Cambodia by the end of September 1989 whether or not a political solution were reached by then. And this was precisely what Vietnam did when all efforts to get the United States and China to support a political settlement failed.

For almost a whole year after its complete withdrawal from Cambodia Vietnam lobbied for improved relations with the United States, saying that all stumbling blocks to normalization of relations had been removed. But the United States insisted that Vietnam should make the Hun Sen government in

*A pedicab driver in Hanoi pauses to read his morning paper. Vietnamese newspapers, long mouthpieces for official pronouncements, are venturing onto the uncertain ground of investigative reporting. (Copyright © 1988 John Spragens, Jr. Reprinted with permission.)*

Cambodia accept a "comprehensive" political settlement with the other Cambodian parties, which was precisely China's position of forcing the Khmer Rouge–dominated coalition on that hapless country. Faced with another year of bloodletting in Cambodia, the real prospect of a Khmer Rouge return to power, and with increasing domestic criticism and international pressures, Secretary of State James A. Baker announced on 18 July 1990 that the United States would withdraw its recognition of the Khmer Rouge–dominated coalition at the United Nations and would discuss settlement of the conflict with Vietnam. The Vietnamese government saw this as a positive gesture and immediately seized the opportunity to enter into talks with the United States. In late September 1990 Nguyen Co Thach, foreign minister and deputy prime minister of the Socialist Republic of Vietnam (SRV), arrived in the United States for talks with James Baker and other U.S. officials. However, in two weeks of meetings Thach was told consistently that normalization of diplomatic and economic relations can occur only after the Cambodian civil war is settled and Vietnam has helped account for 1,677 American servicemen still listed as missing in action. Although Vietnam has made valiant efforts to find and return the remains of Americans since the end of the war while its own 300,000 MIAs are still unaccounted for, Thach nevertheless promised that Vietnam would do all it could on both issues. At a meeting in Washington, D.C., on 17 October, for example, Thach accepted without any hesitation a U.S. proposal to station a permanent U.S. representative in Hanoi to deal with efforts to account for U.S. MIAs.[101]

But the prospects for U.S.-Vietnam normalization of relations are very chancy if the United States insists on the "comprehensive political solution" to the Cambodian situation. Mindful of this trap the chairperson of the Senate Foreign Relations Committee and seven other Democratic and Republican senators wrote to President Bush in early November 1990 saying that the administration was mistaken to link the Cambodian conflict to an improvement in relations with Vietnam. As quoted in the 4 November 1990 issue of the *New York Times*, the letter said: "We should not allow the prolonged end game in the Cambodian peace negotiations to prevent us from taking the next step of lifting the trade embargo with Vietnam. Conclusion of a comprehensive peace in Cambodia, establishment of a substantial U.N. presence, and conduct of a free and fair election in war-torn Cambodia could take years. . . . In addition, we are heartened by the significant support for market economic principles that have been demonstrated by some members of the Vietnamese Government. These developments warrant a significant U.S. response."

Vietnam has embarked on a bold and far-reaching economic reform that, according to the World Bank, has put it in the forefront of socialist economies attempting to rejuvenate their economic systems. In order to guarantee that this will succeed, the Vietnamese need regional peace and access to international markets and foreign aid, both of which would be greatly facilitated by the lifting of the U.S. trade embargo and normalization of relations with the United States. However, more than fifteen years after the end of the war the U.S. government is still not ready to come to terms with Vietnam. China is still the reason, although there is a cynical twist this time around: Partly because the United States needed China's support for its policy in the Gulf, it was willing to toe China's vindictive line against Vietnam. The irony here is that the United States is now in the best position ever to promote its own interests by playing a constructive role in Indochina.

## NOTES

1. *Relief and Rehabilitation of War Victims in Indochina, Part 4: South Vietnam and Regional Problems,* hearing before the Subcommittee to Investigate Problems Connected with Refugees and Escapees of the Committee on the Judiciary, United States Senate, 93rd Congress (Washington: U.S. Government Printing Office, 1973), p. 8. For a brief reference on statistics of U.S. bombings see James Pinckney Harrison, *The Endless War: Vietnam's Struggle for Independence* (New York: McGraw-Hill, 1983), pp. 3–4, 276–277.

2. Quoted in Harrison, *The Endless War,* p. 4.

3. Joseph Buttinger, *Vietnam: The Unforgettable Tragedy* (New York: Horizon Press, 1977), p. 17.

4. Helen B. Lamb, *Vietnam's Will to Live: Resistance to Foreign Aggression from Early Times Through the Nineteenth Century* (New York: Monthly Review Press, 1972); David G. Marr, *Vietnamese Anticolonialism, 1885–1925* (Berkeley: University of California Press, 1971); Huynh Kim Khanh, *Vietnamese Communism, 1925–1945* (Ithaca, NY: Cornell University Press, 1986); Wilfred Burchett, *Catapult to Freedom: The Survival of the Vietnamese People* (London: Quartet Books, 1978).

5. Leopold Pallu, *Histoire de l'Expédition de Cochinchine en 1861* (Paris, 1864), quoted in Burchett, *Catapult to Freedom,* pp. 83–84.

6. See Ngo Vinh Long, *Before the Revolution: The Vietnamese Peasants Under the French* (Cambridge, MA: The MIT Press, 1973) and *Vietnamese Women in Society and Revolution: The French Colonial Period* (Cambridge, MA: Vietnam Resource Center, 1974).

7. "Canh Nha Que" (The Scene in the Countryside), *Phu Nu Tan Van*, 15 August 1929, p. 1–6. This was the largest magazine in circulation in Indochina at the time.

8. Truong Chinh and Vo Nguyen Giap, *The Peasant Question*, translated and with an introduction by Christine P. White (Ithaca, NY: Southeast Asia Program, Cornell University, 1974), pp. 31–32.

9. For a detailed breakdown of the number of workers see *Résumé statistique relatif aux années, 1913–1940* (Hanoi: 1941), p. 9, and *Annuaire statistiques de l'Indochine, 1941–1942*, p. 278. These sources were published by the colonial government. For the number of workers in commercial, industrial, and agricultural enterprises, see Rene Bunout, *La main d'oeuvre et la legislation du travail en Indochine* (Bordeaux: Delmas, 1936), p. 9. Official French statistics for 1930 listed 49,000 persons in the rubber and other agricultural plantations in Cochinchina. But Bunout (p. 112) estimated that if women and children workers were included, about 100,000 persons worked in the rubber plantations alone.

10. Official French source cited in Paul Monet, *Les Jaunièrs: Histoire Vraie* (Paris: Gallimard, 1931), p. 204.

11. Nguyen Thi Sanh, "Cuoc tong bai cong thang 11-1936 cua tho mo cong ty Phap mo than Bac-ky (SCFT)" [The General Strike of November 1936 of the miners of the Société Française de charbonage du Tonkin], *Nghien Cuu Lich Su* (Historical Research), no. 138 (Hanoi: Institute of Historical Research, May–June 1971), p. 33.

12. Paul Bernard, *Le Problème Économique Indochinois* (Paris: Nouvelles Editions Latines, 1934), p. 21; Charles Robequain, *L'Évolution Économique de l'Indochine Française* (Paris: Centre d'Études de Politique Étrangère, 1939), pp. 87–89.

13. Ngo Van Hoa, "Nhung tien de cua Lien, Minh Cong Nong truoc Khi dang ra doi" (The premises of the Peasant-Worker Alliance before the birth of the Party), *Nghien Cuu Lich Su*, no. 152 (Hanoi: Institute of Historical Research, September–October 1973), p. 23.

14. Ibid.

15. Ibid.; René Bunout, *La main d'oeuvre*, p. 8.

16. Ngo Vinh Long, *Before the Revolution*, pp. 101–120.

17. Nghiem Xuan Yem, "Nan Dan Doi" (The Starvation Crisis of the People), *Thanh Nghi*, no. 107 (5 May 1945), p. 18.

18. For discussion and original documents relating to this event, see Tran Huy Lieu et al., *Tai Lieu Tham Khao Lich Su: Cach Mang Can Dai Viet Nam* (Reference Documents: Modern Vietnamese Revolution) (Hanoi: Ban Nghien Cuu Van Su Dia xuat ban, 1956), vol. 5, pp. 98–102, and vol. 6, pp. 51–52 and 134–140. For a detailed treatment in English see Huynh Kim Khanh, *Vietnamese Communism*, pp. 90–141.

19. For the most detailed discussion of this period see Ngo Vinh Long, "The Indochinese Communist Party and Peasant Rebellion in Central Vietnam, 1930–1931," *Bulletin of Concerned Asian Scholars*, vol. 10, no. 4 (1978), pp. 15–35; also see Huynh Kim Khanh, *Vietnamese Communism*, pp. 142–160.

20. For the most detailed study of the 1930s in English, see Ngo Vinh Long, *Peasant Revolutionary Struggles in Vietnam in the 1930s* (Ph. D. diss., Harvard University, 1978, 745 pp.). For the "Popular Front" period of 1936–1939, also see Huynh Kim Khanh, *Vietnamese Communism*, pp. 218–231.

21. Cited in *History of the August Revolution* (Hanoi: Foreign Languages Publishing House, 1972), p. 8. Twenty years later, in his book *Deux actes du drame indochinois* (Paris: Plon, 1959) Georges Catroux reaffirmed his policy in great detail.

22. Joseph Buttinger, *Vietnam: A Dragon Embattled* (New York: Praeger Publishers, Inc., 1967), vol. 1: pp. 200–240; Ngo Vinh Long (1973), *Before the Revolution*, pp. 122–132.

23. *Temoignages et Documents Français Relatifs a la Colonisation Française au Viet Nam* (Hanoi: Association Culturelle pour le Salut du Vietnam), vol. 1, pp. 10–11.

24. *History of the August Revolution*, pp. 23–30, 115–134; Philippe Devillers, *Histoire du Vietnam de 1940 a 1952* (Paris: Edition du Seil, 1952), pp. 1–129. Tran Huy Lieu and Van Tao, *Tong Khoi Nghia Thang Tam* (The General Uprising of August) (Hanoi: Van Su Dia, 1957), pp. 7–121, contains all the original documents of the August Revolution, the full text of Bao Dai's abdication speech, and the full text of the Declaration of Independence.

25. For a translation of the Declaration of Independence see Marvin E. Gettleman, ed., *Vietnam: History, Documents, and Opinions on a Major World Crisis* (New York: Fawcett World Library, 1966), pp. 57–59.

26. Van Tao et al., *Lich Su Cach Mang Thang Tam* (History of the August Revolution) (Hanoi: Su Hoc, 1960), pp. 149–181. For the most detailed first-hand account of the August Revolution and subsequent developments by an American, see Archimedes L.A. Patti, *Why Vietnam: Prelude To America's Albatross* (University of California Press, 1980). Patti was the head of the Indochina mission of the Office of Strategic Services and a special envoy sent by President Franklin D. Roosevelt to Vietnam to meet and cooperate with Ho Chi Minh and the Viet Minh.

27. George McT. Kahin, *Intervention: How America Became Involved in Vietnam* (New York: Anchor Books, 1987), p. 27.

28. Ibid., pp. 7–8.

29. Buttinger, *Vietnam: The Unforgettable Tragedy*, p. 20. For a more detailed account of the maneuvers to bring the French back into power in the southern part see Kahin, *Intervention*, pp. 8–26.

30. Buttinger, *Vietnam: The Unforgettable Tragedy*, pp. 21–22.

31. Ibid., p. 22.

32. Ibid., p. 24.

33. See the Senator Gravel Edition of *The Pentagon Papers* (Boston: Beacon Press, 1971), vol. 1, p. 30. This will be referred to hereinafter simply as the *Pentagon Papers*. Officially the "History of the U.S. Decision Making Process on Vietnam Policy," this 47-volume top-secret inquiry into U.S. involvement in Indochina was commissioned by Robert McNamara and headed by Leslie Gelb. It was completed in January 1969 and 43 volumes of it were made public in June and July 1971 by the *New York Times*.

34. Kahin, *Intervention*, pp. 34–35.

35. Nguyen Khac Vien, *The Long Resistance* (Hanoi: Foreign Languages Publishing House, 1975), pp. 128–133; Joseph Starobin, *Eyewitness in Indo-China* (New York: Cameron and Khan, 1954), pp. 10–102; Kahin, *Intervention*, pp. 35–39.

36. Bernard Fall, *Two Vietnams: A Political and Military Analysis* (New York: Praeger, 1967), p. 111.

37. *Pentagon Papers*, vol. 1, p. 67.

38. Nguyen Khac Vien, *The Long Resistance*, pp. 134–136.

39. Kahin, *Intervention*, pp. 38–39.

40. *Pentagon Papers*, vol. 1, p. 85.

41. Ibid., p. 96.

42. Kahin, *Intervention*, p. 45.

43. *Pentagon Papers*, vol. 1, p. 96.

44. Ibid., pp. 87, 442.

45. Dwight D. Eisenhower, *Mandate for Change: The White House Years, 1953–56* (New York: Signet, 1963), p. 412.

46. *Congressional Record* (Washington: U.S. Government Printing Office, 9 July 1954), vol. 100, p. 1037; Sir Anthony Eden, *Full Circle* (London: Cassell, 1953), p. 143; Kahin, *Intervention*, pp. 45–50.

47. *Pentagon Papers*, vol. 1, p. 121.

48. Ibid., pp. 121–132, 149–153.

49. Kahin, *Intervention*, pp. 61–62.

50. *Pentagon Papers*, vol. 1, p. 177.

51. James Gavin, *Crisis Now* (New York: Random House, 1968), pp. 47–48.

52. Cited in Buttinger, *Vietnam: The Unforgettable Tragedy*, p. 33.

53. Gavin, *Crisis Now*, p. 49.

54. Kahin, *Intervention*, pp. 96–98.

55. Gabriel Kolko, *Anatomy of a War* (New York: Pantheon Books, 1985), p. 93.

56. William A. Nighswonger, *Rural Pacification in Vietnam* (New York: Praeger, 1966), p. 46. Colonel Nighswonger was a senior AID (Agency for International Development, a CIA front) officer for the Pacification Program. Milton E. Osborne, *Strategic Hamlets in South Vietnam* (Ithaca, NY: Cornell University, 1965), p. 22. Nguyen Khac Nhan, "Policy of Key Rural Agrovilles," *Asian Culture*, vol. 3, nos. 3 and 4 (July–December 1961), p. 32.

57. Nighswonger, *Rural Pacification*, pp. 46–47.

58. Kahin, *Intervention*, pp. 155–156. For details of the Diem regime, the rise of the NLF, and the overthrow of Diem, pp. 93–181; and Kolko, *Anatomy*, pp. 86–151.

59. Ellen J. Hammer, *A Death in November: America in Vietnam 1963* (New York: Oxford University Press, 1987).

60. Kahin, *Intervention*, p. 181.

61. Nighswonger, *Rural Pacification*, pp. 61–63.

62. Kahin, *Intervention*, pp. 236–285 provides details leading to the decision. See p. 306 for the immediate quote.

63. For details see ibid., pp. 295–305; *Ramparts*, July 1975.

64. Kahin, *Intervention*, p. 307.

65. Recent excellent examples include Neil Sheehan, *A Bright Shining Lie: John Paul Vann and America in Vietnam* (New York: Random House, 1988); James William Gibson, *The Perfect War: Technowar in Vietnam* (Boston: Atlantic Monthly Press, 1986) and in paperback as *The Perfect War: The War We Couldn't Lose and How We Did* (New York: Vintage Books/Random House, 1988); Jonathan Schell, *The Real War: The Classic Reporting on the Vietnam War with a New Essay* (New York: Pantheon Books, 1987).

66. These include Kolko's *Anatomy of a War*; Jeffrey Race, *War Comes to Long An* (University of California Press, 1973); and Truong Nhu Tang, *A Viet Cong Memoir: An Inside Account of the Vietnam War and Its Aftermath* (New York: Vintage Books, 1986).

67. *Pentagon Papers*, vol. 3, p. 139.

68. Cited in *U.S. News and World Report*, 20 March 1967.

69. Ngo Vinh Long, "The Tet Offensive and Its Aftermath," Jan.–April 1988 issues of *Indochina Newsletter*, Asia Resource Center, 2161 Massachusetts Ave., Cambridge, MA 02140; Kolko, *Anatomy*, pp. 303–337; Don Oberdorfer, *Tet!* (New York: Avon Books, 1972); *Nineteen Sixty-Eight*, Time-Life's "The Vietnam Experience" series (Boston: The Boston Publishing Company, 1983).

70. *Pentagon Papers*, vol. 6, p. 539.

71. Kolko, *Anatomy*, p. 309.

72. George C. Herring, *America's Longest War* (New York: Alfred A. Knopf, 1986), p. 194.

73. Kolko, *Anatomy,* pp. 308–309; Oberdorfer, *Tet!,* pp. 256–262; *Nineteen Sixty-Eight,* p. 20.

74. Quotes cited in *Nineteen Sixty-Eight,* pp. 146–147.

75. W. Averell Harriman, *America and Russia in a Changing World* (New York: Doubleday and Co., 1971), pp. 136–140.

76. One of the best treatments of this story is William Shawcross's *Sideshow: Kissinger, Nixon and the Destruction of Cambodia* (New York: Simon & Schuster, 1979).

77. Cited in Nguyen Khac Vien, *The Long Resistance,* p. 178.

78. This period of "talk-fight" struggle from 1971 to 1972 was much more complex than is indicated here. For a more detailed treatment, see Kolko, *Anatomy,* pp. 412–437.

79. For details of this "Christmas bombing" and the signing of the Paris Agreement, see ibid., pp. 439–453.

80. *Fiscal Year 1974 Authorization for Military Procurement, Research and Development, Construction Authorization for Safeguard ABM, and Active Duty and Selected Reserve Strengths,* hearings before the Committee on Armed Services, United States Senate, 93rd Congress, Part 3, Authorizations (U.S. Government Printing Office, 1973), p. 1383.

81. *Vietnam: May 1974,* Staff Report Prepared for the Use of the Committee on Foreign Relations, United States Senate, 5 August 1974, U.S. Government Printing Office, p. 22.

82. Economic aid to the Thieu regime during the same period was also increased and channeled through various programs such as the Foreign Assistance Act and "Food for Peace." For example, on 17 and 18 December 1974 Congress passed the Foreign Assistance Act, authorizing $450 million in economic aid to Saigon. This was $100 million more than the amount authorized by Congress in fiscal year 1974. According to the 16 January 1975 issue of *Dien Tin* (Telegraph, a Saigon daily), 90 percent of U.S. economic aid to the Thieu regime had been used to maintain the war. See *Congressional Record,* 20 May 1974 and 4 June 1974, for details of the hunger and starvation caused by the economic blockade.

83. *Dai Dan Toc* (Saigon daily run by a group of Saigon Lower House deputees), 30 August 1974.

84. *Dien Tin,* 6, 20, 22, and 24 Sept.; and *Dai Dan Toc,* 30 Sept. 1974.

85. *Dien Tin,* 20 Sept. 1974.

86. *Chinh Luan* (CIA-sponsored Saigon newspaper), 20 Sept. 1974.

87. Kolko, *Anatomy,* p. 502.

88. *Washington Post,* 2 November 1974.

89. *Hoa Binh* (Catholic daily in Saigon), 27 September 1974.

90. *Washington Post,* 7 October 1974.

91. Kolko, *Anatomy,* pp. 542–543.

92. Nayan Chanda's *Brother Enemy: The War After the War, A History of Indochina Since the Fall of Saigon* (New York: Macmillan Publishing Company, 1986).

93. Ibid., p. 66.

94. Ibid., pp. 68–73.

95. Ibid., pp. 16–17.

96. These facts are summarized from Vietnamese newspaper reports by this author and can be ascertained by reading the reports of the Foreign Broadcast Information Service (a U.S. government agency) for this period.

97. For a discussion of this estimate see Michael Vickery, "How Many Died in Pol Pot's Kampuchea?" *Bulletin of Concerned Asian Scholars,* vol. 20, no. 1, pp. 70–73.

98. Chanda, *Brother Enemy,* pp. 6–7.

99. David G. Marr and Christine P. White, eds., *Postwar Vietnam: Dilemmas in Socialist Development* (Ithaca, NY: Cornell Southeast Asia Program, 1988), pp. 80–82.

100. Adam Fforde and Stefan de Vylder, *Vietnam—An Economy in Transition* (Stockholm: Swedish International Development Authority, 1988), pp. 62–63. For examples of structural problems and obstacles also see my study in *Postwar Vietnam*, pp. 163–173; and "Agrarian Differentiation in the Southern Region of Vietnam," *Journal of Contemporary Asia*, vol. 14, no. 3 (1984). An excellent study in French is Nguyen Duc Nhuan et al., *Le Viet Nam Post-Revolutionaire: Population, Economie, Societe, 1975–1985* (Paris: Editions L'Harmattan, 1987).

101. *The Boston Globe*, 31 October 1990.

# 2

Ngô Vĩnh
Hải

# Postwar Vietnam: Political Economy

After liberation in April 1975 the new Vietnamese government inherited a legacy of war that, according to official Vietnamese estimates, "included 20,000,000 bomb craters, ten million refugees, 362,000 war invalids, one million widows, 880,000 orphans, 250,000 drug addicts, 300,000 prostitutes and three million unemployed; two-thirds of the villages were destroyed."[1] These statistics describe not even the whole nation but just the southern half of the country.

The objective situation of the economic, political, social, and cultural devastation of the war would have presented a daunting challenge to any new government. Therefore, as Ngo Vinh Long observed in the concluding section to Chapter 1, the foremost priority of Vietnamese policymakers was for postwar reconstruction and economic recovery. The Vietnamese government formulated ambitious targets, and there were some encouraging results from 1975 to 1990; but it seems obvious that most of the priorities and objectives were not realized because of both external developments (such as the costly conflicts with China and Cambodia and the U.S.-imposed trade embargo and economic blockade) and internal developments (such as obstacles to economic policies and programs created by political, social, and personnel-management problems).

Although statistics, such as those provided by the Vietnamese government, often reveal some of the magnitude of the problems confronting postwar Vietnam, they do not tell the whole story. There were other problems that cannot be easily quantified and thus seem less tangible but have also created a tremendous negative impact on postwar developments in Vietnam.

One of these problems was the polarization that has come about as a result of almost a century of French divide-and-rule policy and more than ten thousand days of U.S. intervention that caused a full-fledged fratricidal war. This situation of distrust and hatred among different elements within Vietnamese society has been further worsened by the continuing vindictive policy of the United States against Vietnam that has included an economic embargo and the use of overseas Vietnamese to infiltrate Vietnam and carry out various sabotage activities. In response, the Vietnamese government has on occasion overreacted by suspecting most of those who had formerly worked for the United States and the Saigon government. As a result, many otherwise healthy and skillful persons have become marginalized.

Another problem ironically arose from the euphoria of victory. Many Vietnamese came to think that since they had been able to defeat the richest and most powerful country on earth by mobilizing the population, they could now also succeed in rebuilding the country basically through self-reliance. This led to overemphasizing the negative impact of the U.S. presence and underestimating truly positive economic developments in the South during the war years. For example, in political seminars organized by the Department of Propaganda and Education of the Communist Party that I had to attend, the lecturers frequently said that the value of all the property and holdings of the capitalists in the South was not equal to the cost of two spans of the Thang Long bridge outside of Hanoi. (This bridge was being built with Chinese aid, and the Party Department of Propaganda and Education [PDPE] could have said that to please the Chinese, especially since the PDPE was still full of Maoists.) Fifteen years later Tran Bach Dang, former chief of PDPE in the South, had to admit that Vietnam had been going through a period when "news and information had been filtered with the aim of proving our [the socialist system's] subjective superiority."[2] In any case, this incorrect assessment of the available resources led to misuse, neglect, and waste that—together with the stress and strain created by the conflict with China and the Khmer Rouge—certainly had an important impact on postwar reconstruction and development.

In short, the postwar Vietnamese leadership faced objective structural economic and political problems, but their subjective assessments and responses often exacerbated these problems and even created new problems. A major aim of this chapter is to show that incorrect or inadequate assessment of the legacies of the Vietnam War led the Vietnamese Communist leadership to force through premature "socialist transformation," which is in reality class struggle and not economic development, of the southern region in Vietnam. Although their aim might have been to solve years of social and economic inequities, the results have been only to create a whole array of additional problems that have adversely affected the development of the country from 1975 to 1990. For the sake of treatment in the remainder of the chapter, I will divide the last fifteen years into four periods: 1975–1979, 1979–1981, 1982–1985, and 1986–1990.

## "TOWARD LARGE-SCALE SOCIALIST PRODUCTION": 1975–1979

After the victory on 30 April 1975, the Communist Party declared that Vietnam had already completed its National Revolution for People's Democracy with the liberation of the country from foreign aggression. In August 1975 the Central Committee of the Party declared a new revolutionary phase—the Socialist Revolution—with the following words: "To complete the reunification of the country and take it rapidly, vigorously and steadily to socialism. To speed up socialist construction and perfect the socialist relations of production in the North, to carry out at the same time socialist transformation and construction in the South."[3] This new phase of the revolution was aimed at liberating the nation from hunger and the working people from the exploitation and oppression of the capitalists and the "feudalistic landlords."

At that time, however, there were a number of policymakers who, having realized the complicated nature of the postwar problems, advocated the mobilization of all segments in the society to participate in the tasks of economic restoration. To bolster their view, they cited Marx as having said that the development of capitalism was necessary for the construction of socialism. They claimed that no country had as yet been successful in building socialism without having first gone through the period of capitalist accumulation. But this group of policymakers was not as powerful as those who advocated class struggle. The view of this latter group of policymakers is reflected in the following analysis of Resolution No. 4 of the Central Committee in December 1976: "Vietnam is now in a favorable international situation. The systems of socialist countries have been and are being ceaselessly expanded and strengthened; the national independence movements and the revolutionary working class movements are developing powerfully. Imperialism is increasingly in crisis and is weakening."[4]

Accordingly, in the view of these policymakers, this "favorable international situation" allowed Vietnam to skip the capitalist stage of development and move directly to the socialist stage of development. To this end, profit-seeking and exploitative capitalistic relations of production had to be eradicated. In their place a large-scale socialist mode of production, including central planning, should be constructed with the aim of serving the interests of the laboring populace. The property and means of production of the exploiting class had to be confiscated and turned into the collective property of the working class to be managed by their representative, the government. In the view of these policymakers, at that time capitalism was in decline and socialism was on the rise, and hence it was the most opportune time to carry out "socialist transformation." If one were to allow the capitalists and landlords to increase their activities and enhance their economic power, then it would be very difficult to carry out a socialist revolution at some point in the future without causing some bloodshed. Hence, socialist transformation—defined simply as "eradicating and constructing"—was pushed.

**THE X-1 CAMPAIGN AND THE "FIRST CURRENCY REFORM"**

The "eradicating" phase of the policy began in August 1975, only a little over four months after liberation, with the launching of the so-called "X-1 campaign." The targets of this campaign were the landlords and compradors or those big capitalists and war profiteers who had collaborated with the United States and with the Saigon regime.

There were relatively few targets for the X-1 campaign in the countryside because during the war years most of the big landlords had fled to the cities. The land they left behind had been either confiscated and distributed by the National Liberation Front (NLF), occupied by the peasants, or left fallow. Later on, beginning in 1970, the Thieu regime had carried out the "Land to the Tiller" program, which had paid the landlords several billion U.S. dollars for the land they had abandoned. Therefore, most of the absentee landlords became urban capitalists—if they had not been so already.[5]

After the X-1 campaign started, 670 households in the southern urban centers were considered compradors. The key members of these households were arrested and their property seized. Although the government explained clearly at the beginning that the sole targets of the campaign were the compradors and not the "national capitalists," the dividing line between them narrowed as the campaign widened. In the zeal to emulate the large cities, many smaller urban centers each had to produce a couple of compradors although in reality there were none. Even in Saigon some people who had reasons to believe that they were national capitalists and had even participated in demonstrations denouncing compradors were nevertheless later arrested. An example was the case of Hong Hoa, a producer and trader of domestic silk.

The above situation created a certain amount of panic among the wealthy and even among those who were not yet part of the new power structures in the newly liberated cities and towns. To pacify public fears, the central government reexamined the whole situation and admitted that many people had been wrongly targeted. As a result, the number of the original 670 households that had been considered compradors was now scaled down to 159.[6] However, the X-1 campaign had already enabled the government to transfer into the state sector most of the important industrial, commercial, and service concerns in the South. These were mostly assembly plants that had been almost totally dependent on imported materials and spare parts, import-export companies, and service facilities that had prospered thanks to U.S. economic aid and direct spending by U.S. military personnel in Vietnam. None of these resources was available after the war. However, the new policymakers thought that they could make up for these losses by calling on the working class to "increase creativity, promote technological innovation, and make use of domestic materials in place of imported materials." It must be noted here that only the creativity of the working class was encouraged at that time. Intellectuals and technical and scientific specialists were regarded as petty bourgeois, hence politically unstable and unreliable and not to be trusted. As a result, this led to unavoidable failures in many cases.

One example was the Sinco sewing-machine assembly plant, an affiliate of the Singer Company. Before liberation it had assembled the machines with mostly imported parts to exact specifications from the parent company. Only the unimportant parts were locally produced. After liberation the new board of directors solicited "creative ideas" (*sang kien*) from the workers in the quest of producing all the parts for the new sewing machines, which nevertheless still carried the Sinco brand name. To this end, they went so far as building new machine tools in order to fabricate the parts. The aim was to produce a system of production said to be "standardized and closed" (*dong bo va khep kin*), which were code words for self-reliant and self-sufficient. But the result was a waste of resources and energy. Because the machine tools were not precision made and because the quality of the metals used was not up to standard, the sewing machines produced did not function properly and broke down quickly when put into operation.

In other cases the boards of directors and technicians of the nationalized factories were replaced by government cadres who could not even make inventories of the available materials scattered about the plants. As a result, the factories had to be closed down temporarily and the workers laid off. According to the policy at the time, unemployed urban residents had to choose between going back to their native villages or working in the New Economic Zones (NEZs). Therefore, when the factories were later put back into operation, the former workers could not go back to work because they were no longer legal residents of the urban areas where the factories were located. As a result, the factories had to hire new workers who turned out to be mostly members of cadres' households. The cadres, who had been mostly from peasant background, had moved into the urban areas with their families after liberation. Hence there was a significant amount of trading places: factory workers were now engaging in agricultural activities while peasants were doing factory work. The result was more waste—with the added side effect that the former urbanites, unused to the extremely strenuous tasks of farming, were unable to cope in the countryside and thus returned in droves to the cities, where they became street people because their former homes and jobs were no longer available to them.

As far as commercial activities were concerned, when the owners of the large enterprises and stores felt that they were under attack they closed up shop and dispersed as many of their goods as possible. This led quickly to the collapse of their distribution networks; the government was still unable to set up any kind of effective replacement. Meanwhile, the postwar demands for consumer goods were increasing steadily. During several decades of war the peasants in the South had typically converted their savings into gold, which they buried. The population in the North had also saved because goods had been rationed and subsidized. This available money plus the available goods being dispersed by the capitalists created an unprecedented black market. Suddenly many people were milling around in the streets or sitting in coffee shops, which seemed to mushroom overnight. The government regarded these people as lazy bums. But they were really black marketers at work, finding suppliers and buyers and haggling over prices through whispers and personal contacts. Hence, although the government wanted to eradicate private businesses in order to build a more comprehensive "socialist distribution" system, in reality its policies encouraged a large increase in the number of private traders. Each shop that was closed down was replaced by hundreds of black marketers or middlepersons, thereby producing ever-spiraling price increases.

While the X-1 campaign was still going on, the government also rammed through another program, which Western researchers have generally called "the first currency reform."[7] This was not any new reform per se but only the old "socialist transformation" because the aim was to replace the old currency with a new one; the aim was consistent with the "eradicating and constructing" philosophy. For twenty-four hours (from midnight on 21 September 1975 to the final hour on 22 September) complete secrecy was maintained, a curfew was imposed, and most activities were curtailed. That morning every household was given a form to declare the amount of old money in its possession; the amount would be replaced by the new currency at the rate of 500 to 1. Many people were so frightened of being regarded as capitalists that they either destroyed some of the old money or did not declare the full amount. In any case, even those who declared and turned in the full amount could only receive installments of small amounts of the new currency on a per capita basis. Hence, although this currency exchange scheme did garner some money for the government treasury and create a certain amount of socioeconomic leveling, at the same time it affected most of the population in the South and caused distrust and loss of confidence in the central government, its banking system, and the value of its currency. Partly as a result of this distrust, the new currency steadily lost its value.

## RURAL COLLECTIVIZATION

Although the Fourth Central Committee Plenum of December 1976 issued a resolution recognizing a mixed economy in the South composed of five sectors—individual (private), household, collective, joint venture, and state— and although this policy was to be maintained until 1980, in reality socialist transformation was subsequently pushed even harder than before. This program began in July 1977 with the campaign to "collectivize agriculture" (*hop tac hoa nong nghiep*) and was followed by the campaign of March 1978 to "eradicate commercial capitalists" (*xoa bo tu san thuong nghiep*), and in May 1978 with the new currency exchange scheme for the entire country.

According to the policymakers, the aim of the rural collectivization program was to steer the peasants toward large-scale socialist production, to eradicate rural exploitation, to mechanize agriculture, and to mobilize resources for irrigation. Although all these factors are interconnected, I will comment only on the result of large-scale socialist production because the other factors have been discussed and documented in detail elsewhere.[8]

The call for large-scale socialist production came out of the postwar need to feed the burgeoning urban population and out of the recognition that the individual peasant landholders in the South could not provide a stable and adequate supply of staples if they were left alone. They had shown that they would rather produce for the market than for any long-term food security strategy. Through rural collectivization the government could presumably force the peasants to be more responsive in meeting government production goals and procurement needs. The Second Five-Year Plan of 1976 called for an increase in the production of food staples to 21 million metric tons of

*In addition to rice, the household economy in Vietnam derives about 50 percent of its income from the private garden plot, the pig sty, and a pond that usually supports five different levels of food production: gourds and squash on the trellis above the pond, arrowroots and other tubers around the pond, azolla on the surface, and various types of fish in the water. The pond is also used for washing, as in this picture taken in Ha Son Binh Province. (Photo by Ngo Vinh Long, 1980.)*

*A woman feeds her ducks in a village in Long An province, which is immediately south of Ho Chi Minh City (Saigon). Because of the war and its incredible devastation in the Mekong Delta, a typical peasant house is made of bamboo and thatch and usually has a couple of earthen vases for rainwater outside and two more inside for storing rice. The peasants supplement their income from rice cultivation by raising ducks and chicken. Pigs do not bring as much cash here in the southern provinces as they do in the northern ones. (Photo by Ngo Vinh Long, 1987.)*

paddy and paddy equivalents a year by 1980. In determining equivalents, for example, one kilogram of paddy rice equals five kilograms of manioc or three kilograms of sweet potatoes or one kilogram of maize. Production quotas were given to the provinces, which in turn apportioned them to the districts, the districts to the villages, the villages to the cooperatives, and the cooperatives to the work brigades. All localities were supposed to achieve self-sufficiency in food staples as well as to pay taxes in kind and to meet certain government food-procurement quotas. To this end, the local authorities put up checkpoints everywhere to prevent staples from slipping out of their own areas and to turn lands planted with tea, coffee, durians, rubber, and so on, into manioc and sweet potato farms, although these two roots would earn only a fraction of the monetary values of the other crops.

Meanwhile, the government procurement policy—which included tax and forced sale of a certain percentage of the crop at a fixed price—had a negative

*Two villagers splitting boards out of a tree trunk. Most of the furniture in the rural areas in Vietnam is still made locally with rudimentary tools. Although the workers are skilled and the finished products well made, the work is time consuming and back breaking. (Photo by Ngo Vinh Long, 1980.)*

impact on areas specializing in rice production. Agricultural tax at that time was a progressive tax imposed on the amounts of rice that the peasants produced in excess of their personal consumption quotas. The procurement price was fixed at the 1975 level of 0.45 dong per kilogram in spite of the fact that the runaway inflation during the latter half of the 1970s had made the free-market price many times the official price.[9] In fact, the government purchase price ended up being lower than production costs. Peasants, therefore, had little incentive to produce much more than they actually needed. As a result, staple production (measured in rice) decreased from 13.5 million metric tons in 1976 to 12.5 and 12.3 million metric tons in 1977 and 1978, respectively.[10] Accordingly, procurement also suffered. Two Western economists, Adam Fforde and Stefan de Vylder, have come to the following conclusion based on official Vietnamese statistics: "The state, which earlier sought a monopoly in staples trade, often without complete success, controlled 15.3% of staples production in 1976. By 1980 this had fallen to 13.7%."[11]

The overall impact was widespread shortages and even hunger, which necessitated food smuggling in spite of the checkpoints. In fact, one can go as far as saying that the checkpoints encouraged food smuggling because they produced price differentials between localities. And since it would usually take a whole day for a bus to travel a distance of about one hundred kilometers because of the profusion of checkpoints, many people could simply make a living by packing a few kilograms of meat inside their shirts and their pants

*Most of the fabric used in Vietnamese villages, especially in the northern region, is still literally homespun. Large-scale socialist production is certainly not applicable in this case, although there are some big textile factories in Hanoi, Ho Chi Minh City, and other urban centers. (Photo by Ngo Vinh Long, Ha Son Binh, 1980.)*

and walking through the checkpoints. In any case, the authorities blamed the "commercial capitalists" for having caused the shortages and price fluctuations through their hoarding and manipulation of the market and used this as an excuse for moving against them.

## THE X-2 CAMPAIGN AGAINST COMMERCIAL CAPITALISTS

The blame of commercial capitalists is reflected in the following statement by Melanie Beresford, author of a book on postwar Vietnam: "In fact the ability of Cholon-based rice merchants to undermine the government's grain purchase policy by pushing up free market prices through hoarding and speculation was a key element in the decision to accelerate the nationalization and collectivization of the southern economy. So in March 1978 a campaign of repression against large private traders was launched."[12]

This was known as the X-2 campaign. But by the time it was officially launched not too many "large private traders" were left. As early as the beginning of 1977, even many of the commercial and industrial capitalists in the South who were not listed as compradors had already "volunteered" their enterprises to the government. By the beginning of 1978, according to official sources, 1,500 enterprises in the South had been nationalized and transformed into 650 state-run concerns with a total of 130,000 workers, or 70 percent of the total work force in this sector.[13] All of the large rice mills, together with

*Local trains, like this one just outside of Hanoi, are slow because they are made with flimsy materials produced locally. Any child can just jump on and off the trains at any time. Transporting perishable goods to distant markets is difficult, and this difficulty limits the peasants' capacity to produce and ship crops such as rice and roots. (Photo by Ngo Vinh Long, 1980.)*

the warehouses and transport facilities, were already under government control by this time. Therefore, the capitalists were in no position to compete with the government in terms of hoarding and speculating in bulky commodities like rice. What they were hoarding were items that could be easily concealed, such as gold, diamonds, dollars, and precision machines and their spare parts—the real targets of this X-2 campaign. For a better understanding of this, a few words of explanation are in order.

The Party's Fourth Plenum Resolution of December 1976 stated, "On the basis of developing the socialist economic sector, the capacity of all the other economic sectors has to be fully utilized."[14] Another section of the same resolution also emphasized: "Priority should be given to the rational development of heavy industry on the basis of the development of agricultural and consumer goods. . . . Efforts should be made to basically complete the transformation of our economy from a small-scale production to large-scale socialist production in about twenty years."[15] This resolution was promulgated in a situation where the management structures of the southern economy had disintegrated. Many high officials in the pre-1975 Saigon regime and many of the capitalists had either fled abroad or been sent to reeducation camps. Lower officials were either not accustomed to their responsibilities or did not feel that they had a voice. The cadres of the former National Liberation Front had a lot of experience in military and political struggles but little in economic management. Therefore cadres from the North had to be sent down to manage the economy. Among them were some southerners who had regrouped in the North after the Geneva Agreements were signed in 1954. But after spending many years in the North and in other socialist countries as students, they had become socialist bureaucrats and no longer could understand the South's economy, which was composed of many economic sectors. Therefore they understood the phrase "the capacity of all other economic sectors should be fully utilized" to mean confiscating the South's means of production and utilizing them fully for "developing the socialist economic sector." Likewise, they interpreted the phrase "rational development of heavy industry on the basis of the development of agricultural and consumer goods" to mean forcing the peasants and the producers of consumer goods to bear the costs of developing heavy industries, which had all been nationalized by that time.

During the first years after liberation, direct investment in state-run industries amounted to 40 percent of total government investment. Then there were other forms of indirect investment—such as low-interest loans, sale of imported goods and raw materials at give-away prices, food subsidies, and free or low-rent housing for cadres and workers—that cannot be easily calculated in monetary terms. In addition, the government guaranteed the purchase of all the finished products whether or not they would bring the government any profit. This system is known by the Vietnamese term *bao cap*, which literally means "full guarantee [of purchase] and supply." Hence, the term *subsidy* used by Western writers to describe this system fails to convey its full meaning. In any case, this system led to massive hiring of workers without much regard for productivity and profitability. According to official statistics, during the

1975–1979 period workers' salaries increased by 3 percent while productivity decreased by 1.5 percent a year.[16] In fact, factories in general were running at only 50 percent of capacity.

Because the state sector was operating at a loss and agricultural taxes could not be further increased, the government increased the income tax rate to 12 percent for the general public and 18–20 percent for merchants. Commodity tax ranged from 15 to 50 percent. But this only drove the private economy underground and broadened the problem of bribery. As a result, although the tax rates were increased, the real amount collected by the government actually decreased. From 1976 to 1979, the government budget deficit was estimated to be about 13 percent of the gross domestic product (GDP).[17]

The budget deficit was further worsened by the conflict with China and the Khmer Rouge. This led to the building up of the armed forces to about 1.2 million men, or four times the total number of main troops in the PAVN (People's Army of Vietnam, or North Vietnamese troops) and the National Liberation Front during the war years. In order to support this troop increase the government further pushed collectivization, believing that this would enable it to procure more food and to control more resources from the rural areas. However, as we have seen, both food production and food procurement decreased. This was the reason why the government decided to embark on its X-2 campaign in order to flush out and confiscate those items it had left alone or had missed during the X-1 campaign.

## CURRENCY UNIFICATION

Just as the X-1 campaign was followed up by the money exchange scheme, the X-2 was also accompanied by the replacement of the two different currencies used currently in the northern and southern halves of the country by a standardized dong for both regions. Again, each person could receive only a specified amount of money in each period. The hope here was that after the capitalists' property and hoarded goods had been confiscated and their cash flow limited, they would not be able to use either the goods or the cash to manipulate the market. Meanwhile, the government would presumably be able to move toward large-scale socialist production with the goods it confiscated and the cash it controlled. However, by this time the rich had either dispersed their wealth or transferred it into precious commodities such as gold and diamonds that could be easily hidden, so neither the X-2 campaign nor the currency replacement scheme netted the government much in goods and cash. In fact, the whole program further eroded public trust in the currency in use and pushed people to speculate in gold, thereby artificially increasing the price of gold to the extent that during the 1978–1979 period an ounce of gold could support a family comfortably for the whole year. At that time there were untold households in the South that each had more than ten ounces of gold and could afford to weather any government campaign, but the government itself could ill afford ten more years of ever-increasing budget deficits, especially given the fact that the poor, who had been the main supporters of the regime, became poorer.

In brief, socialist transformation only strengthened the private sector vis-à-vis the state sector while limiting its contribution to the GDP. Decrease in economic activities from the private sector also meant decrease in the amount of taxes collected. Meanwhile, in spite of all the subsidies and privileges, the state sector could not produce enough to make up for the loss of contribution from the private sector. The result was increasing budget deficits and worsening economic problems.

The aim of socialist transformation in Vietnam was supposedly for the benefit of the majority of the population—the peasants who composed about 80 percent of the total population and the poor working class who formed the majority of the urban inhabitants. However, as the description and analyses in the preceding pages have shown, it was precisely the peasants and workers who had to bear the brunt of the process of socialist transformation in the country.

**RELAXATION OF CONTROL: 1979–1981**

By the beginning of 1979 the economic situation became even more critical as a result of the full-scale war with both China and the Khmer Rouge. This created the second mass exodus of refugees out of the country, who took with them most of the fishing boats. Production of staples also decreased, and the government managed to procure only about 10 percent of the crops through taxes and forced sale.

To remedy this situation, in August 1979 the Party Congress criticized what it called the "haste tendency" (*tu tuong nong voi*), ordered all checkpoints to be eliminated, and declared a policy relaxation in order to create a "production burst" (*bung san xuat*) in the nonstate sectors. This new policy allowed all industrial and handicraft enterprises to find their own sources of supplies above and beyond the government subsidized quotas, to sell their products in the free markets or to barter with other enterprises, and to increase their employees' pay in proportion to increase in output. It also allowed the localities to export their products directly to foreign customers once they had met their quotas of goods sold to the government's department of foreign trade. This policy promptly resulted in increased output in all sectors, and the elimination of the checkpoints also facilitated easier trading and lower price differentials between the localities and regions, giving the peasants the needed incentives to produce more.

However, with the new policy the government could no longer force the farmers to sell their produce to the government at depressed prices. In order to procure the necessary amounts of staples, for example, the government had to pay the peasants 6 dong per kilogram of rice. It resold the rice to its employees at the rate of 0.40 dong per kilogram, thus incurring the loss of 5.6 dong. Hence, the government budget deficit during the 1979–1981 period increased by 32.7 percent as compared to the 1977–1978 period.[18]

The deficit, in turn, led to inflation. But because most of the population had for a long time lost all trust in the currency, nobody kept any significant

*In every village in Vietnam there are at least two kindergartens. The children are sent there so that their parents can work in the fields. Lunch is provided, and the children are taught to sing and read. (Photo by Ngo Vinh Long, 1980.)*

amount of cash on hand. Their automatic defense mechanism was to spend the money on durable goods or consumer goods as soon as they got it. This speedy turnover of the money in circulation further increased inflation. But those who controlled goods could barter them and so could protect themselves from inflation. Only those who were on salaries, such as cadres, soldiers, police, and other government employees, had to endure increasing difficulties. The main victims of inflation, therefore, were also the pillars of the new regime.

In order to prop up the system, in June 1981 the government doubled the salaries of all its employees. But this only created a budget deficit of 20 billion dong in 1982, or equivalent to U.S.$1.5 billion at the time.[19] And the increased deficit worsened the inflation; so went the downward spiral.

**THE TRANSFORM/REFORM DUALISM: 1982–1985**

The above situation set the stage for a lengthy debate between the reformers and those Party leaders who supported continued socialist transformation. The latter admitted that the "production burst" policy did increase production, especially in the nonstate sectors, but they also blamed it for exacerbating inflation, thereby creating additional difficulties for government employees. These differences caused the

National Party Congress scheduled for 1981 to be delayed for almost a year. It was finally convened in March 1982 and issued a resolution criticizing the overly ambitious industrialization program of previous years and putting new emphasis on the development of energy sources, agriculture, communication and transportation, consumer goods, and export. Large and unfinished industrial projects that were regarded as unnecessary were abandoned, and an investment freeze was imposed on new projects. However, because salaries for government employees were doubled in late 1981 and because more staples were purchased at market prices to be sold to government employees at the subsidized rate, the budget deficit for 1982 increased by 39 percent over the 1981 level.[20]

In addition to investment cutbacks in the industrial sector, the government also reformed the tax structures for the other sectors in the hope of stimulating production. In agriculture, taxes were now fixed on various categories of land and not imposed on yields as in prior years. As a result, production of staples increased from 14.4 million metric tons in 1980 to nearly 18 million metric tons in 1984. As far as the southern region was concerned, the local authorities also realized that the policy of forcing people into the agricultural cooperatives was counterproductive because this created a loss of incentive that, in turn, decreased production. At that time, therefore, there was tacit recognition that most of the land would remain in private hands, although on paper the government still officially maintained that collectivization would be essentially completed by 1985. Thanks to this so-called "reform from below," in the nine Mekong Delta provinces grain production increased by an average of 9 percent a year during this period.

Taxes were also readjusted for other sectors. Depending on the particular trade, the new taxes amounted to 3–5 percent for handicraft, light industry, and transportation and 6–10 percent for the service sector. The new tax rates and the deregulation mentioned earlier helped production in all sectors—outside of agriculture and state-run industries—to increase by an average of 11.4 percent during the 1980–1985 period.[21] Productivity of the state-run enterprises also increased by over 8.1 percent for the same period due to the incentive provided by the salary increases and the additional supplies beyond government subsidized quotas that these enterprises were now allowed to buy in the free market.[22]

Although production increased in all sectors, government spending outpaced government revenue. The budget deficit for 1984 was 19 billion dong as compared to 3 billion dong for 1980. The budget deficit created more inflation, which in turn lowered the living standard of all salaried government employees. Therefore, in 1984 the government again increased the salaries of all its employees, which only added fuel to the inflation. But some Party leaders blamed this on the "black market" and tried to remedy the situation with a policy for "adjusting prices, wages, and currency." Many Western writers have dubbed this the "price, wage, and currency reform." But for three reasons this reform was in reality intended to be the most far-reaching effort at socialist transformation up to that date. First, in exchanging one new dong for ten old ones and in limiting the amount each family could bring home each time, the government wanted to destroy the economic power of the moneyed class. Second, in setting official prices at the same level with the black market prices the government wanted to increase the amount of cash in its hands by selling the merchandise it was holding in its warehouses. Also, with more cash the government could presumably corner the goods in the free market because most people now supposedly had much less money in hand. Third, by increasing the wages of all its employees the government hoped to strengthen the positions of those individuals working in the public sector. Presumably, with most of the goods and cash in its hands and with the conditions of the work force in the public sector improved, the government could now impose a wage-and-price freeze and the economy would become stabilized.

But the human proposes and reality disposes. Although at that time the banking system was entirely a government monopoly, the total production of the state sector included only one-third of the gross national product (GNP). After the money-exchange scheme had been carried out, the government spent huge sums to buy agricultural produce and other commodities with a view to extending the powerful position of the state sector. However, this only had the effect of increasing the amount of cash in the hands of the people in the private sector who, because of the lack of legal protection for investments and because the interest rates at the time were still much lower than the inflation rates, neither invested their money nor put it in saving accounts. So there was no avenue for the huge amounts of money issued by the government to make their way back to the central banks; and this lack only added to the inflation. But some policymakers even said that this was the kind of inflation that would cure all inflation, the rationale being that it cost almost nothing for the government to print money in order to buy the goods. In reality, however, the resources garnered by the government only went to support a burgeoning bureaucratic behemoth and not to stimulate production and development. Therefore, in 1986, inflation grew to over 700 percent. In the face of this admitted disaster, the government fired To Huu and Tran Phuong, both deputy prime ministers and both considered responsible for the policy. To Huu was also subsequently relieved of his Politburo seat when the Sixth Party Congress met in December 1986. These individuals were sacked so that collective leadership of the Party would not be blamed for the disaster.

**OLD MEN, NEW THINKING: 1986-1990**

The Political Report of the Sixth Party Congress, which was read by the outgoing General Secretary Truong Chinh, contains the following observation:

We set too high targets for capital construction . . . laying much stress on building heavy industry and large-scale projects, failing to pool efforts on solving basically the food problem, on boosting the production of consumer goods and goods for exports. . . . We laid stress on changing the ownership of the means of production, but overlooked the settlement of problems relating to management organization and the system of distribution. We often resorted to campaign-like, coercive measures running after quantity, but neglecting quality and efficiency.[23]

The Congress, therefore, called for "new thinking" (*doi moi tu duy*) in tackling the cancerous problems at hand. Hence the shortened code name *doi moi*—literally, "renovation"—for the reform policies and programs that followed. However, the remedies prescribed from 1987 to 1988, which included the arrests and trials of corrupt officials, were at best only skin ointments. When things deteriorated to an unprecedented level in early 1989, the government decided that more drastic reform measures had to be taken. A few of these measures and their impact will be briefly described.

## LEGALIZATION OF WEALTH
In the attempt to control the entire economy, the government had previously put foreign currencies, gold, and precious stones in the same banned category as hard drugs. The maximum penalty was life imprisonment for those who traded or hoarded these items. This was tantamount to declaring that wealth was illegal because the government realized that no rich person would be stupid enough to stock up on the dong under such an inflationary situation. In fact, gold became the main currency for most business transactions and hence the demand for, the prices of, and the speculation in gold increased. The official currency became marginalized.

To remedy this situation the government legalized the purchase and sale of gold by the private sector. In only a couple of months, over 700 privately owned gold shops sprang up in Ho Chi Minh City alone. In the effort to further assure the public, the new prime minister, Do Muoi (who had formerly been the chief of the socialist transformation campaign), read an important speech calling on people in the private sector to boldly invest their money in all wealth-generating enterprises.

## RESTORING LAND TO THE PEASANTS
It fell upon Politburo member Vo Chi Cong, the man who had been responsible for the collectivization push in the South, to make a speech calling for the return of land to the peasant households as an effort to promote agricultural production. In reality, this policy was tantamount to imposing a fixed rent—paid in taxes and sale quotas set according to various categories of land—for fifteen years. In any case, partly as a result of this, grain production in 1989 totaled 21 million metric tons as compared to 18 million metric tons in 1988. There was a significant rice surplus, and in 1989 Vietnam exported 1.5 million metric tons of milled rice, making it the third largest rice exporter in the world after Thailand and the United States.

## ANTI-INFLATIONARY MEASURES
The government anti-inflation package was now composed of an array of monetary and fiscal measures. Monetary measures included readjustment of

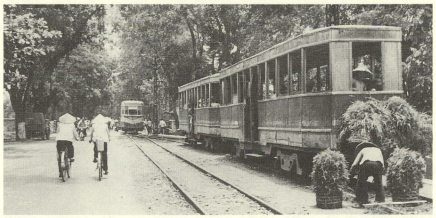

*The lack of infrastructure and means of transport are among the biggest obstacles to economic development in Vietnam. Partly because of the destruction during the war, shortage of foreign exchange, and the trade embargo imposed by the United States and its allies, Vietnam has to rely mostly on outmoded or locally produced means of transportation such as bicycles and trains. (Photo by Ngo Vinh Long, Hanoi, 1986.)*

the official interest rates and the currency exchange rates as well as legalization of the gold trade. Interest rates were now allowed to float above inflation rates. For example, during the first months of 1989 when the inflation rate was about 8–9 percent a month, the short-term interest rate was put at 9 percent a month and long-term interest rates of three months or more were fixed at 12 percent a month. By the beginning of June 1989 when inflation was reduced, short-term and long-term interest rates were also reduced to 7 and 9 percent, respectively. To make things more flexible, the National Bank was now limiting itself to a role comparable to that of the U.S. Federal Reserve Bank, and private commercial banks and saving-and-loan associations were permitted to come into existence.

The National Bank also had a new policy of floating the official currency-exchange rates close to the market rates. The official exchange rate for the U.S. dollar, for example, was raised from 900 to 4,500 dong. The previous low exchange rates had the effect of making export commodities expensive and import goods cheaper than domestic products. In order to enable domestic products to compete on the international market the government either had to subsidize exports or force the producers to sell export goods cheaply, thus discouraging exports. On the other hand, because government import-export agencies had a complete monopoly, they were able to charge exorbitant prices for imported products. A used Honda moped that cost U.S.$50–70 in Japan would be sold in Vietnam for U.S.$800–1,000 according to the black-market exchange rate or from $5,000–7,000 at the official rate. If exchanged with the peasants for rice, a moped was equal to fifteen metric tons of rice, which was the total yield of three hectares of paddy fields a year. Officials in charge of imports could therefore sell the imported goods at any price and would still

*Vietnamese workers unloading pineapples. (Copyright © 1988 John Spragens, Jr. Reprinted with permission.)*

be able to claim that they made huge profits because the exchange rate was set too low in comparison to the market rate. Therefore, the new exchange-rate policy had the effect of encouraging exports and limiting imports. In addition, it also served to reduce the illegal trafficking in foreign currencies. Before the new policy went into effect, overseas Vietnamese who wanted to help their families back home sometimes had to pay smugglers as much as half of the value of their remittances. Otherwise, they would resort to sending small packages of consumer goods since this would still fetch many times more dong than if they were to exchange their money at the official rates. In fact, the formerly low exchange rates made the transfer of money abroad much more profitable than vice versa.

Meanwhile, the legalization of the gold trade brought in large amounts of gold from as far as Switzerland, and this served to reduce its domestic price. In addition to the high interest rates already mentioned, those who had hidden or hoarded gold were now selling it and putting some of the money in the banks to take advantage of the high interest rates, thereby pushing the price of gold down even further. During the first six months of 1989 the price of gold was reduced by 40 percent although inflation was still around 40 percent during those months. But there was another side to this. The state-run enterprises, which were still not cost efficient, did not decrease the prices of the products in relation to the drop in the price of gold. Therefore, during the first six months of 1989 the amount of goods that were still piling up unsold in government warehouses was estimated at one trillion dong. Worse still, because it was now much cheaper to import Thai goods, hordes of smugglers made the run across the borders with bagfuls of gold.

The new fiscal measures involved budget cuts and revenue-raising schemes. Budget cuts included ending subsidies to inefficient and unnecessary state-run enterprises, lowering government investments, replacing food subsidies to government employees with cash payments, reducing the number of effective troops in the armed forces by 700,000 in the immediate future, and terminating government monopoly in social work by involving the Catholic and Buddhist churches and other groups in joint welfare projects.

Revenue-raising measures included: an import tax on state-run import-export enterprises; a new tax on motor vehicles; new school fees amounting to about U.S.$30–80 a year for a college student; new hospital fees that would cost 5–10 U.S. pennies per visit and about U.S.$10 for a serious operation; rents for apartments and houses that the government had allowed its cadres and employees to use practically without cost; and the sale of government-supplied goods at market value instead of at giveaway subsidized prices.

## THE LIMITS OF RENOVATION

As a result of the market-oriented economic reforms, in 1989 the nonstate sector in Vietnam produced 90 percent of the country's rice and accounted for 65 percent of its gross national product, according to the 21 September 1990 issue of *Quan Doi Nhan Dan* (The People's Army). However, the relatively short-term lease of fifteen years of agricultural lands to the peasants does not give them the needed psychological security that would guarantee long-term productivity. The peasants will take whatever they can out of the soil without putting much back unless they are convinced that the land is theirs.

Another trumpeted success of the reform measures has been the reduction of inflation to about 35 percent. But mostly this was not due to increased production or budget cuts but to the sale of government-owned property, to foreign remittances, and to the availability of gold in the country. The revenue from the sale of government-owned property in Ho Chi Minh City alone was estimated at about 500 billion dong, or about U.S.$100 million.[24] As far as the value of the goods that overseas Vietnamese sent home is concerned, previously it was estimated at about U.S.$100 million and the transport costs were equal to $300 million. With the new exchange rates as well as the policy of allowing foreigners to own property in Vietnam, overseas Vietnamese communities were therefore encouraged to send more money home. At least $300 million in cash was made available to the Vietnamese economy this way, and the sale of gold by individual households in order to put some money into saving accounts, as mentioned earlier, also added more cash to the economy. This was why the Vietnamese government could afford to issue 2 trillion more dong—equal to U.S.$400 million—in 1989 without causing further inflation.

However, the government will not be able to attract additional remittances as well as savings unless it provides real incentives for private investment. The Vietnamese capitalists have been burned too many times to trust verbal encouragements, especially as a law code for foreign investors was issued in 1988 but there is none as yet for domestic entrepreneurs. In fact, the following excerpt from an interview with Secretary General Nguyen Van Linh published in the 8 May 1990 issue of *Nhan Dan* shows that in the minds of many Vietnamese policymakers the Vietnamese private sector is still considered "exploitative" and therefore should be used by the socialist government only in the tactical sense:

> The private sector is an objective reality that must be used, developed and managed by the socialist government. . . . Vietnam will issue laws guaranteeing the long and legal existence of the private sector as long as this mode of ownership of the means of production can still contribute effectively to the society. The socialist government firmly controls the nerve centers of the national economy. The present by-laws of the Vietnamese Communist Party require that Party members do not participate in exploitative activities.

Because "exploitative activities" are generally understood to include making profits on the labor of others, those who have money in Vietnam are still hesitant to invest it, and as long as the local residents do not feel safe to invest, overseas Vietnamese and foreign corporations will not participate in droves either. This is the reason why, in an interview given to the Cuban news agency, *La Prensa Latina*, on 8 June 1990, Party Secretary General Nguyen Van Linh disclosed that up to April 1990 only 140 foreign companies had signed on with about U.S.$1 billion in proposed investment funds.

Even so, this money will not all be forthcoming, and economic development in Vietnam will stagnate if the present social and political climate is not further improved. Perhaps due to unfolding events in China and Eastern Europe the government has overreacted by clamping down on the press and suppressing groups that have called for an end to official corruption and the beginning of a multiparty system. In the name of providing stability for economic development the government has arrested and detained a number of former revolutionary leaders as well as peace-movement personalities such as Nguyen Ho, Father Chan Tin, and Huynh Tan Mam. Freedom of the press and of political participation is needed to safeguard against corruption as well as other abuses that will certainly crop up with the "liberalization" of the economy.

## FUTURE PROSPECTS

The Vietnamese policymakers have attributed the failure of their economic policies to a variety of factors such as the legacies of war, the U.S. economic blockade, unusual natural disasters that have been exacerbated by the ecological destruction caused by U.S. bombs and chemical defoliants, and mismanagement by cadres at different levels. In recent years they have also admitted that previous policies had not been appropriate and therefore they have committed themselves to market-economy reforms. But this does not mean that the Vietnamese leaders have surrendered to capitalism and have rejected the principles of Marxism-Leninism. On the contrary, they believe that they are only using the tools of capitalism to build a more efficient system of socialism.

Partly as a result of the population increase that produces more than one million persons of working age yearly and partly as a result of the demobilization of about 700,000 troops, Vietnam is being confronted by increasing unemployment. In addition, the 180,000 Vietnamese "guest workers" in the Soviet Union and in Eastern Europe are being sent back to Vietnam to join the work force there. Meanwhile, the ability of the government to provide new jobs is partly curtailed by the phase-out of aid from the Soviet Union, which amounts to an equivalent of U.S.$2 billion in economic aid and $1 billion in military aid. Therefore, in order be able to provide the necessary jobs the Vietnamese government has had to adopt more flexible tactics such as calling for foreign investments. At a conference on the world economy in Switzerland in February 1990 Vo Van Kiet, vice–prime minister in charge of economic affairs, declared:

> At the present time all private citizens in Vietnam have complete freedom to engage in business activities, to own their own means of production, to enjoy the fruit of their labor and investments, to be treated fairly and equally before the law like the state sector and the collective sector, and to have the right to become rich and have their right to become rich guaranteed by the government. . . . We have changed our system of socialist economic management and have terminated central planning. . . . To state it more clearly, we have accepted a market-economy system.[25]

But Kiet was quick to add: "Reform does not mean the complete eradication of the old and the rejection of socialism but the acceptance of a more precise redefinition for a better socialist humanism whose ideal is to serve the people."[26]

In the quest of achieving old goals with new means it remains to be seen how Vietnam will be able to convince the capitalist owners of the means of production that their rights are fully protected by a dictatorship of the proletariat, how a market economy can develop in a socialist system, how a system designed for only two economic sectors—the state and the collective sectors—can tolerate the existence of many sectors, and how changes in the economic substructures will not undermine the political superstructure.

## NOTES

1. Nguyen Khac Vien, *Vietnam Ten Years After* (Hanoi: Foreign Language Publishing House, 1985), p. 6.

2. Tran Bach Dang, "Nhung Van De cua Chung Ta" (Our Problems), *Saigon Giai Phong* (Liberated Saigon), 13 August 1989, pp. 1–2.

3. *Fifty Years of Activities of the Communist Party of Vietnam* (Hanoi: Foreign Language Publishing House, 1980), p. 255.

4. *Tap Chi Hoc Tap* ("Studies Magazine," official monthly review of the Communist Party), December 1976, p. 54.

5. For details see Ngo Vinh Long, "Agrarian Differentiation in the Southern Region of Vietnam," *Journal of Contemporary Asia* 14, no. 3 (1984), pp. 283–305.

6. About 70 percent of those who were categorized as compradors were Vietnamese citizens of Chinese origin, prompting China to accuse Vietnam of discriminating against ethnic Chinese. The new Vietnamese government responded by saying that they were only carrying out socialist transformation, which was something that China had gone through before. It should also be noted that throughout the French colonial period the Chinese community in Vietnam was used by the French as a class of economic intermediaries and hence was given all kinds of special privileges.

7. David G. Marr and Christine P. White, eds., *Postwar Vietnam: Dilemmas in Socialist Development* (Ithaca, NY: Southeast Asia Program, Cornell University, 1988), p. 233.

8. For details see Ngo Vinh Long, "Some Aspects of Cooperativization in the Mekong Delta," in ibid., pp. 163–176.

9. Nguyen Tran Que, "Tu Moi Quan He Gia-Luong trong Khu Vuc Quoc Doanh den su Can Doi Hang Tien Tren Thi Truong Xa Hoi" (From the Price-Salary Connection in the State Sector to the Balance of Goods and Money in the Social Market), *Nghien Cuu Kinh Te* (Economic Research, official monthly magazine of the Vietnamese government) (Hanoi: Institute for Economic Research, no. 2, 1983), p. 32.

10. General Statistical Office, *Statistical Data of the Socialist Republic of Vietnam* (Hanoi: Statistical Publishing House, 1987), tables 2 and 27; International Monetary Fund reports: *Socialist Republic of Vietnam—Recent Economic Developments* (1979) and *Vietnam: Economic Report* (1990). The statistical appendix to the 1990 report gives detailed statistics on pp. 116–154.

11. Adam Fforde and Stefan de Vylder, *Vietnam—An Economy in Transition* (Stockholm: Swedish International Development Authority, 1989), p. 58.

12. Melanie Beresford, *Vietnam: Politics, Economics and Society* (London: Pinter Publishers Limited, 1988), p. 153.

13. Nguyen Khac Vien, *Vietnam Ten Years After*, p. 17.

14. *Tap Chi Hoc Tap*, December 1976, p. 32.

15. Ibid.

16. General Statistical Office, *Statistical Data of the Socialist Republic of Vietnam* (Hanoi: Statistical Publishing House, 1987–1988); International Monetary Fund reports: *Socialist Republic of Vietnam—Recent Economic Developments* (1979) and *Vietnam: Economic Report* (1990). The statistical appendix to the 1990 report gives detailed statistics on pp. 116–154.

17. General Statistical Office, *Statistical Data of the Socialist Republic of Vietnam* (Hanoi: Statistical Publishing House, 1976–1980); International Monetary Fund reports: *Socialist Republic of Vietnam—Recent Economic Developments* (1979) and *Vietnam: Economic Report* (1990). The statistical appendix to the 1990 report gives detailed statistics on pp. 116–154.

18. Marr and White, *Postwar Vietnam*, p. 124.

19. Ibid., table 7.1.

20. Ibid., p. 124.

21. Fforde and de Vylder, *Vietnam—An Economy in Transition*, table 4.7.

22. Ibid.

23. Beresford, *Vietnam: Politics, Economics and Society*, p. 172.

24. *Dat Moi* ("New Land," a monthly magazine published by the Canadian Vietnamese Congress, Suite 29, 1700 rue Berri, Montreal H3L4E4), June 1990, p. 57.

25. Quoted in *Dat Moi*, March 1990, p. 30.

26. Ibid.

# 3

## Michael Vickery | Cambodia

Cambodia first came to the attention of many in the West as a result of U.S. aggression to perpetuate a dubious regime led by General Lon Nol against what seemed to be popular revolutionary forces patronized by Prince Norodom Sihanouk, whom Lon Nol had overthrown in 1970. Since 1979 the United States has been part of a multination effort to bring back those same "popular forces" against a state that has proven itself much more long-lived, effective, and popular than either the forces backed by the United States now or Lon Nol's Khmer Republic, which the United States supported in the early 1970s.

Never mind the crocodile tears shed by U.S.-regime figures about the fate of the poor Cambodian people under the "genocidal" Pol Pot clique. In 1980 when the Pol Pot remnants were broken and starving on the Thai border, the United States shelled out $54 million toward their rehabilitation and rearmament,[1] encouraged, perhaps even bullied, other countries into providing similar support, and had until 1990 adamantly opposed measures that would effectively have prevented that group from returning to power—because that would inevitably have meant some degree of recognition and support for the People's Republic of Kampuchea (PRK) in Phnom Penh and their Vietnamese allies, who in U.S. demonology were even worse than Pol Pot,[2] in spite of the obvious benefits they have brought to Cambodia after the horrors of 1970–1979. As was written in the *Far Eastern Economic Review* in December 1988, it is time "to give substance to . . . statements on the 'unacceptability' of a Khmer Rouge return to power"; but instead we saw our secretaries of state for ten years making statements that suggested U.S. acquiescence in their return to Phnom Penh.[3]

Political conflict, internal and international, is not new to Cambodia, and in some respects the problems of today mirror those of the past. The following historical sketch may help to illustrate important features of Cambodia's

This chapter is a revised version of Michael Vickery, "Cambodia (Kampuchea): History, Tragedy, and Uncertain Future," *Bulletin of Concerned Asian Scholars* 21, nos. 2–4 (April–Dec. 1989), pp. 35–58. Reprinted with permission.

historical, geographical, and international situation that are relevant for understanding both the past and the present.

**GEOGRAPHIC AND
HISTORICAL BACKGROUND**

The country consists mainly of low plains cut by many rivers, with mountains in the northeast and southwest, and the east-west Dangrek Chain demarcating Cambodia's northern border with Thailand. Most of the rivers flow into the Mekong or the Tonle Sap, the inland sea in the country's center that joins the Mekong at Phnom Penh. An important geographical peculiarity is that during the flood season between June and October the overflow from the Mekong causes the Tonle Sap to reverse its course and expand to several times its normal area, silting and fertilizing the rice plains and providing a large supply of freshwater fish. All important watercourses within Cambodia's modern boundaries feed into the Mekong–Tonle Sap system.

Although this unified watercourse system has always been an integrative factor, especially before the construction of modern roads, the ultimate channels into which everything flows are the Mekong and Bassac rivers, which reach the sea across what is now southern Vietnam. There is no other good southern route to the sea out of central Cambodia. The economy of all of southern and eastern Cambodia, if it is not to be autarchic, depends on control of the mouths of those two rivers. Seen in another way, whoever controls the area around the river mouths can exert strong pressure on Cambodia south of the Tonle Sap.

In the northwest the rivers also flow into the Tonle Sap, but that area is just across a narrow watershed from other rivers flowing into the Gulf of Thailand, and very close to one good, short overland portage to such an alternative river system via the Wattana Gap. There is thus an objective geographical potential for Cambodia's northwest to become oriented toward the west, if political conditions, for instance, should render the eastward orientation precarious. Cambodia thus has an inherent geographical-economic tendency toward division, which has, in fact, been manifest in many instances throughout its history.

The natural wealth of the country lies chiefly in agriculture, forest products, and fishing. Over 80 percent of the population lives in the central plain where rice is the most important product. There also lie the rich fishing grounds of the Tonle Sap inland sea and connecting rivers. The production of industrial raw materials such as rubber and cotton was important before the 1970–1975 war, and they are slowly being redeveloped. Much of the west and northeast consists of forested hills containing valuable timber. Industrial-quality mineral deposits have not been discovered, although iron exists and has traditionally been exploited by local craftsmen.

The first supravillage sociopolitical organization attested in the Cambodian area is known as Funan, the center of which appears to have been near the southern coast in what is now Cambodia or in adjacent areas of Vietnam.

Funan controlled the coast and riverine outlets from the plains of southern and central Cambodia; and it was a maritime society along a trade route linking China, Southeast Asia, and India. Funan society was stratified and its population also practiced advanced techniques of water control and rice agriculture. The ethnic identity of the population is unknown, but could have been Khmer, Cham, Mon, or some other Mon-Khmer group.[4]

During the seventh through the ninth centuries the centers of political power, by then dominated by the Khmer, shifted away from the coast, and an agricultural rather than maritime-trade economy predominated. This trend led to the high point of Khmer civilization, the Angkor state, which between the eleventh and fourteenth centuries dominated much of what is now central and northeastern Thailand as well as central and southern Vietnam, then inhabited by the Cham. Angkor was an agrarian civilization, with tight control of the population exercised by a complex hierarchy of officials acting for semideified kings.[5]

The location of the Angkorean capital at the northern end of the Tonle Sap was favorable for control of both the river system flowing southward and the routes linked to the Gulf of Thailand, and Angkorean expansion north of the Dangrek Mountains ensured control of the Mun river system flowing into the Mekong farther north. In spite of Angkorean strength, the natural divisive tendencies of the Cambodian plain were manifest in nearly continual conflicts between the Cambodian heartland and the southeastern coast, then occupied and ruled by the Cham.

The Angkorean state disappeared in the fifteenth century, and Cambodia's economic and political center shifted southward to the Phnom Penh region. Cambodia and its neighbors, in particular Ayutthaya just north of Bangkok, were again integrated into an international sea-trade network centered on China. Most of the population were still peasant farmers, but probably lived under looser administrative control than in Angkor times, while the state looked toward external trade for wealth accumulation.[6]

With the shift of the capital to the Phnom Penh area the naturally divisive tendencies came to the fore, and the northwest, with Angkor, came increasingly under the influence of the rapidly developing rival center, Ayutthaya, which with its predecessor, Sien, had begun as a maritime trade center in the thirteenth century, then expanded inland up the Chao Phraya Valley and toward Cambodia. Although the core area of Ayutthaya was originally Mon and Khmer, by the fourteenth through the fifteenth centuries they were being displaced by the Thai. The ethnolinguistic change no doubt reinforced the existing economic and political rivalry between Ayutthaya and Cambodia, and from that time on the two powers came to view one another as hereditary enemies.[7]

To Cambodia's east a similar process was underway. As the Mon and Khmer of central Thailand were being absorbed and transformed by the Thai, the Cham of central Vietnam, in a reversal of fortunes that was not clear until the end of the fourteenth century, were being conquered and gradually transformed into Vietnamese, as the latter expanded out of their Red River

Valley homeland and moved down the coast over the narrow central plains, until then occupied by the Cham. This process was partly dependent on objective geographical-economic conditions.

Vietnam, considered within its modern boundaries, consists of two large plains in the north and south joined by an extremely narrow strip of flat land squeezed between mountains and sea, with a few small spots of fertile lowlands at river mouths along the coast. As soon as societal development had progressed beyond the prehistoric-village level, the occupants of the narrow central coast were forced to depend on or seek control of one or both of the large plains in the north and south. Conversely, the societies of the large plains, in reaction to pressure from the central coast peoples, sought to dominate them. These inevitable processes are amply documented, although too often obscured by French-colonial and anti-Vietnamese postcolonial treatments that emphasize the ethnic difference, and depict the process as unilateral Vietnamese aggression. In fact, periods of warfare alternated with times of peace and cooperation, and in the late fourteenth century Cham aggression overran most of northern Vietnam and nearly captured its capital.[8]

Until the sixteenth century the Vietnamese-Cham conflict was of less immediate significance to Cambodia than developments in Thailand, since Champa was off the important maritime trade route of that time, while Cambodia and Thailand were in direct competition for favored status on the international sea-trade route. Indirectly, Vietnamese pressure on Champa may have been of benefit to Cambodia, for Cambodian-Cham conflict, a historical constant since at least the ninth century, was over control of the rivers and ports of southern Cambodia and Vietnam, not competition between alternative centers. Cham interest and influence in Cambodia is manifest in the Iberian reports from Cambodia in the 1590s and in the fact that a Cambodian king in 1638 saw fit to embrace Islam, to which the majority of Cham had converted during the previous two to three centuries. This was the mainland high-water mark of the rapid expansion of Islam in Southeast Asia, and its repulsion, with the return of Cambodian royalty to Buddhism, coincided with the beginning of Cambodia's decline as a Southeast Asian power.[9]

It is important to recognize that tension, rivalry, and conflict between the Cambodian central plain and the southeastern coast have been constants throughout recorded history from Funan times, when the rival groups may both have been Khmer, or related Mon-Khmer, through the Angkor Period, when the contesting groups were Khmer and Cham, to modern times when the Cham have been assimilated and replaced by Vietnamese.

Until the seventeenth century Cambodia competed as an equal with its neighbors both east and west. Thereafter Ayutthaya's more favorable location for international sea trade and its larger hinterland supplying desirable products resulted in greater wealth and state power, while Cambodia gradually became an economic backwater.

By the same time the absorption of Champa by the Vietnamese had brought them close to Khmer territory, and the first record of relations between them, referring to events of about 1613, portrays the king of Hue, then at war with rivals in the north, requesting war elephants from the Cambodian king and offering a daughter in return. The tone of this Cambodian chronicle suggests not only that they did not feel threatened, but they considered the Vietnamese royalty as lower in rank.[10]

Gradually, as the Vietnamese completed their domination of Champa, they occupied areas that made tension between them and Cambodia inevitable; and by the 1690s the Saigon area—an ancient Khmer zone—was in their hands, with the potential to throttle Cambodia's trade. However, it is important to note that the first Vietnamese intervention within Cambodia, in 1658, had been at the invitation of a Cambodian royal faction that was requesting help *against the Cham.* When the Cham danger had disappeared the tendency to rely on outside help in internal power struggles continued, and during the end of the eighteenth and first half of the nineteenth centuries, Cambodian royalty followed traditional economic-political fault lines and split into pro-Thai and pro-Vietnamese factions. In this way the country fell prey to invading armies supporting the Cambodian agents of Bangkok or Hue.[11]

These wars, which nearly destroyed Cambodia, ended in 1846 with a compromise among the parties that permitted a Cambodian prince to reign as joint vassal of both Vietnam and Thailand, sending tribute to both. Then in 1863 the French, having conquered part of southern Vietnam, signed a protectorate treaty with King Norodom, who had succeeded to the Cambodian throne in 1860. The Cambodian court also found the treaty advantageous in that it protected them against Thailand, for although the French forever after claimed their protectorate had saved Cambodia from Vietnam, the Vietnamese danger had ended with the French conquests there during 1859–1861. After a second treaty was imposed by the French in 1884, serious rebellions broke out, and they abated only when King Norodom was allowed to proclaim that the French would continue to respect local customs.

Thereafter the French regime was not threatened until after World War II. This was not because it was benevolent, for living standards were depressed by high taxes and demands for cheap exports, but the protectorate *did* offer some protection to the traditional elites who had first acquiesced in a French protectorate and who controlled the populace through a complex network of traditional relationships.[12]

Before the French Protectorate was established in 1863, Cambodian society consisted of royalty, a bureaucracy-aristocracy, peasants, and a small commercial group, mostly non-Khmer and usually Chinese. The bureaucracy-aristocracy included both those who occupied official positions in the capital and provincial governors. The French did not intend to change the social structure, although they eventually did, as their administration expanded and could not be filled by members of the traditional ruling class. New men who could quickly learn French and modern skills found a path of rapid upward mobility which had not existed earlier.

The most important economic activity of the Khmer population was rice farming, carried out by small farmers working family-sized plots to which they had usufruct rights, but not ownership, under the traditional system in which land belonged to the state. Legal private ownership was introduced by the French, and rice land came to be owned by small proprietors, not, in general, large landlords. Nevertheless, widespread debt to usurers soon made the farmers' situation little better than that of tenants.

Unlike in Vietnam, in Cambodia there was little elite or intellectual opposition to French domination, no doubt simply because the protectorate *did* offer some protection for the status of traditional elites, while "new men" who rose through the very limited educational system were accommodated with prestigious posts.[13] The Cambodian administrative structure continued to grow throughout the early twentieth century alongside and subordinate to the French, and it came to be staffed by a new elite descending partly from former aristocracy, but to a large extent from men who owed their new fortunes to the French Protectorate. Right across the political spectrum of the 1960s and 1970s from Lon Nol to Son Sann, including Sihanouk courtiers like Nhiek Tioulong and much of the left-wing leadership, the modern Cambodian political elite descended from and often themselves had been French colonial functionaries.

Only in the late 1930s was a modern nationalist movement formed, led by Son Ngoc Thanh, with the Khmer-language newspaper *Nagaravatta* as its mouthpiece. Although the members of the movement were quite moderate, the French saw their desire for independence as a threat, and the Cambodian royalty felt endangered by their ideas for social and economic modernization, which may have come close to being a kind of closet republicanism. Their activities were finally suppressed in 1942, and Thanh fled to Japan, for like many Asian nationalists in European colonies he saw Japanese victory as liberation from European hegemony.[14]

It was not only a certain type of Asian nationalism that was comfortable with Japanese policies. In fact, World War II brought little change within Cambodia, because Franco-Japanese agreement maintained the colonial administration in Indochina while giving the Japanese the facilities they desired, until on 9 March 1945 the Japanese interned the French and offered independence to the three Indochina states. King Sihanouk, who had succeeded to the throne in 1941, likewise saw no harm in cooperation with Japan, and he abrogated all treaties with France, promulgated a new Basic (Constitutional) Law, and formed a government of traditionalists who had already made administrative careers under the French. In May, Son Ngoc Thanh was brought back from Japan and appointed minister of foreign affairs, and in August, prime minister.[15]

The Thanh government showed an intention to make the most of its formal independence; and a program that Thanh announced, long since forgotten, is worth reviewing here: (1) support the Great Asian War, which is the emancipation of the peoples of this part of the world (and which illustrates Thanh's pro-Japanese orientation); (2) reawaken the historical grandeur of "Kampuchea" [in French text]; and (3) achieve the union of all peoples in Cambodia, especially the Vietnamese and the Khmer.

The Thanhist group wished to eliminate French influence and remove the French language from primary schools, and among Phnom Penh intellectuals

*Son Ngoc Thanh in the forest in 1953. Thanh was a nationalist who became prime minister of Cambodia under Sihanouk in 1941. He advocated closer relations with Vietnam and tried to rid the country of French influence but was arrested and exiled when the French reestablished themselves in 1945. After his return to Cambodia in 1951, Thanh spent the next twenty years engaged in clandestine anti-Sihanouk activities in South Vietnam and Thailand as the leader of the Khmer Serei, a movement that developed close links with U.S. intelligence and Special Forces. When Sihanouk was overthrown in 1970, Thanh returned to public life. He was prime minister under Lon Nol but soon had a falling out with him and returned to South Vietnam, where he reportedly died in 1976. (Photo courtesy of General Chana Samudavanija.)*

there was a movement to introduce Vietnamese as the primary foreign language. This desire for Khmer-Vietnamese rapprochement included recognition by Thanh of Ho Chi Minh's independent Vietnam on 2 September 1945 and permission for a Vietnamese mission to be established in Phnom Penh. A reformist faction of the Cambodian elite was seeking friendship with an independent Vietnam. These policies, however, came to naught, for King Sihanouk strongly opposed Khmer-Vietnamese rapprochement, and he preferred confrontation over the issue of old Cambodian provinces incorporated in Vietnam since the eighteenth century. When British and French troops arrived in September 1945, Thanh, too weak to resist, was arrested; Sihanouk cooperated enthusiastically, and the French Protectorate was reestablished.[16]

**THE RISE AND FALL OF PARTY POLITICS**

In contrast to the prewar protectorate, French policy after 1945 was designed to attract popular support and permitted promulgation of a constitution similar to that of the French Fourth Republic, with a strong parliament, political parties, and regular elections, but with considerable power reserved for the king in emergencies. The resulting governments would be solely concerned with local affairs, for

France retained control of foreign affairs, defense, and any matter that they deemed crucial to maintenance of the protectorate.

Nevertheless, the position of the traditional ruling group was to be threatened more by these minimally democratic reforms that the French now introduced than by either the Japanese occupation of Indochina or the reestablishment of the protectorate. A modern constitution, elections, and a cabinet responsible to the National Assembly were innovations that would enlarge the possibilities of upward mobility for the new "middle" class created by the French and whose second and third generations had gone to modern schools, occasionally even to universities in France.

The first three elections, in 1946 for a Constitutional Convention, and in 1948 and 1951 for the National Assembly, were won handily by the Democratic Party, vehicle of the "new men" rising through the educational system to prestigious posts and led by a minor prince fresh from a French university. They were both anti-French and anti-Sihanouk, with direct links to the Son Ngoc Thanh nationalists (and to more radical groups), who joined the Democrats as they returned from exile or were released from prison. The goals of this largely urban party were even more threatening because in the rural areas armed resistance against the French was developing along with Vietnam's war for independence.

During the 1940s numerous groups of varying political tendencies had begun armed struggle against the French, some in collaboration with the Vietnamese, some wary of them. Certain of these groups also had vague notions of overthrowing the monarchy and of some form of social revolution.[17] In April 1950 a "Unified Issarak" (freedom) Front was formed, and sometime in mid-1951 a Khmer People's Revolutionary Party (KPRP) was formed, following a decision of the Second Congress of the Indochina Communist Party to split into three national parties. The provisional Central Committee of the new organ was headed by Son Ngoc Minh, with Tou Samouth as a member.[18] Since the Issarak and KPRP forces were winning in the countryside, controlling from one-half to three-fifths of the country, the situation was becoming intolerable for the French and for the Cambodian Right; and the French minister for associated states declared that France would make no concession (toward independence) to a Democratic government.[19]

In these circumstances Sihanouk, with French military support, carried out a coup d'état against his own government in June 1952. Basing his actions on residual powers granted to the king in emergencies by the constitution, he dismissed the Democrat-led government and named himself prime minister while promising to achieve independence within three years. Then, in January 1953, in conflict again with the Democrat-dominated Parliament that refused to grant him emergency powers or to pass his budget, Sihanouk dissolved both houses, proclaimed a national emergency that abridged all democratic rights, and launched a "Royal Crusade for Independence."[20]

The French, hard pressed in Vietnam, were persuaded to negotiate now that the Cambodian government seemed securely in conservative hands, with the result that by November 1953 the attributes of independence had been transferred to Sihanouk. Again, as in 1945, a Cambodian government—against the wishes of the progressive elements of Khmer society—had chosen a course threatening to Vietnam, even collaborating with the colonial power seeking to reimpose its control.

Independence and its confirmation by the Geneva Conference of July 1954 represented a defeat for all progressive currents of Cambodian politics from the KPRP through the Thanhist guerrillas to the urban Democrats. Because Cambodia was already independent, it was Sihanouk's government that had to be represented at Geneva, and his delegation adamantly refused any concessions to the communists. In the end neither China nor the Soviet Union insisted, particularly once the more important question of the partition of Vietnam had been decided against the Vietnamese revolutionary forces. In contrast to Vietnam and Laos, the Cambodian communists were allowed no regroupment zone, and were left with no choice but to lay down their arms and reintegrate with Cambodian society under Sihanouk and his conservative supporters. About 1,000 of the leading KPRP cadre, including Son Ngoc Minh, withdrew to North Vietnam, while the rest who remained active changed from armed to political struggle in order to contest the coming elections as the Krom Pracheachon (Citizens' Group), in fact the new political form of the KPRP.

If Geneva disappointed the Cambodian Left, it also added an unexpected obstacle to the plans of the Right. The latter, under Sihanouk, had hoped to continue the dictatorial regime instituted with Sihanouk's January 1953 coup, but the Geneva Accords required all three Indochina countries to hold elections in Cambodia before the end of 1955, under existing constitutions and with freedom for all factions to participate, including former guerrillas. This made possible the open organization of the Pracheachon, while the old Democratic Party was revitalized and pushed leftward by students who had returned from study in Paris, perhaps even with organizational work by Saloth Sar (Pol Pot). Because of the Democrats' previous successes and the popularity that both groups had gained during the anti-French struggle, it was expected that in an honest election the parties of the Left would at least win enough seats to form an effective parliamentary minority.

However, Sihanouk's dictatorial regime of 1953 was still in control, and was in charge of preparing for the election, which in the end was not honest. The result was total victory for Sihanouk's new Popular Socialist Community Party (Sangkum Reastr Niyum), formed from an alliance of several small right-wing parties that had run unsuccessfully against the Democrats in 1948 and 1951. The International Control Commission established by the Geneva Conference to oversee the election nevertheless certified the procedure as "correct," which shows how little such international supervision may mean.[21] Equally interesting is that in the midst of the Sihanouk government's suppression of opposition candidates in the campaign prior to the election, the United States, true to form, signed a military aid agreement with Cambodia in May 1955.[22] From then until 1970, through subsequent elections in 1958, 1962, and 1966, no non-Sangkum politician sat in the National Assembly, although talented members of the former leftist opposition to Sihanouk were permitted to join the Sangkum and even become ministers.

**ROYAL SOCIALIST DICTATORSHIP**

With open political competition abolished, the remnants of the Left, whether KPRP-Pracheachon or Democratic, either renounced politics or went underground; and with the peaceful, prosperous conditions of the late 1950s and early 1960s, Sihanouk's regime, although antidemocratic, enjoyed wide popular support. A sensible foreign policy widened Cambodia's international relations, particularly with socialist countries, some of whom were very generous with aid projects, which competed for recognition with the large U.S. aid program.

Sihanouk's opening to the Left internationally brought down the ire of the United States, whose diplomats hectored Sihanouk about communist danger and whose agents began to plot with his enemies. The most notorious case was the Dap Chhuon incident of February 1959, which discredited the United States both because of the methods involved and the people chosen as instruments.[23]

Then, in 1963–1964, Cambodia began to fall apart. Early in 1963 a student riot against official brutality and corruption set off a chain reaction that led to government confrontation with leftists, real and imagined. This in turn led to the rejection of needed economic reforms advocated by leftist ministers. Early in 1964 American aid was rejected on the grounds that the United States was supporting Sihanouk's enemies. A nationalization program served to concentrate state-owned businesses in the hands of courtiers who treated them as old-fashioned appanages, while decreases in foreign aid were compensated with increased pressure on the rural population to produce and deliver cheap rice for export.

From 1955 to 1967 roughly 65 percent of the population were rice farmers, and land planted to rice increased from 1.7 to 2.5 million hectares. Production increased from 1.5 million tons of paddy (unhusked rice) in 1955 to 2.7 million tons in 1964, then dropped to 2.38 and 2.28 million tons in 1966 and 1967, respectively. These quantities provided for domestic requirements and an exportable surplus ranging from 197,000 tons in 1957 to 366,000 in 1963, 451,000 in 1964, and 491,000 in 1965, in spite of the decline in total production in the last two years. These exports accounted for 34 percent of total export income in 1957, over 50 percent in 1963–1964, and 38 percent in 1966, slightly behind rubber in that year. After the high point of both export and domestic surplus after export in 1963–1964, there was a decline in rice for domestic consumption in 1965, probably due to squeezing the peasants through debt and tax.

As a result, in 1966 only 172,000 tons were officially exported out of a good crop of 2.38 million tons, which put domestic consumption back at the 1963 level, in spite of an increase in population. It seems also that peasants were selling their surplus illegally across the borders to Thailand and Vietnam for higher prices, thereby depriving the government of revenue. This situation became particularly serious after American aid, which had covered much of the annual budget deficits, was terminated. Faced with this predicament the government organized rice-purchase campaigns by state agencies, which in fact amounted to forcing the peasants to sell their rice to the state at below-market prices. The results were not particularly impressive—219,000, 226,000, and 87,000 tons exported in 1967–1969, out of large crops of 2.5, 3.8, and 2.7 million tons, respectively.[24]

As the economy declined, signs of political opposition, which could only be rebellion, became increasingly frequent. In 1960 the small Communist Party had been reorganized with former Paris students who had begun to return in 1953 gradually taking control. The deteriorating economic and political conditions of the 1960s favored them, but they were frustrated by the insistence of the Vietnamese that conditions for a revolution in Cambodia were not ripe, while the Cambodian leadership felt that Sihanouk's corrupt and increasingly despotic regime should be overthrown. These opposing views conditioned the growth of the revolutionary movement throughout the 1960s, with control increasingly achieved by the nationalist group, of whom Saloth Sar, Ieng Sary, and Son Sen fled Phnom Penh in 1963 to begin organizing a rural revolutionary struggle.[25]

The controversy was ultimately taken out of the hands of both the Cambodian party and their Vietnamese comrades and mentors by a real peasant revolt against direct oppression, the Samlaut uprising in April 1967. At a time when government forces were engaged in an enforced collection of the rice crop at below-market prices and a roundup of suspected communists, peasants in Samlaut in southwestern Battambang Province attacked a state farm. Interestingly, this farm had been organized by one of the pro–Cultural Revolution intellectuals who had agreed to work with Sihanouk in hopes of pushing him leftward domestically as he pursued a policy of international alignment with the major socialist powers. Conflict between peasants and government forces continued into June with considerable brutality, particularly by the army. Although there is disagreement as to whether the Samlaut uprising was part of a nationwide communist plan, other disturbances occurred at the same time elsewhere, and two prominent leftist intellectuals Khieu Samphan and Hou Yuon fled Phnom Penh.[26]

**THE WAR**

The Samlaut uprising and more particularly its continuation in January 1968 deserve to be called the beginning of the Cambodian War, for conflict between left and right continued and increased, both in suppression of individual leftists by the authorities and in armed attacks by both sides in rural areas.

Of course neither the outbreak of armed struggle in Cambodia nor the development of the Communist Party may be understood without reference to the war in Vietnam. Sihanouk had agreed to tolerate sanctuaries for the

Democratic Republic of Vietnam (DRV) and National Liberation Front (NLF) forces on the Cambodian border, and to allow shipment of Chinese arms across the country from the port at Sihanoukville, an operation of great profit for key Cambodian military figures. Advantages such as these contributed to Vietnam's objection to a Cambodian revolution, whatever the objective political-economic conditions.

By 1969 even Sihanouk's neutralist foreign policy, which had endeared him to the local Left and international socialist bloc, was no longer certain. He was moving toward the United States, was increasingly critical of Vietnam, and in spite of formally good relations with that country, he permitted, perhaps even encouraged, anti-Vietnamese tirades in the Khmer-language press.

It now seems certain that the 18 March 1970 coup that overthrew Sihanouk was an internal Cambodian affair. In spite of the great interest in discovering major American responsibility, little evidence has appeared, and given Sihanouk's shifts during 1969 the U.S. government would have seen little reason to remove him. The line taken by those responsible for the coup, that Sihanouk had to be removed because he was selling the country to the Vietnamese, is also difficult to accept, for Sihanouk was then moving away from his earlier position of sympathy for the anti-Saigon Vietnamese, and toward reconciliation with the United States.

Sihanouk was overthrown by men who belonged to the Right, and who were pro-U.S., but Sihanouk's support had always been at that end of the spectrum, and his supporters in Phnom Penh in March 1970 were no less right-wing than his enemies. The two groups represented different factions of the ruling class, and what divided them was rivalry over control of the economy and style of management. Sihanouk's policies since the mid-1960s had favored a courtier-bureaucrat group who treated their offices as appanages, and while they grew conspicuously wealthy the account books of the state enterprises they managed showed red. Their rivals wanted a more modern, rational, capitalist style of economic management, under a functioning bourgeois democratic government, not Sihanouk's rubber-stamp assemblies. Perhaps they considered that it was necessary to get rid of Sihanouk before he secured firm U.S. support.

Following Sihanouk's destitution, the constitution and form of government were changed, until by 1972 Lon Nol, elected president of the Khmer Republic in an apparently fraudulent contest, was able to rule in a quasi-dictatorial manner as Sihanouk had in 1953–1954. The change of regime at first received support from many who had opposed Sihanouk from the Left, even the moderate Left who had no intention of becoming revolutionary combatants. For a few months Phnom Penh lived in a state of euphoria. There was a freedom of speech and press unknown since pre-Sangkum days in the early 1950s, and progressive-minded people tried to believe, against increasing evidence to the contrary, that the new government would keep its promises to reform the system, gain the confidence of the peasantry, and create a more viable national life.

The Lon Nol government, however, did not take long to justify the worst apprehensions of everyone. Its declared policy of free enterprise instead of the strict control and rationing of essential supplies that the situation demanded aggravated the expected inflation, and those in positions of power proved as rapacious as in Sangkum days. The army showed itself inefficient, which could have been forgiven, but it was also corrupt and brutal in its dealings with the peasantry. Within a few months it was common knowledge in Phnom Penh that the enemy troops, whether Khmer revolutionaries or their North Vietnamese and NLF supporters, made a better impression on villagers than the Phnom Penh forces.

Surprising to all parties must have been Sihanouk's moves after his removal. Having received the news of his deposition in Moscow, he continued on his scheduled trip to Peking. Then instead of proceeding to Cambodia to face his enemies with the popular support he was believed to have, or go into comfortable exile in France as his enemies in Phnom Penh may have expected, he remained in Peking and declared that he would lead the struggle against Phnom Penh. His move led to a split in the urban Left, some hating him so much that they remained in Phnom Penh on the government side until the end. With Sihanouk on the revolutionary side, and his popularity maintained among peasants who suffered from attacks by American planes and Lon Nol troops, the revolutionary forces in the short term stood to gain, for any peasant hesitation to attack the towns and government troops would be removed.

Sihanouk's switch also removed Vietnamese objections to Cambodian armed struggle, but meant that Vietnam's Cambodian allies were latecomers on the revolutionary scene and operated under the disadvantage of having advocated apparent theoretical and tactical errors over the previous twenty years. As is now well known, the veterans who returned from Vietnam after 1970 and the domestic intellectuals who may have favored a similar line were pushed aside and for the most part physically eliminated during 1970–1975, while anti-urban, peasantist theories came to dominate the "Pol Pot clique" among the party leadership.[27]

Although the war did not start in 1970, it grew in that year to encompass nearly the entire country—but not immediately. Even before the coup, Lon Nol, seriously out of touch with reality, had permitted massacres of Vietnamese civilians resident in Cambodia and had issued an ultimatum to the Vietnamese to withdraw all troops from Cambodian territory, and on 16 March Vietnamese representatives met with Cambodian officials to discuss the request. Until early May both Vietnamese and Chinese representatives remained in Phnom Penh to try to persuade Lon Nol to continue to tolerate the Vietnamese sanctuaries on the border, and only then did Lon Nol tell them this was out of the question. This was interestingly just when U.S. and South Vietnamese forces had invaded eastern Cambodia, a move that pushed North Vietnamese troops farther into the country, increased the level of civil warfare between the two Cambodian sides, and set the coming disaster on its course.

Not only had Lon Nol's original demands been unrealistic, his speech to the country on 11 May, with its claims that the war was one of religion and foreseen in ancient prophecies, revealed that he was certifiably insane. Unfortunately, his distance from international realities was shared by many of Cambodia's youth, who in 1970 volunteered in far larger numbers than required to drive the Vietnamese out of the country. Poorly armed and singing, they gaily rode off on ancient buses to their slaughter, imagining that they were more than a match for the Vietnamese army.[28]

By the autumn of 1970 the antigovernment forces had occupied nearly all territory east of the Mekong except major towns, and at night flares, Spooky gunships, and tracer bullets were visible from riverside houses in Phnom Penh. Road and rail traffic out of Phnom Penh was blocked most of the time, although daring taxi drivers still made the run from Battambang to Phnom Penh during lulls in the shooting. Over the next four years inflation rose by hundreds of percent, refugees crowded into the city, fleeing both bombing and harassment by revolutionary forces, and by 1974 much of the Phnom Penh population was facing hunger, while the privileged kept up a lavish lifestyle.[29]

Although the Lon Nol army was able to maintain its numbers until the end, because hunger forced young men to join the army for the basic food ration, morale was bad and too many officers were more interested in profit than fighting. Phantom troops were maintained in records so that officers could collect their salaries, weapons were even sold to the enemy, and the army that never had popular support outside Phnom Penh eventually came to be seen by the Phnom Penh population as a liability.

In Paris during January 1973 the United States, the Republic of Vietnam (South Vietnam), the Democratic Republic of Vietnam (DRV, North Vietnam), and the Provisional Revolutionary Government of South Vietnam (PRG) signed an "agreement ending the war and restoring peace in Vietnam." The Cambodian revolutionary forces refused to participate and continued their assault on Phnom Penh. In order to stem the imminent collapse, and with their air force no longer engaged in Vietnam, the United States began an air assault, perhaps the most intensive ever, right through the heart of Cambodia's central agricultural area where most of the population lived. During February to August 1973, 257,000 tons of bombs were dropped, for a total of 540,000 tons since the secret bombing of Cambodia began in 1969. This was nearly three-and-one-half times as many bombs as were dropped on Japan during the entire Second World War.[30]

Although the bombing of 1972 and 1973 physically destroyed most of the heavily populated central agricultural region, it probably stopped an offensive that would have overrun Phnom Penh, but it very likely undermined the more moderate communist leaders, who were sympathetic to Vietnam, for the Paris Peace Agreement was viewed by the Cambodian communists as a stab in the back by Vietnam that allowed the full force of U.S. power to be directed at them. The terror of the bombing also imprinted a hatred of city folk on the young survivors of the raids, who blamed Phnom Penh for having called in the American bombers. It has been reasonably suggested that a communist victory in Cambodia in 1973 under a more moderate leadership would have

*Norodom Sihanouk chairing a meeting of Khmer Rouge leaders in March 1973. Left to right: Ieng Sary, Hou Yuon, Pol Pot, Hu Nim, Khieu Samphan, and Norodom Sihanouk. At that time Sihanouk was the titular head of the resistance to the Lon Nol government, as he is now titular head of the Democratic Kampuchea coalition that is opposing Vietnamese influence in Cambodia. (Photo courtesy of Verso Editions, London.)*

avoided a solution like that carried out after 1975 by the radical communists who then gained control.[31]

After the bombing ceased under orders of the U.S. Congress in August 1973, it took another year and a half for the Communists to regroup and rebuild by exerting ever stricter measures of control over their population base. More significantly, Vietnam was increasingly viewed as an enemy rather than a friend, occasionally even as the principal enemy. This was particularly true after the Paris Agreement, which opened the way for concentration of American bombing on Cambodia.

**DEMOCRATIC KAMPUCHEA**     The last defenses of Phnom Penh collapsed on 17 April 1975, and the Communist troops began marching into the city from several directions. At first they were welcomed by the populace, who had for at least two years hoped for an end to the war at any price. The first measure announced by the victors dispelled the belief that discussions among Khmers at peace would lead to a moderate socialist regime. The entire population of Phnom Penh, swollen by refugees to an estimated 2 million, was ordered to leave the city for rural areas. This was said to be a temporary measure, for three days only, to escape expected U.S. bombing of the captured city, a reasonable fear after wartime experiences. There were also objective economic reasons for the evacuation—inadequate food supplies in Phnom Penh and the inability of existing transport to bring sufficient food there.

At first the new government maintained the form of the Royal Government of National Union headed by Prince Sihanouk that had been established in exile in 1970. Khieu Samphan emerged as deputy prime minister, minister of national defense, and commander-in-chief of the armed forces, but the full composition of the government was not publicly announced, and other names only gradually appeared in disparate news items. Sihanouk and some of his close collaborators returned in September, and their figurehead role was soon apparent.

The real political structure was only revealed in April 1976 when Sihanouk resigned, and Democratic Kampuchea formally emerged, with Khieu Samphan as chairman of the State Presidium, Pol Pot (Saloth Sar) as prime minister, and Ieng Sary in charge of foreign affairs. This structure lasted until 7 January 1979, and the same three men still lead the DK rump group in exile, although most of the rest of the original DK leadership disappeared in purges.[32]

The population of Phnom Penh was at first dispersed at random according to the routes they followed out of the city from their places of residence. Later shifts were directed by the authorities throughout 1975 in attempts to distribute them where labor was most needed. Administratively DK was divided into eight major zones, each subdivided into four to seven regions, in which conditions of life differed widely.[33] In general living was best where evacuees were distributed among established peasant villages, and worst where evacuees were settled on undeveloped land and forced to create and plant fields without either knowledge of how to carry out such work or adequate food supplies pending their first crop.

Democratic Kampuchea attempted to carry out a revolution that, in spite of their rhetoric about "Marxism-Leninism," was different from any previous revolution in modern times. Not only were peasants viewed, reasonably, as the main revolutionary class, but unlike classical Marxism, Leninism, Stalinism, or even Maoism, in Cambodia even the urban working class, along with all other urban groups, were considered class enemies, and were forced to become poor peasants.

If there was any conscious theory behind this policy, it cannot be called "Marxism-Leninism," nor even "Maoism." The total rejection of an urban sector resembles certain non- or even anti-Marxist peasantist theories current in Eastern Europe in the 1930s, or such movements in various parts of the world in earlier times, but it is unlikely that the DK leaders were directly influenced by any of those. The DK aberration is more likely to have arisen strictly from local conditions under pressure of peasantist demands rooted within Cambodian rural society and exacerbated by the war and its destruction.[34]

The imprinting of terror and violence, particularly during the American bombardment, combined with the nature of class conflict already present in Cambodian society, can account adequately for the first wave of the violence for which Democratic Kampuchea has become a paradigm.[35] Besides the evacuation of Phnom Penh, which in itself must have caused thousands of deaths, massacres soon afterward occurred in a number of places. In general they were focused on the military and highest-level civilian officials of the Khmer Republic, and with the exception of the roundup in Phnom Penh of central government personnel they appear to have been local outbursts of anger rather than centrally organized. Throughout 1975 there were also selective arrests of former regime officials, businessmen, and intellectuals, nearly all of whom were accused of contacts with the CIA.[36]

This first period of violence tapered off during 1975, and 1976 was a year of relative calm and relative agricultural recovery in traditional farming areas. There was, however, still a large measure of objective violence in the organization of labor in certain areas. In particular where groups of displaced urban folk were settled in hitherto uncultivated areas, large death rates, sometimes over 50 percent, resulted from overwork, lack of food, and illness.

Violence also resulted from policies to refashion society through abolition of religious practices, traditional ceremonies, normal educational possibilities, and basic everyday freedom of movement or in personal relationships. Such measures were most profound among urban evacuees, and there is no doubt that the majority of peasants were less subject to such harassments, and with some glee participated in their enforcement on their class enemies.

By 1977 the second wave of violence, more centrally planned, had begun. It appears to have been a result of the failures in planned production and distribution that had already caused many deaths—because the expected increases had not happened. Instead of rethinking their ideology and planning, the DK leadership blamed the failures on conscious sabotage and treason. The first arrests and executions that now occurred were among cadres and officials, particularly in those areas in which largely urban evacuees had failed to perform as expected. Such arrests occurred whether or not the cadres in question had behaved leniently or harshly toward their subject populations.[37]

As failures continued, circles of arrests widened. The projected treason behind the failures was blamed on Vietnamese influence, and by late 1977, and more violently during 1978, anti-Vietnamese policies were instituted. Executions spread from suspect cadres to large population groups in the areas they had administered, particularly in the Eastern Zone, still largely under control of cadres associated with the policies of Khmer-Vietnamese cooperation dating back to the 1940s. Extant records of accusations and confessions show that accusations of CIA contact were less frequent, while collaboration with Vietnam was becoming the favorite crime.[38]

Although Cambodian demographic statistics were always rather weak, it is possible, on the basis of the most generally accepted prewar population figure and the number of survivors counted or estimated since 1979, to conclude that between 700,000 and 1 million persons above a normal peacetime death rate, perished during 1975–1979. The total population declined by about 400,000. Perhaps half, based on impressionistic survivor accounts, may have been executed, the rest dying of illness, hunger, and overwork.[39]

DK attitudes toward the Cambodia-Vietnam border were also indicative. The clashes with Vietnamese troops in 1975 may be attributed to honest errors on both sides and were apparently quickly settled by negotiation, but DK intransigence is clear in the refusal to negotiate seriously to establish a border where one has never been properly surveyed nor demarcated on the ground, while insisting that only Cambodia had the right to suggest changes in its favor.[40]

Thus the domestic violence escalated across the border to international violence with increasingly brutal attacks into Vietnam. Beginning in January 1977 Cambodia attacked across the border into civilian settlements in six out of seven of Vietnam's border provinces. Further, such attacks occurred in April, without any previous Vietnamese provocation even alleged by Cambodia. Evidence accumulated since 1979 suggests Phnom Penh may have been intending to reconquer some of the Khmer-populated part of Vietnam, showing the same lack of realism as the youngsters who rushed out of Phnom Penh in 1970 to repel the "Viet Cong."

At first the Vietnamese response was to strengthen border defenses without riposting in kind, and in June a conciliatory letter was sent to Phnom Penh proposing negotiations to resolve the border problem. Pol Pot rejected this, and Cambodian attacks continued. The first vigorous Vietnamese counterattack came in September 1977, and in December they penetrated up to forty kilometers inside Cambodia, and then withdrew by January 1978. That year brought no modification of Democratic Kampuchea's aggressive stance, and after the Eastern Zone purges of May–June 1978 finally wiped out that section of the Cambodian leadership on whom the Vietnamese might have been

*The People's Revolutionary Council of Kampuchea made its public debut at a grand ceremony in Phnom Penh on 25 January 1979 on the occasion of the celebrations of the Kampuchean people's great victory. In this photo a unit of the revolutionary armed forces expresses its determination to defend the revolutionary gains. (Photo from Vietnam News Agency. Collection of Ngo Vinh Long.)*

counting to effect changes in Cambodian policy, Vietnam decided to launch a major invasion to eliminate the continuing danger to its border security. During the two years of Cambodian attacks perhaps 30,000 Vietnamese civilians had been brutally murdered, thousands of buildings destroyed, and large areas of farmland abandoned.[41]

By the time the Vietnamese attack came, in December 1978 and January 1979, terror had also spread so far into peasant circles that were once DK regime supporters that even foreign invasion was felt as a relief. Little resistance was offered by the populace, who welcomed the complete turn-around in policies instituted by the new People's Republic of Kampuchea with Vietnamese encouragement and support.[42]

**THE PEOPLE'S REPUBLIC OF KAMPUCHEA**

The People's Republic of Kampuchea thus came into existence after 7 January 1979 following the destruction of the previous Democratic Kampuchea regime by Vietnamese military forces in response to attacks during 1977–1978 by DK against Vietnamese territory, and in support of Cambodians who had been opposed to, and in some cases resisted the extreme DK policies. These Cambodians became the nucleus of the new state.

The new PRK immediately reversed the basic policies of DK. Freedom of movement and in choice of work was announced, normal urban-rural differences were reestablished, educational, medical, and administrative structures were rebuilt, nonrevolutionary intellectuals, technocrats, and administrators who had been restricted to peasant labor during 1975–1979 were invited to return to work in their former occupational areas. The change in January 1979, in addition to political and economic rationality, represented a vast improvement in personal freedom and human rights.[43]

The first state structure was a People's Revolutionary Council combining executive and legislative functions with Heng Samrin as president. Then in 1981 a constitution was adopted, and the state structure was changed to an executive branch consisting of State Council plus Council of Ministers and a National Assembly. In elections to the latter, 117 members were chosen by province according to size of population. Although there were no competing parties, each provincial list contained more candidates than seats to be filled. Heng Samrin became president of the State Council, and most of the Revolutionary Council ministers remained in equivalent posts in the new structure.

Changes in leading state personnel in terms of their political background—whether revolutionary veterans who spent from 1954 through the 1970s in Vietnam, DK cadres without such Vietnam experience, or others—show an interesting evolution since 1979. In the Revolutionary Council of 1979 there were twelve of the people who had spent time in Vietnam, against five former DK cadre, with one person of nonrevolutionary background as minister of education. After May 1981 there were eleven of the above Vietnam veterans, eight former DK, and five nonrevolutionaries, in education, agriculture, health, culture/information, and as the secretary-general of the State Council.[44]

Since then this tendency has gone even further, and by 1986–1987 there were six or seven of the Vietnam veteran group at the ministerial level, only three former DK officers, and at least eleven of the former bourgeois nonrevolutionaries. The latter, moreover, were being given ever more significant departments. In addition to the powerful Interior Ministry, assigned to Nay Pena in 1985, agriculture, Cambodia's most important economic sector, was under Kong Samol, who obtained his degree in agricultural science from the United States, and people of similar nonleftist backgrounds headed finance, trade, and education, the last particularly significant given the controversy over the direction being taken by Cambodia's cultural development.

The same evolution in factional tendencies is even clearer in the People's Revolutionary Party of Kampuchea, which was only formally revealed to the public after its Fourth Congress in May 1981. In 1981 eleven full members of the Central Committee and one alternate were of the Vietnam group, and seven had served in the DK administration. Then, following the Fifth Party Conference of October 1985 the Central Committee was enlarged to thirty-one full and fourteen alternate members, only five of whom were of the Vietnam group, while nine or ten were DK cadres, nine were revolutionary combatants who broke with Pol Pot by 1975, and at least twenty were young professionals who neither went to Vietnam nor joined Pol Pot.

Even more of these new people who are rapidly moving up to the top ranks of the state bureaucracy and party are to be found in subministerial and provincial government positions. They represent the pre-1975 upwardly mobile "middle class," that is, Khmer who were moving upward socially and economically via modern education and state employment, often out of a peasant or nonelite urban family background. In general they found places then as schoolteachers, administrators, technicians, or were still students in 1975. Without the war and revolution they would have served, and sometimes did serve, the regimes of Sihanouk and Lon Nol.

Although these members of the upwardly mobile "middle class" could have fled abroad, they have chosen to stay in Cambodia and work for the PRK out of nationalist commitment, ideology, idealism, or of course in some cases inertia. Noteworthy is the fact that because of the great loss of skilled manpower between 1970 and 1979, most of them now have higher positions than they could have expected under a peaceful evolution of Cambodia after 1970.

## THE POLITICAL ECONOMY

The economic situation facing the PRK in January 1979 was one of nearly absolute zero. Democratic Kampuchea had succeeded in its goal of creating a classless society, but at the price of neglecting all sectors but basic agriculture, a few related industries, and some hastily conceived irrigation works, not all of which functioned usefully. Because of the emphasis on poor peasants as the only worthy class, trained personnel had been ignored, their abilities unused, and in 1979 most were dead or dispersed. All infrastructure such as roads, transport, and buildings had been allowed to deteriorate. There had been no money, no private exchange, no personal income, and no taxes since 1975, in large parts of the country since 1970. Neither had there been written records, formal judicial proceedings, codified laws, or conservation of archives.

The PRK program was to reverse nearly all policies associated with DK. Their announced intention was to move toward authentic socialism with a planned and market economy in which currency, banking, and commercial transactions would be restored. This meant revival of an urban sector, schools, formal administration, and private possessions. Land, however, remained state property, and thus it cannot be used for speculation or loan collateral, and cannot be lost to usurers for nonpayment of debt, a major cause of social and political tension before 1975.

The PRK proposed to create from scratch a nonproductive administrative and service sector, reactivate and restore a small essential industrial sector, and persuade the majority food-producing sector to support the administration and industry with minimal return for the immediate future. That is, the PRK inherited a truly classless society, yet in order to move toward socialism they had to recreate social classes.

*Revolutionary troops in 1979 in Svay Rieng Province, Kampuchea, help local people harvest the first rice crop raised after liberation. (Photo from Vietnam News Agency. Collection of Ngo Vinh Long.)*

This involved potential risks. Cambodia's majority agricultural sector could have continued to live on its own at basic subsistence level without cities, industries, or officials. There must have been peasants who, although welcoming the freedom of movement and the freedom to organize their own lives after the DK was destroyed, would see no reason to welcome the reconstruction of a class structure that had in the past been inimical to them.

It was also problematical to what extent the former urban sector would return to work without the status and possibilities for wealth accumulation to which they had been accustomed before 1975, for even though the PRK acknowledged the necessity to recreate class differences, there was no intention to permit the same wide status and income differentials or property relations that had characterized prerevolutionary society. Survivors were invited to join the new administration, but as examples of the problems that were faced, only 7,000 of 20,000 pre-1975 teachers reappeared, only 50 of 500 doctors, and only 3 people with legal training.[45]

The procedure adopted to achieve the social restructuring was at first nearly complete laissez-faire. There was sudden freedom of movement, freedom in choice of work or to not work, and, pending reconstruction of a national economy, freedom to trade. Since Cambodia after DK was starved of commodities, and anything could turn over a quick profit, the markets quickly

*Phnom Penh in October 1979 when people were gradually returning to the devastated city, deserted for four years following its enforced evacuation by the Pol Pot regime. (Photo by Marcus Thompson, courtesy of Oxfam.)*

became a favorite area of work for people fleeing the fields, even for many who had not previously worked as traders. This market freedom, and the absence of taxation until 1983, achieved a mobilization of concealed liquid capital, hoarded and hidden since 1975, for what at the time was a productive purpose: the acquisition of essential commodities that the state could not have purchased, confiscated, or obtained through foreign aid.

The more enterprising took the recently dug up cash, gold, jewels, or silks to the border to purchase goods from Thailand to bring back to the markets of Battambang, Phnom Penh, and other towns. Others established themselves in those markets, buying for resale the goods brought from the border and financing further trading ventures. The final purchasers in the towns used their own prewar hoards, where they existed, or the products that they made at home for sale, or even their government rice rations, when these could be spared. Ultimately this capital was exported abroad, principally to Thailand, but in the meantime it had financed a necessary part of the country's reconstruction that the state alone could not have managed. Moreover, used in this way it did not generate severe inflationary pressure, and it did not contribute to the reemergence of wide class differentiation.[46]

By 1979 conditions had improved to some degree. State employees received government rations from international food aid supplies; the market sector, which included large numbers of spouses, relatives, and friends of state employees, could offer adequate prices to entice surplus food from the rural areas; and the latter could feed themselves from the land.

As the state gradually formed, the total laissez-faire policy was modified. The 1981 constitution consecrated three economic sectors—state, cooperative, and family—the latter referring to small-scale agricultural and artisanal work. To these, following the Fifth Party Congress of October 1985, has been added a fourth, the private sector, where individuals may invest funds in small-scale manufacturing with hired labor, with profit constituting the entrepreneur's income. In 1987–1988 the private sector received further encouragement, and still more privatization seems planned. Taxation was introduced in 1983, and by 1986 had been seriously implemented as a source of state income.[47]

Although the flourishing markets have been good for re-creation of towns, they are not the backbone of Cambodia's economy, which is acknowledged to be agriculture, and which supports the 80 percent or more of the population who live in rural areas. In comparison with the prewar situation, agricultural production since 1979 might seem disappointing, since the production levels of the 1960s have not been regained, and no rice is yet available for export. On the other hand, considering the near-starvation level of 1979 and the continuing need for food aid from abroad for several years thereafter, a rather encouraging recovery has been made. In 1982, 1.4 million hectares were planted (as compared to 2.5 million in 1967), producing 1.5 million tons, not quite enough for the then 6.8 million population. By 1986, 1.8 million hectares of wet-season rice were planted, which together with other crops was theoretically just barely sufficient.

Immediate recovery to the prewar production level could not be achieved because of the population dislocation resulting from the Pol Pot years and the 1979 warfare, and also the destruction of seed varieties under DK, disruption of the water supply in some areas by misconceived irrigation projects of DK, unexpected flooding during several years after 1979, the disproportion of women in a work force in which plowing, harrowing, and care of draft animals were traditionally men's tasks, and particularly because of the destruction of draft animals. For example, when 2.5 million hectares were planted in 1967 there were 1.2 million head of draft animals (water buffalo and cattle), but by 1979 only 760,000 survived. By 1986 the prewar number of animals had been reached, but organizational, seed, and water factors were still keeping the area planted below the prewar norm.[48]

Peasants were free to sell their produce on the free market until taxes began to be imposed in 1983, and since 1984 there has been strong exhortation to sell at fixed low prices to the state, accompanied by increasing obstacles to free market access. This plus the guaranteed use of state-owned land may diminish the incentive to plant large surpluses, and many peasants may be limiting production to their own needs. A continued laissez-faire policy is not an answer, for without a state center, which had to be recreated, the agricultural sector would have become attached to the markets of Thailand and Vietnam, with de facto disappearance of Cambodia as a state. After DK, Cambodia could have independence or laissez-faire—not both.[49]

Industry is acknowledged to be subordinate to agriculture, and its function is to produce what agriculture needs, based as much as possible on local raw materials. Perhaps fifty to sixty factories are in operation, none of them up to capacity, need, or plan, except those producing cigarettes and soft drinks. The reasons for the poor performance of industry—even in those areas such as rubber and cotton for which Cambodia is well endowed with primary raw materials—are the obsolete plants that cannot be rebuilt in present conditions and the inability to import certain materials for industry, such as chemicals. Local capital, even if more rationally mobilized, is insufficient.

Moreover, Cambodia is forced to depend on its own meager resources to a much greater degree than most disaster areas because of a U.S.-imposed embargo, not only on government or private aid from the United States, but on normal channels of aid from international financial institutions, as well as normal trade and investment from countries who wish to enjoy U.S. favor. Under the Trading With the Enemy Act and the Export Administration Act, Cambodia has been designated an enemy of the United States and subject to a complete embargo on trade and development assistance, a weapon that was never used against the Soviet Union, even in the worst days of Stalinism and the cold war.[50]

As there was no Cambodian currency in 1979, state employees were given rations instead, while market activity was conducted through barter, in gold and silver, or with foreign currency, such as Vietnamese dong and Thai baht. A new riel (that is, Cambodian currency) was established in April 1980, with 1 riel based on the market value of one kilogram of rice, and salaries were set very low, intended as basic subsistence only. The 1981 salary level in riel ranged from 65 for a worker to 260 for the three highest state officers; in 1984 these salaries were raised to 140 and 500 respectively, with no further raise as of early 1986 when I last checked. To see what this means, in 1981 some sample market prices were: 14 to 20 riel per kilogram for meat, 2.5 to 3 riel per kilogram for rice, 1 riel per single egg, and 3 riel for a piece of laundry soap. By 1984 these prices had risen to 16 riel for chicken, 40 to 45 riel for beef and pork, 4 to 6 riel for rice, 2 riel for an egg, and 12 riel for soap; and by 1986 the price of meat was around 60 riel, with rice up to at least 10. By the end of 1988 there had been a moderate increase in prices, accompanied by another rise in salaries, although the latter are still far from sufficient.

In Cambodia's best prewar years of the 1960s basic food prices in riel were nearly the same, but salaries were about ten times their present level. This means the rural/urban income ratio has shifted drastically in favor of peasants, and the state salary structure no longer gives its occupants an economically privileged position.

Cambodian currency management has been much more successful than monetary policy in Vietnam, and the movement of the riel shows that the two currencies are quite independent. When the new riel was established in 1980 it was assigned a quite arbitrary official rate of 4 riel=U.S.$1. A year later the free market rate was 50 riel=U.S.$1, in 1984 over 140, in 1986, 155, in late 1987, 120, then back to 150 at the end of 1988. These figures show de facto

*The Democratic Kampuchea regime for the most part did away with motor vehicles, and, as a result, the few trains, buses, and trucks now in operation in Cambodia are usually heavily crowded with passengers. This bus is at a highway crossroads in Kandal Province in December 1983. The billboard in the background shows the revolution crushing Sihanouk and Pol Pot. (Copyright © 1983 John Spragens, Jr. Reprinted with permission.)*

inflation and devaluation rates no worse than many Third World capitalist countries, while in Vietnam the currency has declined disastrously, by hundreds of percent.[51]

The economic policies so far followed, in part purposeful, in part ad hoc responses to difficult situations, surprisingly satisfy most of the demands made of Third World countries by the International Monetary Fund and World Bank in order to qualify for aid from those institutions. Thus Cambodia has (1) concentrated on agriculture, (2) avoided too much industrialization, (3) liberalized imports, (4) increased the domestic tax burden, (5) frozen wages, and (6) allowed the currency to depreciate until it found a stable level at which it has recently seemed to be recovering on its own. Another standard IMF/World Bank demand, attraction of foreign investment, does not depend on Cambodia, but first requires relaxation of the U.S.-led embargo on normal economic relations with the PRK.[52]

Encouraging progress has been made in basic primary education, which started from zero after the disastrous DK policies. Since 1979 the Ministry of Education has been in the hands of professional teachers who were trained before 1970 and were not associated with any revolutionary faction before 1979. By 1984 new primary teachers had been trained in adequate numbers, and school enrollment was comparable to the best prewar years. The syllabus for primary and secondary schools is very nationalist in content, with all instruction in Khmer; stories of Vietnamization of schools and culture in the PRK are nothing more than disinformation.[53]

**THE PRK AND THE INTERNATIONAL COMMUNITY**

Unfortunately, all efforts to restore essential services and improve the quality of life are impeded by the necessary investment of scarce resources in rearmament and defense against attacks by the DK coalition supported in sanctuaries along the Thai border by China, the United States, and ASEAN (Brunei, Indonesia, Malaysia, the Philippines, Singapore, and Thailand). In the autumn of 1979 the nearly destroyed Democratic Kampuchea armed forces, with tens of thousands of civilian supporters or impressed workers, reached the Thai border after several months' retreat from the Vietnamese attack. Very quickly an international rehabilitation and reequipment operation was set in motion, much of it disguised within the large refugee camp network that was being created.[54] The foreign-sponsored reconstruction of the DK forces ensured that Vietnamese troops would have to undertake the defense of Cambodia for some time to come.

An international diplomatic campaign was also mounted against the PRK. It has proceeded through numerous phases, from the International Conference on Kampuchea in July 1981 to the two Jakarta Informal Meetings in July 1988 and February 1989. In all of the various proposals and formats that have been developed over the years, the principal demands made by opponents of the PRK have centered on withdrawal of the Vietnamese troops in Cambodia and free elections. The assumption behind this emphasis was that the PRK only existed by virtue of the Vietnamese presence: once they were gone it would quickly fall, and in free elections the present PRK leaders would stand no chance. As it gradually became clear that the PRK would not just fade away, the proposals have called for formation of a coalition government of the PRK and its Cambodian enemies.

The latter are the Coalition Government of Democratic Kampuchea, formed in 1982 under pressure by ASEAN and the United States. Three parties are involved. The largest is the Democratic Kampuchea group led by Pol Pot, Ieng Sary, and Khieu Samphan, and believed to have about 40,000 experienced troops. Although they were reviled by all Western countries during their time in power, there has been no hesitation to use them against Vietnam after 1979. In fact they were deemed essential to any serious resistance against the PRK. To make them more respectable their backers insisted on a coalition with two noncommunist groups that had formed on the border after 1979, the Khmer People's National Liberation Front (KPNLF), under Son Sann, which has been reported to have between ten and fifteen thousand troops, and an even smaller group under Prince Sihanouk. Son Sann and most of the other older leaders of his group trace their political descent from the Democratic Party of the 1940s and 1950s, although some of them were supporters of Lon

Nol during 1970–1975. The Sihanoukist leadership, naturally, consists of his traditional supporters. There is thus no natural affinity among the three coalition partners. The KPNLF leaders have a history of anti-Sihanoukism since prewar days, while both they and the Sihanoukists are violently anti-communist, particularly anti-DK. The only thing the two groups have in common is a desire both to remove the Vietnamese from Cambodia, which is occurring by itself, and to destroy the PRK because of its friendship with Vietnam.

Because of the internal animosities, the coalition hardly functions as such, and it never would have formed without the insistence of its foreign backers. Indeed, the KPNLF and Sihanoukist groups represent governments from whom international recognition had long been withdrawn, and which had also lost popular support before being forced from office. They are truly foreign creations as much as the PRK is alleged to be. In addition, the KPNLF has nearly destroyed itself with factional infighting, and the record on human rights within its camps is nearly as bad as the fierce discipline attributed to the Pol Pot authorities in their camps.[55]

The coalition, however, holds Cambodia's seat in the United Nations and is recognized by most important Western governments, including the United States. The nonrecognition of the PRK has been based on its alleged unrepresentative character and the alleged violation of international law through which it was established. The improvement in human rights, reconstruction, and the evolution in state personnel as outlined above are ignored. According to the coalition and its backers, particularly the United States, China, and ASEAN, the PRK government is a collection of Vietnamese puppets who only remain in power because the country is occupied by the Vietnamese army.

The demands made by the international enemies of the PRK, and the assumptions behind them, have shown an amazing lack of realism or attention to the facts of the situation within Cambodia. In 1979–1980 it might have been possible to achieve quick withdrawal of Vietnamese troops, if it was guaranteed that sanctuaries and support would not be offered to anti-PRK and anti-Vietnamese groups on the Thai border, in particular the universally discredited DK. The ASEAN proposal to the International Conference on Kampuchea in 1981 showed awareness of this with its call for disarmament of Cambodian factions and exclusion of DK, but it was blocked by China and the United States, who preferred to rearm and rehabilitate the DK forces in an effort to destroy the PRK by force.

Nevertheless, the Vietnamese troops are being withdrawn in a gradual phase-out that began in 1982 when, according to an American expert, their numbers fell from 180,000 to 150,000. Each year thereafter Vietnam announced a further partial withdrawal, only grudgingly acknowledged by their enemies with some delay, until by early 1988 the latter were admitting a figure of 120,000 against Vietnam's claim of 100,000 remaining troops.[56]

Removal of the Vietnamese required the creation of a PRK army capable of defending the country; and the possibility of achieving this is regularly denied by those who also deny the reality of Vietnamese troop withdrawal.

Until recently the conventional figure for PRK forces was 30,000, of poor quality and prone to desertion. This figure was calculated in 1982 by the American diplomat-scholar Timothy Carney, based on careful analysis of all available sources.[57] Since then, however, development of the army has been a major PRK goal, with five-year conscription, much internal propaganda to encourage voluntary service, and always the awareness that the Vietnamese, whose departure is desired, will only leave when the PRK can defend itself. By 1986 a U.S. Embassy official in Bangkok was willing to estimate PRK forces of 39,000; in 1988 an authoritative American journal allowed a figure of 50,000; and by early 1989 a figure of 70,000 was being floated by both serious observers and propagandist enemies of the PRK.[58] With forces like that the PRK has numerical superiority over its enemies, although their battle experience may be inferior to that of the DK troops.

A realistic picture of Cambodia today, then, reveals a PRK that has endured longer than its two predecessors, has built up a new state apparatus staffed by nationalist Khmers, and is slowly developing a defense capability. Its enemies have not been able to destroy the PRK, and it is not a mere client that will collapse when its foreign support troops have been withdrawn.

Over the last two years interesting signals showing awareness of the changing situation were emitted by some of the key international players in the Cambodian game. Chinese policy on Cambodia since 1975 has always been more related to its dispute with the Soviet Union than to approval of DK ideology and domestic policies, particularly since the reforms of Deng Xiaoping. With Sino-Soviet relations improving, as they clearly are, China's interest in DK is certain to diminish. Indeed, in a little-noticed statement to the Malaysian Institute for Strategic and International Studies a specialist from the Institute for International Studies in Shanghai said that "recent steps of the Chinese government may be interpreted as leading toward withdrawal of support" for the Khmer Rouge.[59] Of course China will not change positions overnight, but it has accepted the Sihanouk-PRK dialogue and agreed that the DK group should not come to power again, although it still insists on replacement of the PRK by a coalition of all four Cambodian parties.

Encouraging sounds have also come from Thailand, through which all aid for the DK coalition must pass, and which could quickly end the struggle with a change of policy. In a 1986 ASEAN Series publication of the Malaysian Institute of Strategic and International Studies, M. R. Sukhumbband Paribatra, one of the most influential of Thailand's younger political scientists, argued that "perhaps the best ASEAN can hope for in Cambodia is 'a Finland solution'." Then on two occasions in November 1987 General Chavalit Yongchaiyut, commander of the Thai army, declared that the Cambodian dispute was mainly an internal conflict, and that Vietnam did not constitute a threat to Thailand. Still more encouraging was the statement of the new prime minister, Chatichai Choonhavan, that Indochina should be Thailand's market, not its battlefield, a position reflecting the Thai business community's unhappiness with the policies followed since 1979. Chatichai, moreover, appointed M. R. Sukhumbband Paribatra to a new group of special prime ministerial advisers.[60]

The Vietnamese, too, did their part, announcing credibly that they would hasten their departure and pull out half their remaining 100,000 troops in 1988, with the rest leaving by September 1989 if there was an overall political settlement, or at the latest by the end of 1990, settlement or not. After the first obligatory round of congratulations, however, the anti-PRK forces began to show nearly as much consternation as was caused by Vietnam's move into Cambodia ten years ago. Vietnam had called their propaganda bluff. They really intended to leave, and the PRK was not going to collapse as a result.

In the face of clear Vietnamese intentions to get out fast, ASEAN began to engage in delaying tactics. Just before the first Jakarta Informal Meeting in July 1988, an ASEAN foreign ministers' joint communique expressed "deep concern over the continued illegal occupation of Kampuchea by Vietnamese military forces," as though there had been no changes since 1979. But by this time the Vietnamese forces had been reduced to 50,000–70,000. A subtle new approach was the foreign ministers' "call for a durable and comprehensive political settlement in Kampuchea which *will lead to* [my emphasis—MV] the total withdrawal . . . under international supervision."[61] The Vietnamese were not to be permitted to simply leave, and the ASEAN foreign ministers were even seeking to delay their departure until new machinery could be set up to undermine the PRK. As Indonesian foreign minister Ali Alatas told a Thai journalist, the question is no longer just "the unilateral withdrawal of Vietnamese troops," but withdrawal "in a context of an overall comprehensive solution," meaning within a framework supervised by those powers that desire a change in the Cambodian government.[62]

Although Alatas claimed to be concerned about the DK forces that might continue fighting after Vietnamese withdrawal, they could easily be blocked by ASEAN pressure; and his remarks implied that it was PRK durability that was causing concern. ASEAN even seemed to be calling for another foreign occupation named the "International Peacekeeping Force" in the embarrassing event of a real Vietnamese withdrawal. All ASEAN and China would have to do would be to cut off aid to the anti-PRK coalition, and the PRK could take care of its own peacekeeping. The U.S. also chimed in with "uncertainty about Vietnamese intentions," and the "direct threat to Thailand of continuing Vietnamese occupation."[63]

The enemies of the PRK are now caught in a dilemma created by a too-wishful belief in their own propaganda. Behind all of the moves since 1979 was a conviction that the PRK could never become anything more than a Vietnamese puppet state, without any national base, which would collapse as soon as the Vietnamese could be made to leave, of course unwillingly. The maintenance of this view against all the accumulating evidence to the contrary resulted from a rare dialectical reinforcement between official U.S. and ASEAN disinformation and housebroken journalists who with witless reverence repeated whatever their favorite "Western diplomats" said, until apparently they all came to believe their own propaganda. Now they cannot avoid perceiving that the Vietnamese really intend to leave, and embarrassment is caused by the sudden realization that the PRK is a real Cambodian government that might survive.

*Students in an eleventh-grade biology class copying drawings from the blackboard at January 10 High School. Cambodia has so few textbooks that they are available to students only in the school library, and thus lessons like this one on chromosomes must be copied into notebooks in great detail. (Copyright © 1988 John Spragens, Jr. Reprinted with permission.)*

The position of the anti-PRK parties at the end of 1988 was that the PRK must not be allowed to survive the Vietnamese withdrawal as the government of Cambodia. The international settlement planned to precede or coincide with the Vietnamese withdrawal would require replacement of the PRK with a four-power coalition (DK, KPNLF, Sihanouk, PRK) in which no party would be dominant, and the arrangement would be assured by an international force. Naturally the PRK refuses to dissolve itself after having rather successfully governed for ten years. PRK leaders have agreed to some kind of participation of their enemies, minus eight DK leaders, in a new government that would be in fact an enlarged PRK. They have also agreed to hold elections under international observation and to abide by the results even if they lose their dominant position. Together with this is a warning that by 1990 at the latest the Vietnamese forces will be gone, and then the problem will have resolved itself and no longer require any concessions to the coalition. Their apparent success in building an army, restoring agriculture to near self-sufficiency, and providing impetus to economic growth by their new encouragement for privatization indicate that this may be no idle threat.

An unexpected breakthrough came in January 1989 when Thai Prime Minister Chatichai Choonhavan invited Cambodian Prime Minister Hun Sen to visit Bangkok. Although Prime Minister Chatichai denied this meant a change in Thai policy, that it was merely a get-acquainted meeting to facilitate the negotiations desired by ASEAN, it was a coup for Hun Sen and a moral defeat for the coalition and Prince Sihanouk. The visit was not even coordinated with Thai Foreign Minister Siddhi Savetsila, one of the most energetic proponents of the standard ASEAN hard line against Cambodia. It clearly signaled Prime Minister Chatichai's intention to break with the old policy and a realization that the PRK was a viable government. This was in line with the views of his new advisers and probably of the then army commander General Chavalit Yongchaiyut.

To realize the full international impact of Chatichai's sudden move, we must recall that ASEAN policy has always been to maintain unity and, on the Cambodian question, to follow the lead of Thailand, the "front line state," even when it seemed that Indonesia and Malaysia were not enthusiastic about a confrontation with Vietnam, and the Philippines were too preoccupied with other matters to be greatly concerned. Furthermore, the United States has always claimed that its policy on Cambodia was to follow ASEAN.

Unfortunately, the United States was no more willing to obey its own dictum of "following" ASEAN than in 1981 or 1985. U.S. "officials do not hide their displeasure" with "Thailand for its policy switch," and they warned that Thailand "would have to pay a price," that "Thailand should consider whether the total value of any new Indochinese trade would even cover the United States trade access privileges it still gets" and which implicitly might be cut.[64] More threatening were the March 1989 announcements that the United States would strengthen the KPNLF and Sihanouk forces and would even countenance the participation of the Pol Pot group in a Cambodian coalition, after years of insisting that no return of the Khmer Rouge could be accepted.[65]

The anti-PRK ASEAN groups and enemies of the PRK in the United States became more insistent than ever that Vietnam must not just go off and leave Cambodia to itself. With a rare degree of doublespeak they evoked an imagined Afghan parallel with Vietnam, by its unilateral withdrawal, which we must recall had been their demand since 1979, allegedly imposing civil war on Cambodia, pushing aside the obvious circumstance that it is precisely the enemies of Phnom Penh, both Cambodian and their foreign supporters, who threaten civil war.

Ironically it is the PRK whose position most approximates the stated objectives of the United States. The PRK are unalterably opposed to the return of the DK leadership (the Khmer Rouge); they agree to free multiparty elections; they accept in principle Sihanouk's return as chief of state; they want foreign investment and trade; they have reestablished the traditional official religion; and they have been moving toward an increasingly free economy since 1985.

Of course one might question PRK's sincerity. Would they proceed in the same direction if their international enemies declared peace and allowed them to make their own arrangements with other Cambodian groups? We cannot know the answer in advance, but at least they have a record of moving steadily in those directions.

Sihanouk, on whom the U.S. administration pins its hopes, also has a record that is even clearer. Once he got control of the political system in 1955, free elections were unknown, and after 1958 no other organized party than his own Sangkum party dared to contest an election. As for the Khmer Rouge (the DK nucleus in exile on the Thai border), Sihanouk, like the United States, has insisted on their inclusion in a four-party coalition government to replace the PRK. He has preferred this to the bipartite merger offered him by Phnom Penh, because instead of the powerless, if ceremonially prestigious, position of figurehead chief of state that the PRK solution implies, a coalition of four factions that hate and distrust one another would provide Sihanouk with considerable opportunities to maneuver and thereby to acquire some real power, such as resulted from the internationally supervised settlement in 1955. Sihanouk, in a desperate attempt to salvage maximum authority for himself, has been willing to risk civil war and the return to power of the DK leadership.

Until July 1990 the U.S. administration's position was equally dangerous and without even any apparent justification in self-interest, once Phnom Penh had offered to establish the type of political and economic system that the United States has pretended to favor. Indeed, as laid out in an interview by Assistant Secretary of State for East Asia and the Pacific Robert Solomon, which was broadcast to Southeast Asia on 29 June 1989,[66] the U.S. position, demanding "self-determination for the Cambodian people" but also "a process of national reconciliation," was dangerously contradictory, if, as seems likely to people who have observed life within Cambodia, the majority of the 8 million population should prefer the present government, and if "national reconciliation" meant forcing them to accept integration with feared and despised coalition elements under international pressure. This would also increase the danger of civil war, which the U.S. administration pretends to be trying to avoid.

It was perhaps not just a coincidence that Solomon gave his policy statement interview on the same day that Sihanouk announced a hardening of his position. This included a demand that a precondition for his participation in the Paris talks was "a dismantling of the Phnom Penh regime in exchange for his government." Solomon emphasized several times that the United States wanted "Sihanouk to play *the* [my emphasis—MV] leadership role," and is "making efforts . . . to strengthen the position of Prince Sihanouk," implicitly against the perceived wishes of the Cambodian majority who, through their present leadership, have indicated their acceptance of Sihanouk as ceremonial leader, but not with strengthened authority.[67]

The efforts to "strengthen the position of Prince Sihanouk" have included "nonlethal" aid as well as proposals from the U.S. government to provide lethal aid, which at least in overt form have so far been blocked by Congress. What would happen to guns sent to the Sihanoukists was well illustrated by the fate of U.S.-supplied uniforms, mosquito nets, and knapsacks sold by soldiers of the noncommunist forces to Thai merchants "as soon as they get back from the battlefield, and sometimes even before."[68]

In his interview Solomon avoided answering questions about the dangers of increased U.S. aid to the noncommunist groups, which are incapable of using it. "The issue," he said, "does not really begin with assistance of one form or another"; "We do not want to see the issue defined strictly as a matter of lethal aid or one form of assistance or another." The "core question is: Will there be a political process to resolve the situation in Cambodia or not?" A political process, he added, "is the broader framework within which to view our efforts to bring peace to Cambodia," as though increased aid to one faction were not designed to influence the political process, in fact to delay or block a political process that seemed feasible as soon as Vietnam set a definite date for withdrawal and Prime Minister Chatichai inaugurated a switch in Thai policy.[69]

Subsequent developments in 1989–1990 have not justified the optimism that followed the Thai policy change. The international players—in whatever slightly changed formula: Jakarta Informal Meetings, Tokyo Conference, Australia Plan, or UN Plan—still insist on weakening, if not destroying, Cambodia with a four-power arrangement termed Supreme National Council in which national sovereignty will be vested pending the outcome of elections under international supervision. China has continued to maintain its support for the tripartite coalition and for the Democratic Kampuchea faction within it. Even within Thailand, Prime Minister Chatichai has not been able to persuade his army to terminate the supply lines across Thai territory to the DK forces.

In the circumstances now prevailing not even the surprising announcement on 18 July 1990 that the United States would no longer support the DK coalition in the UN augurs as well as it might have if undertaken a few years ago. The change seems certainly to have been made primarily for domestic political reasons, and it is not clear yet what concrete measures it implies. Will the United States now urge recognition of Phnom Penh or even vacating the UN seat? Probably not. Will U.S. aid to the coalition now be cut off and persuasion exerted on the Thais to block supplies to the coalition? Even this is not assured. In fact, U.S. policy is still (October 1990) to aid the two noncommunist coalition members, pretending that aid to them will not get into the hands of their more powerful ally, while urging them to keep a distance from the Khmer Rouge. With respect to Phnom Penh, the United States says there must be internationally supervised elections within a comprehensive settlement, which means Phnom Penh must give up some of its sovereignty to its enemies before the United States will recognize any democratic progress within the country.

The U.S. administration, with its ostensible but perhaps only cosmetic change of policy, may only have decided to finesse domestic critics while leaving the situation on the ground in Southeast Asia as it is; and with the new U.S. preoccupation in the Middle East, Cambodia is not likely to get much attention from Washington.[70] Behind the declarations of interest in assuring choice to the Cambodian people there is still the hardly concealed U.S. hostility to Phnom Penh and to Vietnam.

The Thai government, although more interested in peace in Cambodia and more friendly to Phnom Penh than the other interested powers, is dominated by businesspeople. They want an economically liberal, free-market Cambodia, not even the moderate socialism of the PRK. This is not because of any special commitment to democracy. Thailand needs raw materials, particularly timber, after denuding its own territory, and Thai companies have already begun to make agreements with Cambodian factions to begin extracting timber from Cambodia's northwest. A well-run Cambodian forestry service with lumbering and timber export strictly monitored and in state hands is certainly contrary to Thai interests.

Washington is perhaps counting on the Nicaragua syndrome to effect the long-desired outcome—elimination of the Phnom Penh government. Beginning in late 1988 Phnom Penh undertook a series of economic liberalization measures. They were partly, no doubt, to remain in line with Vietnam, which was doing the same thing, in order to qualify for IMF and World Bank aid, partly also in the hope that the United States, Western Europe, and ASEAN would view Cambodia more sympathetically. As in all cases of new economic liberalism in poor countries, the immediate effects have been disastrous, with even less prospect for the subsequent progress dreamt of by neoclassical and monetarist economists than in Eastern Europe.

Moreover, the lesson of Vietnam demonstrates that as far as the United States is concerned, insistence on such liberalization is intended to destroy the economy, not just to put it onto a track that U.S. theory says leads to development and qualifies the country for normal international economic relations.

Vietnam carried through the reforms recommended by the IMF and World Bank, and very successfully, but the United States has still blocked loans from those institutions on the pretext that Vietnam has not persuaded the Phnom Penh government to cooperate in its own demise.[71]

In Cambodia, after ten years of a well-managed currency and low inflation, there has been over 100 percent devaluation in 1988–1990, without the state being able to raise salaries commensurately. The small class of local merchants with enough capital to invest in imports are thriving while the population as a whole sinks into even worse poverty than before. International carpetbaggers are also thriving, apparently encouraged by Phnom Penh in the dream that they will bring tourists and foreign investment.

And if the rural population, unable to sell its products at adequate prices to an impoverished city and unable to receive protection from Phnom Penh against coalition depredations, becomes dissatisfied with urban-rural disparity, Cambodia will be back in the same situation it faced at the beginning of its revolution in 1969–1970. In spite of the clear opportunism of the Western press campaign in favor of the Khmer Rouge, urging that to save Cambodia from them they must be taken into the government, there is probably some truth in the claims that they are making progress with hearts and minds in rural Cambodia.[72]

In a last-ditch attempt to avoid further decline, the Phnom Penh government has moved further toward its enemies, accepting in principle the UN plan, which calls for formation of a Supreme National Council as repository of sovereignty while a UN administrative and security force, which might number up to 20,000, takes over administration pending supervised national elections to form a new government. In Jakarta on 10 September 1990 all four Cambodian factions accepted a formula for the council. It is to consist of twelve members, six from the State of Cambodia, and six from the coalition, that is, two from each partner in the latter. This represents a small Phnom Penh victory, for the coalition, in particular its Democratic Kampuchea segment, had been insisting on equal representation for each of the four parties. Nevertheless, peace and return to prosperity in Cambodia are not likely in the near future.

**NOTES**

1. Letter of Jonathan Winer, counsel to Senator John Kerry, dated 22 October 1986, to Larry Chartieness, Vietnam Veterans of America, "The Khmer Rouge received no funds from the U.S. from fiscal year 1976 through 1979. In the years from 1980–1986 they received . . . in FY 87 dollars: 1980 $54.55 million . . . 1981 $18.29 million. . . ."

2. In 1981, at the International Conference on Kampuchea, the United States sided with China against an Association of Southeast Asian Nations (ASEAN) formula that sought to disarm all three Cambodian parties (the Partie [sic] of Democratic Kampuchea, Son Sann's Khmer People's National Liberation Front [KPNLF], and Sihanouk's group) and exclude the Democratic Kampuchea (DK) group; in 1985 George Shultz warned ASEAN against formulating peace proposals that Vietnam might accept (*Bangkok Post*, 13 July 1985); and as I showed in "Democratic Kampuchea: CIA to the Rescue," *Bulletin of Concerned Asian Scholars*, vol. 14, no. 4 (1982), the CIA tried to make the People's Republic of Kampuchea in 1979 look worse than Democratic Kampuchea.

3. Peter Carey, "Prospects for Peace in Cambodia," *Far Eastern Economic Review*, 22 December 1988, pp. 17–18.

4. See George Coedes, *The Indianized States of Southeast Asia* (Honolulu: East-West Center Press, 1968), sections on Funan; Claude Jacques, " 'Funan,' 'Zhenla,' the Reality Concealed by These Chinese Views of Indochina," in R. B. Smith and W. Watson, eds., *Early South-East Asia, Essays in Archaeology, History and Historical Geography*, (London: Oxford University Press, 1979).

5. Coedes, *States*, pp. 171–172. This type of society resembles the "Asiatic Mode of Production," concerning which see Lawrence Krader, *The Asiatic Mode of Production: Sources, Development and Critique in the Writings of Karl Marx* (Assen: Van Gorcum, 1975); Marian Sawer, *Marxism and the Question of the Asiatic Mode of Production* (The Hague: Nijhoff, 1977); and on its possible application to Cambodia, L. A. Sedov, *Angkorskaia imperiia* [in Russian] (Moscow, 1967).

6. Michael T. Vickery, "The Fall of Angkor: a New Perspective," in "Cambodia After Angkor: The Chronicular Evidence for the Fourteenth to Sixteenth Centuries" (Ph.D. diss., Yale University [Ann Arbor: University Microfilms, 1977]), pp. 509–522 and further references.

7. The ideas put forward here are not part of mainstream Thai historiography, and they have been propounded in the following writings by Michael Vickery: "The Khmer Inscriptions of Tenasserim: A Reinterpretation," *Journal of the Siam Society (JSS)* vol. 61, no. 1 (January 1973), pp. 51–70; review of Robert B. Jones, *Thai Titles and Ranks, etc.*, *JSS*, vol. 62, no. 1 (January 1974), pp. 159–174; "The 2/K.125 Fragment. A Lost Chronicle of Ayutthaya," *JSS*, vol. 65, no. 1 (January 1977), pp. 1–80; and "A New *Tamnan* about Ayudhya," *JSS*, vol. 67, no. 2 (July 1979), pp. 123–186. In his book *Thailand: A Short*

*History* (New Haven: Yale University Press, 1984), David K. Wyatt has ignored this aspect of the history of Thailand.

8. Although Vietnamese-Cham struggles had long been a regular feature of the area's history, the two sides had been equal, and the Cham had nearly conquered the political center of Vietnam in the 1370–1380s. See Coedes, *States*, pp. 237–238.

9. For the Cambodian Moslem king, see Francis Garnier, "Chronique royale du Cambodge," *Journal Asiatique* ser. 6, 18 (Oct.–Dec. 1871), pp. 365–373, and Dr. Hendrick P.N. Muller, ed., *De Oost-Indische Compagnie in Cambodja en Laos* (The Hague: Martinus Nijhoff, 1917), pp. 20–21; for the Iberian sources, see discussion in Vickery, "Cambodia After Angkor," pp. 205–211, 243–256.

10. See Vickery, "Cambodia After Angkor," pp. 200–218.

11. David P. Chandler, *A History of Cambodia* (Boulder: Westview Press, 1983), chaps. 6–7.

12. Chandler, *A History*, p. 156.

13. Many of the issues mentioned here have been discussed in more detail in Michael Vickery, "Looking Back at Cambodia, 1942–1976" in Ben Kiernan and Chanthou Boua, eds., *Peasants and Politics in Kampuchea, 1942–1981* (Armonk, NY: M. E. Sharpe, and London: Zed Press, 1982); Vickery, *Cambodia 1975–1982* (Hempstead, England: Allen and Unwin, and Boston: South End Press, 1984); Vickery, *Kampuchea Politics, Economics and Society* (London: Frances Pinter and Boulder: Lynne Rienner, 1986); and Ben Kiernan, *How Pol Pot Came to Power* (London: Verso, 1985), cited below as "Looking," *Cambodia, Kampuchea,* and *How,* respectively. See Vickery, *Kampuchea,* pp. 5–6.

14. Vickery, *Kampuchea,* pp. 8–10; Kiernan, *How,* pp. 21–24.

15. Vickery, *Kampuchea,* pp. 8–10; Kiernan, *How,* pp. 63–64.

16. Vickery, *Kampuchea,* p. 9. Note that the "Phnom Penh intellectuals" of the time would have included the Thiounn brothers who are now among the DK leadership and Son Sann. On the Thiounns, see Vickery, *Kampuchea,* pp. 5–6 and Kiernan, *How,* pp. 29–33.

17. Vickery, *Kampuchea,* pp. 10–12; Kiernan, *How,* chap. 3.

18. Kiernan, *How,* chap. 3, p. 83 on date of KPRP; Vickery, *Kampuchea,* chap. 6.

19. Vickery, "Looking," pp. 94–96; Kiernan, *How,* pp. 99, 126.

20. See Vickery, "Looking"; but the best treatment of this period will be in David Chandler's history of the period 1945–1979, forthcoming.

21. Vickery, "Looking," pp. 96–99; Kiernan, *How,* pp. 153–164. Foreign-imposed elections now, as proposed by enemies of the PRK, would probably be similar and are naturally opposed by the surviving victims of the 1955 charade and their political descendants who today govern in Phnom Penh. This accounts for the concern among all parties about the composition of the preelection government.

22. Vickery, "Looking," pp. 98, 103–104.

23. Dap Chhuon started out as an independence fighter when Lon Nol and Son Sann were making careers as *functionnaires* under the French, and Sihanouk was abetting the French in arresting true nationalists. In 1949 Chhuon joined Sihanouk and became a serious rival of Lon Nol, and in 1959 Chhuon emerged as leader of a U.S.-supported plot to overthrow Sihanouk. The outcome, destruction of Dap Chhuon, was very favorable to Lon Nol, and there were always rumors that Lon Nol was involved but betrayed his accomplices. Wilfred Burchett (*The Second Indochina War,* p. 45, fn.) reported the rumor but fudged the record in saying "according to one version which I heard in Kampuchea at the time, Lon Nol was involved." "At the time," in February 1959, Burchett was nowhere near Cambodia. The most thorough treatment of the

incident will appear in David Chandler's forthcoming book on post–World War II Cambodia.

24. Laura Summers, Introduction to Khieu Samphan, *Cambodia's Economy and Industrial Development*, Data Paper 111, Southeast Asia Program (Cornell, 1979); Vickery, "Looking," pp. 104–106; Kiernan, *How*, chap. 6. Some of the statistics are from *Annuaire statistique du cambodge*. It is possible that the post-1966 statistics were distorted for domestic political reasons.

25. Kiernan, *How*, chap. 6.

26. The major work on Samlaut is in the following publications by Ben Kiernan: Kiernan, *The Samlaut Rebellion and its Aftermath, 1967–1970: The Origins of Cambodia's Liberation Movement* (Melbourne: Monash University, Centre of Southeast Asian Studies, Working Papers, nos. 4–5, 1975–1976); Kiernan, "Conflict in the Kampuchean Communist Movement," *Journal of Contemporary Asia*, vol. 10, nos. 1–2 (1980); Kiernan and Boua, *Peasants and Politics;* and Kiernan, *How*. Note the different nuances in interpretation from one to the other. Kiernan insists that the 1967 rebellion was organized by the Communist Party, but his shifts with respect to *who* was involved and *where* are anything but confidence inspiring. The present author is agnostic on the question, but so far favors the view that Samlaut 1967 was a local uprising, not centrally directed.

27. Vickery, *Cambodia*, chap. 5; Kiernan, *How*, chap. 8.

28. Lon Nol's 11 May speech in Jonathan S. Grant et al., eds.; *Cambodia: The Widening War in Indochina* (New York: Washington Square Press, 1971), pp. 109–112. The lack of realism was to be repeated in DK attacks on Vietnam in 1977–1978.

29. William Shawcross, *Sideshow: Kissinger, Nixon and the Destruction of Cambodia* (New York: Simon and Schuster, 1979), pp. 183–185, 348–349; Vickery, *Cambodia*, pp. 78–80.

30. Shawcross, pp. 259–267, 297; and Ben Kiernan, "The American Bombardment of Kampuchea, 1969–1973," *The Vietnam Generation* (New Haven, CT), vol. 1, no. 1 (1988 or 1989).

31. Shawcross, *Sideshow*, chaps. 18–19, particularly pp. 298–299; Kiernan, *How*, pp. 390–393.

32. Vickery, *Cambodia*, p. 146, chap. 3, n. 5.

33. Vickery, *Cambodia*, chap. 3.

34. Vickery, *Cambodia*, chap. 5.

35. Although innocent of any theoretical background, Shawcross, *Sideshow*, pp. 298–299, described eloquently the effect on peasant soldiers of bombing with a rate of losses that cannot be sustained "without suffering often irreversible psychological damage," and "which bred a dreadful hatred of their enemy and a contempt for the attitudes of the outside world." In search of mainstream respectability he has carefully expunged this from his later work, *The Quality of Mercy: Cambodia, Holocaust and Modern Conscience* (Bangkok: DD Books, 1984; also New York: Simon and Schuster, and London: Andre Deutsch, 1984), pp. 48–50. Recent research, published in the article referred to in n. 30 above, by Kiernan among survivors has confirmed the effects of the bombing. See a description of the equivalent phenomenon among U.S. soldiers in Vietnam in "Treating War's Psychic Wounds," *Newsweek*, 29 August 1988, pp. 46–48.

36. This has been determined from confessions in the Tuol Sleng Prison archives.

37. Vickery, *Cambodia*, chap. 3.

38. On the Eastern Zone, see Vickery, *Cambodia*, pp. 131–143.

39. For discussion of population and death statistics see Vickery, "Democratic Kampuchea: CIA to the Rescue"; *Cambodia*, pp. 184–188; *Kampuchea*, p. 3; "How Many

Died in Pol Pot's Kampuchea," correspondence, *BCAS*, vol. 20, no. 1 (Jan.–Mar. 1988), pp. 70–73.

40. A little-known detail of Indochinese history—an error in the original French Indochina map survey and emplacement of triangulation points resulted in objective errors in all maps, and the greatest errors were in the southern Cambodia-Vietnam border region. See Victor Delahaye, *La plaine des joncs et sa mise en valeur* (Rennes: Imprimerie de l'Ouest Eclair, 1928); and L. Malleret, *L'Archeologie du Delta du Mekong*, tome I, p. 67. See also Vickery, *Cambodia*, pp. 195–196.

41. Grant Evans and Kelvin Rowley, *Red Brotherhood at War* (London: Verso, 1984), pp. 115–126.

42. Vickery, *Cambodia*, chap. 4.

43. Vickery, *Cambodia*, chap. 4; Vickery, *Kampuchea*.

44. For more detail see Vickery, *Kampuchea*, chaps. 4, 6, and 8. Further changes have been made since then, and the same trend has been maintained.

45. Not all were killed. At least half of the pre-1975 number of doctors had escaped overseas, mostly to France, before the end of the war in 1975.

46. On wealth crossing the border to Thailand, see Vickery, "Refugee Politics: The Khmer Camp System in Thailand," pp. 293–331, in David A. Ablen and Marlowe Hood, eds., *The Cambodian Agony* (Armonk: M. E. Sharpe, Inc., 1987), pp. 293–331.

47. Vickery, *Kampuchea*, chap. 9. Taxes have increased even more since 1986.

48. Perhaps the best-informed specialist on contemporary Cambodian agriculture is the French agronomist-engineer François Grunewald, to whom I am indebted for much of my information, in particular from his "Le Kampuchea contemporain et ses problèmes de developpement agricole" (Paris: Rapport de Mission ASCODEKA, 1983); and "Du côte des rizières: réussites, échecs, et tendances dé l'agriculture du Kampuchea," in *Les Cahiers de la Recherche Developpement*, no. 16 (December 1978), pp. 51–66.

49. Had Vietnam not overseen the re-creation of a new state center, they could have absorbed half of Cambodia simply via a free market.

50. Joel Charny, John Spragens, Jr., *Obstacles to Recovery in Vietnam and Kampuchea*, *U.S. Embargo of Humanitarian Aid* (Boston: Oxfam America, 1984).

51. See Murray Hiebert, *Far Eastern Economic Review*, 13 October 1988, p. 12, for the latest PRK currency move, which Hiebert, evidently mesmerized by the anti-PRK propaganda line, treats as a *new departure* from Vietnamese policy.

52. It was precisely such IMF/World Bank–imposed policies that Philippine communist leader Jose Maria Sison said a Communist-led Philippine government would refuse to implement, and for which he criticized Aquino, in an interview in Bangkok in July 1986. See *The Nation* (Bangkok), 7 July 1986, p. 5.

53. Vickery, *Kampuchea*, chap. 10.

54. Vickery, "Refugee Politics."

55. Sihanouk lost his legitimacy, apart from association with DK, when the world recognized the Khmer Republic in 1970; and most of the KPNLF leadership, though not Son Sann, are holdovers from the Khmer Republic, which lost recognition after 1975. Interestingly, Son Sann's first notable job was in December 1940 as a member of the French Economic Delegation to Tokyo to discuss Japanese purchase of Cambodian rice.

56. Edmund McWilliams, "Vietnam in 1982: Onward into the Quagmire," *Asian Survey*, January 1983, pp. 62, 70.

57. Timothy Carney, "The Heng Samrin Armed Forces and the Military Balance in Cambodia," pp. 180–212, in *The Cambodian Agony*.

58. In June 1986 a U.S. Embassy official in Bangkok (*Bangkok Post*, 4 June 1986, p. 4) estimated PRK forces as possibly up to 39,000, a 3,000-per-year increase since Carney presented his figure. More recently Gareth Porter, "Cambodia: Sihanouk's Initiative," *Foreign Affairs* (Spring 1988), pp. 809–826, especially p. 821, reported without indication of source an estimate of 50,000 for PRK "regular troop strength." The 70,000 figure is in Peter Carey, *Far Eastern Economic Review*, 22 December 1988, pp. 17–18, and in Esmeralda Luciolli, *Le mur de bambou* (Paris: Editions Regine Deforges, 1988), p. 128.

59. *The Nation* (Bangkok), 8 July 1988; *Berita Harian* (Kuala Lumpur), 9 July 1988.

60. Sukhumbband Paribatra, *Kampuchea Without Delusion*, pp. 15, 16, and 20; General Chavalit's remarks in *The Nation*, 4, 5, 6, and 8 November 1987; *Bangkok Post*, 6 November 1987.

61. "ASEAN Joint Communique," *The Nation*, 6 July 1988.

62. *The Nation*, 10 July 1988, pp. 6–7.

63. *Bangkok Post*, 2 July 1988; *The Nation*, 6 and 8 July 1988.

64. *Far Eastern Economic Review* (FEER), 2 March 1989, pp. 9, 10–11; for U.S. actions in 1981 and 1985 see note 2 above.

65. Recently President Bush appointed a former KPNLF representative, Sichan Siv, as deputy assistant for public liaison, according to the *Bangkok Post*, 14 March 1989: "Khmer refugee finds top spot in the White House," by Joan Mower, Associated Press reporter in Washington. In a 22 April 1985 letter to the *Washington Post*, Sichan Siv identified himself as "KPNLF Representative to the United Nations."

66. Reported in *The Nation* (Bangkok), 1 July 1989.

67. Sihanouk statement reported in *Bangkok Post*, 30 June 1989, "Sihanouk makes threat to boycott Paris peace talks."

68. Michael Adler, "Brisk Trade in US Aid Material at Site 2 Camp," *The Nation*, 4 July 1989.

69. Solomon interview cited above.

70. Given the near impossibility that Washington did not have intelligence on the coming Iraqi moves in Kuwait, it is not unlikely that Washington announced its switch on Cambodia knowing that other matters would soon push it out of public view.

71. Susumu Awanohara, "US, Japan block IMF effort to support Vietnam, fiscal interdiction," FEER, 28 September 1989, pp. 22–23.

72. Nate Thayer, "Despite record, Khmer Rouge gaining support," *Bangkok Post*, 9 May 1990; Steve Erlanger, "United Nations' Cambodia plan dodging vital issues" in the *New Straits Times* (Kuala Lumpur), 31 August 1990; Nate Thayer, "Resistance routs P. Penh troops in countryside," *Bangkok Post*, 17 July 1990, reporting Khmer Rouge claims as truth. At least the Khmer Rouge have been winning some hearts and minds among the Western press corps in Thailand.

# 4

W. Randall
Ireson
&
Carol J.
Ireson | Laos

Laos was, and still is, fundamentally a rural, subsistence agrarian society, and its history and development of the last forty years can be understood only in that context. Its population of about 4 million is divided among over forty ethnic groups, with the dominant lowland Lao constituting almost half. The remaining half is made up of other lowland Tai[1] groups, midland (Lao Theung) groups of predominantly Austronesian origin, and highland (Lao Sung) groups that have migrated from China. Lowland Lao and Tai tend to cultivate paddy rice in the river valleys, and the other groups subsist on swidden (slash-and-burn) rice agriculture on the mountainsides. Except in the more heavily populated areas along the Mekong River and some interior valleys, villages tend to be isolated and to rely on their own production to meet all their needs. Barter between villages is proportional to their proximity, and it is only recently that one can speak of a market economy expanding beyond major provincial towns.

Ethnic and linguistic diversity has been a barrier to the development of a unified national identity. Prior to 1945, only lowland Lao held the few colonial administrative positions open to Lao, and, in general, lowland Lao have viewed their upland neighbors with indifference or contempt. One important aspect of the Laotian Communist movement has been an effort to include minority groups in party and military affairs, and this aspect bore fruit with significant minority support for the movement during the war years.[2] However, the lower formal education and language disadvantage of minorities continue to be barriers to their integration in national affairs.

Lowland Lao and Tai typically live in wooden or bamboo houses built on stilts and grouped in villages of from ten to several hundred families. Households may include three generations, but seldom more than one married

This chapter is a revised version of W. Randall Ireson and Carol J. Ireson, "Laos: Marxism in a Subsistence Rural Economy," *Bulletin of Concerned Asian Scholars* 21, nos. 2–4 (April–Dec. 1989), pp. 59–75. Reprinted with permission.

couple of the middle generation, other couples of that generation having already established their own home nearby. Average family size is six persons.[3] Related households often farm together, either as a single economic unit with regard to paddy rice production or in loose cooperative groups that exchange labor during the intense work periods of transplanting and harvest. Help is also available from neighbors for major activities such as house raisings, weddings, or funerals. The household economy is based on rice production, using water buffalo to pull the plow. Buffalo and oxen are a significant aspect of family wealth, and many families also raise a few pigs or poultry. Small family gardens provide seasonal vegetables, peppers and other spices, and occasionally fruit. Cotton or tobacco may also be grown, again primarily for household consumption. Gathering wild plants and hunting forest animals also contribute significantly to the diet.

The lowland Lao are Buddhist, and the *wat* or temple plays an important role in most villages as a center for weekly prayers and monthly *bouns* or religious festivals. Traditionally, all men were expected to join the monkhood for a period of their lives, which could be as little as a few weeks during adolescence; however, the practice has gradually weakened over the decades. Generally a small number have entered the monkhood for a much longer period, and through their study of the scriptures and Buddha's precepts provide a repository of social and religious knowledge for Lao society. Wat schools also served as an important source of basic education for boys prior to the gradual expansion of a secular education system after 1945.

Intervillage contact is maintained through petty marketing networks as well as visiting among relatives in an extended kin network that may spread throughout a province. Major Buddhist festivals also provide a stimulus for travel and visiting between nearby villages. Most villages are connected, however tenuously, to a marketing network. Villagers themselves may take their products to sell in the nearest market town, or village marketing cooperatives may buy and sell from district or provincial state stores. Even in remote areas, private merchants travel to purchase village products and pay with household goods or money, but the total volume of trade is quite small. A village woman may sell her few kilos of garlic to a traveling market woman, who in turn sells it in the provincial capital. State stores also exchange whatever goods are in stock—suitcases, pots, cloth, sewing machines—for rice and other agricultural produce. State store pricing is commonly calculated in both rice and kip (the Lao currency), reflecting the subsistence economic base common throughout most of the country. State stores are an addition since 1975. They never functioned efficiently and, following the economic liberalization of the late 1980s, have now been largely supplanted by private merchants.

In summary, lowland Lao have lived simply but adequately, traded and traveled occasionally within a limited area, and have ignored and been ignored by the government.

Lao Theung and Lao Sung groups, coming from several widely different traditions, cannot be characterized uniformly.[4] In general, their villages are only semipermanent, due to the need to move every decade or two as the land cultivated as swidden in one area becomes exhausted. The physical standard of living tends to be somewhat lower than that of lowlanders because highland rice yields are often only half that of paddy, and villages rely more on hunting and gathering than on animal husbandry and gardening for food supply. The Hmong, however, are well known for their animal raising. Opium production and trade provided a significant income source for some groups. Most upland ethnic groups have patrilineal descent groups and patrilocal residence after marriage, in contrast to the bilateral, uxorilocal pattern of the lowland Lao.[5]

For the Hmong and Mien, the main Lao Sung groups, clan membership forms an important basis for establishing and maintaining relationships between distant villages. This became of strategic importance during the war because if a clan chief decided to support either the Royal or Pathet Lao (Communist) side, the other members of the clan were expected to share that allegiance. Contact with government officials, however, was typically even less than for lowland Lao.

Upland Lao religions are universally based on animist principles, though there are significant differences among them. Ancestral spirit cults often serve as a uniting force, but do not stimulate the intervillage exchanges typified by Buddhist *bouns.*

**EARLY LAO KINGDOMS**

The history and development of Laos as a nation has been heavily influenced by its stronger neighbors. From precolonial times Lao states have been affected by neighboring kingdoms in Burma, Thailand, and Vietnam. French colonial policy, with British acquiescence, set Laos as a buffer between Siam and its more profitable colony in Vietnam; after World War II, Laos was inextricably bound up in the great-powers struggle for the future of Indochina.

Prior to the French entry into Laos in 1893, Laos had been unified only twice as a nation with something approximating its present boundaries. The first time occurred under Fa Ngum in 1353 with the founding of the Kingdom of Lan Xang (literally "million elephants"). Fa Ngum united several small kingdoms and established his capital at Luang Prabang; its borders extended from Chiang Mai and Sukhothai south to the northern border of Cambodia, and east to the Annamite range.[6] The kingdom generally prospered for two centuries before its dissolution.

Under Souligna Vongsa (r. ca. 1637–ca. 1694), Lan Xang was once more reunited and experienced a half-century of peace and prosperity. The kingdom covered much of the Korat Plateau, reached to about the present border with Kampuchea, and to the crest of the Annamite range, except that Xieng Khouang remained independent, paying tribute both to Vietnam and Lan Xang. Souligna's only son had been executed for adultery, so on the king's death the succession was contested, and by 1713 Lan Xang was divided into three petty kingdoms centered at Luang Prabang, Vientiane, and Champassak. Vientiane and Luang Prabang were plagued by Thai occupation and Vietnamese encroachment until the coming of the French at the close of the nineteenth century.

But to speak of a Lao "kingdom" in many ways gives the impression of more unity than is justified. The Tai and Burmese states of the thirteenth and fourteenth centuries were characterized by large tracts of undeveloped land and scant populations, and a primary goal of statecraft was to exercise control over enough people, concentrated in a region, to bring land into production and to provide for military defense. Except in the Thai kingdom of Ayudhya, areas distant from the capital were thus under only loose and indirect administration through a series of vassals and overlords, and villagers were unlikely to be aware of a ruler higher than their local *chao muang* (lord of a district).[7]

**LAOS UNDER THE FRENCH**

Following the French conquest of Cambodia and Vietnam, a Siamese army was dispatched in 1885 to Luang Prabang, ostensibly to suppress Chinese (Hô) bandits, but not incidentally to reassert claims to the Lao state. August Pavie, the French vice-consul in Luang Prabang, was able to persuade the Lao king to accept French protection in the context of reasserting "inherited" Vietnamese claims to the area. With Britain motivated to establish Siam as a strong and independent buffer between the two expanding colonial powers, and the French mounting a military advance up the Mekong into Champassak and Khammouane, Siam was forced in 1893 to accept a treaty ceding all territories east of the Mekong to France. Treaties in 1904 and 1907 further modified the frontier to French advantage.[8]

French administration of its colony in Laos was informed by the low economic importance attached to this relatively isolated region with difficult transportation routes and few easily exploitable natural resources. The French contented themselves with posting a small number of colonial officers and enlisting Vietnamese civil servants to undertake the bulk of the administrative tasks. Only a few hundred French were posted in Laos at the height of the colonial period.

In contrast to their activities in Vietnam and Cambodia, the French in Laos built no universities, no railroads, and few roads. Aside from a small tin mine in Khammouane, there was no development of raw material exports. Small numbers of the Lao nobility were educated in Vietnam, Cambodia, and France, and what secular education existed in Laos was in French rather than Lao. Outside the main towns, French presence was scarcely felt, except as requirements for corvée labor along the few roads constructed.

**THE INDEPENDENCE MOVEMENT**

With the fall of France to the Nazis in 1940, its Indochina colonies came under de facto Japanese domination, though in Laos the immediate impact of the occupation on village life was slight. Across the Mekong, an underground group of Lao nationalists, the Lao Seri (Free Lao), were organized and supported by the Free Thai movement and the United States. Beginning in January 1945, French, British, and U.S. guerrilla units were inserted into Laos to join with the Lao in harassing the Japanese and preparing for the reassertion of Allied authority in the region.[9]

After Japan's defeat in 1945, Laos was occupied by the Chinese in the north and the British in the south, in accordance with the Potsdam conference. Considerable maneuvering among the various Lao nationalist factions followed. Prince Phetsarath declared the unification of Laos, and was a month later dismissed from office by King Sisavang Vong. Lao Seri activists from Thailand then formed a new committee, the Lao Issara.[10] About the same time, Prince Souphanouvong arrived in Savannakhet with a Vietnamese military escort[11] and helped form a provisional Lao Issara government including Souphanouvong, Phetsarath, Oun Sananikhone, and Khammao Vilay. However, a Franco-Chinese agreement in February 1946 opened the way for the return of French troops, who moved north from Pakse and defeated Souphanouvong and a detachment of Vietnamese at Thakhek on 21 March. The leadership of the Lao Issara fled to Thailand, where a provisional government in exile was formed under Phetsarath.[12] For a year resistance raids were launched across the Mekong into western Laos, but internal disagreements among the leadership of the Lao Issara led to the resignation of Souphanouvong in 1947 and the mounting of a new resistance effort from the east, with significant Viet Minh support and leadership.

For the next seven years, the various forces jockeyed for advantage in a number of ways. The French and the Lao royal family reached an agreement for a more independent state in 1949, and shortly afterward the majority of the Issara dissidents in Thailand reconciled with the king and returned to Laos. Meanwhile, the Viet Minh increased its guerrilla activities in Vietnam and provided assistance to Lao Communist forces, which were beginning to establish base areas in the northern and northeast parts of the country. In 1950 a resistance government was established with Viet Minh assistance, headed by Souphanouvong, and also including Kaysone Phomvihane, Nouhak Phounsavan, and Phoumi Vongvichit, all members of the present Politburo of Laos. Though opposed to the reestablishment of French rule, the United States gave limited economic assistance to the royalist Lao government.

As the Viet Minh brought more pressure on the French in Vietnam, in combination with small numbers of Lao troops they also expanded their influence west of the Annamite Mountains. In 1953, the northern province of Sam Neua came under resistance control, together with parts of the neighboring provinces of Phong Saly, Xieng Khouang, and Luang Prabang. The Viet Minh also briefly occupied the central Meking town of Thakhek. A few months later, the fate of the French was sealed at Dien Bien Phu, and the Geneva Conference turned to the question of Indochina.

## BEGINNINGS OF THE SECOND INDOCHINA WAR

Despite the Viet Minh military victory, the Geneva Conference did not turn out entirely to their benefit. With pressure from China, the Soviet Union, and the United States, an

*Prince Souphanouvong at work in a cave in the mountains in 1950. (Free Lao photo. Collection of Ngo Vinh Long.)*

agreement was reached calling for the withdrawal of France from Indochina, the removal of "volunteer" troops from Laos, the partition of Vietnam pending national elections, and the formation of a coalition Government of National Unity in Laos.

For the Lao, the main problems created by the Geneva Agreements were the integration of Royalist and Pathet Lao (PL) (resistance) troops, the administrative status of the provinces of Phong Saly and Sam Neua, and the division of ministries among the two factions. National elections in 1955 gave the leftists 8 of 39 seats in the National Assembly.[13] The United States began an effort to strengthen the rightist forces with economic aid and political pressure; the effort was stepped up after the 1958 elections for the National Assembly gave 13 of 20 new seats to the leftist Neo Lao Hak Sat (NLHS) and Santiphap parties.

Accused by the United States of leftist sympathies and faced with a cutoff of aid, Souvanna Phouma attempted to organize a reform government without the NLHS. But a rightist group funded by the CIA, the Committee for the Defense of National Interests, was able to block his attempt and to constitute a government, led by Phoui Sananikone, that excluded the NLHS. Phoui dismissed many government personnel with leftist sympathies, attempted to force the absorption of PL troops into the national army, and otherwise effectively eliminated any official avenue for PL influence, thus further polarizing the two sides. Phoui's government soon came under pressure for being ineffective and corrupt, but it used exaggerated reports of Viet Minh incursions to acquire additional U.S. military aid and clandestine advisers.[14] In August

*The Central Committee of the Free Lao Front during the resistance against the French colonialists. In August 1950 Prince Souphanouvong (with mustache) became prime minister of the Pathet Lao ("Land of the Lao") and Kaysone Phomvihane (on Souphanouvong's right) defense minister. (Free Lao photo. Collection of Ngo Vinh Long.)*

1959, Souphanouvong and fifteen other PL leaders were jailed by Phoui, signaling the end of any pretense at compromise between the sides.

The Pathet Lao now began a campaign of increased guerrilla warfare and political action, initially in the mountainous areas under their influence, but gradually spreading toward the Mekong. The Royal Lao Government (RLG) countered with rigged elections and increased accusations of Vietnamese invasions. In May 1960, Souphanouvong and his colleagues escaped from prison and made their way back to the liberated areas, which became their base until their final victory in 1975.

On 9 August, Captain Kong Le, the idealistic twenty-six-year-old leader of a paratroop battalion, executed a coup in Vientiane and successfully took control of the government, giving his support to a reconstituted government with Souvanna Phouma as prime minister. Souvanna made overtures to the Pathet Lao to join in a reconciliation, but was met by counterdemands. General Phoumi Nosavan and his rightist supporters declared martial law in Savannakhet and moved their forces north toward Vientiane. Kong Le resisted him, but the United States had meanwhile cut off cash grants for military pay to Souvanna's government, successfully pressuring Souvanna to accommodate the rightists and restrain Kong Le. At the same time the United States was supplying and paying Phoumi's rightist troops directly. The king and most Lao political figures rallied to Phoumi's cause, labeling Kong Le a pro-

*First conference for political alliance between the Pathet Lao Front and the Neutralist Patriotic Lao Forces (15 October 1965). (Photo from Pathet Lao News Agency. Collection of Ngo Vinh Long.)*

Communist rebel; his forces were defeated in Vientiane in mid-December. With about 500 troops, Kong Le made his way to Xieng Khouang, where he joined with the PL forces.

**INCREASED ROLE OF THE GREAT POWERS**

Amid growing international sentiment for another coalition government in Laos, Souvanna Phouma and Souphanouvong met in early 1961 on the Plain of Jars. PL military action had secured much of the eastern two-thirds of the country prior to the convening of the second Geneva Conference on 16 May. Despite an early agreement in principle to form a coalition government with Souphanouvong, Souvanna Phouma, and Boun Oum heading the leftist, neutral, and rightist factions, respectively, a final agreement was not obtained until June 1962, after another PL victory at Nam Tha.

*While the U.S. CIA was training Meo tribesmen to kill and to produce opium for them, the Pathet Lao was trying to educate the Meo youngsters as well as older people (in the background) to read and write in their own script. This class was held in a mountain cave (1968). (Photo from Lao News Agency. Collection of Ngo Vinh Long.)*

The permanence of this settlement depended not only on internal Lao politics, but on the willingness of external powers to accede to the agreement as well as maintain pressure on the Royalist and PL factions to accept a coalition government. These conditions did not hold. Although a neutral Laos had value as a diplomatic fiction, neither side had any interest in abiding by the convention. PL actions were in accord with the overall North Vietnamese strategy for expansion of Communist control in Indochina; the United States saw the situation in Laos as related to its own efforts to support the South Vietnamese government and to prevent the spread of Communism in Asia. Both sides successfully attempted to draw strength from the neutralists. From 1960, CIA operatives had also given more support to rightist forces than the State Department may have intended, further polarizing the situation.

More and more the situation in Laos became connected with the escalating conflict in Vietnam. After the Tonkin Gulf incident, President Johnson ordered retaliatory air raids on North Vietnam, and expanded bombing began in early 1965. U.S. bombing raids on Laos had begun in October 1964, at first accompanying Royal Lao Air Force sorties, but soon proceeding independently against the Ho Chi Minh Trail and other targets in northern Laos.

From 1963 onward, Laos was, in fact, under two separate governments. Souvanna Phouma headed the so-called coalition, the RLG based in Vientiane, while the PL established a separate government based in Sam Neua. The RLG received extensive economic and military aid from the United States as well

*At the successful conclusion of the Indochinese Summit Conference of April 1970, Prince Sihanouk (center) embraces Prime Minister Pham Van Dong of the Democratic Republic of Vietnam. President Nguyen Huu Tho (far left) of the National Liberation of Vietnam smiles and hugs Prince Souphanouvong of Laos. The purpose of the meeting was to coordinate the common struggles of the Indochinese peoples against U.S. aggression. This was a big turning point in the war. (Photo from Vietnam News Agency. Collection of Ngo Vinh Long.)*

as economic assistance from several Western European nations. Thai mercenaries and the *armée clandestine*, a CIA-financed irregular force composed primarily of Hmong and Mien tribespeople, also augmented the RLG military. At its peak, it numbered 30,000.[15] PL forces were similarly aided by North Vietnam and China, and according to Macalister Brown and Joseph J. Zasloff were under substantial Vietnamese direction.[16]

For the next eight years, the military situation remained one of small seasonal changes from generally stable areas of control, with few large battles. However the PL gradually expanded their influence through a combination of political and military action. By 1972, nearly three-fourths of the country was under de facto PL control, with only narrow areas around the Mekong river towns still administered by the RLG. During this same period, the RLG was supported almost entirely by foreign aid, principally from the United States. A large U.S. Agency for International Development (USAID) mission carried out strategic development projects, including relief and resettlement for the hundreds of thousands of people displaced by the war and by the intense bombing of contested areas. USAID also acted as a conduit for funds for CIA activities and supported the aerial supply of food and weapons to armée clandestine guerrillas fighting in the mountainous regions.

The U.S. "Secret War" in Laos included extensive aerial bombing of much of the country. The total 2.1 million tons dropped was equal to all that

DURANT LES 15 ANNÉES DE LUTTE CONTRE LES IMPÉRIALISTES AMÉRICAINS ET LEURS VALETS (7/1954 A 7/1970) L'ARMÉE ET LE PEUPLE LAO ONT: DURING 15 YEARS OF STRUGGLE AGAINST THE U.S. IMPERIALISTS AND THEIR HENCHMEN (JULY 1954 — JULY 1970), THE LAO ARMED FORCES AND PEOPLE HAVE :

-MIS HORS DE COMBAT 145.223 ENNEMIS      - PUT OUT OF ACTION  145,223 ENEMY TROOPS
-SAISI 50.527 ARMES DE DIVERS TYPES      - SEIZED 50,527 GUNS OF VARIOUS TYPES
-DESCENDU ET DÉTRUIT 1500 AVIONS AMÉRICAINS. - SHOT DOWN OR DESTROYED 1,500 U.S. AIRCRAFT

*A 1970 collage exhibits photos of downed U.S. pilots and planes, captured weapons and prisoners, and (though not intentionally so) the extent of destruction of a land that was once thickly forested. (Photo from Pathet Lao News Agency. Collection of Ngo Vinh Long.)*

dropped by the United States in the European and Pacific theatres in World War II and amounted to two-thirds of a ton per Laotian.[17] All towns in the liberated zones of PL control in Phong Saly, Houa Phan, and Xieng Khouang provinces were decimated, and the people either lived in caves in the limestone mountains or in the forests, farming by night and hiding by day. Similarly, the Ho Chi Minh Trail, which passed through the rugged mountains of eastern Laos from Khammouane Province south to Saravane and Attopeu, was subject to carpet bombing from B-52s based in Thailand and South Vietnam as well as raids by fighter-bombers.

For all its intensity, however, the strategic effect of the bombing was minimal. Traffic along the Ho Chi Minh Trail continued, and while food production in the liberated areas was substantially disrupted, the scattered population was able to survive and carry on the guerrilla struggle, often with their dependents moving to refugee camps in RLG-controlled areas to wait out the war at U.S. expense.

Despite its apparent superiority in resources and foreign support, the RLG was unable to prevail over the PL. Arthur J. Dommen attributes this failure to a combination of inadequate U.S. analysis of the strategic and political situation, an ineffective and alienating aid program, and lack of national commitment on the part of Royalist leaders.[18] Brown and Zasloff also emphasize the well-planned and coordinated nature of the PL/North Vietnamese struggle, their ability to speak effectively to the rural people of Laos, and the readiness to exploit unexpected events to their advantage.[19] Brown and Zasloff contrast this orchestrated struggle to the feudal, family-centered, and self-interested behavior of RLG elites.

## THE IMPACT OF THE WAR ON VILLAGE SOCIETY

Thirty years of war had significant effects on traditional Lao society. The greatest impact was undoubtedly during the 1960–1975 period, when great-power support intensified and broadened the conflict. There were four major effects of the war: destruction of the agricultural base and dislocation of the population, recruitment of men into the various armies, propaganda and development efforts to enlist the population to support one side or the other, and the distortion of the economy in Royalist areas by foreign aid.

The intense bombing carried out by the United States from 1963 to 1973 had a significant impact on agricultural production in the targeted areas. Because the people living in the PL zones had to hide in the forest or caves during the day and could farm their fields only at night, the area harvested was much reduced. Laos was not subjected to massive defoliation as Vietnam was, but the intensity of bombing, which reached over 700 sorties a day at its peak,[20] made agriculture a very risky activity. Additionally, the widespread use of antipersonnel bomblets served to deny large areas of paddy and swidden fields to the people.

Tribal groups were recruited into the armies of both sides. Entire Hmong villages recruited by the CIA were moved according to tactical considerations, and as farming was disrupted, the villages were supported with air drops of rice and other supplies by Air America. With U.S. support, the RLG also carried out a policy of removing people from contested areas; for example, thousands of families from the eastern valleys of Khammouane and Savannakhet provinces were resettled in refugee villages near the Mekong on Route 13 and Route 9. Their only alternative was to risk living under intense bombing. By 1973, nearly 1 million Lao, or a third of the population, were living as refugees.

The military draft also disrupted village society. With able-bodied men involved in the war, family agricultural production frequently became the responsibility of the women. Women relate how during the war they carried out the farming tasks usually done by men and managed the family in the absence of their husbands. As the needs of the military continued, the draft

*After the Pathet Lao took back the Plain of Jars in February 1970, the United States evacuated 20,000 progovernment civilians and Meo mercenaries and began to systematically bomb the Plain of Jars and Pathet Lao territory. Six hundred thousand refugees (about a quarter of the country's population) fled the region. In this picture Lao peasants in the Plain of Jars are being helped by Pathet Lao fighters to reap their rice. (Photo from Pathet Lao News Agency. Collection of Ngo Vinh Long.)*

age on both sides fell to fifteen, with even twelve-year-old boys being taken into the army.[21]

In efforts to win the people over to their side, both factions undertook propaganda and development efforts. On the PL side, cadres worked at the village level to convince people of the nationalist goals and rightness of their cause. Basic education and adult literacy efforts, together with training of village medics, composed the bulk of development efforts, which in general were hampered by scarcity of resources and difficulty of transport. However, these programs were used as a vehicle for political awareness, evidently with some effect. The PL also effectively exploited tensions between the secular government and education system of the RLG and traditional Lao values and *wat*-centered education carried out by the Buddhist *sangha* (clergy),[22] convincing many Buddhist monks to support the liberation effort through sermons and religious guidance of the people.

The RLG similarly attempted to recruit the Sangha to their side, but their heavy-handed attempt to control the order for political purposes backfired. More effective in spreading the RLG "presence" was an expanded range of elementary schools and village health posts, improvement of roads, and construction of village wells, irrigation systems, and district or province hospitals. Virtually all these projects were financed through grants from USAID.

*Early 1970: Lao militia women helping members of the Lao People's Liberation Army get an artillery piece into position for the attempt to retake the Plain of Jars in early 1970 from the Meo army and their U.S. CIA backers. (Photo from Pathet Lao News Agency. Collection of Ngo Vinh Long.)*

The immense amounts of military and economic aid granted to the RLG drastically changed the character of the Lao economy, particularly in areas near the Mekong Valley provincial capitals. Import support programs, wages paid to Lao military and officials from U.S. funds, expenditures by foreign personnel, and particularly gains from the endemic corruption in the RLG military and government all served to stimulate a thriving luxury consumer economy in the towns that had only basic markets prior to 1960. In Vientiane, European cars and motorcycles, imported liquor, gold, drugs, and women were all for sale, though the average Lao income was around $100 per year. The artificial nature of this economy became immediately evident after the abrupt termination of Western aid in 1975, when shops closed and goods were exhausted almost overnight.

**THE THIRD COALITION AND
THE PATHET LAO VICTORY**

By the early 1970s, U.S. commitment to the Vietnam war was ebbing. President Nixon delegated Henry Kissinger to engage in talks with the North Vietnamese, represented by Le Duc Tho, with a view to withdrawing U.S. troops "with honor." As one consequence of those negotiations, a final cease-fire and political agreement were signed by the two Lao factions in Vientiane on 21 February 1973.[23] Continuing negotiations ultimately led to the formation of a Provisional

Government of National Union in April 1974, with Souvanna Phouma as prime minister. The ministries were divided among the Royalists and PL. The police forces of Luang Prabang and Vientiane were "integrated," meaning in practice that PL and RLG police patrolled alternating intersections in the cities. More important, perhaps, for the majority of Lao, U.S. bombing raids stopped in 1973, and overall military activity declined.

A National Political Consultative Council (NPCC) was created as a parallel force to the Council of Representatives and soon came under PL domination. An eighteen-point program of liberal democratic reforms was proposed, and after July 1974, a series of strikes and agitations in favor of the program was led by "student advisers." As the rightist military situation in Vietnam and Cambodia steadily deteriorated through early 1975, the Lao royalists lost heart in the face of continual PL pressure and political gains. Shortly after the victories of the Khmer Rouge in Cambodia and the NVA in Vietnam, the flight of the rightist governmental, commercial, and military elite began. The PL, by now identified as the Lao Peoples' Liberation Army, moved without opposition into Vientiane, and the administration was purged of its remaining rightist elements.[24]

The May "student-led" occupation of the USAID compound in Vientiane signaled the end of U.S. support for the RLG side, and by September the Lao People's Revolutionary Party (LPRP) began to play a public role in political affairs. On 1 and 2 December a secret Congress of People's Representatives met in Vientiane, accepted the abdication of the king, and proclaimed the Lao People's Democratic Republic (PDR), completing the transfer of power to the Pathet Lao. In contrast to Vietnam and Kampuchea, the final change of power in Laos was accomplished without military action.

**CONSOLIDATING THE NEW GOVERNMENT**

The new Lao PDR was faced with extreme difficulties and needed five years to begin to cope adequately with them. Western aid, which had funded over 90 percent of the RLG budget and the import of food for the cities, was immediately withdrawn, and a large number of government officials and commercial leaders fled to Thailand, creating an acute shortage of trained administrators. The value of the kip plummeted, adding to the government's difficulties in buying food from Thailand, or even rice from Lao farmers. Most rightist Hmong and Mien guerrilla forces also fled, but kept up a resistance struggle in the north, which took the new government over two years to quell. Laos was still not really a nation, but divided by regional and ethnic differences reflecting the ancient petty kingdoms as well as the previous thirty years' struggle.

In its initial policies, the government gave priority to agricultural production, national security, and the consolidation of political control. The eighteen-point program of the NPCC was abandoned, higher ranking civil service and military personnel from the RLG were sent to reeducation camps, a series of controls was placed on private commerce and travel, and taxes were instituted on rice production and other activities. Cadres in the villages began mandatory political education sessions, where the evils of bourgeois capitalism and the virtues of socialism were discussed, and people were exhorted to follow the "three cleans"—clean living, clean dress, and clean eating—interpreted to mean live in simple houses, wear simple clothes and no jewelry, and eat simple food with little meat or fish.

The collectivization of agriculture was encouraged, but with little success. In 1978, the Politburo declared a policy of accelerated organization of village-based cooperatives, but farmers did not understand the program; principles for compensating the use of land, draft animals, and farm tools were not made clear; and some cadres were overzealous in their actions. Resistance to the program was widespread. Coming after a drought in 1977 and floods in 1978, the harvest for 1979 would have been disastrous, and the collectivization program was abruptly suspended in mid-1979.[25]

For the many Lao who had become used to the free-wheeling economy of the U.S.-RLG period, the hardships during the first years, combined with the strict political control by the new government, provided sufficient motivation to leave the country. By the end of 1978, about 80,000 Lao had left the country, a number that would climb to 350,000, or 10 percent of the population, by the mid-1980s.[26] Aside from the large numbers involved, the refugee population included the vast majority of educated Lao, thus leaving the country with a critical shortage of able administrators and technical cadres. Martin Stuart-Fox estimates that this drain has retarded Lao development by at least a generation.[27]

At the same time, hundreds of thousands of internal refugees began to make their way back to their homes and reestablish their livelihoods. In some cases, the new government was able to provide truck or air transportation and some assistance in rebuilding destroyed villages. Considerable aid was also granted by the UN High Commission for Refugees. Particularly in the old liberated areas, rebuilt villages were laid out in an orderly pattern, and operational village agricultural cooperatives established.

In 1976, an adult literacy campaign was instituted, with literate people in villages mobilized to teach classes to all adults who could not read. Using simple teaching materials, these teachers were effective in reaching large numbers of previously uneducated adults throughout the country.[28] Although present governmental literacy statistics are undoubtedly inflated, at the very least a tripling from the pre-1975 rate of about 20 percent has occurred. The Lao language was also modified, with spelling rendered completely phonetic, thus making reading and writing much easier to learn.

Administrative integration of the country has also been an important goal. Communication and travel between provinces and to remote districts has been difficult and problematic, but recent improvements in radio-telegraph links and in some roads have helped bind the country together. Communications move through a five-tiered administrative structure (national, province, district, subdistrict, village), with major policy decisions made at the national level but implementation decisions delegated successively lower in the system.[29] Particularly since 1987, provinces have been given autonomy to develop their own programs and to become responsible for their own financial affairs in response to a policy of devolution and increased emphasis on individual accountability articulated at the Fourth Party Congress in 1986. National and provincial officials frequently travel to district centers and to Vientiane to consult on policy matters and to report or consult on individual programs.

During the first several years after 1975, senior government officials were almost all long-time PL cadres selected for their political orthodoxy rather than their technical or administrative competence. The poor performance of the Lao economy, combined with a number of failures in development efforts, led to a modification of this policy, and after about 1979, former RLG officials began to be reincorporated into the bureaucracy, though not at the top levels. Frequent political seminars, arranged at all levels from national ministries down to the villages, provide a means of communicating national policy decisions, and more importantly, some understanding of the implications of those decisions to officials and villagers. Given the lack of effective media penetration to rural areas, the rudimentary educational system, and the low literacy level of most Lao, these seminars are the functional equivalent of elementary-school civics classes and the nightly TV news in the United States and offer an important measure of identification with the new Laos that did not exist before.

The celebration in 1985 of the tenth anniversary of the founding of the Lao PDR also provided an occasion for self-congratulation and government efforts to stimulate national pride. Preparations began over a year in advance, and statistics (of doubtful accuracy) supporting achievements in every sector from agricultural production to provision of basic health services were published daily in the newspaper and read over the radio. On 2 December celebrations took place in virtually every district center around the country.

## CONTINUING PROBLEMS AND ISSUES

Compared to conditions in early 1976, those under the aegis of the Lao PDR are substantially improved in terms of national consolidation, agricultural production and food self-sufficiency, national fiscal accountability, and provision of basic education and health services. Much remains to be done, however. National development is also affected by a number of continuing issues that are not entirely under Lao control. Some of these issues are the result of the war, some are related to political relations between neighboring or allied countries, and some to continuing relations with the United States.

### WAR-RELATED ISSUES

Antipersonnel bomblets dropped by the thousands during the conflict are an immediate threat to many Lao. Broadcast by the United States in an effort to deny wide areas to the enemy, the bomblets, about the size of a baseball, do not necessarily explode on impact, but remain in the ground until they are disturbed. When moved or struck, they explode, spreading shrapnel over about a 10-meter radius. Hidden by fallen leaves or covered by eroding earth, these bomblets are still live, and Lao who are clearing fields with hoe, machete, or by fire may cause one to explode, with often fatal consequences. Precise statistics are not available, but fifteen years after the last bomb was dropped, several hundred people are yearly blinded, burned, or lose limbs, and several score are killed. The most seriously affected areas are Xieng Khouang Province and the eastern districts of Khammouane, Savannakhet, and Sekhong provinces.

"Yellow rain" was, for several years, also thought to be a threat to some Lao. Beginning in 1979, rumors began to appear about the use of chemical warfare agents on Hmong villages and guerrillas in Laos and against Khmer resistance fighters in Kampuchea. Evidence was difficult to acquire, but after obtaining analyses of several minuscule samples, the U.S. State Department accused the Lao, with Vietnamese and Soviet assistance, of using mycotoxins in some kind of aerial delivery system. The chemical was termed "yellow rain" because some Hmong reported a yellow substance falling from the sky prior to the sudden deaths of villagers by internal hemorrhaging. An acrimonious controversy followed in the scientific and diplomatic communities over the accuracy of these allegations. By 1984, the bulk of the evidence seemed to indicate that yellow rain was bee feces dropped during massive cleansing flights.[30]

## RELATIONS WITH NEIGHBORING COUNTRIES

Laos maintains very cordial relations with Vietnam and Kampuchea and has received considerable economic and military aid from Vietnam. The role of Vietnamese advisers in the Lao government has been the object of some concern in Western quarters, with the fear expressed that Laos may become a Vietnamese colony. This concern seems quite unfounded. Vietnamese advisers are present at high levels in most if not all Lao ministries, but policymaking and implementation are always subject to Lao perceptions of reality and limitations in capability. Overall Lao policies are undoubtedly influenced by the Vietnamese but have been generally more liberal than those implemented east of the Annamite cordillera. Vietnamese technical-assistance personnel work in the field in the same way as aid workers do anywhere and are subject to the same frustrations.

Lao-Thai relations have been much less constant. Tensions were high in the first years after 1975, with numerous shooting incidents across the Mekong. A period of improvement followed, with increased trade and diplomatic expressions of the desire for friendly relations. In 1984, however, the Lao protested incursions by Thai military in the border area between Sayabouli and Loei provinces. Several months of military skirmishing followed, but a cease-fire was eventually arranged, even though the demarcation of the border remains in dispute. Relations again improved, but in November 1987 another war broke out further to the southeast along the border between Sayabouli and Phitsanuloke. The fighting in this case was intense. Losses were high on both sides, though the Thai seemed to get the worst of it. The conflict died down in February 1988, but tensions remain.

Small numbers of Lao resistance elements operating from Thailand have also had a deleterious effect on Thai-Lao relations. Since 1978, they have not posed a significant threat, but through harassment provoke a continuing drain on the resources of Laos. These guerrillas seem to be recruited from Hmong and lowland Lao refugees who were associated with the royalist forces, and they undoubtedly have bases in the border regions with northeast Thailand.

With the relaxation of many trade restrictions in 1988, cross-border trade with Thailand has increased markedly, and growing numbers of Thai tourists are also visiting Laos. Some Thai businesspeople and entrepreneurs are investing in Lao ventures; construction, imports of consumer goods, garment production, and particularly log and lumber export are the initial areas of interest.

Relations with China have until recently been strained, particularly after the Vietnamese invasion of Kampuchea in 1979 and Chinese attacks on Vietnam and support for the Khmer Rouge. A Chinese embassy staffed at the chargé level was maintained in Vientiane, but in early 1988 relations were normalized and ambassadors exchanged. During the war, the Chinese provided significant military aid to the Pathet Lao and maintained a consulate at Phong Saly for a time. From the late 1960s to 1973, they constructed a 600-kilometer network of asphalted roads linking the northern provincial capitals, which includes today some of the best roads in the country. Informal cross-border trade also continued, despite diplomatic tensions, and now with improved formal ties and a Lao economic policy that encourages foreign trade, volume is increasing. Much trade is conducted by barter: Chinese consumer goods and construction materials for Lao forest products, specialty crops, and rice.

## LAO/U.S. RELATIONS AND CONTINUING ISSUES

In contrast to its policy toward Vietnam and Kampuchea, the United States did not sever diplomatic relations with Laos after 1975, but both embassies in Vientiane and Washington were downgraded to representation by a chargé d'affaires. U.S. contacts with Laos have in large degree focused on the issue of Americans missing in action from the war. In Laos, as in Vietnam, "MIAs" are primarily fliers who were shot down with no positive confirmation of death or who were at one time reported to be in captivity. Families of MIAs and politicians in the United States have directed considerable pressure at the government to obtain a "full accounting" from the Indochinese governments of the fate of the over 2,000 men classified in this category. The United States has in turn pressured the Vietnamese and Lao governments for cooperation on what the State Department terms a "humanitarian issue." Accusations that Americans are still held in Lao POW camps have been repeatedly met with forceful denials. Excavations of several crash sites in Laos by joint U.S.-Lao teams have produced some identifiable remains. The United States has successfully encouraged a private U.S. organization to construct a clinic in a village near the site of the second joint excavation.

The United States is attempting to encourage other U.S. private voluntary organizations to initiate assistance to Laos. Working either through a United Nations agency or private organizations, the Americans have also given emergency rice and medicines in recent years. Official Lao tolerance of the U.S. government MIA focus, the success of the excavations, and the willingness of the U.S. embassy to give limited emergency assistance have enabled relations between governments to slowly warm. Lao officials are cautiously optimistic that this trend will continue.

The continued existence of reeducation camps and the drug trade from Laos have been obstacles to improved U.S.-Lao relations. After 1975, over 10,000 people, mostly with military or police positions in the former RLG, but also including civil officials and villagers who had worked closely with the United States, were rounded up and sent to prison camps in eastern districts from Phong Saly to Attopeu. There they were required to perform hard and menial labor and to attend political seminars to learn the "error" of their ways. Because of limited food rations and lack of medicines, an unknown number died, though now all but perhaps a hundred have been released. Many former prisoners fled to Thailand as refugees after their release, but some have again taken up positions in the government or pursued a private life in Laos. The Lao government claims that all the camps have been closed, but it appears that in reality there may be one or two prison camps remaining for a small number of former high officials.[31] In addition, a larger number of former detainees are still under a loose house arrest and constrained to live within a particular district remote from their homes, but otherwise may farm for a livelihood, have their family come live with them, and write and receive letters and packages from their families in Vientiane.

During the war, Laos was an important producer of drugs, particularly marijuana and opium. RLG military and civilian officials as well as the CIA were involved in opium smuggling for both private gain and to augment budgets for clandestine operations.[32] For the first several years after 1975, the new government discouraged opium production and arrested drug addicts, though it recognized that hill tribes continued to grow and sell the crop through private channels. Some opium was also legally purchased by state stores for trade to Eastern Europe for pharmaceutical use. As narcotics control in Thailand and Burma has gained effectiveness in recent years, more production has moved to Laos. Since 1986, the Lao PDR government has responded positively, but insubstantially, to increased international pressure for suppression of narcotics production. In August 1988, participants in a heroin refinery operation in Oudomsay Province were convicted in a Vientiane show trial. The defendants included the provincial party secretary and several other officials. It is not clear whether the convictions represented a genuine effort to restrict trafficking or if they were merely a public relations ploy. Shortly afterward, however, the United States accused Laos of official collusion in drug trafficking. A year later, the United States agreed to fund a six-year $8.7

million project in Houa Phan province with the ostensible goal of replacing opium with other crops. A significant component of the project will be funding for construction of roads, schools, and clinics. These grants are undoubtedly related to continued Lao cooperation on the MIA/POW issue as well as narcotics control.

## CONTEMPORARY LAOS: THE OVERALL VIEW

The Lao People's Democratic Republic is one of the least developed nations of Asia by all measures. Economic activity is limited, health conditions are harsh, and the educational system is poor. But economic liberalization coupled with a mostly literate population indicate future developmental possibilities.[33] We will consider the current economic, political, health, and educational situation in Laos, both on a national level and as it is experienced by the majority of people living in rural villages.

### ECONOMY AND POLITY

With an estimated GDP per capita of less than $200, Laos remains one of the poorest Asian nations. The economy is based on subsistence rice production, ill connected to a monetized market network with a few industrial, extractive, and trading enterprises. The agricultural base is at present adequate for the population, however, and provides a vitally important foundation to the economy that enables people to live at a very basic level regardless of other events. Over 85 percent of the labor force works in agriculture. In 1985 eighteen small factories run by the Ministry of Industry, all located near Vientiane, accounted for about three-quarters of industrial production.[34]

With the exception of electricity from a single hydroelectric dam, the Laotian export profile indicates its mainly agricultural and extractive economy. The other main exports are timber, forest products, tin, gypsum, and coffee.[35] The meager exports of agricultural products reflect not only the mainly subsistence orientation of most farmers but also the trade obstacles affecting landlocked nations.

As in all Marxist nations, politics and economics are inextricably related. The Lao People's Revolutionary Party is central to present and future developments in Laos.[36] Political leaders and civil servants situated in two parallel structures govern Laos: the Party hierarchy and the administrative hierarchy. Overlapping memberships and the overall policy authority of the Party facilitate coordination. The LPRP is organized like most Communist parties, with a secretary general presiding over a Politburo guiding a Central Committee to which Party committees and provincial and lower-level Party organizations report. Governmental administration is accomplished by a Council of Ministers, which is responsible for the overall operation of the various ministries and state committees and which oversees, at some distance, the operation of provincial governments. With the election of district assemblies in mid-1988 and the election of provincial assemblies and an expanded national Supreme People's Assembly in early 1989, a quasilegislative branch of the government may form. A draft constitution, the first since 1975, was released for discussion and comment in 1990 and is expected to be adopted by 1991. The judiciary is inadequately developed, because of the lack of both a constitution and a code of socialist law. A Supreme People's Court was established in 1983.[37]

Party economic theoreticians aim to bypass the capitalist stage of production, advancing directly from small-scale subsistence farm production to technologically advanced socialist production. During the transition phase, five forms of economic organization are allowed to coexist, ranging from state-owned enterprises to private companies.[38] Nevertheless, the Third Party Congress in April 1982 promulgated several resolutions to liberalize economic activity, though increased taxation and regulation of private traders limited their impact. The Fourth Party Congress in November 1986 elaborated these resolutions in more detail and called for a "new perspective" for "opening the door" to economic development. The Investment Code of 1988 allows for the continued existence of all five forms of economic activity and particularly encourages the development of joint enterprises and capitalist organizations. A recent sharp upsurge in trade, availability of consumer goods, and home construction as well as the beginnings of foreign investment are visible results of the changes reinforced by the Fourth Congress.

Although 15 percent of the population is considered urban, many city dwellers are really peasants who happen to live within town boundaries. These urban farmers grow much of their own food, though one or two family members may earn a small salary as a civil servant or worker. In rural areas, most Lao are subsistence agriculturalists who provide most of their own needs through farming. There is little occupational specialization in the villages. Traditionally, a headman was responsible for organizing community projects and mediating disputes and a few villagers may have had special ritual or healing skills, but even those part-time specialists had to meet their own subsistence needs. Today most villages are governed by a village committee. In more accessible villages, one or more of the mass organizations—the Women's Union, the Youth Organization, the Front for National Construction—may have village-level branches responsible for some village activities. The local Women's Union, for example, may organize a women's "seminar" to discuss what it means to be a proper socialist woman or it may organize a money-raising project to support its activities. Party membership often reaches to the village level, though the one or two Party members in a village may be insufficient to constitute a branch of the Party.[39]

Rice remains the staple crop. Overall national self-sufficiency masks local shortages that are not filled because of limited transport infrastructure. The forest remains an important and reliable food reserve for rural dwellers in difficult years. Near towns, some farmers use tractors and mechanized threshers. Traditional farming practices provide little control over pests and weather. Government emphasis on food self-sufficiency has led to substantial aid and budget expenditures for agriculture; some projects are successful, but farmer adoption of improved practices remains low.

## HEALTH

A Lao baby born today can expect to live for only about fifty years,[40] indicating that the health situation for most Lao people is poorer than for most other Asians. High infant mortality accounts for most of this difference; nearly 12 of 100 babies born do not survive their first year (a higher figure than in neighboring and poorer Vietnam) and 30 to 50 percent of children experience moderate malnutrition.[41] Children are "exposed to endemic, transmissible, respiratory and gastrointestinal diseases from birth."[42] Malaria is the premier child killer, with one study of twenty villages indicating that nearly 4 of every 10 children had at some time contracted this mosquito-borne disease. Diarrhea is common; one UNICEF study indicates the incidence to be more than three attacks per year for children under five years of age.[43]

Although the Laotian population is small (3.9 million) for its land area, the crude birth rate of 47 per 1,000 ensures growth of 2.9 percent per year and a population doubling time of twenty-four years.[44] Contraception was outlawed for the first twelve years of the new regime. Frequent births, poor medical care and nutrition, and a heavy workload ensure women's poor health and a high proportion of low birth-weight babies.[45]

Illness and lack of energy are everyday facts of life for most villagers. During one day in a northern Lao Theung village three of eight women interviewed were sick or had been sick the previous day. In another nearby village, nearly all of the children had runny noses, coughs, and conjunctivitis on the day that aid personnel visited. Most village women and children draw their families' water from muddy streams or unlined wells. Most villagers boil drinking water, but also drink unboiled water. Food markets, even in provincial capitals, are often makeshift arrangements of low tables placed in a muddy field. Latrines are used in towns, but are rarely found in rural areas. The brushy area around a village is the common latrine for villagers, with excreta disposed of by the free-ranging pigs or the monsoon rains.

Few villages have medical services, though many have traditional health practitioners who employ herbal remedies. Even if a village has a regularly staffed health post, the health worker usually has received only three months of training and few medicines. Villagers with no health post or with medical needs requiring more than simple first aid remain untreated or must travel to district or provincial hospitals. Only some provincial hospitals have the doctors, equipment, and medicines to deal with injuries and the most common diseases. Facilities are commonly not sanitary and a family member must stay at the hospital to care for a patient's nonmedical needs.

## EDUCATION

Most adult Lao are literate, a surprising finding considering the country's poverty. Schools were conducted "in thick forests or caverns" during the war years, while adults were "eliminated from illiteracy" village by village in the old liberated zones before 1975.[46] The Buddhist temple's traditional role as an educational center for boys has also contributed to higher male literacy.

The postwar adult literacy campaign was successful in educating most adults in basic number and letter skills. Schools of one or two grades have been built in most villages and are attended by nearly all of the villages' children. These educational developments account for the high literacy and school attendance statistics of the LPDR. According to government statistics, most men (92 percent) and three-fourths of women (76 percent) are literate, and six of ten people age ten and over have attended school at some time.[47] Although literacy is much higher than during the "preliberation" era, the reality is short of these figures. Extrapolated from several studies in and near urban areas, a national average of about 60 percent seems more reasonable.[48]

All too frequently, a village school is a two-room shelter made of bamboo. It leans to one side, and the thatched roof has visible holes. A teacher cradles her baby in a sling on her back while she stands before a piece of plywood painted black, writing a lesson for her textbook-sharing pupils. Most village children who have not yet completed the two grades attend the school whenever the teachers teach. The teachers, though, are paid little and must attend to their own subsistence needs. They have received a five-year elementary education and a three-year teacher-training course before being assigned to this school.

Lao Theung and Lao Sung children from isolated villages may attend boarding schools built for non-Lao speakers. Their schools are especially ramshackle, since little of the small national or provincial education budget is allocated to these "minority" schools. School buildings and boarding facilities may consist only of temporary thatch and bamboo shelters. Such schools, though, offer these children their best opportunity to study and to be integrated into the national life of Laos.[49]

Some successful students continue their schooling beyond primary school; they may attend three years of "middle" school in the district center and two or three years of high school or technical training in the provincial capital, with a progressively smaller proportion of girls attending at each higher level. Most students return home or are assigned to nearby districts as teachers or technicians where they bring some more experience of the "outside world" to the villagers. A very few are selected to attend technical or teacher-training "universities" in Vientiane and fewer still for technical study in Eastern Europe or the Soviet Union. These highly trained youth are assigned government jobs on their return to Laos but do not return to their villages.

**CONTEMPORARY LAOS:
BEYOND THE VILLAGE**

In general, the structure of Lao village life still revolves around meeting basic needs, as it has for centuries. However, there have been important changes in the last fifteen years. More adults have rudimentary literacy skills, more children attend a few grades of school, and some villages have health posts. Some villagers work together not only in traditional labor-exchange networks, but in formalized cooperative work groups. National and provincial government is more visible to villagers as they pay taxes, receive occasional government services, organize village governing committees or cooperatives, and attempt to respond to other government directives.

Villages today are more connected, both economically and politically, to other villages and to an idea of Laos as a nation. Neighboring villages are linked by regular exchanges of products or services or by the need to coordinate construction or ritual activities. The women of one northern Lao Lue village specialize in making indigo-dyed cotton cloth for work clothing. Some of the cloth is used in their own families and the surplus exchanged for rice, animals, baskets, and other products from neighboring villages.

Two other examples of village cooperation are as follows. In a forest in south central Laos, hundreds of people from several neighboring villages felled trees and cleared brush for a track into a new village. This form of intervillage cooperation is an innovation of the current government. Next year the collective work party will benefit a different village in the area.

In southern Laos, a district center made up of seven villagelike sections celebrated Boun Kathin, an annual Buddhist festival. The inhabitants of neighboring villages were invited to attend. In the district center each group of eight to ten houses was assigned hosting responsibilities for one of the invited villages. The men built temporary shelters to house the visitors, while the women prepare food for them. Both the hosts and the guests augmented their store of spiritual merit during this activity and also solidified social and economic ties.

Most villages are connected to markets, either through private traders or the state store. Province governments now have authority to make direct trade agreements across the border with China, Thailand, Burma, Vietnam, or Kampuchea. The agriculture department of one northern province, for example, can purchase Chinese veterinary supplies in exchange for rice and forest products such as sticlac (a resin collected from certain trees and used in manufacturing lacquerware). Vientiane and other towns are dependent upon surrounding villages for rice and other food, so these villages have some incentive to produce an agricultural surplus for the nearby market. With recent economic liberalization, food imports from Thailand have also increased, often competing with locally produced goods.

**ECONOMIC AND POLITICAL LIBERALIZATION**

National and provincial policies can have a strong effect on village life. Policies regarding taxes, private trade, agricultural cooperativization, and religion have all had an impact on villages. Even village self-sufficiency, seemingly a consequence of isolation and poverty, has been influenced by government controls on private trade following the wartime disruption of the production base and the market network. Primary education and village political seminars foster a sense of national identity and pride.

Beginning with the Third Party Congress and continuing with the Fourth, the Party has resolved to open some economic opportunities to foreign capitalist investors, to encourage private Lao investment, and to carefully expand the political process in a limited way. Results of these resolutions are only recently visible. With the relaxing of restrictions on border trade in 1988, Thai and Chinese goods have become much more available. Formerly meager shops are now filled with toys, hardware, clothing, and household goods. Numerous small shops, restaurants, and even discos have opened. Some "tuk-tuks," small three-wheeled Thai taxis, cruise the streets. Vientiane teenagers frequent the new video arcade, and some young women wear jeans. District centers in more isolated northern provinces may now boast a soup shop and a store stocked with imported beer. New houses are under construction and the number of family shops for petty trade has increased.

In the countryside, travel restrictions eased for a while, with Lao citizens now free to visit between provinces without requesting approval, and even to cross the Mekong to neighboring villages in Thailand. Some restrictions were reimposed in 1990, however.

The elections for peoples' assemblies held in 1988–1989 heralded a tentative opening of the political process. Nearly all candidates were Party members, but still local people. The number of government personnel is being reduced, and some officials are moving to jobs with private or state-private companies. This exodus reduces the government payroll, but continued insistence on centralized decisionmaking in many sectors has led to delays and bottlenecks in the administrative process. Corruption is also increasing and cynicism regarding the government's role is now verbalized by both officials and ordinary citizens. The government has allowed more open criticism of its performance, including publishing critiques in the party daily, *Siang Pasason*, but there remains a significant tension between the roles of the Party and the technocrats in planning and executing programs.

With the decision to implement a "new economic mechanism" domestically, the government is also seeking external investment and increased foreign aid, though perhaps with an incomplete understanding of the effect this will have on Lao economic and social life. So far, the new policies have yielded little new industry or increased production, though negotiations are underway with several potential investors. With advice from the United Nations and Asian Development Bank, the government is attempting to change from command planning to an indicative planning model in preparing the Third Five-Year Plan (1991–1995). If implemented effectively, this reorientation could have a significant impact on the Lao economy. The present "boomlet" one sees in market activity is one-sided: the Lao are buying more imported consumer goods but have not increased either the number or the variety of their exports. Purchases seem to be financed mainly by hoarded savings or remittances from relatives abroad.

With all these changes, the potential for an improvement in living standards and national development is quite real. Some Lao say that now "things are different" and "the refugees should come back." Others complain that the country is returning to the cronyism and inequalities of the prerevolutionary years. Many uncertainties and obstacles remain, which will challenge the political vision and management ability of the Lao leadership in the years ahead. Economic development will undoubtedly continue at an uneven pace, but the subsistence economic base has helped smooth past ups and downs and may continue to provide a stabilizing force for the overall quality of life of the average Lao. Political liberalization is likely to be slower as the party attempts to maintain control over the direction of development. As with glasnost and perestroika in the Soviet Union, the process of opening the Lao PDR and restructuring some of its institutions is challenging and difficult, and the outcome is not predictable. At present, many Lao are appreciative of the changes that have taken place, but cautious about the ultimate outcome.

## NOTES

1. "Tai" refers to the group of cultures encompassing both Thai and Lao culture.

2. Joseph Zasloff, *The Pathet Lao: Leadership and Organization* (Lexington, MA: Lexington Books, 1973), p. 81.

3. National Committee of Plan, *Lao Census of 1985* (mimeo), (n.p.: National Committee of Plan, 1986).

4. See Frank M. Lebar, Gerald C. Hickey, and John K. Musgrave, *Ethnic Groups of Mainland Southeast Asia* (New Haven: Yale University Human Relations Area Files, 1964).

5. Jacques Lemoine, *Un Village Hmong Vert du Haut Laos* (Paris: Centre National de la Recherche Scientifique, 1972); G. Linwood Barney, "The Meo of Xieng Khouang Province, Laos," in Peter Kunstadter, ed., *South East Asian Tribes, Minorities, and Nations* (Princeton: Princeton Univ. Press, 1967), p. 285.

6. D.G.E. Hall, *A History of South-East Asia* (New York: St. Martin's Press, 1964), p. 238.

7. David K. Wyatt, *Thailand: A Short History* (New Haven: Yale University Press, 1982), chaps. 3, 4.

8. Hall, *A History*, ch. 37.

9. See Michel Caply, *Guérilla au Laos* (Paris: Presses de la Cité, 1966).

10. Macalister Brown and Joseph J. Zasloff, *Apprentice Revolutionaries: The Communist Movement in Laos, 1930–1985* (Stanford, CA: Hoover Institution Press, 1986), p. 30.

11. Souphanouvong, a half-brother to Prince Phetsarath and Prince Souvanna Phouma (the latter was to play an important role as prime minister of several coalition governments), was educated in Vietnam and had early chosen to work for independence through the Indochinese Communist Party and in close cooperation with Ho Chi Minh. His arrival in Laos was part of an overall ICP strategy aimed at preventing the reintroduction of colonial powers to Indochina. See Brown and Zasloff, *Apprentice Revolutionaries*, p. 31.

12. Brown and Zasloff, *Apprentice Revolutionaries*, p. 38.

13. Ibid., p. 56.

14. Hugh Toye, *Laos: Buffer State or Battleground* (New York: Oxford University Press, 1968), p. 129; Brown and Zasloff, *Apprentice Revolutionaries*, p. 68.

15. Brown and Zasloff, *Apprentice Revolutionaries*, p. 100.

16. Ibid., pp. 95ff.

17. Arnold R. Issacs, *Without Honor: Defeat in Vietnam and Cambodia* (Baltimore: Johns Hopkins Press, 1983), p. 161.

18. Arthur J. Dommen, *Conflict in Laos: The Politics of Neutralization* (New York: Fredrick Praeger, 1964), chap. 12.

19. Brown and Zasloff, *Apprentice Revolutionaries*, ch. 9.

20. Issacs, *Without Honor*, p. 161.

21. Zasloff, *The Pathet Lao*, p. 81.

22. Martin Stuart-Fox and Rod Bucknell, "The Politicization of the Sangha in Laos," *Journal of Southeast Asian Studies*, 13 (1982), pp. 60–80.

23. Brown and Zasloff, *Apprentice Revolutionaries*, p. 104.

24. Ibid., pp. 111ff.

25. Martin Stuart-Fox, "The Initial Failure of Agricultural Cooperativization in Laos," *Asia Quarterly* 4 (1980), pp. 273–299.

26. UN High Commission for Refugees, "Refugees and Displaced Persons from Indochina as of 30 April, 1984" (n.p.: UN High Commission for Refugees, 1984).

27. Martin Stuart-Fox, "The First Ten Years of Communist Rule in Laos," *Asia Pacific Community*, (Winter 1986), pp. 55–81.

28. Ministry of Education, *Adult/Education Training Situations in Laos Before/After the Liberation* (mimeo), (Vientiane: Ministry of Education, 1985); Jacqui Chagnon and Roger Rumpf, "Education: The Prerequisite to Change in Laos," in Martin Stuart-Fox, ed., *Contemporary Laos* (St. Lucia, QLD: University of Queensland Press, 1982).

29. Randall Ireson, "Laos: Building a Nation Under Socialism," *Indochina Issues*, no. 79 (1988), pp. 1–7.

30. See Lois R. Embree, "Yellow Rain," *Chemical and Engineering News* (9 Jan. 1984), pp. 8–34; Grant Evans, *The Yellow Rainmakers* (London: Verso, 1983); Julien Robinson, Jeanne Gueillemin, and Matthew Meselson, "Yellow Rain: The Story Collapses," *Foreign Affairs* 68 (Fall 1987), pp. 100–117; Sterling Seagrave, *Yellow Rain: A Journey Through the Terror of Chemical Warfare* (New York: M. Evans, 1981).

31. Amnesty International, *Amnesty International Report 1990* (London: Amnesty International, 1990); Amnesty International, *Amnesty International Report 1988* (London: Amnesty International, 1988); Amnesty International, *Amnesty International Report 1986* (London: Amnesty International, 1986); Amnesty International, "'Re-Education' in Attapeu Province: The Democratic People's Republic of Laos" (mimeo) (London: Amnesty International, 1986).

32. Alfred W. McCoy, *The Politics of Heroin in Southeast Asia* (New York: Harper and Row, 1972).

33. Statistics on most aspects of the Lao PDR are scanty or unreliable, so many of the presented statistics are based on micro or regional studies or are estimates. The first population census of Laos conducted in 1985 is a notable exception.

34. Asian Development Bank, *Economic Survey of the Lao People's Democratic Republic* (n.p.: Asian Development Bank, 1986), p. 6; Martin Stuart-Fox, *Laos: Politics, Economics and Society* (London: Frances Pinter, 1986), p. 120.

35. Asia Yearbook, *Asia 1989 Yearbook* (Hong Kong: Far Eastern Economic Review, 1989), p. 172; Asian Development Bank, *Economic Survey*, p. iv.

36. Y. Mikhayev, "Laos: Towards the Building of Socialism," *International Affairs* (Moscow) (April 1982), pp. 13–18; Macalister Brown and Joseph J. Zasloff, "Laos: Gearing up for National Development," *Southeast Asian Affairs* (1985), pp. 189–208.

37. Stuart-Fox, *Laos: Politics, Economics and Society*.

38. Hans U. Luther, *Socialism in a Subsistence Economy: The Laotian Way* (Bangkok: Chulalongkorn University Social Research Institute, 1983).

39. Stuart-Fox, *Laos: Politics, Economics and Society*, p. 64.

40. Ibid., p. 149; UNICEF, *An Analysis of the Situation of Children and Women in the Lao People's Democratic Republic* (Vientiane: UNICEF, 1987), p. 17.

41. Robert Kripps, "1984 Nutrition Survey: Phase 1," WHO Assignment Report (Vientiane: World Health Organization, 1984), p. 18, cited in UNICEF, *An Analysis;* Elizabeth Kennard, personal communication, 1988.

42. UNICEF, *An Analysis,* p. 19.

43. Ibid., pp. 19–20.

44. National Committee of Plan, *Lao Census.*

45. UNICEF, *An Analysis,* p. 68.

46. Ministry of Education, *Adult/Education Training Situations,* pp. 19, 26.

47. UNICEF, *State of the World's Children 1988* (New York: Oxford Univ. Press, 1988).

48. Chandan Mukherjee and A.V. Jose, *Report of a Survey of Rural Households in the Hat Xai Fong District in Vientiane Province of the Lao People's Democratic Republic* (Bangkok: Asian Employment Programme, International Labor Organisation, 1982), p. 12; ARTEP, *Rural Development in Vientiane Province, 1986* (Vientiane: ILO, 1986).

49. Chagnon and Rumpf, "Education: the Prerequisite to Change."

# PART TWO

## The United States and the War

# 5

# The United States and Indochina: Far from an Aberration

## Noam Chomsky

In one of his sermons on human rights, President Carter explained that we owe Vietnam no debt and have no responsibility to render it any assistance because "the destruction was mutual."[1] If words have meaning, this must stand among the most astonishing statements in diplomatic history. What is most interesting about this statement is the reaction to it among educated Americans: null. Furthermore, the occasional reference to it, and what it means, evokes no comment and no interest. It is considered neither appalling, nor even noteworthy, and is felt to have no bearing on Carter's standing as patron saint of human rights, any more than do his actions: dedicated support for Indonesian atrocities in Timor and the successful terrorist campaign undertaken in El Salvador to destroy the popular organizations that were defended by the assassinated archbishop; a huge increase in arms flow to Israel in parallel with its 1978 invasion of Lebanon, its subsequent large-scale bombing of civilians, and its rapid expansion into the occupied territories; etc. All of this is a tribute to the successes of a system of indoctrination that has few if any peers.

Some of the remarks in this article are adapted from Noam Chomsky's articles "Dominoes," *Granta* 15 (1985), pp. 129–133; and "Forgotten History of the War in Vietnam," *In These Times*, vol. 9, no. 24 (15–21 May 1985), p. 11. This article appeared with the title "Visions of Righteousness" in *Cultural Critique*, no. 3 (Spring 1986). It is reprinted here with some minor modifications by permission of Noam Chomsky and *Cultural Critique*, which holds the copyright.

These successes permit the commissars to issue pronouncements of quite impressive audacity. Thus, Zbigniew Brzezinski thunders that the Soviet invasion of Afghanistan is

> a classical foreign invasion, waged with Nazi-like brutality. Scorched villages, executed hostages, massive bombings, even chemical warfare . . . [with] several hundred thousand killed and maimed by Soviet military operations that qualify as genocidal in their intent and effect. . . . It needs to be said directly, and over and over again, that Soviet policy in Afghanistan is the fourth greatest exercise in social holocaust of our contemporary age: it ranks only after Stalin's multimillion massacres; after Hitler's genocide of the European Jews and partially of the Slavs; and after Pol Pot's decimation of his own people; it is, moreover, happening right now.[2]

While the descriptive words are fair enough, when issuing from this source they merit all the admiration accorded similar pronouncements by Brzezinski's Soviet models with regard to American crimes, which he somehow seems to have overlooked in his ranking of atrocities of the modern age. To mention a few: the U.S. wars in Indochina, to which his condemnation applies in full except that there were *many millions* "killed and maimed" and the level of destruction was far greater; the Indonesian massacres of 1965 backed enthusiastically by the United States with half a million murdered; the Timor massacres conducted under Brzezinski's aegis with hundreds of thousands "killed and maimed" and the remnants left in the state of Biafra and the Thai-Cambodian border, an operation that is "happening right now" thanks to U.S. silence and support; the murder, often with hideous torture and mutilation, of over 100,000 people in El Salvador and Guatemala since 1978, operations carried out thanks to the support of the United States and its proxies, and most definitely "happening right now." But the readers of the *National Interest* will find nothing amiss in Brzezinski's presentation, since in Vietnam "the destruction was mutual" and the other cases, if known at all, have been easily assimilated into the preferred model of American benevolence. An auspicious opening for a new "conservative" journal of international affairs.

"It is scandalous," Brzezinski writes, "that so much of the conventionally liberal community, always so ready to embrace victims of American or Israeli or any other unfashionable 'imperialism', is so reticent on the subject" of Afghanistan. Surely one might expect liberals in Congress or the press to desist from their ceaseless efforts on behalf of the PLO [Palestine Liberation Organization] and the guerrillas in El Salvador long enough to notice Soviet crimes; perhaps they might even follow Brzezinski to the Khyber Pass so that they can strike heroic poses there before a camera crew. One should not, incidentally, dismiss this characterization of the "liberal community" on the grounds of its transparent absurdity. Rather, it should be understood as a typical example of a campaign carefully designed to eliminate even the limited critique of crimes by the United States and its clients that sometimes is voiced, a campaign that reflects the natural commitments of the totalitarian right, which regards anything less than full subservience as an intolerable deviation from political correctness.

Some feel that there was a debt but that it has been amply repaid. Under the headline "The Debt to the Indochinese Is Becoming a Fiscal Drain," Bernard Gwertzman of the *New York Times* quotes a State Department official who "said he believed the United States has now paid its moral debt for its involvement on the losing side in Indochina." The remark, which passed without comment, is illuminating: we owe no debt for mass slaughter and for leaving three countries in ruins, no debt to the millions of maimed and orphaned, to the peasants who still die today from unexploded ordnance. Rather, our moral debt results only from the fact that we did not win—or as the party line has it, that South Vietnam (namely, the client regime that we established as a cover for our attack against South Vietnam, which had as much legitimacy as the Afghan regime established by the USSR) lost the war to North Vietnam—the official enemy, since the U.S. attack against the south cannot be conceded. By this logic, if the Soviets win in Afghanistan, they will have no moral debt at all. Proceeding further, how have we paid our moral debt for failing to win? By resettling Vietnamese refugees fleeing the lands we ravaged, "one of the largest, most dramatic humanitarian efforts in history" according to Roger Winter, director of the U.S. Committee for Refugees. But "despite the pride," Gwertzman reports, "some voices in the Reagan Administration and in Congress are once again asking whether the war debt has now been paid. . . ."[3]

Invariably, the reader of the press who believes that the lowest depths have already been reached is proven wrong. In March 1968, as U.S. atrocities in South Vietnam were reaching their peak, the *New York Times* ran an item headed "Army Exhibit Bars Simulating Shooting at Vietnamese Hut," reporting an attempt by demonstrators to disrupt an exhibit in the Chicago Museum of Science and Industry: "Beginning today, visitors can no longer enter a helicopter for simulated firing of a machine gun at targets in a diorama of the Vietnam Central Highlands. The targets were a hut, two bridges and an ammunition dump, and a light flashed when a hit was scored." The *Times* is bitterly scornful of the peaceniks who demonstrated in protest at this amusing exhibit, which was such great fun for the kiddies, even objecting "to children being permitted to 'fire' at the hut, even though no people appear. . . ." Citing this item at the time, I asked whether "what is needed in the United States is dissent—or denazification," a question that elicited much outrage; the question stands, however.[4]

To see how the moral level has improved since, we may turn to the *New York Times* sixteen years later, where we find a report on a new board game designed by a Princeton student called "Vietnam: 1965–1975." One player "takes the role of the United States and South Vietnam, and the other represents North Vietnam and the Vietcong." The inventor hopes the game will lead people to "experiment with new ideas, new approaches" to the war. We may ask another question: how would we react to a report in *Pravda* of a board game sold in Moscow, in which one player "takes the role of the USSR and Afghanistan, and the other represents Pakistan, the CIA, China, and the rebels," designed to lead people to "experiment with new ideas, new approaches" to the war—perhaps supplied with some accessory information concerning the "bandits terrorizing Afghanistan," who, according to Western sources, initiated their attacks from Pakistan with support from this U.S.-Chinese ally in 1973, six years before the USSR sent forces to "defend the legitimate government"?[5]

The American system of indoctrination is not satisfied with "mutual destruction" that effaces all responsibility for some of the major war crimes of the modern era. Rather, the perpetrator of the crimes must be seen as the injured party. We find headlines in the nation's press reading: "Vietnam, Trying to Be Nicer, Still Has a Long Way to Go."[6] "It's about time the Vietnamese demonstrated some good will," said Charles Printz of Human Rights Advocates International, referring to negotiations about Amerasian children who constitute a tiny fraction of the victims of the savage U.S. aggression in Indochina. Crossette adds that the Vietnamese have also not been sufficiently forthcoming on the matter of the remains of American soldiers, though their behavior is improving somewhat: "There has been progress, albeit slow, on the missing Americans." The unresolved problem of the war is what they did to us. This point of view may be understood by invoking the terminology contrived by Adlai Stevenson—the hero of Brzezinski's "liberal community"—at the United Nations in May 1964, when he explained that we were in South Vietnam to combat "internal aggression," that is, the aggression of South Vietnamese peasants against U.S. military forces and their clients in South Vietnam. Since we were simply defending ourselves from aggression, it makes sense to consider ourselves the victims of the Vietnamese.[7]

**VISIONS OF RIGHTEOUSNESS**

This picture of aggrieved innocence, carefully crafted by the propaganda system and lovingly nurtured by the educated classes, must surely count as one of the most remarkable phenomena of the modern age. Its roots lie deep in the national culture. "The conquerors of America glorified the devastation they wrought in visions of righteousness," Francis Jennings observes, "and their descendants have been reluctant to peer through the aura."[8] No one who surveys the story of the conquest of the national territory, or the reaction to it over three and a half centuries, can doubt the accuracy of this indictment. In Memphis in 1831, Alexis de Tocqueville watched in "the middle of the winter" when the "cold was unusually severe" as "three or four thousand soldiers drive before them the wandering races of the aborigines," who "brought in their train the wounded and the sick, with children newly born and old men on the verge of death," a "solemn spectacle" that would never fade from his memory: "the triumphal march of civilization across the desert." They were the lucky ones, the ones who had escaped the ravages of Andrew Jackson who, years earlier, had urged his men to exterminate the "blood thirsty barbarians" and "cannibals" and to "distroy [sic] those deluded victims doomed to distruction [sic] by their own restless and savage conduct"—as they did, killing women and children, stripping the skin from the bodies of the dead for bridle reins and cutting the tip of each dead Indian's nose to count the number of "savage dogs" who had been removed from the path of civilization. De Tocqueville was particularly impressed by the way the pioneers could deprive Indians of their rights and exterminate them "with singular felicity, tranquilly, legally, philanthropically, without shedding blood, and without violating a single great principle of morality in the eyes of the world." It was impossible to destroy people with "more respect for the laws of humanity." Still earlier, the Founding Fathers, in their bill of indictment in the Declaration of Independence, had accused the King of England of inciting against the suffering colonies "the merciless Indian Savages, whose known rule of warfare, is an undistinguished destruction of all ages, sexes and conditions"; they were referring to the response of the native population to the genocidal assaults launched against them by the saintly Puritans and other merciless European savages who had taught the Indians that warfare, European-style, is a program of mass extermination of women and children, a lesson that George Washington was soon to teach the Iroquois as he sent his forces to destroy their society and civilization, quite advanced by the standards of the era, in 1779. Rarely have hypocrisy and moral cowardice been so explicit, and admired with such awe for centuries.[9]

The story continues with no essential change in later years. The U.S. conquest of the Philippines, led by men who had learned their craft in the Indian wars, ranks among the most barbaric episodes of modern history. In the island of Luzon alone, some 600,000 natives perished from the war or diseases caused by it. General Jacob Smith, who gave orders to turn the island of Samar into a "howling wilderness," to "kill and burn"—"the more you kill and burn the better you will please me"—was retired with no punishment by President Roosevelt, who made it clear that Smith's only sin was his "loose and violent talk." Roosevelt, who went on to receive the Nobel Peace Prize, explained that "I also heartily approve of the employment of the sternest measures necessary" against the cruel and treacherous savages who "disregard . . . the rules of civilized warfare," and who had furthermore "assailed our sovereignty" (President McKinley) in an earlier act of internal aggression. The director of all Presbyterian missions hailed the conquest as "a great step toward the civilization and the evangelization of the world," while another missionary explained that the notorious "water cure" was not really "torture" because "the victim has it in his own power to stop the process" by divulging what he knows "before the operation has gone far enough to seriously hurt him," and a leading Episcopal bishop lauded General Smith's tactics as necessary "to purge the natives," who were "treacherous and barbarous," of the "evil effects" of "a degenerate form of Christianity." The press chimed in with similar sentiments. "Whether we like it or not," the *New York Criterion* explained, "we must go on slaughtering the natives in English fashion, and taking what muddy glory lies in the wholesale killing until they have learned to respect our arms. The more difficult task of getting them to respect our intentions will follow." Similar thoughts were expressed as we were slaughtering the natives of South Vietnam, and we hear them again today, often in almost these words, with regard to our current exploits in Central America. The reference to the "English fashion" will be understood by any student of American history.

For Theodore Roosevelt, the murderers in the Philippines were fighting "for the triumph of civilization over the black chaos of savagery and barbarism," while President Taft observed that "there never was a war conducted, whether against inferior races or not, in which there were more compassion and more restraint and more generosity" than in this campaign of wholesale slaughter and mass torture and terror. Stuart Creighton Miller, who records these horrors and the reaction to them in some detail and observes that they have largely disappeared from history, assures the reader that "the American interventions both in Vietnam and in the Philippines were motivated in part by good intentions to elevate or to aid the victims"; Soviet scholars say the same about Afghanistan, with comparable justice.[10]

General Smith's subordinate Littleton Waller was acquitted in court-martial proceedings, since he had only been following orders: namely, to kill every male Filipino over the age of ten. He went on to become a major general, and to take charge of Woodrow Wilson's atrocities as he celebrated his doctrine of self-determination by invading Haiti and the Dominican Republic, where his warriors murdered, raped, burned villages, established concentration camps that provided labor for U.S. companies, reinstituted virtual slavery, demolished the political system and any vestige of intellectual freedom, and generally reduced the countries to misery while enriching U.S. sugar companies. According to the approved version, these exploits not only illustrate the Wilsonian doctrine of self-determination to which we are dedicated as a matter of definition, but also serve as a notable example of how "the overall effect of American power on other societies was to further liberty, pluralism, and democracy." So we are informed by Harvard scholar Samuel Huntington, who adds that "No Dominican could doubt but that his country was a far, far better place to live in 1922 than it was in 1916," including those tortured by the benefactors and those whose families they murdered or whose villages they burned for the benefit of U.S. sugar companies.[11]

The record of U.S. intervention in Central America and the Caribbean, to the present day, adds further shameful chapters to the story of terror, torture, slavery, starvation, and repression, all conducted with the most touching innocence, and with endless benevolence—particularly with regard to the U.S. investors whose representatives design these admirable exercises. The worst period in this sordid history was initiated by the Kennedy administration, which established the basic structure of state terrorism that has since massacred tens of thousands as an integral part of the Alliance for Progress; this cynical program, devised in fear of "another Castro," fostered a form of "development" in which croplands were converted to export for the benefit of U.S. corporations and their local associates while the population sank into misery and starvation, necessitating an efficient system of state terror to ensure "stability" and "order." We can witness its achievements today, for example, in El Salvador, where Presidents Carter and Reagan organized the slaughter of some 60,000 people, to mounting applause in the United States as the terror appeared to be showing signs of success. During the post–World War II period, as U.S. power greatly expanded, similar projects were undertaken over a much wider range, with massacres in Greece, Korea (prior to what we call "the Korean War," some 100,000 had been killed in South Korea, primarily in U.S.-run counterinsurgency campaigns undertaken as part of our successful effort to destroy the indigenous political system and install our chosen clients), Southeast Asia, and elsewhere, all with inspiring professions of noble intent and the enthusiastic acclaim of the educated classes, as long as violence appears to be successful.[12]

In brief, a major theme of our history from the earliest days has been a combination of hideous atrocities and protestations of awesome benevolence. It should come as no great surprise to students of U.S. history that we are the injured party in Indochina.

Contrary to much illusion, there was little principled opposition to the Indochina War among the articulate intelligentsia. One detailed study undertaken in 1970, at the peak of antiwar protest, revealed that the "American intellectual elite" came to oppose the war for the same "pragmatic reasons" that had convinced business circles that this investment should be liquidated. Very few opposed the war on the grounds that led all to condemn the Soviet invasion of Czechoslovakia: not that it failed, or that it was too bloody, but that aggression is wrong. In striking contrast, as late as 1982—after years of unremitting propaganda with virtually no dissenting voice permitted expression to a large audience—over 70 percent of the general population (but far fewer "opinion leaders") still regarded the war as "fundamentally wrong and immoral," not merely "a mistake."[13]

The technical term for this failure of the indoctrination system is the "Vietnam syndrome," a dread disease that spread over the population with such symptoms as distaste for aggression and massacre, what Norman Podhoretz calls the "sickly inhibitions against the use of military force," which he hopes were finally overcome with the grand triumph of U.S. arms in Grenada.[14] The malady, however, persists, and continues to inhibit the state executive in Central America and elsewhere. The major U.S. defeat in Indochina was at home: much of the population rejected the approved stance of passivity, apathy, and obedience. Great efforts were made through the 1970s to overcome this "crisis of democracy," as it was called, but with less success than reliance on articulate opinion would suggest.

There was, to be sure, debate over the wisdom of the war. The hawks, such as Joseph Alsop, argued that with sufficient violence the United States could succeed in its aims, while the doves doubted this conclusion, though emphasizing that "we all pray that Mr. Alsop will be right" and that "we may all be saluting the wisdom and statesmanship of the American government" if it succeeds in subjugating Vietnam (what we would call: "liberating Vietnam") while leaving it "a land of ruin and wreck" (Arthur Schlesinger). Few would deny that the war began with "blundering efforts to do good" (Anthony Lewis) in "an excess of righteousness and disinterested benevolence" (John King Fairbank), that it was "a failed crusade" undertaken for motives that were "noble" though "illusory" and with the "loftiest intentions" (Stanley Karnow, in his best-selling history). These are the voices of the doves. As noted, much of the population rejected the hawk-dove consensus of elite circles, a fact of lasting significance. It was that part of the population that concerned the planners in Washington, for example, Defense Secretary Robert McNamara, who asked in a secret memo of 19 May 1967 whether expansion of the American war might "polarize opinion to the extent that 'doves' in the US will get out of hand—massive refusals to serve, or to fight, or to cooperate, or worse?"[15]

**"DEFENDING" SOUTH VIETNAM**

It is worth recalling a few facts. The United States was deeply committed to the French effort to reconquer their former colony, recognizing throughout that the enemy was the nationalist movement of Vietnam. The death toll was about a half million. When France withdrew, the United States dedicated itself at once to subverting the 1954 Geneva settlement, installing in the south a terrorist regime that had killed perhaps 70,000 "Viet Cong" by 1961, evoking resistance which, from 1959, was supported from the northern half of the country temporarily divided by the 1954 settlement that the United States had undermined. In 1961–1962, President Kennedy launched a direct attack against rural South Vietnam with large-scale bombing and defoliation as part of a program designed to drive millions of people to camps where they would be "protected" by armed guards and barbed wire from the guerrillas whom, the United States conceded, they were willingly supporting. The United States maintained that it was invited in, but as the London *Economist* accurately observed, "an invader is an invader unless invited in by a government with a claim to legitimacy." The United States never regarded the clients it installed as having any such claim, and in fact regularly replaced them when they failed to exhibit sufficient enthusiasm for the American attack or sought to implement the neutralist settlement that was advocated on all sides and was considered the prime danger by the aggressors, since it would undermine the basis for their war against South Vietnam. In short, the United States invaded South Vietnam, where it proceeded to compound the crime of aggression with numerous and quite appalling crimes against humanity throughout Indochina.

The *Economist*, of course, was not referring to Vietnam but to a similar Soviet fraud concerning Afghanistan. With regard to official enemies, Western intellectuals are able to perceive that 2 + 2 = 4. Their Soviet counterparts have the same clear vision with regard to the United States.

From 1961 to 1965, the United States expanded the war against South Vietnam while fending off the threat of neutralization and political settlement,

*Headquarters of the U.S. Operations Mission (USOM) in Laos. A U.S. general shakes the hand of the defense minister of the Souvanna Phouma government in 1962. (Photo courtesy of Ngo Vinh Long.)*

which was severe at the time. This was regarded as an intolerable prospect, since our "minnow" could not compete politically with their "whale," as explained by Douglas Pike, the leading government specialist on the National Liberation Front (in essence, the former Viet Minh, the anti-French resistance, "Viet Cong" in U.S. propaganda). Pike further explained that the NLF "maintained that its contest with the GVN [the U.S.-installed client regime] and the United States should be fought out at the political level and that the use of massed military might was in itself illegitimate" until forced by the United States "to use counter-force to survive." The aggressors succeeded in shifting the conflict from the political to the military arena, a major victory since it is in that arena alone that they reign supreme, while the propaganda system then exploited the use of "counter-force to survive" by the South Vietnamese enemy as proof that they were "terrorists" from whom we must defend South Vietnam by attacking and destroying it. Still more interestingly, this version of history is now close to received doctrine.

In 1965, the United States began the direct land invasion of South Vietnam, along with the bombing of the north, and at three times the level, the systematic bombardment of the south, which bore the brunt of U.S. aggression throughout. By then, probably some 170,000 South Vietnamese had been killed, many of them "under the crushing weight of American armor, napalm, jet bombers and, finally, vomiting gases," in the words of the hawkish military historian Bernard Fall. The United States then escalated the war against the

*An American with the USOM in Laos training Meo mercenaries. Most Americans working with the Meo tribesmen were CIA agents. (Photo, ca. 1963, from the Pathet Lao News Agency. Collection of Ngo Vinh Long.)*

south, also extending it to Laos and Cambodia where perhaps another one-half million to a million were killed, while the Vietnamese death toll may well have reached or passed 3 million, while the land was destroyed and the societies demolished in one of the major catastrophes of the modern era[16]—a respectable achievement in the days before we fell victim to the "sickly inhibitions against the use of military force."

The devastation that the United States left as its legacy has been quickly removed from consciousness here, and indeed, was little appreciated at the time. Its extent is worth recalling. In the south, 9,000 out of 15,000 hamlets were damaged or destroyed along with some 25 million acres of farmland and 12 million acres of forest: 1.5 million cattle were killed; and there are 1 million widows and some 800,000 orphans. In the north, all six industrial cities were damaged (three razed to the ground) along with 28 of 30 provincial towns (12 completely destroyed), 96 of 116 district towns, and 4,000 of some 5,800 communes; 400,000 cattle were killed and over a million acres of farmland were damaged. Much of the land is a moonscape, where people live on the edge of famine with rice rations lower than Bangladesh. In a recent study unreported here in the mainstream, the respected Swiss-based environmental group IUCN (International Union for Conservation of Nature and Natural Resources) concluded that the ecology is not only refusing to heal but is worsening, so that a "catastrophe" may result unless billions of dollars are spent to "reconstruct" the land that has been destroyed, a "monumental" task that could be addressed only if the United States were to offer the reparations that it owes, a possibility that cannot be considered in a cultural climate as depraved and cowardly as ours. Forests have not recovered, fisheries remain reduced in variety and productivity, cropland productivity has not yet regained normal levels, and there is a great increase in toxin-related disease and cancer, with 4 million acres affected by the 18 million gallons of poisons dumped on cropland and forest in U.S. chemical warfare operations. Destruction of forests has increased the frequency of floods and droughts and aggravated the impact of typhoons, and war damage to dikes (some of which, in the south, were completely destroyed by U.S. bombardment) and other agricultural systems has yet to be repaired. The report notes that "humanitarian and conservationist groups, particularly in the United States, have encountered official resistance and red tape when requesting their governments' authorization to send assistance to Vietnam"—naturally enough, since the United States remains committed to ensure that its victory is not threatened by recovery of the countries it has destroyed.[17]

Throughout 1964, as the United States planned the extension of its aggression to North Vietnam, planners were aware that heightened U.S. military actions might lead to North Vietnamese "ground action in South Vietnam or Laos" in retaliation (William Bundy, November 1964). The United States later claimed that North Vietnamese troops began leaving for the south in October 1964, two months after the U.S. bombing of North Vietnam during the fabricated Tonkin Gulf incident. As late as July 1965, the Pentagon was still concerned over the "probability" that there might be North Vietnamese units in or near the south—five months after the regular bombing of North Vietnam, three months after the direct U.S. land invasion of the south, over three years after the beginning of U.S. bombing of the south, ten years after the U.S. subversion of the political accords that were to unify the country, and with the death toll in the south probably approaching 200,000. Thankfully, North Vietnamese units finally arrived as anticipated, thus making it possible for the propaganda system to shift from defense of South Vietnam against internal aggression to defense against North Vietnamese aggression. As late as the Tet Offensive in January 1968, North Vietnamese troops appear to have been at about the level of the mercenary forces (Korean, Thai) brought in by the United States from January 1965 as part of the effort to subjugate South Vietnam, and according to the Pentagon there were still only South Vietnamese fighting in the Mekong Delta, where the most savage fighting took place at the time. U.S. military forces, of course, vastly exceeded all others in numbers, firepower, and atrocities.

The party line holds that "North Vietnam, not the Vietcong, was always the enemy," as John Corry observes in reporting the basic message of an NBC "White Paper" on the war.[18] This stand is conventional in the mainstream. Corry is particularly indignant that anyone should question this Higher Truth propounded by the state propaganda system. As proof of the absurdity of such "liberal mythology," he cites the battle of Ia Drang Valley in November 1965: "It was clear then that North Vietnam was in the war. Nonetheless, liberal mythology insisted that the war was being waged only by the Vietcong, mostly righteous peasants." Corry presents no example of anyone who denied that there were North Vietnamese troops in the south in November 1965, since there were none, even among the few opponents of the war, who at that time and for several years after included very few representatives of mainstream liberalism. As noted earlier, principled objection to the war was a highly marginal phenomenon among American intellectuals even at the height of opposition to it. Corry's argument for North Vietnamese aggression, however, is as impressive as any that has been presented.

**"THE WAR THAT WENT WRONG, THE LESSONS IT TAUGHT"**

The NBC "White Paper" was one of a rash of retrospectives on the tenth anniversary of the war's end, devoted to "The War that Went Wrong, The Lessons It Taught."[19] They present a sad picture of U.S. intellectual culture, a picture of dishonesty and moral cowardice. Their most striking feature is what is missing: the American wars in Indochina. It is a classic example of Hamlet without the Prince of Denmark. Apart from a few scattered sentences, the rare allusions to the war in these lengthy presentations are devoted to the suffering of the American invaders. The *Wall Street Journal*, for example, refers to "the $180 million in chemical companies' compensation to Agent Orange victims"—U.S. soldiers, not the South Vietnamese victims, whose suffering was and is vastly greater.[20] It is difficult to exaggerate the significance of these startling facts.

There is an occasional glimpse of reality. *Time* opens its inquiry by recalling the trauma of the American soldiers, facing an enemy that "dissolved by day into the villages, into the other Vietnamese. They maddened the Americans with the mystery of who they were—the unseen man who shot from the tree line, or laid a wire across the trail with a Claymore mine at the other end, the mama-san who did the wash, the child concealing a grenade." No doubt one could find similar complaints in the Nazi press about the Balkans.

The meaning of these facts is almost never perceived. *Time* goes so far as to claim that the "subversion" was "orchestrated" by Moscow, so that the United States had to send troops to "defend" South Vietnam, echoing the fantasies concocted in scholarship, for example, by Walt Rostow, who maintains that in his effort "to gain the balance of power in Eurasia," Stalin turned "to the East, to back Mao and to enflame the North Korean and Indochinese Communists."[21] Few can comprehend—surely not the editors of *Time*—the significance of the analysis by the military command and civilian officials of the aggressors:

> The success of this unique system of war depends upon almost complete unity of action of the entire population. That such unity is a fact is too obvious to admit of discussion: how it is brought about and maintained is not so plain. Intimidation has undoubtedly accomplished much to this end, but fear as the only motive is hardly sufficient to account for the united and apparently spon-

taneous action of several millions of people. . . . [The only collaborators are] intriguers, disreputable or ignorant, who we had rigged out with sometimes high ranks, which became tools in their hands for plundering the country without scruple. . . . Despised, they possessed neither the spiritual culture nor the moral fibre that would have allowed them to understand and carry out their task.

The words are those of General Arthur MacArthur describing the Philippine war of national liberation in 1900 and the French resident minister in Vietnam in 1897,[22] but they apply with considerable accuracy to the U.S. war against Vietnam, as the *Time* quote illustrates, in its own way.

Throughout, the familiar convenient innocence served admirably, as in the days when we were "slaughtering the natives" in the Philippines, Latin America, and elsewhere, preparing the way to "getting them to respect our intentions." In February 1965, the United States initiated the regular bombardment of North Vietnam, and more significantly, as Bernard Fall observed, began "to wage unlimited aerial warfare inside [South Vietnam] at the price of literally pounding the place to bits," the decision that "changed the character of the Vietnam war" more than any other.[23] These moves inspired the distinguished liberal commentator of the *New York Times*, James Reston, "to clarify America's present and future policy in Vietnam":

The guiding principle of American foreign policy since 1945 has been that no state shall use military force or the threat of military force to achieve its political objectives. And the companion of this principle has been that the United States would use its influence and power, when necessary and where it could be effective, against any state that defied this principle.

This is the principle that was "at stake in Vietnam," where "the United States is now challenging the Communist effort to seek power by the more cunning technique of military subversion" (the United States having blocked all efforts at political settlement because it knew the indigenous opposition would easily win a political contest, and after ten years of murderous repression and three years of U.S. Air Force bombing in the south).[24]

In November 1967, when Bernard Fall, long a committed advocate of U.S. support for the Saigon regime, pleaded for an end to the war because "Viet-Nam as a cultural and historic entity . . . is threatened with extinction . . . [as] the countryside literally dies under the blows of the largest military machine ever unleashed on an area of this size," Reston explained that America

is fighting a war now on the principle that military power shall not compel South Vietnam to do what it does not want to do, that man does not belong to the state. This is the deepest conviction of Western Civilization, and rests on the old doctrine that the individual belongs not to the state but to his Creator, and therefore, has "inalienable rights" as a person, which no magistrate or political force may violate.[25]

The same touching faith in American innocence and benevolence in Indochina—as elsewhere throughout our history—persists until today in any commentary that can reach a substantial audience, untroubled by the plain facts. Much of the population understood and still remembers the truth, though this too will pass as the system of indoctrination erases historical memories and establishes the "truths" that are deemed more satisfactory.

By 1967, popular protest had reached a significant scale, although elite groups remained loyal to the cause, apart from the bombing of North Vietnam, which was regarded as a potential threat to us since it might lead to a broader war drawing in China and the USSR, from which we might not be immune—the "toughest" question, according to the McNamara memo cited earlier, and the only serious question among "respectable" critics of the war. The massacre of innocents is a problem only among emotional or irresponsible types, or among the "aging adolescents on college faculties who found it rejuvenating to play 'revolution'," in Stuart Creighton Miller's words. Decent and respectable people remain silent and obedient, devoting themselves to personal gain, concerned only that we too might ultimately face unacceptable threat—a stance not without recent historical precedent elsewhere. In contrast to the war protestors, two commentators explain, "decent, patriotic Americans demanded—and in the person of Ronald Reagan have apparently achieved—a return to pride and patriotism, a reaffirmation of the values and virtues that had been trampled upon by the Vietnam-spawned counterculture,"[26] most crucially the virtues of marching in the parade chanting praises for their leaders as they conduct their necessary chores, as in Indochina and El Salvador.

The U.S. attack reached its peak of intensity and horror after the Tet Offensive, with the post-Tet pacification campaigns—actually mass murder operations launched against defenceless civilians, as in Operation Speedy Express in the Mekong Delta—and mounting atrocities in Laos and Cambodia, called here "secret wars," a technical term referring to executive wars that the press does not expose though it has ample evidence concerning them, and that are later denounced with much outrage, when the proper time has come, and attributed to evil men whom we have sternly excluded from the body politic, another sign of our profound decency and honor. By 1970, if not before, it was becoming clear that U.S. policy would "create a situation in which, indeed, North Vietnam will necessarily dominate Indochina, for no other viable society will remain."[27] This predictable consequence of U.S. savagery would later be used as a post hoc justification for it, in another propaganda achievement that Goebbels would have admired.

It is a most revealing fact that there is no such event in history as the American attack against South Vietnam launched by Kennedy and escalated by his successors. Rather, history records only "a defense of freedom,"[28] a "failed crusade" (Stanley Karnow) that was perhaps unwise, the doves maintain. At a comparable level of integrity, Soviet party hacks extol the "defense of Afghanistan" against "bandits" and "terrorists" organized by the CIA. They, at least, can plead fear of totalitarian violence, while their Western counterparts can offer no such excuse for their servility.

The extent of this servility is revealed throughout the tenth anniversary retrospectives, not only by the omission of the war itself, but also by the interpretation provided. The *New York Times* writes sardonically of the "ignorance" of the American people, only 60 percent of whom are aware that the United States "sided with South Vietnam"[29]—as Nazi Germany sided with France, as the USSR now sides with Afghanistan. Given that we were defending South Vietnam, it must be that the critics of this noble if flawed enterprise sided with Hanoi, and that is indeed what the party line maintains; that opposition to American aggression entails no such support, just as opposition to Soviet aggression entails no support for either the feudalist forces of the Afghan resistance or Pakistan or the United States, is an elementary point that would not surpass the capacity of an intelligent ten-year-old, though it inevitably escapes the mind of the commissar. The *Times* alleges that North Vietnam was "portrayed by some American intellectuals as the repository of moral rectitude." No examples are given, nor is evidence presented to support these charges, and the actual record is, as always, scrupulously ignored. Critics of the antiwar movement are quoted on its "moral failure of terrifying proportions," but those who opposed U.S. atrocities are given no opportunity to explain the basis for their opposition to U.S. aggression and massacre or to assign these critics and the *Times* their proper place in history, including those who regard themselves as "doves" because of their occasional twitters of protest when the cost to us became too great. We learn that the opponents of the war "brandished moral principles and brushed aside complexity," but hear nothing of what they had to say—exactly as was the case throughout the war. A current pretense is that the mainstream media were open to principled critics of the war during these years, indeed that they dominated the media. In fact, they were almost entirely excluded, as is easily demonstrated, and now we are permitted to hear accounts of their alleged crimes, but not, of course, their actual words, exactly as one would expect in a properly functioning system of indoctrination.

The *Times* informs us that Vietnam "now stands exposed as the Prussia of Southeast Asia" because since 1975 they have "unleashed a series of pitiless attacks against their neighbors," referring to the Vietnamese invasion that overthrew the Pol Pot regime (after two years of border attacks from Cambodia), the regime that we now support despite pretenses to the contrary, emphasizing the "continuity" of the current Khmer Rouge–based coalition with the Pol Pot regime (see below). The Khmer Rouge receive "massive support" from our ally China, Nayan Chanda reports, while the United States has more than doubled its support to the coalition. Deng Xiaoping, expressing the Chinese stand (which we tacitly and materially support), states: "I do not understand why some want to remove Pol Pot. It is true that he made some mistakes in the past but now he is leading the fight against the Vietnamese aggressors."[30] As explained by the government's leading specialist on Indochinese communism, now director of the Indochina archives at the University of California in Berkeley, Pol Pot was the "charismatic" leader of a "bloody but successful peasant revolution with a substantial residue of popular support," under which "on a statistical basis, most [peasants] . . . did not experience much in the way of brutality."[31] Though the *Times* is outraged at the Prussian-style aggression that overthrew our current Khmer Rouge ally, and at the current Vietnamese insistence that a political settlement must exclude Pol Pot, the reader of its pages will find little factual material about any of these matters. There are, incidentally, countries that have "unleashed a series of pitiless attacks against their neighbors" in these years, for example, Israel, with its invasions of Lebanon in 1978 and 1982. But as an American client state, Israel inherits the right of aggression so that it does not merit the bitter criticism that Vietnam deserves for overthrowing Pol Pot; and in any event, its invasion of Lebanon was a "liberation," as the *Times* explained at the time, always carefully excluding Lebanese opinion on the matter as obviously irrelevant.[32]

The *Times* recognizes that the United States did suffer "shame" during its Indochina wars: "the shame of defeat." Victory, we are to assume, would not have been shameful, and the record of aggression and atrocities supported by the *Times* obviously evokes no shame. Rather, the United States thought it was "resisting" Communists "when it intervened in Indochina": how we "resist" the natives in their land, the *Times* does not explain.

That the United States lost the war in Indochina is "an inescapable fact" (*Wall Street Journal*), repeated without question throughout the retrospectives and in American commentary generally. When some doctrine is universally proclaimed without qualification, a rational mind will at once inquire as to whether it is true. In this case, it is false, though to see why, it is necessary to escape the confines of the propaganda system and to investigate the rich documentary record that lays out the planning and motives for the American war against the Indochinese, which persisted for almost thirty years. Those who undertake this task will discover that a rather different conclusion is in order.

The United States did not achieve its maximal goals in Indochina, but it did gain a partial victory. Despite talk by Eisenhower and others about Vietnamese raw materials, the primary U.S. concern was not Indochina, but rather the "domino effect," the demonstration effect of successful independent development that might cause "the rot to spread" to Thailand and beyond, possibly ultimately drawing Japan into a "New Order" from which the United States would be excluded. This threat was averted. The countries of Indochina will be lucky to survive: They will not endanger global order by social and economic success in a framework that denies the West the freedom to exploit, infecting regions beyond, as had been feared. It might parenthetically be noted that although this interpretation of the American aggression is supported by substantial evidence, there is no hint of its existence, and surely no reference to the extensive documentation substantiating it, in the standard histories, since such facts do not conform to the required image of aggrieved benevolence. Again, we see here the operation of the Orwellian principle that Ignorance is Strength.

Meanwhile, the United States moved forcefully to buttress the second line of defense. In 1965, the United States backed a military coup in Indonesia (the most important "domino," short of Japan) while American liberals lauded the "dramatic changes" that took place there—the most dramatic being the massacre of hundreds of thousands of landless peasants—as a proof that we were right to defend South Vietnam by demolishing it, thus encouraging the Indonesian generals to prevent any rot from spreading there. In 1972, the United States backed the overthrow of Philippine democracy behind the "shield" provided by its successes in Indochina, thus averting the threat of national capitalism there with a terror-and-torture state on the preferred Latin American model. A move towards democracy in Thailand in 1973 evoked some concern, and a reduction in economic aid and increase in military aid in preparation for the military coup that took place with U.S. support in 1976. Thailand had a particularly important role in the U.S. regional system since 1954, when the National Security Council laid out a plan for subversion and eventual aggression throughout Southeast Asia in response to the Geneva Accords, with Thailand "as the focal point of U.S. covert and psychological operations," including "covert operations on a large and effective scale" throughout Indochina, with the explicit intention of "making more difficult the control by the Viet Minh of North Vietnam." Subsequently Thailand served as a major base for the U.S. attacks on Vietnam and Laos.[33]

In short, the United States won a regional victory, and even a substantial local victory in Indochina, left in ruins. That the United States suffered a "defeat" in Indochina is a natural perception on the part of those of limitless ambition, who understand "defeat" to mean the achievement only of major goals, while certain minor ones remain beyond our grasp.

Postwar U.S. policy has been designed to ensure that the victory is maintained by maximizing suffering and oppression in Indochina, which then evokes further joy and gloating here. Since "the destruction is mutual," as is readily demonstrated by a stroll through New York, Boston, Vinh, Quang Ngai Province, and the Plain of Jars, we are entitled to deny reparations, aid, and trade, and to block development funds. The extent of U.S. sadism is noteworthy, as is the (null) reaction to it. In 1977, when India tried to send 100 buffalos to Vietnam to replenish the herds destroyed by U.S. violence, the United States threatened to cancel "food for peace" aid while the press featured photographs of peasants in Cambodia pulling plows as proof of communist barbarity; the photographs in this case turned out to be fabrications of Thai intelligence, but authentic ones could no doubt have been obtained, throughout Indochina. The Carter administration even denied rice to Laos (despite a cynical pretense to the contrary), where the agricultural system was destroyed by U.S. terror bombing. Oxfam America was not permitted to send ten solar pumps to Cambodia for irrigation in 1983; in 1981, the U.S. government sought to block a shipment of school supplies and educational kits to Cambodia by the Mennonite church. Meanwhile, from the first days of the Khmer Rouge takeover in 1975, the West was consumed with horror over their atrocities, described as "genocide" at a time when deaths had reached the thousands in mid-1975. The Khmer Rouge may be responsible for a half-million to a million dead, so current scholarship indicates (in conformity to the estimates of U.S. intelligence at the time), primarily in 1978, when the worst atrocities took place, largely unknown to the West, in the context of the escalating war with Vietnam.[34]

The nature of the profound Western agony over Cambodia as a sociocultural phenomenon can be assessed by comparing it to the reaction to comparable and simultaneous atrocities in Timor. There, the United States bore primary responsibility, and the atrocities could have been terminated at once, as distinct from Cambodia, where nothing could be done but the blame could be placed on the official enemy. The excuses now produced for this shameful behavior are instructive. Thus, William Shawcross rejects the obvious (and obviously correct) interpretation of the comparative response to Timor and Cambodia in favor of a "more structurally serious explanation"; "a comparative lack of sources" and lack of access to refugees.[35] Lisbon is a two-hour flight from London, and even Australia is not notably harder to reach than the Thai-Cambodia border, but the many Timorese refugees in Lisbon and Australia were ignored by the media, which preferred "facts" offered by State Department handouts and Indonesian generals. Similarly, the media ignored readily available refugee studies from sources at least as credible as those used as the basis for the impotent but ideologically serviceable outrage over the Khmer Rouge, and disregarded highly credible witnesses who reached New York and Washington along with additional evidence from church sources and others. The coverage of Timor actually declined sharply as massacres increased. The real reason for this difference in scope and character of coverage is not difficult to discern, though not very comfortable for Western opinion, and becomes still more obvious when a broader range of cases is considered.[36]

The latest phase of this tragicomedy is the current pretense, initiated by William Shawcross in an inspired agitprop achievement,[37] that there was relative silence in the West over the Khmer Rouge. This is a variant of the Brzezinski ploy concerning the "liberal community" noted earlier; in the real world, condemnations virtually unprecedented in their severity extended from mass circulation journals such as the *Reader's Digest* and *TV Guide* to the *New York Review of Books*, including the press quite generally (1976–early 1977). Furthermore, Shawcross argues, this "silence" was the result of "left-wing skepticism" so powerful that it silenced governments and journals throughout the West; even had such "skepticism" existed on the part of people systematically excluded from the media and mainstream discussion, the idea that this consequence could ensue is a construction of such audacity that one must admire its creators, Shawcross in particular.[38]

I do not, incidentally, exclude myself from this critique with regard to Cambodia and Timor. I condemned the "barbarity" and "brutal practice" of the Khmer Rouge in 1977,[39] long before speaking or writing a word on the U.S.-backed atrocities in Timor, which on moral grounds posed a far more serious issue for Westerners. It is difficult even for those who try to be alert to such matters to extricate themselves from a propaganda system of overwhelming efficiency and power.

Now, Western moralists remain silent as their governments provide the means for the Indonesian generals to consummate their massacres, while the United States backs the Democratic Kampuchea coalition, largely based on the Khmer Rouge, because of its "continuity" with the Pol Pot regime, so the

State Department explains, adding that this Khmer Rouge–based coalition is "unquestionably" more representative of the Cambodian people than the resistance is of the Timorese.[40] The reason for this stance was explained by our ally Deng Xiaoping: "It is wise for China to force the Vietnamese to stay in Kampuchea because that way they will suffer more and more. . . ."[41] This makes good sense, since the prime motive is to "bleed Vietnam," to ensure that suffering and brutality reach the maximum possible level so that we can exult in our benevolence in undertaking our "noble crusade" in earlier years.

The elementary truths about these terrible years survive in the memories of those who opposed the U.S. war against South Vietnam, then all of Indochina, but there is no doubt that the approved version will sooner or later be established by the custodians of history, perhaps to be exposed by crusading intellectuals a century or two hence, if "Western civilization" endures that long.

**WILSONIAN IDEALS**

As the earlier discussion indicated, the creation of convenient "visions of righteousness" is not an invention of the intellectuals of the Vietnam era; nor, of course, is the malady confined to the United States, though one might wonder how many others compare with us in virulence. Each atrocity has been readily handled, either forgotten, or dismissed as an unfortunate error due to our naiveté, or revised to serve as a proof of the magnificence of our intentions. Furthermore, the record of historical fact is not permitted to disturb the basic principles of interpretation of U.S. foreign policy over quite a broad spectrum of mainstream opinion, even by those who recognize that something may be amiss. Thus, Norman Graebner, a historian of the "realist" school influenced by George Kennan, formulates as unquestioned fact the conventional doctrine that U.S. foreign policy has been guided by the "Wilsonian principles of peace and self-determination." But he notices—and this is unusual—that the United States "generally ignored the principles of self-determination in Asia and Africa [he excludes the most obvious case: Latin America] where it had some chance of success and promoted it behind the Iron and Bamboo curtains where it had no chance of success at all." That is, in regions where our influence and power might have led to the realization of our principles, we ignored them, while we proclaimed them with enthusiasm with regard to enemy terrain. His conclusion is that this is "ironic," but the facts do not shake the conviction that we are committed to the Wilsonian principle of self-determination.[42] That doctrine holds, even if refuted by the historical facts. If only natural scientists were permitted such convenient methods, how easy their tasks would be.

Commentators who keep to the party line have an easy task; they need not consider mere facts, always a great convenience for writers and political analysts. Thus, Charles Krauthammer asserts that "left isolationism" has become "the ideology of the Democratic Party"; "There is no retreat from the grand Wilsonian commitment to the spread of American values," namely human rights and democracy, but these "isolationists" reject the use of force to achieve our noble objectives. In contrast, "right isolationism" (Irving Kristol, Caspar Weinberger, and the Joint Chiefs, etc.) calls for "retreat from Wilsonian goals" in favor of defense of interests. He also speaks of "the selectivity of the fervor for reforming the world" among "left isolationists," who have an "obsessive" focus on the Philippines, El Salvador, Korea, and Taiwan, but, he would like us to believe, would never be heard voicing a criticism of the Soviet Union, Cuba, or Libya. The latter allegation might be considered too exotic to merit discussion among sane people, but, as noted earlier, that would miss the point, which is to eliminate even that margin of criticism that might constrain state violence, for example, the occasional peep of protest over U.S.-organized terror in El Salvador which, if truth be told, is comparable to that attributable to Pol Pot at the time when the chorus of condemnation was reaching an early peak of intensity in 1977. Crucially, it is unnecessary to establish that there is or ever was a "grand Wilsonian commitment," apart from rhetoric; that is a given, a premise for respectable discussion.

To take an example from the field of scholarship, consider the study of the "Vietnam trauma" by Paul Kattenburg, one of the few early dissenters on Vietnam within the U.S. government and now Jacobson Professor of Public Affairs at the University of South Carolina.[43] Kattenburg is concerned to identify the "salient features central to the American traditions and experience which have made the United States perform its superpower role in what we might term a particularistic way." He holds that "principles and ideals hold a cardinal place in the U.S. national ethos and crucially distinguish U.S. performance in the superpower role"—a standard view, commonly set forth in the United States, Britain, and elsewhere in scholarly work on modern history. These principles and ideals, he explains, were "laid down by the founding fathers, those pure geniuses of detached contemplation," and "refined by subsequent leading figures of thought and action" from John Adams to Theodore Roosevelt, Woodrow Wilson and Franklin Roosevelt; such Kim Il Sung-ism with regard to the "pure geniuses," etc., is also far from rare. These principles, he continues, were "tested and retested in the process of settling the continent [as Indians, blacks, Mexicans, immigrant workers, and others can testify], healing the North-South breach, developing the economy from the wilderness in the spirit of free enterprise, and fighting World Wars I and II, not so much for interests as for the survival of the very principles by which most Americans were guiding their lives."

It is this unique legacy that explains the way Americans act "in the superpower role." The Americans approached this role, "devoid of artifice or deception," with "the mind set of an emancipator":

> In such a mind set, one need not feel or act superior, or believe one is imposing one's ethos or values on others, since one senses naturally that others cannot doubt the emancipator's righteous cause any more than his capacities. In this respect, the American role as superpower, particularly in the early postwar years, is very analogous to the role that can be attributed to a professor, mentor, or other type of emancipator.

Thus, "the professor is obviously capable," and "he is clearly disinterested." "Moreover, like the American superpower, the professor does not control the lives or destinies of his students: they remain free to come or go," just like the peasants of South Vietnam or the Guazapa Mountains in El Salvador. "It will help us understand America's performance and psychology as a super-power, and the whys and wherefores of its Indochina involvement, if we bear in mind this analogy of the American performance in the superpower role with that of the benevolent but clearly egocentric professor, dispensing eman-cipation through knowledge of both righteousness and the right way to the deprived students of the world."

The reader must bear in mind that this is not intended as irony or caricature, but is rather presented seriously, is taken seriously, and is not untypical of what we find in the literature, not at the lunatic fringe, but at the respectable and moderately dissident extreme of the mainstream spectrum.

The standard drivel about Wilsonian principles of self-determination—unaffected by Wilson's behavior, for example in Hispaniola, or in succeeding to eliminate consideration of U.S. domination in the Americas from the Versailles deliberations—by no means stands alone. Kennedy's Camelot merits similar acclaim among the faithful. In a fairly critical study, Robert Packenham writes that Kennedy's policies toward Latin America in 1962–1963 "utilized principally diplomatic techniques to promote liberal democratic rule," and cites with approval Arthur Schlesinger's comment that the Kennedy approach to development, based on designing aid for "take off" into self-sustaining economic growth, was "a very American effort to persuade the developing countries to base their revolutions on Locke rather than on Marx."[44] In the real world, the Kennedy administration succeeded in blocking capitalist de-mocracy in Central America and the Caribbean and laying the basis for the establishment of a network of National Security States on the Nazi model throughout the hemisphere; and the aid program, as the facts of aid disburse-ment make clear, was designed largely to "improve the productivity of Central America's agricultural exporters and at the same time to advance the sales of American companies that manufacture pesticides and fertilizer," which is why nutritional levels declined in the course of "economic miracles" that—quite predictably—benefited U.S. agribusiness and their local associates.[45] Locke deserves better treatment than that. But these again are mere facts, not relevant to the higher domains of political commentary.

Open the latest issue of any major journal of U.S. foreign policy and one is likely to find something similar. Thus the lead article in the current issue of *Foreign Affairs*, as I write, is by James Schlesinger, now at Georgetown University after having served as secretary of defense, director of Central Intelligence, and in other high positions.[46] He contrasts the U.S. and Soviet stance over the years. "The American desire was to fulfill the promise of Wilsonian idealism, of the Four Freedoms. . . . The themes of realpolitik remain contrary to the spirit of American democracy," while the Soviets, so unlike us, are guided by "deep-seated impulses never to flag in the quest for marginal advantages." The United States seeks all good things, but "almost inevitably, the Polands and the Afghanistans lead to confrontation, even if the Angolas and the Nicaraguas do not"—and most assuredly, the Guatemalas, Chiles, Vietnams, Irans, Lebanons, Dominican Republics, etc., do not have the same effect; indeed, the idea would not be comprehensible in these circles, given that in each such case the United States is acting in defense against internal aggression, and with intent so noble that words can barely express it.

True, one is not often treated to such delicacies as Huntington's ode to the Holy State cited earlier, but it is, nevertheless, not too far from the norm.

The official doctrine as propounded by government spokesmen, the U.S. media, and a broad range of scholarship is illustrated, for example, in the report of the National Bipartisan (Kissinger) Commission on Central America: "The international purposes of the United States in the late twentieth century are cooperation, not hegemony or domination; partnership, not confrontation; a decent life for all, not exploitation." Similarly, Irving Kristol informs us that the United States

is not a "have" nation in the sense that it exercises or seeks to maintain any kind of "hegemony" over distant areas of the globe. Indeed, that very word, "hegemony," with all its deliberate vagueness and ambiguity, was appropriated by latter-day Marxists in order to give American foreign policy an "imperialist" substance it is supposed to have but does not.

Among these "Marxists," he fails to observe, are such figures as Samuel Huntington, who, accurately this time, describes the 1945–1970 period as one in which "the U.S. was the hegemonic power in a system of world order."[47] And again, the idea that the United States does not exercise or seek any kind of "hegemony," alone among the great powers of history, requires no evidence and stands as a Truth irrespective of the historical facts.

Similar thoughts are familiar among the culturally colonized elites elsewhere. Thus, according to Michael Howard, Regius Professor of Modern History at Oxford, "For 200 years the United States has preserved almost unsullied the original ideals of the Enlightenment: the belief in the God-given rights of the individual, the inherent rights of free assembly and free speech, the blessings of free enterprise, the perfectibility of man, and, above all, the universality of these values." In this nearly ideal society, the influence of elites is "quite limited." The world, however, does not appreciate this magnificence: "the United States does not enjoy the place in the world that it should have earned through its achievements, its generosity, and its goodwill since World War II"—as illustrated in such contemporary paradises as Indochina, the Dominican Republic, El Salvador, and Guatemala, to mention a few of the many candidates, just as belief in the "God-given rights of the individual" and the universality of this doctrine for 200 years is illustrated by a century of literal human slavery and effective disenfranchisement of blacks for another century, genocidal assaults on the native population, the slaughter of hundreds of thousands of Filipinos at the turn of the century and millions of Indochinese, and a host of other examples.[48]

Such commentary, again, need not be burdened by evidence; it suffices to assert what people of power and privilege would like to believe, including those criticized, e.g., the "left isolationists" of Krauthammer's fancies, who are delighted to hear of their commitment to Wilsonian goals. Presupposed throughout, without argument or evidence, is that the United States has been committed to such goals as self-determination, human rights, democracy, economic development, and so on. It is considered unnecessary to demonstrate or even argue for these assumptions, in political commentary and much of scholarship, particularly what is intended for a general audience. These assumptions have the status of truths of doctrine, and it would be as pointless to face them with evidence as it is with doctrines of other religious faiths.

The evidence, in fact, shows with considerable clarity that the proclaimed ideals were not the goals of Woodrow Wilson, or his predecessors, or any of his successors.[49] A more accurate account of Wilson's actual goals is given by the interpretation of the Monroe Doctrine presented to him by his secretary of state, Robert Lansing, an argument that Wilson found "unanswerable" though he thought it would be "impolitic" to make it public:

> In its advocacy of the Monroe Doctrine the United States considers its own interests. The integrity of other American nations is an incident, not an end. While this may seem based on selfishness alone, the author of the Doctrine had no higher or more generous motive in its declaration.[50]

The category of those who function as "an incident, not an end" expanded along with U.S. power in subsequent years. How planners perceived the world, when they were not addressing the general public, is illustrated in a perceptive and typically acute analysis by George Kennan, one of the most thoughtful and humane of those who established the structure of the postwar world:

> . . . We have about 50% of the world's wealth, but only 6.3% of its population. . . . In this situation, we cannot fail to be the object of envy and resentment. Our real task in the coming period is to devise a pattern of relationships which will permit us to maintain this position of disparity without positive detriment to our national security. To do so, we will have to dispense with all sentimentality and day-dreaming; and our attention will have to be concentrated everywhere on our immediate national objectives. We need not deceive ourselves that we can afford today the luxury of altruism and world-benefaction. . . . We should cease to talk about vague and—for the Far East—unreal objectives such as human rights, the raising of the living standards, and democratization. The day is not far off when we are going to have to deal in straight power concepts. The less we are then hampered by idealistic slogans, the better.[51]

The subsequent historical record shows that Kennan's prescriptions proved close to the mark, though a closer analysis indicates that he understated the case, and that the United States did not simply disregard "human rights, the raising of the living standards, and democratization," but evinced positive hostility towards them in much of the world, particularly democratization in any meaningful sense, any sense that would permit genuine participation of substantial parts of the population in the formation of public policy, since such tendencies would interfere with the one form of freedom that really counts: the freedom to rob and to exploit. But again, these are only consider-ations of empirical fact, as little relevant to political theology as is the fact that the United States attacked South Vietnam.

Given these lasting and deep-seated features of the intellectual culture, it is less surprising perhaps—though still, it would seem, rather shocking—that the man who is criticized for his extreme devotion to human rights should say that we owe Vietnam no debt because "the destruction was mutual," without this evoking even a raised eyebrow.

## THE GUARDIANS OF THE FAITH

The reasons for the rather general and probably quite unconscious subordination of large segments of the educated classes to the system of power and domination do not seem very difficult to discern. At any given stage, one is exposed to little that questions the basic doctrines of the faith: that the United States is unique in the contemporary world and in history in its devotion to such ideals as freedom and self-determination, that it is not an actor in world affairs but rather an "emancipator," responding to the hostile or brutal acts of other powers, but apart from that, seeking nothing but justice, human rights, and democracy. Intellectual laziness alone tends to induce acceptance of the doctrines that "everyone believes." There are no courses in "intellectual self-defense," where students are helped to find ways to protect themselves from the deluge of received opinion. Furthermore, it is convenient to conform: that way lies privilege and power, while the rational skeptic faces obloquy and marginalization—not death squads or psychiatric prison, as elsewhere all too often, but still a degree of unpleasantness, and very likely, exclusion from the guilds. The national tendencies to conform are thus refined by institutional pressures that tend to exclude those who do not toe the line. In the sciences, critical thought and reasoned skepticism are values highly to be prized. Elsewhere, they are often considered heresies to be stamped out; obedience is what yields rewards. The structural basis for conformity is obvious enough, given the distribution of domestic power. Political power resides essentially in those groups that can mobilize the resources to shape affairs of state—in our society, primarily an elite of corporations, law firms that cater to their interests, financial institutions and the like—and the same is true of power in the cultural domains. Those segments of the media that can reach a large audience are simply part of the system of concentrated economic-political power, and naturally enough, journals that are well funded and influential are those that appeal to the tastes and interest of those who own and manage the society. Similarly, to qualify as an "expert," as Henry Kissinger explained on the basis of his not inconsiderable experience in these matters, one must know how to serve power. The "expert has his constituency," Kissinger explained:

"those who have a vested interest in commonly held opinions: elaborating and defining its consensus at a high level has, after all, made him an expert."[52] We need only proceed a step further, identifying those whose vested interest is operative within the social nexus.

The result is a system of principles that gives comfort to the powerful—though in private, they speak to one another in a different and more realistic voice, offering "unanswerable" arguments that it would be "impolitic" to make public—and is rarely subjected to challenge. There are departures, when segments of the normally quiescent population become organized in efforts to enter the political arena or influence public policy, giving rise to what elite groups call a "crisis of democracy" which must be combated so that order can be restored. We have recently passed through such a crisis, which led to an awakening on the part of much of the population to the realities of the world in which they live, and it predictably evoked great fear and concern, and a dedicated and committed effort to restore obedience. This is the source of the reactionary jingoism that has misappropriated the term "conservatism" in recent years, and of the general support for its major goals on the part of the mainstream of contemporary liberalism, now with a "neo" affixed. The purpose is to extirpate heresy and to restore domestic and international order for the benefit of the privileged and powerful. That the mainstream intelligentsia associate themselves with these tendencies while proclaiming their independence and integrity and adversarial stance vis à vis established power should hardly come as a surprise to people familiar with modern history and capable of reasoned and critical thought.

## NOTES

1. News conference, 24 March 1977; *New York Times* (*NYT*), 25 March 1977.

2. Zbigniew Brzezinski, "Afghanistan and Nicaragua," *The National Interest* 1 (Fall 1985), pp. 48–51.

3. Bernard Gwertzman, "The Debt to the Indochinese Is Becoming a Fiscal Drain," *NYT*, 3 March 1985.

4. *NYT*, 18 March 1968; Chomsky, *American Power and the New Mandarins* (New York: Pantheon Books, 1969), p. 14.

5. "A Vietnam War Board Game Created by Princeton Senior," *NYT*, 1 April 1984; Lawrence Lifschultz, "The Not-So-New Rebellion," *Far Eastern Economic Review*, 30 January 1981, pp. 32–33.

6. Barbara Crossette, *NYT*, 10 November 1985.

7. For documentation and further discussion of the interesting concept "internal aggression" as developed by U.S. officials, see my *For Reasons of State* (New York: Pantheon Books, 1973), pp. 114ff.

8. Francis Jennings, *The Invasion of America* (Chapel Hill: University of North Carolina Press, 1975), p. 6.

9. Alexis de Tocqueville, *Democracy in America* (New York: Knopf, 1945), p. 1; General Andrew Jackson, General Orders, 1813, cited by Ronald Takaki, *Iron Cages* (New York: Knopf, 1979), pp. 80–81, 95–96. See Richard Drinnon, *Facing West: The Metaphysics of Indian-Hating and Empire-Building* (Minneapolis: University of Minnesota Press, 1980), for a penetrating discussion of these matters. For an upbeat and enthu-

siastic account of the destruction of the Iroquois civilization, see Fairfax Downey, *Indian Wars of the U.S. Army* (Garden City, NY: Doubleday, 1963), pp. 32ff.

10. Daniel Boone Schirmer, *Republic or Empire* (Cambridge, MA: Schenkman, 1972), p. 231; Stuart Creighton Miller, *"Benevolent Assimilation"* (New Haven: Yale University Press, 1982), pp. 220, 225, 248ff., 78, 213, 269; David Bain, *Sitting in Darkness* (Boston: Houghton Mifflin, 1984), p. 78.

11. Samuel Huntington, "American Ideals versus American Institutions," *Political Science Quarterly*, vol. 97, no. 1 (Spring 1982), p. 25; Correspondence, vol. 97, no. 4 (Winter 1982–1983), p. 753. On Wilson's achievements, see Lester Langley, *The Banana Wars* (Lexington: University of Kentucky Press, 1983); Bruce Calder, *The Impact of Intervention* (Austin: University of Texas Press, 1984).

12. For extensive discussion of these matters and their sources in U.S. planning, see my *Turning the Tide* (Boston: South End Press, 1985), and sources cited there.

13. For references to material not specifically cited, here and below, and discussion in more general context, see my *Towards a New Cold War* (New York: Pantheon Books, 1982), *Turning the Tide*, and sources cited there.

14. Norman Podhoretz, "Proper Uses of Power," *NYT*, 30 October 1983.

15. Mark McCain, *Boston Globe*, 9 December 1984; memo released during the Westmoreland-CBS libel trial.

16. Bernard Fall, "Viet Cong: The Unseen Enemy in Vietnam," *New Society*, 22 April 1965, pp. 10–12; Paul Quinn-Judge, "The Confusion and Mystery Surrounding Vietnam's War Dead," *Far Eastern Economic Review*, 11 October 1984, p. 49.

17. Ton That Thien, "Vietnam's New Economic Policy," *Pacific Affairs*, vol. 56, no. 4 (Winter 1983–1984), pp. 691–708; Chitra Subramaniam, *Philippine News Service*, 15 November 1985; both writing from Geneva. For detailed discussion of the effects of U.S. chemical and environmental warfare in Vietnam, unprecedented in scale and character, see Stockholm International Peace Research Institute, *Ecological Consequences of the Second Indochina War* (Stockholm: Almqvist Wiksell, 1976), concluding that "the ecological debilitation from such attack is likely to be of long duration."

18. John Corry, *NYT*, 27 April 1985.

19. *Time*, 15 April 1985, pp. 16–61.

20. *Wall Street Journal*, 4 April 1985. An exception was *Newsweek*, 15 April 1985, which devoted four pages of its 33-page account to a report by Tony Clifton and Ron Moreau on the effects of the war on the "wounded land."

21. Walt W. Rostow, *The View from the Seventh Floor* (New York: Harper & Row, 1964), p. 244. On the facts concerning Indochina, see the documentation reviewed in *For Reasons of State*. Rostow's account of Mao and North Korea is also fanciful, as the record of serious scholarship shows.

22. Cited in *American Power and the New Mandarins*, pp. 253, 238.

23. "Vietnam Blitz: A Report on the Impersonal War," *New Republic*, 9 October 1965, p. 19.

24. James Reston, *NYT*, 26 February 1965.

25. Bernard Fall, *Last Reflections on a War* (Garden City, NY: Doubleday, 1967), p. 33, 47; James Reston, *NYT*, 24 November 1967.

26. Allan E. Goodman and Seth P. Tillman, *NYT*, 24 March 1985.

27. Chomsky, *At War with Asia* (New York: Pantheon Books, 1970), p. 286.

28. Charles Krauthammer, "Isolationism, Left and Right," *New Republic*, 4 March 1985, pp. 18–25.

29. *NYT*, 31 March 1985.

30. Nayan Chanda, "CIA No, US Aid Yes," "Sihanouk Stonewalled," *Far Eastern Economic Review*, 16 August 1984, pp. 16–18; 1 November 1984, p. 30.

31. Douglas Pike, *St. Louis Post-Dispatch*, 29 November 1979; *Christian Science Monitor*, 4 December 1979. Cited by Michael Vickery, *Cambodia* (Boston: South End Press, 1983), pp. 65–66.

32. On Lebanese opinion and the scandalous refusal of the media to consider it, and the general context, see my *Fateful Triangle* (Boston: South End Press, 1983).

33. Chomsky and Edward S. Herman, *Political Economy of Human Rights*, I (Boston: South End Press, 1979), chapter 4.

34. The major scholarly study of the Pol Pot period, Vickery's *Cambodia*, has been widely and favorably reviewed in England, Australia, and elsewhere, but never here. The one major governmental study, by a Finnish Inquiry Commission, was also ignored here: Kimmo Kiljunen, ed., *Kampuchea: Decade of the Genocide* (London: Zed Books, 1984). See Kiljunen, "Power Politics and the Tragedy of Kampuchea in the '70s," *Bulletin of Concerned Asian Scholars*, vol. 17, no. 2 (April–June 1985), pp. 49–64, for a brief account of the Finnish study; and my "Decade of the Genocide in Review," *Inside Asia*, vol. 2 (February–March 1985), pp. 31–34, for review of this and other material. Note that the Finnish study is entitled *Decade of the Genocide*, in recognition of the fact that the killings during the U.S.-run war were roughly comparable to those under Pol Pot. The facts are of little interest in the U.S., where the Khmer Rouge have a specific role to play: namely, to provide a justification for U.S. atrocities.

35. Shawcross, in David Chandler and Ben Kiernan, eds., *Revolution and Its Aftermath in Kampuchea* (New Haven: Yale University Press, 1983); see my "Decade of Genocide" for further discussion.

36. See *Political Economy of Human Rights* and Edward S. Herman, *The Real Terror Network*, for extensive evidence.

37. Shawcross, *Revolution and Its Aftermath in Kampuchea* and *Quality of Mercy* (New York: Simon & Schuster, 1984); see my "Decade of Genocide" for discussion. Perhaps I may take credit for suggesting this clever idea to him. In a 1978 essay (reprinted in *Towards a New Cold War*, p. 95), I wrote that "it is not gratifying to the ego merely to march in a parade; therefore, those who join in ritual condemnation of an official enemy must show that they are engaged in a courageous struggle against powerful forces that defend it. Since these rarely exist, even on a meager scale [and in the case of the Khmer Rouge, were undetectable outside of marginal Maoist groups], they must be concocted; if nothing else is at hand, those who propose a minimal concern for fact will do. The system that has been constructed enables one to lie freely with regard to the crimes, real or alleged, of an official enemy, while suppressing the systematic involvement of one's own state in atrocities, repression, or aggression. . . ." These comments accurately anticipate the subsequent antics.

38. On Shawcross's fabrication of evidence in support of his thesis, see my "Decade of Genocide" and Christopher Hitchens, "The Chorus and Cassandra: What Everyone Knows About Noam Chomsky," *Grand Street*, vol. 5, no. 1 (Autumn 1985), pp. 106–131.

39. *Nation*, 25 June 1977.

40. John Holdridge of the State Department. Hearing before the Subcommittee on Asian and Pacific Affairs of the Committee on Foreign Affairs, House of Representatives, 97th Congress, Second Session, 14 September 1982, p. 71.

41. Cited by Ben Kiernan, *Tribune* (Australia), 20 March 1985.

42. Norman A. Graebner, *Cold War Diplomacy* (New York: Van Nostrand Books, 1962).

43. Paul M. Kattenburg, *The Vietnam Trauma in American Foreign Policy, 1945–75* (New Brunswick, NJ: Transaction Books, 1982), pp. 69ff.

44. Robert A. Packenham, *Liberal America and the Third World* (Princeton: Princeton University Press, 1973), pp. 156, 163.

45. Lester Langley, *Central America: The Real Stakes* (New York: Crown, 1985), p. 128; see *Turning the Tide* for discussion and further sources on these matters.

46. James Schlesinger, "The Eagle and the Bear: Ruminations on Forty Years of Superpower Relations," *Foreign Affairs*, vol. 63, no. 5 (Summer 1985), pp. 938, 939, 940, 947.

47. Irving Kristol, "Foreign Policy in an Age of Ideology," *The National Interest* 1 (Fall 1985); Huntington, in M. J. Crozier, S. P. Huntington, and J. Watanuki, *The Crisis of Democracy* (New York: New York University Press, 1975).

48. Michael Howard, "The Bewildered American Raj," *Harper's*, vol. 270, no. 1618 (March 1985), pp. 55–60.

49. For a review of the facts of the matter, see *Turning the Tide* and sources cited.

50. Gabriel Kolko, *Main Currents in American History* (New York: Pantheon Books, 1984), p. 47.

51. Policy Planning Study (PPS) 23, 24 February 1948, *FRUS 1948*, I (part 2); reprinted in part in Thomas Etzold and John Lewis Gaddis, *Containment* (New York: Columbia University Press, 1978), pp. 226ff.

52. Henry Kissinger, *American Foreign Policy* (New York: Norton, 1969), p. 28.

# 6

## George R. Vickers

# The Vietnam Antiwar Movement

In early 1965 President Lyndon Johnson ordered U.S. military forces to begin combat operations in South Vietnam, and by April of that year about 25,000 U.S. troops were stationed in that country. On 17 April 1965, more than 20,000 Americans demonstrated in Washington, D.C., to protest the U.S. intervention. It was a pattern that would be repeated for the duration of U.S. involvement in the Vietnam War: Escalation in the size and intensity of U.S. intervention was met by escalation in the size and intensity of opposition to the war here at home.

Twenty years later new debates over the U.S. role in the world and the possibility of U.S. direct intervention in regional conflicts have led to a reexamination of the U.S. experience in Vietnam, including the role of domestic opposition to that war.[1] All too frequently, however, discussion of the antiwar movement centers on a caricature that abstracts one small moment in time and a tiny sector of the opposition. Broadcast media need dramatic imagery, and the images of small bands of youths carrying Viet Cong flags battling with police, or a few revolutionaries going underground to wage war against "Amerika," are far more dramatic than middle-aged white men in business suits signing petitions.

In promoting an image of the antiwar movement as a band of violent Hanoi supporters, those who supported U.S. intervention at the time or who have since come to believe that the war was justified make three main types of assertions about the significance and impact of the movement:

1. Some argue that the movement was a critical factor in preventing the United States from achieving victory over Communist forces in Vietnam, saying, for example, that "American public opinion indeed turned out to be a crucial 'domino'; it influenced military morale in the field, the

---

This chapter is a revised version of George R. Vickers, "The Vietnam Antiwar Movement in Perspective," *Bulletin of Concerned Asian Scholars* 21, nos. 2–4 (April–Dec. 1989), pp. 100–111. Reprinted with permission.

long drawn-out negotiations in Paris, the settlement of 1973, and the cuts in aid to South Vietnam in 1974, a prelude to final abandonment in 1975."[2]

2. A second accusation is the charge that the antiwar movement was manipulated by North Vietnamese officials who "provided tactical advice and helped coordinate worldwide antiwar demonstrations."[3] Some go so far as to claim that antiwar activists were conscious, willing agents of an enemy state and "agreed to collaborate with their war effort by providing propaganda advice and orchestrating a campaign to demoralize American troops in the field and to create disorder and disruption back home. . . ."[4]

3. Another prevalent argument is the claim that the fall of Cambodia and Laos and the crimes and abuses committed by Communist regimes in Southeast Asia after the U.S. defeat prove that the "domino theory" was correct and that administration justifications for U.S. intervention have been retroactively confirmed. "New Left orthodoxy had scorned the idea that the war was at least partly about Soviet expansion, but soon after the American pullout, the Soviets were in Da Nang and Cam Ranh Bay. . . . Far from being liberated, South Vietnam was occupied by its former 'ally' in the North. Large numbers of 'indigenous' revolutionaries of the NLF whom we had supported were in 'political reeducation' camps set up by Hanoi or taking their chances on the open seas. . . . In Cambodia two million peasants were dead, slaughtered by the Communist Khmer Rouge, protégés of Hanoi and beneficiaries of the New Left's 'solidarity.' It was a daunting lesson: more people had been killed in three years of a Communist peace than in thirteen years of American war."[5]

These are significant allegations, and they raise essential questions about the efficacy, motivations, and justifications of the antiwar movement. Assessing the accuracy of such charges, however, requires us to penetrate the media portrait to recover something of the actual origins and history of the movement.

**BUILDING A STRUCTURE**

Describing the origins of the southern civil rights movement in the 1950s and early 1960s, Aldon Morris emphasized the extent to which "pre-existing institutions, leaders and organizations were critically involved in all phases of the movement and were especially important in the beginning stages, when the action was planned and resources mobilized."[6] The early spread and growth of the antiwar movement also utilized preexisting institutions and organizations—including the civil rights movement and the network of national support built up to assist the civil rights organizations. These preexisting organizations included adult political and issue-oriented organizations such as the Committee for a SANE Nuclear Policy, Turn Toward

Peace, and the Americans for Democratic Action; pacifist and religiously motivated social-action organizations like the American Friends Service Committee, Committee for Nonviolent Action, Fellowship of Reconciliation, and so on; Old Left organizations that ranged from Communist to Trotskyist to Socialist to Social Democratic; and a younger social-action–oriented constituency centered around the Students for a Democratic Society (SDS), Student Peace Union (SPU), National Student Association (NSA), and Student Nonviolent Coordinating Committee (SNCC).[7]

There was considerable overlap in membership and issue-focus among these organizations, but they also provided entree into several fairly distinct broader constituencies as the antiwar movement began to articulate a comprehensive critique of U.S. policy in Vietnam. The development of that critique went public in March 1965, with the first teach-in at the University of Michigan. That event inaugurated a tactic whereby scholars and intellectuals challenged the administration's facts and assumptions. Although the administration's justifications for U.S. intervention frequently shifted, in the early years there were five principal arguments:[8]

1. The United States was legally obligated to fight;
2. The United States was responding to an emergency plea from the Vietnamese people;
3. The global reputation or credibility of the United States was at stake;
4. The United States was resisting an invasion because the National Liberation Front was a creature of North Vietnam, and North Vietnamese troops were fighting in South Vietnam;
5. If the United States failed to contain Communist expansion in Vietnam, it would have to contain it elsewhere closer to home, and a Communist victory would lead to a "domino effect" throughout Southeast Asia.

In later years the administration added a new argument, saying that abandoning the struggle would lead to a "bloodbath" of North Vietnamese reprisals against South Vietnamese.

The antiwar movement challenged each of these arguments on empirical and logical grounds. Challenging the factual claims in administration arguments, the movement critique also constructed a sophisticated counterargument.[9] Thus, while denying that the NLF was solely an instrument of North Vietnam, the movement argued that the revolution in the South had popular support independent of northern influence: "Concede that Hanoi . . . intrigued to create and retain control over the NLF. . . . But much more important than questions about the bureaucratic origins of the NLF is the question, Why did it grow? . . . How could it be that this illegitimate invasion from without was experienced by so many South Vietnamese as an entirely legitimate revolution from within?"[10] Moreover, argued movement analysts, the South Vietnamese government was no less a creation of the United States than the NLF might be a creation of Hanoi.

To the charge that North Vietnamese troops were fighting in South Vietnam, the movement responded that even U.S. documents showed that the U.S.

intervention preceded significant North Vietnamese infiltration, and in any case the U.S. claim that North and South Vietnam were separate countries was contrary to fact and international agreements such as the Geneva Accords.[11]

The articulation of a critique of U.S. policy went hand-in-hand with efforts to organize and mobilize the constituencies represented in the network of preexisting institutions and organizations. The first national antiwar demonstration in April 1965 drew about 20,000 demonstrators and was sponsored by Students for a Democratic Society. Since the neoconservative critics of the antiwar movement often accuse SDS of denying the "communist" character of the Viet Cong and of romantic glorification of the North Vietnamese, it is worth noting that the major speech at the demonstration by Paul Potter, the president of SDS at the time, argued: "We must accept the consequences that calling for an end of the War in Vietnam is in fact allowing for the likelihood that a Vietnam without war will be a self-styled Communist Vietnam. . . . I would rather see Vietnam Communist than see it under continuous subjugation of the ruin that American domination has brought."[12] The other speakers at the march were Senator Ernest Gruening, historian Staughton Lynd, I. F. Stone, and Robert Moses (the SNCC worker who directed the Mississippi Summer Project in 1964). The major thrust of the march was a petition to Congress to act to stop the war.

In November of that year, SANE organized another march in Washington that was even more mainstream, featuring Coretta Scott King, Benjamin Spock, and Norman Thomas. The speech by the new SDS president, Carl Oglesby, however, reflected a significant radicalization of the youth sector represented by SDS. In his speech, Oglesby noted: "We are here to protest against a growing war. Since it is a very bad war, we acquire the habit of thinking that it must be caused by very bad men." But, he argued, the war was originated and expanded by mainstream liberals: "They are not moral monsters. They are all honorable men. They are all liberals."[13] The speech reflected a growing conviction that the war was not simply the result of mistaken facts, but was a logical outgrowth of a bipartisan cold-war foreign policy that would not change easily.

During 1966 the base of the antiwar movement was broadened, and organizational structures were developed at local and regional levels. In January, Senator J. William Fulbright held Foreign Relations Committee hearings about the war. The lonely dissenters against the war, Senators Wayne Morse and Ernest Gruening, for the first time gained a powerful ally, but congressional dissent of significant proportions was still years away. With both the executive and legislative branches of government controlled by the same political party, many in Congress who had doubts about the war were hesitant to act because of the political cost.

One result was that the antiwar movement developed as an extraparliamentary movement—a fact that shaped both its ideology and its structural forms. SDS had decided in 1965 *not* to take the lead in building an antiwar movement because of a commitment to community organizing. In 1966 several

*Benjamin Spock, Martin Luther King, Jr., and Charles Owen Rice heading the 15 April 1967 protest march of more than 100,000 in New York. Some feel that Martin Luther King, Jr., was assassinated the following year primarily because in his opposition to the Vietnam War he not only challenged U.S. dependence on military solutions and anticommunist crusades, but also called for a radical redistribution of wealth and power in the United States and throughout the world. (Photo by Eli Finer. Reprinted by permission of Pathfinder Press.)*

efforts to forge a national coalition of groups opposing the war foundered on sectarian differences.[14] While this was going on, there were a number of demonstrations in different cities that drew crowds similar to the 1965 demonstrations. Finally, in November a conference in Cleveland created a national structure intended to organize a much more massive national demonstration scheduled for 15 April 1967.

The structure was called the Spring Mobilization Committee to End the War in Vietnam, and it would be followed by the National Mobilization Committee to End the War in Vietnam and the New Mobilization Committee to End the War in Vietnam—coalitions based on the same basic model that would organize national demonstrations in 1968 and 1969. The key to these coalitions was *nonexclusion*—the principle that any organization opposed to the war could participate, and a focus on single demonstrations rather than an ongoing program that would have required a much higher degree of political agreement among the participating organizations. Around the same time, a national Student Mobilization Committee that was organizationally independent was formed to support the call for a demonstration on 15 April. With SDS drawing back, this provided a much needed vehicle to mobilize student participation.

The 15 April 1967 march in New York City not only broadened the base of the movement by getting some labor unions and mainstream religious denominations to participate, but for the first time also brought in organized sections of the civil rights movement. Just as Democratic Party politicians who were opposed to the war hesitated to speak out against their own president, civil rights leaders who had forged an effective alliance with the Johnson administration were hesitant to jeopardize that alliance by challenging his war policy. But on 4 April 1967 at Riverside Church, Dr. Martin Luther King, Jr., spoke out publicly against the war for the first time and agreed to be the featured speaker at the 15 April march. More than 100,000 joined in the march.

This first stage of the antiwar movement drew to a close in early 1967. Although the movement was successful in developing a powerful critique of the war, in building an organizational structure capable of spreading that critique and mobilizing opposition to U.S. intervention, and in broadening the social base of opposition, there was a growing sense of frustration and impotence within the movement. U.S. troop strength continued to grow throughout this period so that by the end of 1966 there were 385,000 U.S. troops in South Vietnam. Despite the broadening of the social base of opposition, public opinion polls continued to show majority (though declining) support for administration policy.[15]

## FROM PROTEST TO RESISTANCE

The combination of a growing sense of power in numbers and a growing frustration at the lack of any visible response by the administration to the movement's growth led to a new stage beginning sometime in 1967 and lasting into 1969, during which the focus of the movement changed. The movement began to emphasize *resistance* to continued conduct of the war in the form of draft resistance, organization of active-duty GI's, obstruction of induction centers, troop trains, and other war-related efforts, and by increasingly engaging in both substantive and symbolic civil disobedience. During Stop the Draft Week in Oakland, California, in October 1967, demonstrators began to use "mobile tactics" against police that led to much more violent countermeasures, as police beat demonstrators who in turn blocked intersections with objects as well as with their bodies.

Later that same month, a national demonstration at the Pentagon drew about 100,000 participants, many of whom stayed on after the peaceful assembly to conduct a nonviolent sit-down to block the building. National Guard troops were called in, and again there were assaults on demonstrators and many arrests. During the siege, several hundred draft cards were publicly burned.

Even as the confrontational character of the extraparliamentary antiwar movement became more massive and pronounced, internal divisions within the Democratic Party generated by the war and opposition to it finally broke into the open as a portion of the movement began active electoral campaigning to defeat prowar congressional candidates, elect antiwar candidates, and even to mount a campaign to "dump Johnson" by nominating an antiwar candidate for president. Led by Allard Lowenstein, the dump-Johnson forces enlisted Senator Eugene McCarthy in what seemed a futile exercise to challenge the renomination of Johnson. As 1967 drew to a close there were more than 500,000 U.S. troops in Vietnam, and a Louis Harris poll in December found that 58 percent of the persons interviewed favored seeing the war through and stepping up U.S. pressure.

In early 1968, however, a series of events transformed the political landscape and gave new impetus to antiwar forces. The most important was the Tet Offensive by NLF and North Vietnamese forces at the end of January. The offensive decisively discredited the optimistic projections of administration and military leaders about the status of the war and provided visible support for the antiwar movement critique. Most importantly, it was the final element needed to convince key members of the business and political elite that U.S. intervention must end.

During the week of 25 March the Wise Men, an unofficial presidential advisory group consisting of powerful men who had served in government but were mostly now in business,[16] met in Washington at the president's request to receive briefings on the war. The next day they presented President Johnson with their consensus that the war could not be won. On 31 March Johnson addressed the nation to announce that he was ending the bombing of North Vietnam and asking "again" for North Vietnam to enter into negotiations. At the end of his speech he dropped a political bombshell by saying that he would not run for another term as president.

The most immediate effect of these events on the antiwar movement was to shift the struggle against the war into the electoral arena. Robert Kennedy had declared his candidacy on 16 March, and while antiwar forces were torn between his campaign and loyalty to the pioneer effort of McCarthy, Johnson and his allies sought to retain control of events through the candidacy of Vice-President Hubert Humphrey.

The assassinations of Martin Luther King in April and Robert Kennedy in June heightened feelings that peaceful change within the electoral and legal framework of U.S. society could not succeed at the very moment that prospects for such change seemed to be improving. A growing minority, particularly in the student wing of the movement, felt that the government was declaring war on the movement and vowed to fight back. At the Democratic Party convention in Chicago that August, the Chicago police confirmed their worst nightmares.

The antiwar protest in Chicago during that convention is probably the commonest image of the antiwar movement. Covered by national and international media, the daily images of street battles between long-haired, youthful demonstrators and Mayor Richard Daley's brutal police were burned into the collective memory of the nation. What is forgotten is that only about 5,000 demonstrators came to Chicago.[17] Most antiwar organizations refused to participate in the Chicago demonstrations because the threatening rhetoric on both sides made them certain that peaceful protest was unlikely.

This second stage was extremely effective in that key members of the national business and political elite became convinced by late 1967 that the war could not be won at an acceptable cost. Their shift, in turn, led Johnson to drop out of the race for reelection and to stop escalating U.S. involvement. There was a high price for success, however, as the more militant tactics and strategy generated internal conflict and fragmentation within the movement. Although public opinion polls finally turned against the war, they also showed growing hostility to the organized antiwar movement. It became increasingly difficult for the diverse constituencies represented within the movement to agree on common actions.

**WINNING AND LOSING**

The defeat of Hubert Humphrey marked another important turn in the antiwar movement. With a president of one party and Congress controlled by the other, new leverage developed within the political system for the antiwar movement to exploit. The year 1969 was transitional in that the most powerful antiwar demonstrations yet seen took place that fall. At the same time, President Nixon's (and Congress's) reactions to those demonstrations introduced new dynamics into the antiwar struggle.

One of the first signs of a changing relationship between the legislative and executive branches was the introduction by Republican Senator Charles Goodell (on 25 September 1969) of a resolution calling on the president to withdraw all U.S. troops from Vietnam by December 1970. Within a month more than ten resolutions generally opposed to continuation of the war were introduced into Congress.

On 15 October 1969, literally millions of Americans participated in a one-day (or part of one day) work stoppage and demonstration that dramatically illustrated both the breadth and the depth of antiwar sentiment in the country. Organized by four activists who had worked in Eugene McCarthy's presidential campaign, the call for a moratorium on business-as-usual to protest the war was endorsed quickly by Representative Morris Udall and then dozens of senators and representatives. Averell Harriman, former Supreme Court justice Arthur Goldberg, the United Auto Workers, and other mainstream figures and groups followed suit. Although no accurate estimate of the total number who participated was possible, estimates ranged as high as 10 million.[18]

A month later, in November, approximately 1 million people participated in simultaneous mass demonstrations in Washington and San Francisco. In response to the growing antiwar sentiment, President Nixon moved to defuse some of the key issues of the movement. On 3 November 1969 he declared in a televised speech that the U.S. objective was to "Vietnamize" the war by turning over combat duties to South Vietnamese forces and gradually withdrawing U.S. troops.[19] In December of that year a draft lottery was introduced to remove some of the personal uncertainty that helped motivate antiwar

*Mayor Daley's police officers brandishing their clubs as they wade into an antiwar rally at Grant Park in Chicago on 28 August 1968 during the Democratic Party convention. Dramatic photos like this one became the stereotyped image of the antiwar movement. (Photo by Brian Shannon. Reprinted by permission of Pathfinder Press.)*

activism by those of draft age. This was followed by actions to remove many of the grounds for draft deferment that made the old system so unfair.

Along with such measures intended to slow the growth of antiwar sentiments in mainstream elements of the population, Nixon also undertook a campaign of intimidation and repression against organized sectors of the movement. The use of COINTELPRO (a program of infiltration and subversion of antiwar movement organizations by FBI agents and informants) was supplemented by a series of conspiracy indictments and by a public attack on the media and the antiwar movement designed to crush or at least place on the defensive the organized antiwar movement. These actions were quite effective, and nationally organized antiwar actions declined dramatically in the winter of 1970.[20]

Government repression was not the only cause of the decline in antiwar activity. Just as it seemed that the antiwar movement was speaking for a majority of the people, conflicts among and within organizations in the antiwar movement induced a process of disintegration that greatly weakened it. In the

*Part of the crowd of some 750,000 in Washington, D.C., on 15 November 1969. With the simultaneous demonstration of 250,000 in San Francisco, this was the largest political demonstration of any kind in U.S. history until that time. Because of the many people protesting in the streets in the fall of 1969, Nixon realized that he would not be able to carry out the threats he had made to the North Vietnamese. (Photo by Brian Shannon. Reprinted by permission of Pathfinder Press.)*

student wing, SDS dissolved in a parody of infantile leftist sectarianism during 1969, while control of the Student Mobilization Committee was seized by the Young Socialist Alliance (youth wing of the Trotskyist Socialist Workers Party). The adult antiwar coalition, the New Mobilization Committee, also split into Trotskyist and non-Trotskyist factions. One result was that the non-Trotskyist sector no longer had an organizational mechanism for mobilizing people on college campuses.[21]

The lull in antiwar organizing came to a sudden end on 30 April 1970, when President Nixon announced that he had ordered U.S. troops to invade Cambodia to attack North Vietnamese and Viet Cong base camps. He also ordered renewed air attacks against North Vietnam. The announcement shocked those who had accepted at face value his claim that the U.S. combat role in Vietnam was winding down. Within hours of his speech college students across the country began demonstrations, and within a week more than one hundred campuses went on strike. Support for the strike spread after National Guard troops killed four students during demonstrations at

Kent State University in Ohio on 4 May, and city police and state highway patrolmen killed two students and wounded fourteen at Jackson State College in Mississippi on 14 May. Before the end of the semester more than 80 percent of the college and university campuses announced some kind of strike action.[22]

The Cambodia invasion also generated new congressional opposition to the war. In June the Senate voted to repeal the Tonkin Gulf Resolution that President Johnson had used as authorization for conducting the war, and the House of Representatives followed suit in December. Although the earlier Goodell resolution and the repeal of the Tonkin Gulf Resolution were more symbolic than substantive, more serious congressional efforts to end the war now began. The Cooper-Church amendment proposed to cut off all funding for U.S. forces in Cambodia after 1 July 1970, and the McGovern-Hatfield amendment aimed at cutting off funding for all U.S. military operations in Southeast Asia and withdrawing all U.S. troops unless Congress voted to declare war. Although the McGovern-Hatfield amendment was defeated by a vote of 55 to 39 on 1 September 1970, the vote reflected the growing influence of antiwar sentiment on Congress.

In early 1971 a new and powerful constituency began to join in antiwar activity. While the trial of Lieutenant William Calley for directing a massacre of Vietnamese civilians in My Lai was the subject of great media attention, the Vietnam Veterans Against the War organized public hearings at the end of January for Vietnam veterans to testify about their participation in other abuses and atrocities. Frustrated by the lack of media attention to their testimony, the veterans announced a march on Washington—"Operation Dewey Canyon III, a limited incursion into the country of Congress"—to make their case.

The veterans' march helped temporarily reunite the fragmented national coalitions of the antiwar movement. Several thousand veterans participated in the Dewey Canyon III protest from 19 April through 23 April, which ended with more than 1,000 Vietnam veterans returning their combat medals to the government. The following day, 24 April, a national rally at the Capitol drew half a million people. From 25 April through 2 May a combined lobbying and civil disobedience campaign at different government agencies focused attention on the domestic costs of the war. On 3 May the predominantly student "Mayday Tribe" initiated massive "mobile tactics" in Washington with the stated intent that "if the Government won't stop the war, we'll stop the government." More than 7,000 were arrested the first day.[23]

The spring antiwar actions in 1971 marked the high point of antiwar mobilization. For most of the remainder of the war, so long as U.S. casualties and troop levels decreased, antiwar actions tended to decrease in size and effectiveness. At the same time any new public signs of U.S. intensified intervention produced massive antiwar reactions. Thus, for example, when President Nixon launched new bombing raids against North Vietnam on 15 April 1972, by 21 April a national student strike had begun. The "Christmas bombing" of Hanoi in December also provoked new protests.

This pattern ended on 27 January 1973, when U.S. and Vietnamese leaders signed the Agreement on Ending the War and Restoring Peace in Vietnam.[24]

*Rusty Sachs, who had been a marine in Vietnam, hurls his Bronze Star onto the Capitol steps on 23 April 1971, the last day of the five-day Operation Dewey Canyon III protest in Washington, D.C. In addition to a thousand Vietnam veterans returning their medals to the government, during this protest veterans attended hearings of the Senate Foreign Relations Committee on proposals to end the war, lobbied Congress, attended ceremonies for the war dead, turned themselves in at the Pentagon as war criminals, performed guerrilla theater in front of the Justice Department, and marched to the Supreme Court to ask why it had not ruled on the constitutionality of the war. (Photo by Bernard Edelman. Reprinted with permission.)*

The accord called for the withdrawal of all remaining U.S. troops from Vietnam within sixty days and for the release of U.S. prisoners of war. With the implementation of the accord, the antiwar movement in the United States faded into memory. Although the agreement permitted the North Vietnamese to keep troops in South Vietnam, recognized that boundaries between North and South Vietnam were "temporary" and not "political," and in most other respects accepted the terms for ending the war offered by Hanoi, many in the antiwar movement believed that Nixon had once again defused the movement and that antiwar movement actions played no role in the outcome.

This sense of impotence and failure was one reflection of how difficult it is to sustain a movement focused on foreign policy issues. The government has such control over information and the definition of events that even while giving in to demands of the movement it is able to control public perceptions of events. During the Nixon presidency government repression against the movement combined with careful efforts to reduce U.S. casualties and visibility in Vietnam led to a gradual decrease in the antiwar movement's ability to mobilize resistance to the war. This gave President Nixon some breathing time to pursue negotiations and to attempt to strengthen South Vietnamese forces. Throughout this period Nixon claimed to be unaffected by the antiwar movement, and despite clear evidence that the U.S. failed to achieve any of its stated objectives in Vietnam, it is surprising how many activists came to believe that the antiwar movement had little impact.

**THE ANTIWAR MOVEMENT AS SOCIAL MOVEMENT**

Whatever else it may be, political activity is *organized* activity. The similarities or differences in the backgrounds and motivations of persons engaged in political activity have their most immediate impact on the structure and programs of the organizations through which individuals participate politically. Political organizations become crucial reference points for those involved in political activity—the place where the significance of events is interpreted, where analysis of events is developed, and where the common bonds of membership take on form and substance.[25]

Precisely because political activity *begins* as organized activity, any investigation of major shifts in the character of political activity must begin with the origins, structure, program, and composition of the political organizations that initiate such shifts. Sometimes these are the result of "splits" within preexisting organizations and sometimes they are "new" organizations without formal ties to the past. Always they emerge from a process of change that begins within the prior framework of organized activity.[26]

Although the movement opposing U.S. policy in Vietnam was never a cohesive entity in the sense that there was a centralized directorate that could make policy for the movement as a whole, the antiwar movement was nevertheless more an organized phenomenon than it was a spontaneous happening. The demands, slogans, strategies, and tactics of the movement did not emerge from amorphous collections of individuals but were developed within organizational settings and negotiated between diverse organizations. The debates over goals, strategies, and tactics were shaped as much by preexisting networks, organizational histories and rivalries, personality conflicts, and ideological differences as they were by any common commitment to ending the war.[27]

Some antiwar groups were multi-issue organizations for whom opposition to the war was one element of a broader program. Others were focused solely on ending U.S. involvement in the war. Some were national organizations with branches in many states, and others were local groups or coalitions that joined together specifically to organize antiwar protests.

There were also many different strategies and tactics pursued by these organizations. Some favored pressuring Congress by petitions, demonstrations, and other forms of legitimate protest. Others concentrated on public education campaigns to change attitudes about the war and worked in electoral politics to elect antiwar candidates and to oppose prowar advocates. Still others eschewed electoral politics in favor of civil disobedience and more direct efforts to obstruct the conduct of the war.

The antiwar movement evolved through several relatively distinct phases. During the first stage, which lasted from the beginning of U.S. escalation in 1965 into 1967, the primary focus was on mobilizing and organizing resources for struggle. This included building an organizational framework capable of organizing and coordinating opposition to the war. This framework emerged out of an environment of preexisting organizations and institutions rooted in several relatively distinct constituencies.

During a second stage of development lasting from 1967 through the U.S. presidential election in 1968, the strategies and tactics of the antiwar movement were tested and refined, and the ideology of the movement became more defined. A critical factor in this development was the fact that both the executive and legislative branches of government were controlled by the Democratic Party, which forced the movement to operate as an extraparliamentary opposition with little access to institutionalized resources in the mainstream political community. This fostered a radicalization of ideology, increased militancy in tactics, and a tendency to define the potential universe of supporters for the movement in terms of "victims" of the dominant political system.

After 1969 this latter situation changed dramatically. With a Republican president and a Democratic Congress, the antiwar movement gained access to important new resources in the institutionalized system to oppose the war. Most notable was the publishing of the *Pentagon Papers* by the *New York Times* in June and July 1971. This top-secret "History of the U.S. Decision-Making Process on Vietnam Policy" had been leaked to the *Times* by two disillusioned RAND Corporation analysts for the Pentagon, Daniel Ellsberg and Anthony Russo, and its revelation of government deception and illegality shocked the nation and greatly strengthened anti–Vietnam War sentiments and positions. Such new resources and the politically divided state of the elected officials running the country opened up the possibility of reaching new constituencies and generated ideological and tactical divisions within the antiwar movement. At the same time, much more overt policies of repression against the movement were adopted under President Nixon, and these policies exacerbated internal tensions and contradictions within the antiwar movement.

The primary impact of the antiwar movement after 1969 was to act as both a factor in, and constraint upon, policy planning by U.S. officials prosecuting the war effort. Nixon's quick retreat from the Cambodia incursion after it produced a massive protest (he announced that troops would be out of Cambodia by 1 July) demonstrated the movement's ability to act as a constraint on policy options. Unknown to the public at the time, however, President Nixon and Henry Kissinger had earlier given up on plans to dramatically escalate the war because of the success of antiwar demonstrations in the fall of 1969. The secret bombing of Cambodia and the creation of a covert team known as the "plumbers" within the White House were also responses to the antiwar movement. The whole policy of Vietnamization was designed to reduce U.S. casualties and visibility in the war effort. Public negotiations with North Vietnam were also undertaken with a specific intent to minimize antiwar activities.[28]

---

**THE "LESSONS" OF VIETNAM**    The antiwar movement mobilized opposition to the U.S. intervention in Vietnam, and in doing so became—itself—a factor affecting policy considerations concerning the war. The domestic social turmoil and political consequences of specific policy options (e.g., the invasion of Cambodia) were a part of the equation policymakers had to solve before deciding on a course of action. After 1969, and especially after 1972, the movement was able also to get Congress to impose legal constraints on policy options in the war.

Despite these very significant impacts, it would be a serious mistake to suggest that the antiwar movement was the *primary* cause of the defeat of U.S. policy in Vietnam. A more accurate view would be that the growth of the antiwar movement reflected and was fueled by the failure of U.S. political and military policies during the war.

### THE ANTIWAR MOVEMENT AND THE MILITARY EFFORT

Neoconservative and prowar critics have treated the antiwar movement as *responsible* for the U.S. defeat in Vietnam, but military analysts have taken a quite different stance. Although the analysts agree that lack of public support for the U.S. war effort was a crucial factor in the U.S. defeat, they generally view the antiwar movement not as a principal *cause* of U.S. defeat, but rather as one *effect* of failed U.S. strategy.

The military has carried out extensive analyses of the reasons for U.S. failure, and there is a growing consensus among military analysts on what were the key elements of the failure.[29] The first failure was that of emphasizing the military aspects of the conflict without recognizing that the war was primarily *political*. Unlike the Viet Cong and North Vietnam, U.S. leaders "never *acted* on the principle that victory in the political war in South Vietnam required major reforms within the government of South Vietnam,"[30] and the "battle for the 'hearts and minds of the American people' was never seen as an integral—and *the* crucial—battlefield of the war."[31]

A related failure was that we gave first priority to the defeat of enemy regular forces in the field using U.S. forces almost exclusively, which played into Hanoi's hands by giving credibility to their charge of U.S. imperialism and allowing them to inflict maximum casualties on U.S. forces. As General Palmer put it, "we paid insufficient attention to our number one military job, which was to develop South Vietnamese armed forces that could successfully pacify and defend their own country."[32]

Col. Harry G. Summers, General Bruce Palmer, Jr., and Lt. General Phillip B. Davidson all agree that warfare, whether "limited" or otherwise, requires the full support and mobilization of the population, and all attribute the decline in U.S. public support to a failure on the part of leaders to seek a public consensus and commitment in the form of a declaration of war.[33] Palmer wrote: "From the beginning our leaders realized that South Vietnam was not vital to U.S. interests."[34] Summers argued: "A declaration of war is a clear statement of *initial* public support which focuses the nation's attention on the enemy. . . . It was the lack of such focus on the enemy and on the political objectives to be obtained by the use of military force that was the cause of our strategic failure."[35] Davidson, too, emphasized that Johnson should have asked for a declaration of war from Congress: "If Congress had refused to declare war, then the President would know that he did not have the support of the people, and that the war could not be won."[36]

Thus, although all these analysts of the strategy and tactics of the Vietnam War recognize that North Vietnam sought to weaken U.S. public support for the war effort, they do not view the antiwar movement as composed of "dupes" manipulated by Hanoi so much as they view antiwar sentiments as a logical consequence of failure on the part of political leaders here to define a clear U.S. objective in Vietnam and to win support for achieving that objective. There are differences between them over the extent to which they think such an objective really existed, but they are united in a view that Johnson and other architects of the war never made an effective case that one did. In this sense, they also support the initial argument of the antiwar movement back in 1965 that administration rationales for U.S. intervention were contradictory, vague, or simply wrong.

### THE ANTIWAR MOVEMENT AND HISTORICAL RESPONSIBILITY

For the military analysts cited above, the central reasons for the U.S. failure in Vietnam were that the United States did not define its objectives clearly, did not understand the character of the war it fought, and was unprepared to fight that kind of war. Although there have been efforts within the military to blame civilian authorities or other outside causes for the defeat,[37] military analysts have been far more self-critical than their civilian counterparts in trying to honestly understand the lessons of the war for future planning.

In stark contrast, civilian supporters of the U.S. intervention in Vietnam have aggressively argued that postwar events have confirmed the original justification for that intervention and have exposed the antiwar movement as a dupe of Hanoi. Moreover, they argue, the antiwar movement bears a heavy moral responsibility for the tremendous suffering that (in their view) has afflicted the peoples of Indochina since the Communist victory in Vietnam.

In constructing this argument, critics of the antiwar movement have used argument-by-assertion and disinformation to rewrite the historical record. This is particularly evident in the case they make for the validity of two justifications offered for the U.S. intervention: the domino theory and the bloodbath argument.

In its original formulation the domino theory argued that a U.S. withdrawal from Vietnam would lead to Communist takeovers not only in Indochina but throughout all of Southeast Asia and possibly beyond. "If we fail to draw the line in Viet-Nam . . . we may find ourselves compelled to draw a defense line as far back as Seattle and Alaska, with Hawaii as a solitary outpost in mid-Pacific," one prominent proponent of the domino theory argued, and the fall of Vietnam would lead to likely Communist victories in the Congo, Philippines, Thailand, Okinawa, Venezuela, and possibly even Japan.[38]

In fact, only Laos and Cambodia have come under Communist domination or pressure, and in both of these countries the process began years before the "fall" of Vietnam in 1975. Indeed, U.S. actions in these countries weakened their chances of withstanding challenges by Communist-led movements.

Cambodia was relatively stable until the overthrow of Norodom Sihanouk by the right-wing Lon Nol in 1970, and the United States supported Lon Nol and exploited the coup by expanding U.S. activities in Cambodia with the approval of his regime. The abuses of the Lon Nol government and the extensive "secret" bombing of Cambodia by the United States from 1969 through 1973 served to strengthen support for the Communist Khmer Rouge, who overthrew the Lon Nol regime in 1975 a few days *before* the takeover of Saigon by Vietnamese Communists. Thus the "fall" of Cambodia to communism began with the destabilization brought about by the removal of Sihanouk in 1970, not with the U.S. withdrawal from Vietnam.

Laos provides somewhat stronger evidence for proponents of the domino theory. The rightist governmental, commercial, and military elite of Laos began to flee soon after the victories of the Khmer Rouge in Cambodia and of the North Vietnamese Army and the National Liberation Front in Vietnam. Communist military forces were able to move into the capital unopposed, and the administration was then purged of its remaining rightist elements, with the final transfer of power to the Communists taking place in December 1975.

Even in Laos, however, internal conflicts among indigenous groups and United States actions *within Laos* were probably more important in shaping the Communist victory there than was the U.S. withdrawal from Vietnam. Conflicts between Communist and non-Communist groups in Laos had been going on since the 1950s, and negotiations to form coalition governments including Communist elements had been held as early as the Kennedy

"Hi, everybody! Look who's here!" (Douglas M. Marlette, the Charlotte Observer. Reprinted by permission.)

administration. The heavy bombing of parts of Laos by the United States from 1963 through 1973 and the U.S. economic support of the right-wing Royal Lao Government—amounting to 90 percent of the operating budget—helped that government stave off a military defeat by Laotian Communist forces.[39] Those same actions, however, created an artificial economy and intensified polarization among political groups that might otherwise have worked together in a coalition government. Thus the strength of indigenous Communist forces in Laos, together with the almost complete dependence of rightist elements on U.S. support, were probably the most important factors in the collapse of the pro-U.S. elements, irrespective of pressure from North Vietnam.

The other major argument used by critics of the antiwar movement as evidence of moral turpitude is the argument that a Communist victory in Vietnam would be followed by a bloodbath in which the victorious Vietnamese Communists would slaughter millions of innocent victims. As one of the original formulators of the argument put it,

> Vietnamese communism is characterized by the utter disregard for human life of Stalinism and Maoism. What will happen to the more than one million refugees from North Viet-Nam? What will happen to the millions of peasants who resisted or bore arms against the Viet-Cong? I shudder to think of it. The massacre of innocents in Viet-Nam will be repeated in every Southeast Asian country that falls to communism in its wake, in a gigantic bloodletting that will dwarf the agony and suffering of the war in Viet-Nam.[40]

Critics of the antiwar movement seem especially thrilled to cite statistics proving that "more people had been killed in three years of a Communist peace than in thirteen years of American war" as an ultimate moral judgment against the antiwar movement, and antiwar veterans have been defensive in response. It must be plainly said, however, that the bloodbath argument was, and is, without merit.

By lumping together killings in Vietnam, Laos, and Cambodia after the end of the war, the movement's critics try to obscure the fact that *virtually all* the killings took place in Cambodia, by a regime that was both hostile to and independent of the North Vietnamese, and against which the Vietnamese themselves intervened militarily. *There was no bloodbath in Vietnam* after the war.

The fact that hundreds of thousands of South Vietnamese who worked for the United States or its client regime were jailed or penalized in a variety of ways is neither surprising nor morally repugnant in any absolute sense. What is more surprising, given the length and intensity of the civil conflict in Vietnam, is that reprisals were not more severe.

It is true that a number of NLF activists and other supporters of the revolution in South Vietnam were denied a role in the victorious regime, were often treated with suspicion or persecuted by cadres from the North, and that a number turned against the Hanoi regime. But infighting among victors who have been in a united front is also nothing new, and, if anything, the emergence of such internal conflicts in the aftermath of the war lends support to the notion that the NLF and the struggle in the South was never purely an extension of the DRV's policies in the North.

My point here is not that the death of more than a million Cambodians (the exact number remains a matter of debate among historians) is acceptable nor that we should cheer because hundreds of thousands of South Vietnamese were jailed or fled the country; nor am I trying to employ a "double standard" to excuse Communist-instigated terror and repression. There is no denying that many activists in the antiwar movement, particularly in the student wing, glorified both Vietnamese revolutionaries and revolution in the abstract. It is also true that many had a naive view (or no view) of the likely consequences of a North Vietnamese victory for the people of Indochina.

It must also be plainly said, however, that the aftermath of the war has not vindicated those who promoted and promulgated it in the first place. The domestic legacy of the Vietnam War includes a profound skepticism on the part of the American people in committing U.S. troops abroad, and a deep suspicion of government assurances that interventionist policies will bring positive results. This "Vietnam syndrome" may not always be an appropriate response to concrete circumstances, but there is little in what we know so far about the Vietnam War itself that challenges the evidence on which it is based.

Another lesson of the war is the reminder that in certain historical epochs profound social transformations shape the formation of "political generations" sharing a texture of feelings and assumptions that frame political instincts for a long period of time, even while the members of that generation are divided by class, race, geography, and other causes of political conflict. It is no accident that people speak of a "Vietnam generation" in talking about all those who were coming of age in the 1960s and that it is often easier for antiwar activists and Vietnam veterans to communicate with each other than it is for either to communicate with that political generation forged in World War II.

## NOTES

1. The United States military, in particular, has undertaken a major effort to understand the lessons of Vietnam and their implications for future wars. Among the best products of this reexamination of the Vietnam War are, Colonel Harry G. Summers, Jr., *On Strategy: A Critical Analysis of the Vietnam War* (Novato, CA: Presidio Press, 1982); General Bruce Palmer, Jr., *The 25-Year War: America's Military Role in Vietnam* (Lexington, KY: University Press of Kentucky, 1984); Lt. General Phillip B. Davidson, USA (Ret.), *Vietnam at War: The History, 1946–1975* (Novato, CA: Presidio Press, 1988).

2. Guenter Lewy, *America in Vietnam* (New York: Oxford University Press, 1978), p. 436.

3. Ibid., p. 436.

4. Peter Collier & David Horowitz, "Another 'Low Dishonest Decade' on the Left," *Commentary*, January 1987, p. 17.

5. Ibid., p. 19.

6. Aldon Morris, *The Origins of the Civil Rights Movement: Black Communities Organizing for Change* (New York: The Free Press, 1984), pp. 277–278.

7. A good historical account of the chronology of events and roles played by different organizations and individuals is Nancy Zaroulis and Gerald Sullivan, *Who Spoke Up?: American Protest Against the War in Vietnam, 1963–1975* (New York: Doubleday, 1984).

8. For an excellent discussion of the shifting and vague statements of U.S. objectives, and the consequences of this for the military, see Andrew F. Krepinevich, Jr., *The Army and Vietnam* (Baltimore: Johns Hopkins University Press, 1986).

9. One of the most comprehensive and widely read critiques of U.S. policy by the antiwar movement in those years was Carl Oglesby and Richard Shaull, *Containment and Change* (New York: The Macmillan Co., 1967).

10. Ibid., pp. 9–10.

11. See, for example, *The Viet-Nam Reader*, Marcus G. Raskin and Bernard B. Fall, eds. (New York: Vintage Books, 1965). Documents substantiating this position are found in *Vietnam: A History in Documents*, Gareth Porter, ed. (New York: New American Library, 1979), and in *Vietnam and America: A Documentary History*, Marvin E. Gettleman, Jane Franklin, Marilyn Young, and H. Bruce Franklin, eds. (New York: Grove Press, 1985).

12. *National Guardian*, 29 April 1965.

13. Excerpted in *The New Left: A Documentary History*, Massimo Teodori, ed. (New York: Bobbs-Merrill, 1969), pp. 182–188.

14. Often these were conflicts within the Old Left between Communist, Socialist, and Trotskyist groupings. For a detailed history of the antiwar movement written totally from a Trotskyist perspective, see Fred Halstead, *Out Now! A Participant Account of the American Movement Against the Vietnam War* (New York: Monad Press, 1978). A much more balanced perspective is found in Zaroulis and Sullivan, *Who Spoke Up?*

15. See, for example, Zaroulis and Sullivan, *Who Spoke Up?*, p. 116.

16. The group consisted of Dean Acheson, George Ball, General Omar Bradley, McGeorge Bundy, Arthur Dean, Douglas Dillon, Abe Fortas, Arthur Goldberg, Henry

Cabot Lodge, John J. McCloy, Robert Murphy, General Matthew Ridgeway, General Maxwell Taylor, and Cyrus Vance. For an account of their meeting see Zaroulis and Sullivan, *Who Spoke Up?*, pp. 159–160.

17. See Zaroulis and Sullivan, *Who Spoke Up?*, pp. 175–208.

18. Ibid., p. 271.

19. The speech is reprinted in Gettleman et al., *Vietnam and America*, pp. 428–439.

20. For a good discussion of Nixon's covert and overt campaign against the antiwar movement and its leaders see Zaroulis and Sullivan, *Who Spoke Up?*, pp. 217–236, 275–342.

21. For a more detailed discussion of the internal organizational conflicts within the antiwar movement see George R. Vickers, "The American Peace Movement," *Bridge*, vol. 4, no. 1 (November, 1975), pp. 66–73.

22. See Zaroulis and Sullivan, *Who Spoke Up?*, pp. 318–320.

23. Ibid., pp. 354–363.

24. See Gettleman et al., *Vietnam and America*, pp. 469–487.

25. See, for example, George R. Vickers, *The Formation of the New Left: The Early Years* (Springfield, MA: D.C. Heath & Co., 1975). Todd Gitlin highlights the importance of organizations in his account of the 1960s, *The Sixties: Years of Hope, Days of Rage* (New York: Bantam, 1987). Doug McAdam also stresses organizational influences on individuals in the civil rights movement in *Freedom Summer* (New York: Oxford University Press, 1988). The general thrust of this argument is consistent with what has come to be known as Resource Mobilization perspectives on social movements.

26. See, for example, Vickers, *The Formation of the New Left*. In *The Origins of the Civil Rights Movement* Aldon Morris argues that preexisting organizations were crucial in the development of the civil rights movement.

27. See, for example, Vickers, "The American Peace Movement."

28. See, for example, George R. Vickers, "The New Left and the American Future," in *Trying Times: American Politics in Transition from the Sixties to the Seventies* (Geneva: WSCF Publications, 1970).

29. See, for example, Krepinevich, Jr., *The Army in Vietnam*. Although Krepinevich does not devote time to the antiwar movement, General Palmer and General Davidson do discuss the movement in their analyses (cited in Note 1 above).

30. Davidson, *Vietnam at War*, p. 720.

31. Ibid., p. 721.

32. Palmer, *The 25-Year War*, p. 179.

33. Palmer makes the fullest argument for this approach: "Public acceptance and support of a war requires a consensus of understanding among our people that the effort is in our own best interests. To achieve such a consensus the American people must perceive a clear threat, or need, to cause the United States to go to war. . . . It seems rather obvious that a nation cannot fight a war in cold blood . . . without arousing the emotions of the people. I know of no way to accomplish that result short of a declaration of war by the Congress and national mobilization. But such public and Congressional support is not attainable unless our governmental leaders, particularly those in the executive branch, themselves fully understand the enormous consequences of taking the nation to war and agree that such a step is necessary." Palmer, *The 25-Year War*, pp. 189–190.

34. Ibid., p. 189.

35. Summers, *On Strategy*, p. 20.

36. Davidson, *Vietnam at War*, p. 728.

37. Krepinevich, *The Army in Vietnam*, offers a detailed criticism of such efforts, most of which try to argue that the Vietnam War was "really" a conventional war

rather than a revolutionary war, that the army won all the major battles it fought, and that it was "political" considerations that prevented the military from taking the steps that would have brought victory. For a good example of such reasoning, see Summers, *On Strategy.*

38. Senator Thomas J. Dodd, Sr., "The New Isolationism," speech in the United States Senate, 23 February 1965. Reprinted in Raskin and Fall, *The Viet-Nam Reader*, pp. 164–194.

39. See, for example, W. Randall Ireson and Carol J. Ireson, Chapter 4 of this book.

40. Dodd, "The New Isolationism," p. 171.

# 7

## Douglas Allen

## Scholars of Asia and the War

Students and others interested in Vietnam, Cambodia, and Laos and in the domestic and international consequences of U.S. policies toward Indochina usually are unaware of key issues defining much of Asian studies. How, for example, has the personal history of scholars of Asia, especially their relation to the traumatic experiences of the Indochina War, affected how and what they teach and write? How have the corporate, governmental, military, and foundational sources of funding determined what research has been funded and what articles and books have been published and widely promoted? Have scholars of Asia supported, resisted, or tried to ignore U.S. and global economic and political power relations that so define their field? Answers to such questions are often crucial in determining which books are available or which issues and interpretations are presented as worthy of consideration.

The war in Vietnam, and more generally in the Indochinese nations of Vietnam, Cambodia, and Laos, was, on the one hand, profoundly influenced by the involvement of U.S. scholars of Asia and, on the other hand, profoundly influenced the lives and careers of those scholars. Involvement took many forms. Especially due to a general stereotype of universities in the 1960s and early 1970s as hotbeds of antiwar teach-ins and demonstrations, few people realize the extent to which professors, administrators, and other members of university communities were involved in planning, carrying out, and legitimizing the war.

At the time of U.S. escalation in Vietnam in the mid-1960s, most members of any university community as well as the general public had a view of professors' scholarly activities as restricted to teaching courses and doing "objective" research. Universities, it was generally assumed, were havens largely isolated and insulated from the hierarchically defined goals, central profit motives, and other pressures of the "real world." Few realized the extent to which universities with Asian studies programs were dependent on governmental and corporate funding, often with strings attached. It took many years of research to uncover the extent to which various scholars of Asia served as highly paid consultants and planners for the State Department, the Defense Department, and the Central Intelligence Agency, working on new weapons of massive destruction and brutal methods of counterinsurgency; research also brought to light the extent to which Asia scholars worked for war-dependent corporations such as Dow, Monsanto, and other agrochemical corporations manufacturing defoliants, napalm, and other chemical weapons.

A few highly visible scholars, such as Robert McNamara, Henry Kissinger, Walt Rostow, and McGeorge and William Bundy, who rarely had any particular expertise on Asia or Indochina, became key policymakers. A larger number of Asia scholars, such as Wesley Fishel of Michigan State University, Ithiel de Sola Pool of the Massachusetts Institute of Technology, Samuel Huntington of Harvard University, and Robert Scalapino of the University of California at Berkeley, were less visible but had some influence in shaping U.S. Indochina policy as, for example, in the establishment and consolidation of power of Ngo Dinh Diem as "our" first president in Saigon[1] or the formulation of technical studies on counterinsurgency and rural pacification in southern Vietnam.[2] And a far greater number of Asia scholars were anonymous cogs in what Senator William Fulbright and others began to call the military-industrial-academic complex.[3]

Without the involvement of many hundreds of scholars from political science, public administration, economics, anthropology, sociology, social work, agriculture, education, criminology, and other disciplines, not to mention the more "transparent" participation of scholars in engineering, physics, and the natural sciences in developing new weapons of destruction and working in other clearly defined war-related projects, the Indochina War would have been far different. In this chapter, I shall cite several major university projects in Vietnam as well as the participation of individual scholars in war-related research, but my major focus will be on antiwar scholars.

By the late 1960s, there was a dramatic shift in the positions taken by Asia scholars on the war. In the early and even mid-1960s, taking a public antiwar stance was often lonely, sometimes risky, and frequently dismissed as "unscholarly" and "political." In contrast, political scientists working for governmental agencies or business administration professors or scientists working for corporations to further the power interests of the status quo were not condemned for "politicizing" their fields. By 1969 and 1970, especially after the Tet Offensive had turned most of the U.S. public against the war, the overwhelming majority of Indochina scholars also had become critical of U.S. Indochina policies. Universities became a key, often most visible, part of the U.S. antiwar movement. As part of this antiwar movement, scholars of Asia increasingly criticized Washington's policies toward Indochina, even if for many this was simply on the pragmatic grounds that the U.S. could not win the war. In a minority of cases, scholars began to question the role of the field of Asian studies and of some of their colleagues in remaining silent or in attempting to legitimize and win the war.

The overwhelming majority of these antiwar U.S. Asia specialists were young faculty and especially graduate students at Cornell University, Harvard University, the University of California at Berkeley, the University of Wisconsin at Madison, the University of Michigan at Ann Arbor, and other elite

Asian studies programs in the late 1960s and early 1970s. These graduate students and young faculty were, to use David Halberstam's title, "the best and the brightest," seemingly destined to become the leading voices in the next generation of Indochina scholars. Who were/are these scholars who teach and do research on Indochina? What part did the Indochina War play as a key formative influence in shaping their teaching methods and research projects, in defining their future academic careers and personal lives? And what part did the Indochina War play in redefining and often destroying any possibilities for an academic future in Asian studies for so many of the young antiwar scholars?

The impact of the war on the lives of these young scholars and on the field of Indochina studies cannot be overemphasized. In any generation, there are a few decisive historical events that radically and permanently change the assumptions, perceptions, values, relationships, and basic orientation of those who experience the events. The Vietnam and Indochina War was one such watershed, a decisive historical and personal break in which individuals were cut off from the security and identity of their pre-Vietnam world.

Most of us who went through such a radical transformation and defined ourselves as antiwar and anti-imperialist Asia and Indochina scholars had at an earlier stage raised many specific concerns about our studies, but we had not seriously challenged the basic academic context within which we had functioned as students. In general, we uncritically accepted the assumption that our field operated within the context of value-free "facts," "objectivity," "rationality," and "progress." That we were usually high achievers, successful students who were rewarded for our acceptance of the scholarly environment, reinforced the perpetuation of the pre-Vietnam academic status quo.

Few of us realized the extent to which our professors had already made significant value-laden decisions for us long before the very first day of classes. For instance, the very selection of published Asian studies and other texts necessarily involved assumptions, biases, and value commitments, either consciously or unconsciously, on the part of our teachers. Yet such assumptions and value judgments were hardly ever rendered explicit. We rarely questioned why some texts were selected and others excluded. And fewer of us realized the extent to which the availability of texts went far beyond the specific choices of our professors. We rarely analyzed such a seemingly simple issue as assigned readings on Indochina in terms of much larger issues of the fundamental economic, political, and cultural relations of the power that defines contemporary U.S. society: What were the funding sources for Asian studies that encouraged and supported certain kinds of research and not others? How did the fact that a rapidly increasing number of book publishers were becoming subsidiaries of U.S. multinational corporations, concerned with running their operations on a profit basis, affect the kinds of texts from which our professor, with his or her own biases, could choose?

In short, although many students of Asia became aware of explicitly repressive censorships of the past, especially McCarthyism of the early 1950s, which destroyed the careers of many and continued to affect the apprehensions and self-censorship of an earlier generation of our teachers,[4] we were not aware of the pervasive, power-defined censorship of the status quo in which alternative voices and viewpoints were effectively silenced. Silenced were those scholars dissenting from the status quo, and, as we gradually came to realize, silenced were the voices of the Indochinese people.

We rarely asked our professors those questions that a few years later, in light of the formative influences of the Indochina War, seemed so obvious. Why was our syllabus structured the way it was? On what basis was it determined that these were the major terms, concepts, categories, and units of study? Who determined that terms such as "imperialism" were "subjective" and not essential to the study of Indochina or that we might finally speak of past French imperialism but not present U.S. imperialism? Who determined that the Vietnam War, as it became increasingly unpopular and unwinnable, could be analyzed as an "aberration," "unworthy" of what the United States had always stood for, but not analyzed as consistent with U.S. economic and political policies in Latin America, Africa, and other parts of Asia?

In striving for "balance" and "objectivity," presenting "both sides" of an issue, who determined that these were "both sides" and that other possible "sides" were not even acknowledged? For example, as widespread debate over the war began to develop, why was the scholarly debate, mirroring the debate within the mass media and U.S. government, usually restricted to variations of the more conservative position (the United States is justified, we must stay the course, and so on) and variations of a liberal antiwar position (we should not have become involved in this "civil war," the policy can't work, and so on)?

By contrast, many in Asian studies gradually concluded that both the mainstream conservative and prowar and antiwar liberal approaches were fundamentally flawed and had limited explanatory power in helping us to understand Indochina. Scholars began to formulate alternative methodological approaches and interpretive frameworks for understanding Indochina; these were often more cognizant of Indochina's history, economy, politics, and culture and used key terms such as "colonialism," "neocolonialism," and "imperialism" when analyzing U.S. and other foreign interventions. By the early 1970s, after the transforming effects of the war, Daniel Ellsberg in the film *Hearts and Minds* certainly spoke for millions when he concluded with the dramatic judgment that we Americans were not just on the wrong side in Vietnam; "we were the wrong side."

In the following three sections, we shall examine different relations between U.S. Asia scholars and the Indochina War. First, we shall consider how Asia scholars, who either actively or tacitly supported the U.S. war effort, related to Indochina. We shall note some of the relations between U.S. policy and universities, citing a number of Vietnam projects and concluding with a case study of the Vietnam Center at Southern Illinois University, which became the most controversial university project in Asian studies in the early 1970s. Next, we shall present interviews with four antiwar scholars, whose personal lives and careers were strongly redefined by the experience of the Indochina

War. Finally, we shall formulate key issues that affected antiwar Asian studies scholars during and after the Indochina War. Some of those issues, such as the reality of academic complicity or the tension between scholarship and activism, remain central issues for antiwar and anti-imperialist scholars today.

**NEOCOLONIALISM AND UNIVERSITIES**

In 1969, when the Center for Vietnamese Studies and Programs was established at Southern Illinois University at Carbondale, U.S. policy toward Vietnam was usually described by the term "Vietnamization." In its broadest sense, Vietnamization was a U.S. policy by which Washington attempted to have Vietnamese—with the help of massive military and economic aid, training programs, and the threat (and use) of nearby air and naval power—create and maintain an "independent" pro–United States, anti-Communist Saigon regime that would have enough stability and legitimacy to govern and would be sympathetic to U.S. economic and political interests.[5] In addition to the funding and training of Saigon's military forces, this policy included multileveled interdependent economic, social, and cultural objectives vital to Washington's goals in Indochina.

Vietnamization, usually identified as the policy of the Nixon administration, was a specific form of neocolonialism. In earlier colonial relations, as in French Indochina, there was no question that the foreign colonizing power directly ruled and dominated its colony. With later neocolonial relations, the domination by a foreign power usually became more indirect, complex, and often less transparent, since the less powerful nation, typically a former colony, seemed to be an independent sovereign state. U.S. neocolonial policies can be seen in Vietnam as early as 1954, and neocolonial policies have determined Washington's basic orientation toward most former colonies in the Third World nations of Latin America, Africa, and Asia.

With regard to Vietnam, neocolonialism brought out a certain asymmetrical relationship between Washington and Saigon. True, there seemed on the surface to be an independent Vietnamese government in Saigon, and it was Vietnamese who were conspicuous: Vietnamese doing the fighting and dying at the hands of other Vietnamese; peasants starving and turned into refugees because of policies carried out by the Saigon regime. But, in reality, the power and control rested in Washington. Neocolonialism was first and foremost a U.S. policy. Major policy decisions were dictated by U.S. priorities and funds and worked against the interests of the vast majority of Vietnamese. Washington's Saigon allies were basically puppets being rewarded for carrying out what the U.S. government defined to be its own regional and global interests.

Toward the end of the French-Indochinese war, the United States was an active participant on behalf of the French, especially in assuming most of France's war costs. With the defeat of the French, Washington had to decide whether to accept Vietnamese independence or to move from the former French colonialism to a new policy of neocolonialism. Starting in 1954–1955,

Washington replaced France and the French-created puppet state under Bao Dai with a U.S. client state under Ngo Dinh Diem.

Before considering the vital role of universities in Washington's policies of neocolonialism, it is important to note that much of the massively funded research, especially by the Department of Defense, was part of a permanent war economy, a military-industrial complex that took hold in World War II and has continued since the end of the Indochina War in 1975. Some of the Indochina War–related research, typical of Johnson's policies in the mid-1960s, was defined by the direct application of force to win the war and achieve U.S. objectives without much concern for neocolonialism. This kind of research was consistent with Johnson's policies of applying direct U.S. military force starting in the mid-1960s.

Concerning the relationship that Michael Klare dubbed "the university-military complex," he wrote that without the support of universities "the United States would not have acquired the intercontinental ballistic missile, and would not have developed a counterinsurgency strategy for intervention in Vietnam. . . . Since the only reservoir of trained scientific manpower available for such work (scientific research for expanding the military sector) is the university campus, it was thus inevitable that the Pentagon should call upon the universities to collaborate in the foundation of a military research network."[6]

The Massachusetts Institute of Technology (MIT) has been an integral part of the permanent war economy and a significant participant in the academic-military-industrial complex through massively funded research projects either on campus or at centers and laboratories off campus. "In the 1960s, MIT and Johns Hopkins ran centers which designed missiles, and half of the MIT budget and three-quarters of Johns Hopkins' budget came from running defense labs. These universities are still major bases for military research and have been among the top 100 Department of Defense contractors year after year." For fiscal year 1987, MIT received contracts from the Defense Department for "research, development, test and evaluation" amounting to $407,640,000; Johns Hopkins, in second place, received contracts amounting to $354,925,000.[7]

We may note the Center for International Studies at MIT, which according to David Wise and Thomas Ross, was "the prototype" for the kind of secret relationship worked out by the Central Intelligence Agency with individuals and institutes at dozens of universities and research centers, including, as we shall see, secret arrangements with the Michigan State University Group in Vietnam (MSUG).

> The Center was founded in 1951 with CIA money, and the following year Max F. Millikan, assistant director of the CIA, became its head. From its start, another key figure at the Center was former OSS (Office of Strategic Services) man Walt Whitman Rostow, an economics professor who became President Johnson's personal adviser on national security and foreign affairs, as well as his principal link with the intelligence community. MIT declared in 1966 that the Center had severed all connection with the agency. . . . When it publicly severed the CIA

link it conceded that the Center was receiving fifteen to twenty percent of its budget from Langley.[8]

Ithiel de Sola Pool, who was chairman of political science at MIT, consultant to the Defense Department, and directed research on pacification and insurgency in Vietnam, in "The Necessity for Social Scientists Doing Research for Governments" and other publications is often quite explicit in justifying "scholarly" research for the CIA and other governmental agencies. Noam Chomsky, citing statements in the 15 September 1969 issue of *Scientific Research*, noted: "One of the initiators of Project Cambridge at MIT, Professor Ithiel Pool, states that this $7.6 million project will 'strengthen' research in counterinsurgency." The entire August 1967 issue of *Asian Survey* was devoted to "Vietnam: A Symposium," and the participants assumed U.S. benevolence toward Vietnam and the need to overcome obstacles and render Washington's policies more successful. Pool's contribution, for example, assumed that the inclusion of the "Viet Cong" in a Saigon government is "not acceptable" and we must provide them with "a political rationalization for changing sides." Pool then discussed how we could induce a change in the "image of reality" of the Vietcong cadres, replace their "naive ideology," and win them over to the Saigon government and U.S. policies.[9]

The chairman of the board of MIT, James R. Killian, Jr., put together the Institute for Defense Analysis (IDA) in 1955.

> MIT had been asked by Charles Wilson, then the Secretary of Defense, to evaluate our weapons systems. . . . Killian got five schools to go along (as part of the IDA consortium): Case Institute of Technology, MIT, Stanford, Tulane, and California Institute of Technology. The Ford Foundation made a grant of $500,000, and Killian became the first chairman of the board of the Institute for Defense Analysis. Later the University of California, Michigan, Penn State, Princeton, Columbia, Chicago and Illinois joined the group. The institute's main headquarters is in Washington. IDA also maintains a code-breaking center at Princeton . . . linked to the National Security Agency.[10]

According to James Ridgeway, by 1968 the only continuing IDA link to the universities seemed to be through its Jason Division, a Defense Department think tank in which the twelve universities "made studies for the military on missile re-entry problems, counterinsurgency, and tactical uses of nuclear warfare in Southeast Asia."[11]

> The Jason organization comprises a team of forty-four academics across the country who meet each summer to study military products for the Defense Department, the CIA and the Department of Energy. The Organization was created in 1960 to reunite the military and academia, both of which suffered from the shock of the Soviet Union's successful launching of the Sputnik spacecraft in 1957. During the Vietnam War, Jason devised the "electronic" or "automated" battlefield, an anti-infiltration system which was criticized as leading to the deaths of thousands of civilians. The Red Cross deplored this invention as a violation of international law because it did not discriminate

between soldiers and civilians. Jason's more recent efforts have concentrated on the development of new nuclear weapons and anti-submarine warfare.[12]

Perhaps the academic institution receiving the most publicity for its involvement in IDA/Jason Indochina War–related research was Columbia University. Professor Marvin Harris, writing at the time of the student protests of 1968, noted that Columbia had been involved in CIA cold-war research, especially through its Regional Institutes and School of International Affairs, long before its 1960 affiliation with the Institute for Defense Analysis. Columbia President Grayson Kirk was a member of IDA's Board of Trustees, and student protesters raised the issue of university affiliation with IDA and its Jason Division. "Recently IDA has turned to research more directly associated with the Vietnamese War, concentrating on such projects as: Small Arms for Counter-Guerrilla Operations, Tactical Nuclear Weapons, Chemical Control of Vegetation, Night Vision for Counter-Insurgents, Interdiction of Trucks from the Air at Night, and Helicopter Aural Detection of Tactical Situations."[13]

Writing four years later, another Columbia University professor, Frank Baldwin, indicated that the university's direct institutional relationship with IDA was terminated after the student protests of 1968, but individual faculty quietly retained their affiliation with Jason. In April 1972, forty faculty from Columbia protested the activities of five Columbia physics professors for their responsibility for "a U.S. air war pouring death on Indochina." They charged these five Jason Division members with "participation in the scientific research that had led to the electronic battlefield, the air war and the use of heinous weapons in Indochina."[14]

One could continue with numerous other illustrations of Indochina War military-related research by university professors. The University of Pennsylvania, for example, had contracts from the Department of Defense to do chemical and biological warfare research for the U.S. Army and Air Force. Critics included leading anti-imperialist scholars Gabriel Kolko and Edward Herman. It turned out that the university had "committed itself to classified poison gas and bacteriological warfare before and during the Indochina conflict."[15]

Most of what we have just been considering has been military-oriented research by universities. As I previously discussed, even more indirect neocolonial Vietnamization involved the funding and training of Saigon's huge military forces and the threat and use of massive direct U.S. military force. Now we shall consider more nonmilitary-oriented university projects that assumed a higher priority during periods of Vietnamization.

It becomes clear that many neocolonial policies are not possible without university participation. The military, even with its close allies in corporate America, was simply not equipped to carry out many vital aspects of Vietnamization. It was necessary to look to "outside" assistance in designing and implementing various kinds of educational, cultural, economic, social, and political programs intended, for example, to create illusions of progress and to restructure the attitudes and behavioral patterns of the Indochinese peoples. Needed was the input of political scientists, anthropologists, sociologists, and historians, of schools of agriculture and technology, and of many other disciplines within the academic community.

Michigan State University was quite willing to fulfill such a role to assist in Vietnam's transition from French colonialism to U.S. neocolonialism. As described by Robert Scigliano and Guy Fox of the MSUG, the university took an active part in U.S. technical assistance to Vietnam and in Saigon's administrative and security matters between May 1955 and June 1962. "Its operations closely coincided with the tenure of Ngo Dinh Diem," and Diem's policies and practices

> set the perimeters within which MSUG operated and was able to achieve success.
>
> In July, 1950, Wesley R. Fishel, then an assistant professor of political science at Michigan State College, met Ngo Dinh Diem, a Vietnamese politician out of power, in Tokyo. . . . In 1951, Fishel had his friend made a consultant to Michigan State's Governmental Research Bureau. . . . In July, 1954, Diem became Premier of Vietnam . . . [and] arranged for the American government to send Fishel to Saigon as an advisor to himself and to the American ambassador.

A team of four MSU professors soon followed Fishel to Saigon and wrote a report recommending that Michigan State "provide, and the Foreign Operations Administration (later the Agency for International Development) underwrite, a massive program of foreign assistance."[16]

The MSUG "conducted the largest technical assistance program of any American university," expending approximately $25 million (including $15 million in equipment and other material aid programs charged to the U.S. economic aid mission). The MSUG contained individuals who armed and trained Diem's secret police, formulated methods of repression and population control, provided professorial cover for the CIA, and Americanized various educational, political, and social institutions.[17] Whether providing cover for the CIA or formulating methods of population control or attempting to "reform" the Saigon bureaucracy, all of these programs were funded by Washington as part of a neocolonial policy.

> In 1954, in the professed belief that it ought to extend the "American way" abroad, Michigan State University (MSU) offered to provide the government of Vietnam with a huge technical assistance program in four areas: public information, public administration, finance and economics, and police and security services. The contract was approved in early 1955, shortly after the National Security Council (NSC) had endorsed Diem, and over the next seven years MSU's Police Administration Division spent fifteen million dollars of U.S. taxpayers' money building up the GVN's (Saigon's Government of Vietnam) internal security program. In exchange for the lucrative contract, the Michigan State University Group (MSUG) became the vehicle through which the CIA secretly managed the South Vietnamese "special police."[18]

Douglas Valentine goes on to analyze how MSUG's Police Administration Division reorganized Diem's police and security forces. He focuses primarily on the Vietnamese Bureau of Investigations (VBI), the most powerful security force which "received the lion's share of American 'technical' aid." The VBI, which existed primarily to suppress Diem's domestic opposition and also served the CIA, had its most promising officers "trained by the CIA and FBI at the International Police Academy at Georgetown University in agent handling, criminal investigation, and counterinsurgency." The VBI became "one of the two foundation stones of Phoenix," the program responsible for rounding up hundreds of thousands of "Vietcong sympathizers," killing approximately 40,000 Vietnamese, and committing countless atrocities. "Whereas the majority of Michigan State's police advisers were former state troopers or big-city detectives, the men who advised the VBI and trained Diem's Secret Service were CIA officers working under cover as professors in the Michigan State University Group."[19]

The MSU-CIA association, especially in providing professorial cover for five known CIA agents, has been confirmed by former coordinator of the MSU Vietnam Project Stanley Sheinbaum, assistant MSUG project chief Robert Scigliano, head of the project at the time of its termination Guy Fox, CIA Inspector General Lyman B. Kirkpatrick, Jr., and others. The CIA involvement in the MSUG was not terminated until 1959. "However, the fact of the CIA relationship receives too much of the attention. The Michigan State professors had their own roles—and at all levels. They helped with fingerprinting techniques, bureaucratic procedures, economic policy, the drafting of South Vietnam's Constitution, and even in the choice of Ngo Dinh Diem as President."[20]

Washington was successful in utilizing Michigan State University in its neocolonial designs. Much to the disgrace of academe, almost all of the analysis and opposition to the MSUG was provided by a few scholars long after the technical assistance program had been terminated. In addition, the major motivation for finally terminating this neocolonial program came more from Diem's disenchantment with the United States and a few critical MSU professors than with university disenchantment with neocolonialism. If the programs of the MSUG eventually proved to be unsuccessful and if Washington's general neocolonial policy from 1954 until 1964 failed miserably, this was not because of opposition from scholars of Asia or from the U.S. public, but rather because of Vietnamese resistance to foreign intervention and imperialism, be it French or American.

By 1964, with the failure of neocolonialism and with Saigon about to "fall" to the southern Vietnamese National Liberation Front (NLF), President Lyndon Johnson was left with only two alternatives: He could either escalate or withdraw. He escalated to a full-scale war, determined to have U.S. troops do what the armed forces of the Republic of Vietnam with U.S. assistance had been unable to do. And this policy of direct, massive U.S. military involvement also failed miserably. Johnson realized that the U.S. public would no longer stand for such a policy. He agreed to the Paris talks and had begun to institute a policy of Vietnamization at the time he was forced out of office.

Once again, Washington faced a choice: It could allow the Vietnamese to determine their own future or it could move from full-scale direct U.S. military involvement to a new stage of neocolonialism. The beginning of the Nixon administration is the time we usually identify with the next stage of neocolonialism: Vietnamization.

It was also in 1969 that the Center for Vietnamese Studies and Programs was established at Southern Illinois University (SIU).[21] SIU received government funding for this Vietnam Center because of its aggressive lobbying, sheer opportunism to cash in on anticipated Indochina money,[22] and a proven record of willingness to participate in U.S. objectives in Vietnam.[23]

From 1961 through 1969, SIU actively participated in Washington's neo-colonial goals in Indochina through technical assistance contracts for education and police and prison training. In addition to elementary teacher training contracts funded at several million dollars, SIU had a vocational-technical education contract discussed by the U.S. Agency for International Development (USAID) under "hamlet schools": "This project was conceived as a pacification project aimed at winning the loyalty of the rural populace to the Central (Saigon) Government."[24]

SIU did not qualify for the Vietnam Center grant from USAID on academic or scholarly grounds. Although forty-one individuals from SIU had served in Vietnam during the 1960s, not one had ever written a scholarly article or book on Vietnam. Not one course on Vietnam was taught at the Carbondale, Illinois, campus. Indeed, the first permanent director of the Vietnam Center, Professor H. B. Jacobini, did not know Vietnamese and had never published anything on Vietnam.

Under the leadership of President Delyte Morris, Southern Illinois University, like Michigan State under his friend John Hannah, embodied what President Clark Kerr of the University of California at Berkeley had termed the new "multiversity," easily performing "service" for the government and corporations. Kerr wrote that the "intellect has also become an instrument of national purpose, a component part of the 'military-industrial complex.' "[25] Some of us on the faculty joked that "the sun never set on the SIU empire," with university projects in Brazil, Afghanistan, Nepal, Nigeria, Mali, and other parts of the world. SIU included faculty and administrators, many of whom were involved in the Vietnam Center, who did little or no teaching and research and whose main "academic" qualifications were past connections with the State Department, CIA, and other funding sources and willingness to serve governmental and corporate interests.

In assuming the justification of Washington's policy objectives, including the need to create and support an anti-Communist nationalist alternative in Saigon (now Thieu rather than Diem), a willingness to engage in neocolonial projects, and the decisive role played by several individuals, SIU's Vietnam Center can be seen as a continuation of the Michigan State project. (Soon after its founding, anticenter bumper stickers proclaimed "MSU + CIA = SIU.") The former president of Michigan State University and former assistant secretary of defense, John A. Hannah, served as the head of the USAID during most of the Nixon administration and awarded SIU the grant to establish the center. The man who had helped bring Ngo Dinh Diem to the United States as a consultant to Michigan State University, served as personal friend and advisor to Diem in Saigon, and was the initial contact most responsible for establishing the MSUG was Wesley Fishel. Fishel became the most influential person involved in establishing the Vietnam Center at SIU.[26]

Typical of Fishel's thinking about the Vietnam Center were the following statements made in 1969: "The idea of a Center for Vietnamese Studies is a project that has intrigued me for years. . . . There are a number of obstacles; but the payoff will be great. . . . There are limitless ways you could involve (SIU) students: IVS (International Voluntary Services), AID (Agency for International Development), Navy." Fishel used his contacts to line up a long list of Asia scholars and other individuals to serve as consultants, visiting speakers, and members of the editorial board of a new journal, *Southeast Asia*. With the exception of a few token scholars, who were deceived by Fishel and quickly submitted letters of resignation, not one of Fishel's contacts was known for having an antiwar position or opposing university neocolonial participation.[27]

Next to Fishel, the U.S. scholar of Asia closely associated with the center and most known for complicity with Washington's designs for Indochina was I. Milton Sacks of Brandeis University, who had served as a consultant to the previously described CIA-funded Center for International Studies at MIT; as a consultant with Simulmatics Corporation (another connection with Ithiel de Sola Pool), which conducted secret research in Vietnam for the Pentagon; and as a consultant for the Pentagon's RAND Corporation. In the previously cited August 1967 issue of *Asian Survey* on Vietnam, Sacks contributed an article in which he assumed that the United States had the right to restructure Saigon's government in terms of what Washington determined to be an acceptable anti-Communist nationalism. On 23 October 1970, while at SIU, Sacks reaffirmed his position: "I approve of social scientists performing intelligence work for the CIA."[28]

The grant establishing SIU's Vietnam Center came under the Foreign Assistance Act of 1966, Section 211(d): "Not to exceed $10,000,000 of funds . . . may be used for assistance, on such terms and conditions as the President may specify, to research and educational institutions in the United States for the purpose of strengthening their capacity to develop and carry out programs concerned with the economic and social development of less developed countries."

According to the title of the original USAID grant (CSD-2514 of 29 June 1969) establishing the Vietnam Center, the initial grant of $1 million was intended to "Strengthen within Southern Illinois University Competency in Vietnamese Studies and Programs Related to the Economic and Social Development of Vietnam and its Post-War Reconstruction." SIU claimed to have this capacity through the previous eight years of AID-funded technical assistance projects, which included providing "training to more than 4,000 Vietnamese professionals—including over 200 Province Chiefs."[29]

Task force meetings of the Vietnam Center reveal the thinking of influential people at SIU following the establishment of the Vietnam Center. For example,

John E. King, first acting director, said that the center "will try to prepare people to work in North and South Vietnam, Red China or anywhere. Doing this to support American foreign policy." Howard R. Long, chairperson of the Department of Journalism, claimed: "Bringing people into an advanced program and giving them research capabilities will be useful to the government." Vice President Ralph W. Ruffner stated that "VET was dreamed up as an alternative of the contract to keep us involved in Vietnam. . . . Poats, Asst. Administrator of AID, indicated that AID would favorably consider furnishing the underwriting, $600,000, in addition to the $1,000,000 for such a program (retraining U.S. and Saigon veterans). . . . If one result (of the VET program) would make it better for a small percentage (of veterans participating with antiwar dissenters), we would be making progress."[30]

According to the grant and other sources (such as the *Congressional Record* of 23 June 1969, letters from Hannah and other USAID officials, and the Newsletters and Task Force minutes of the Center), the Vietnam Center was intended to provide "special consultant and training services" for U.S. corporations and for Washington and Saigon governmental agencies; "to retrain" U.S. and Saigon veterans; to engage, through separately funded contracts, in all sorts of technical assistance and postwar reconstruction projects. Clearly SIU was guilty of active and willing complicity with U.S. policies of Vietnamization under Nixon and Kissinger. SIU administrators, assuming some sort of U.S. victory in war, anticipated that the university would be in an advantageous position to secure many millions of dollars of future contracts essential to Washington's neocolonial policies in Indochina.

I shall not present a detailed description and analysis of the successful antiwar and anti-imperialist campaign against SIU's Center for Vietnamese Studies, but this was certainly one of the most intense, dramatic, protracted, and successful Indochina struggles that took place on any U.S. campus during the war.[31] The contrast between Michigan State's earlier participation in neocolonialism of the 1950s and early 1960s and SIU's participation in Vietnamization of the late 1960s and early 1970s is striking. Both universities were unsuccessful in their ambitious Vietnam goals, but the MSUG did manage to undertake important neocolonial projects and evoked little or no opposition from scholars of Asia or other critics of the war until long after its termination. SIU's Center, by contrast, was from its start a source of great controversy. Founded at the height of the antiwar movement and when scholars of Asia were becoming increasingly disillusioned with U.S. policies, the center was never able to realize its neocolonial objectives.

The most important role in the successful anticenter struggle was played by the Vietnamese, who made the issues of Washington-funded technical assistance and postwar reconstruction projects moot.[32] Second in importance were the local antiwar activists, who kept continuous pressure on the center for years after antiwar activism had dissipated on most campuses; who organized numerous teach-ins, protests, exposures, marches, guerrilla theater, and other militant activities; and who suffered hundreds of arrests, beatings, expulsions, and firings.[33] Third in importance was the indispensable role

*A number of scholars integrated their scholarship with activism. Pictured here is an affinity group sitting with other demonstrators in Lafayette Park near the White House. They had come to Washington, D.C., for the big 1971 May Day demonstration to "Stop the War or We'll Stop the Government." Thirteen thousand people were arrested later that day in connection with the demonstration. From left to right in the foreground are Mitchell Goodman, Zee Gamson, and Cynthia Fredrick (national coordinator for the Committee of Concerned Asian Scholars). From left to right in the background are the members of the affinity group—Marilyn Young, Mark Ptashne, Fred Branfman, Howard Zinn, Daniel Ellsberg, and Noam Chomsky. (Photo courtesy of Daniel Ellsberg.)*

played by antiwar scholars of Asia, especially those in the Committee of Concerned Asian Scholars (CCAS), who had special skills and contacts and whose efforts were complementary to those of the Vietnamese and local antiwar activists.

The Vietnam Center became the major university issue for CCAS and the most controversial Indochina–U.S. university issue in the Association for Asian Studies. CCAS played a major role in organizing a number of national conferences in Carbondale and an effective international boycott of the Vietnam Center by Asia scholars. The struggle against the Vietnam Center represented one of the few clear-cut victories over academic support for and involvement in U.S. neocolonial designs for Indochina. In many respects, the campaign against the USAID-funded Center represented what antiwar scholars of Asia could do best: presenting scholarly analysis of U.S. policies and what was happening in Indochina, documenting the role funding agencies played in carrying out Washington's priorities and in shaping the field of Asian studies, revealing the role individual scholars and academic institutions played as an integral part of U.S. Indochina policies, and integrating such scholarship with intense anti-imperialist activism.

**REDEFINING THE LIVES
OF ASIA SCHOLARS**

Throughout the 1970s, most U.S. scholars of Asia with a strong antiwar and anti-imperialist position were either members of the CCAS or identified with the CCAS orientation as formulated in its "National Statement of Purpose" quoted below. Although CCAS chapters no longer exist, the CCAS orientation is continued through its international journal, the *Bulletin of Concerned Asian Scholars (BCAS)*.[34]

During the past fifteen years, many of these antiwar Asia scholars have shared with me some of their thoughts, feelings, commitments, and expectations in the late 1960s and early 1970s and how subsequent developments (in Indochina and other parts of Asia, in U.S. policy, and in Asian studies) influenced their analysis, commitments, and careers. Their personal histories revealed not only nostalgia, regret, bitterness, and dedication, but also much about the nature of the field of Asian studies, U.S. policies toward Indochina, developments within Indochina, and the struggles of progressive scholars to make sense of these power relations and to analyze and support anti-imperialist forces in Asia. For this reason, it seemed that contacting these antiwar scholars would be a valuable means for revealing some of the effects of Asia scholars on the Vietnam/Indochina War, and, even more so, the effects of the war on scholars of Asia.

My focus was on progressive scholars of Asia who identified easily with the "National Statement of Purpose" of the CCAS:

> We first came together in opposition to the brutal aggression of the United States in Vietnam and to the complicity of silence of our profession with regard to that policy. Those in the field of Asian Studies bear responsibility for the consequences of their research and the political posture of their profession. We are concerned about the present unwillingness of specialists to speak out against the implications of an Asian policy committed to ensuring American domination of much of Asia. We reject the legitimacy of this aim and attempt to change this policy. We recognize that the present structure of the profession has often perverted scholarship and alienated many people in the field.
>
> The Committee of Concerned Asian Scholars seeks to develop a humane and knowledgeable understanding of Asian societies and their efforts to maintain cultural integrity and to confront such problems as poverty, oppression, and imperialism. We realize that to be students of other peoples, we must first understand our relations to them.
>
> The Committee of Concerned Asian Scholars wishes to create alternatives to the prevailing trends in scholarship on Asia which too often spring from a parochial cultural perspective and serve selfish interests and expansionism. Our

organization is designed to function as a catalyst, a communications network, for both Asian and Western scholars, a provider of central resources for local chapters, and a community for the development of anti-imperialist research.[35]

In May 1988, a questionnaire was sent to twenty-two antiwar and anti-imperialist scholars of Asia, and thirteen responded.[36] I was determined not to slant the survey in the direction of those who have impressive publication records and have had more "normal" academic careers. It was important to include the majority of those promising scholars of Asia who left, or were forced to leave, the field of Asian studies or have had a series of short-term academic appointments without any job security.

Each of the following four antiwar scholars is taken as representative of an increasingly larger grouping. The first and by far smallest group of scholars, well established by the late 1960s, is represented by Noam Chomsky, already recognized by then as the world's foremost linguist; this group includes such influential professors as Howard Zinn, Franz Schurmann, Gabriel Kolko, and George McT. Kahin. A number of these well-known scholars were Indochina and Asia specialists; others like Chomsky and Zinn might never have directed much of their attention to Asia had it not been for the war.[37]

A second and larger group, represented by Mark Selden, consists of young faculty members starting out in the late 1960s or early 1970s, who, while they have usually had far from "normal" academic careers, have managed to remain productive anti-imperialist scholars within the field of Asian studies.

A third and much larger group, represented by Nina Adams, consists of those earlier Asian studies graduate students, often in Vietnam and Indochina studies, whose Indochina experiences redefined their lives and academic careers in unexpected directions; they have survived within an academic context either by shifting their focus away from any Indochina or Asia specialization or by accepting a series of unattractive short-term positions.

The fourth and by far largest group, represented by Martha Winnacker, consists of graduate students and some young faculty, whose Indochina experiences redefined their lives so that they were never given the opportunity to pursue an academic career or had short-lived careers because of lack of funding as well as firings and tenure denials. Some of these scholars tried to relate to Indochina and Asia through limited alternative nonuniversity ways; most simply gave up on any possibility for a scholarly career as an Asian studies specialist.

## THE ESTABLISHED SCHOLAR: NOAM CHOMSKY

Noam Chomsky, Institute Professor at the Massachusetts Institute of Technology, is not only one of the world's foremost linguists and a major influence in many other disciplines, but he is also one of the leading radical critics of U.S. foreign policy. In confronting the Indochina War, he felt that he could not do otherwise than drastically redefine his scholarly priorities and his personal life.

DOUG ALLEN: How did you become involved in the antiwar movement?

NOAM CHOMSKY: In the mid-1960s, when I became seriously committed to antiwar activity, I felt that it was a completely hopeless effort, and undertook it only because it seemed impossible to refrain. In the early years, it was largely a matter of speaking to very small groups in the hope that the audience would outnumber the organizers. I tried my hand at congressional lobbying of the Massachusetts delegation; serious issues, such as the U.S. attack against South Vietnam, could not be raised at the time; the words could not even be heard.

Public events were not easy to manage in Boston. The first major demonstration on the Boston Common in October 1965, where I was a speaker, was broken up by a hostile crowd, including many students; all of this with the enthusiastic support of the media, who were as scandalized as liberal senators such as Mike Mansfield that anyone should dare to criticize the bombing of North Vietnam.

When a few of us tried to organize tax resistance, we sent out 10,000 letters to people whose names had appeared in ads and received about 50 responses. When Paul Lauter asked me to help organize support efforts for draft resisters, it seemed like a hopeless cause, though one that could not be evaded.

DA: How did this rather grim situation change?

NC: By the end of 1966, things were beginning to change, and 1967 was very different, with the huge Pentagon demonstration and many other actions. By then, there was a government response to resistance, and several of us anticipated spending years in jail—which, I expect, would have happened had the Tet Offensive not changed elite policy with regard to the prosecution of the war and the treatment of domestic opposition. Meanwhile, speaking and demonstrations, including much civil disobedience and many arrests, were a regular occurrence, and popular involvement grew enormously, much to my surprise.

By 1968, the student movement began to self-destruct. I recall a leading SDS (Students for a Democratic Society) intellectual telling an audience that the war was now "a liberal issue" and we should turn to more serious concerns. But popular opposition to the war, among students as well, continued to grow; and with it, a change in the cultural climate of profound and long-lasting significance, with the rise of the women's movement, the ethnic movements, and others, a phenomenon that continued, contrary to much propaganda, through the 1970s. Dissidence is now, in my opinion, more widespread and solidly rooted in substantial parts of the population than ever, and the general sophistication, outside of elite intellectuals, has also deepened considerably. I now give talks anywhere in the country of a sort that would have been virtually impossible even in peace movement circles at the peak of antiwar activism.

DA: What were your feelings about Indochina?

NC: My feelings in the late 1960s were rather grim. Particularly with the murderous post-Tet accelerated pacification campaign, I felt that the U.S. had substantially won the war, in terms of its minimal, not its maximal objectives. As I wrote at the time, the possible outcomes seemed to me either virtually

*Noam Chomsky speaking at Social Responsibility Week at the University of California at Berkeley, May 1982. (Copyright © 1982 John Spragens, Jr. Reprinted with permission.)*

complete destruction of Indochina or North Vietnamese domination over the whole region, since "no other viable society will remain," local forces elsewhere being unable to sustain the increasingly violent U.S. assault. That view I have not changed.

The U.S. did not attain its goals of reincorporating Indochina within the global system it came to dominate after World War II, but it did succeed in ensuring that the "virus" of successful independent development would not "infect" regions beyond, to use the terminology of Kissinger and others. In Indochina, the virus was destroyed, and surrounding areas were "inoculated" with murderous coups and terror (Indonesia, Thailand, the Philippines, and elsewhere). Sophisticated elements in the business community came to the same view. I think there has been overwhelming documentary evidence available for years showing this was the primary U.S. war aim, and it falls quite naturally out of a much more comprehensive global vision.

DA: What were some of your personal commitments at the time?

NC: Those years became a ceaseless engagement in travel and speaking, demonstrating and supporting resistance, and writing when possible. The latter was barely possible apart from movement journals such as *Ramparts* and *Liberation*, with the exception of the *New York Review* for a brief period, effectively terminated in 1972; the media were almost entirely closed, much more so than today, contrary to much illusion. U.S. policy was becoming far better understood in wider circles. The field of Asian studies barely participated with a few notable exceptions, and the founding of CCAS seemed to me then a very promising development, as it has, I believe, proven to be. I am not an Asia scholar. I was then primarily an activist. My prime concern was not really Asia, but U.S. policy and society. That remains so, for me.

DA: How did such commitments change your life and career?

NC: My career and life are very different from what they were twenty-five years ago. I was well aware, when undertaking protest and resistance, that such changes were inevitable, and I was not, quite frankly, very happy to contemplate them. If the world were different, there are other things I'd much rather do. I have tried, over the years, to maintain two quite separate careers, one in research and teaching in several areas that I find intellectually most interesting, and a second as an activist, lecturer, and writer on international affairs and foreign policy. Each of these careers amounts to a full-time commitment, which meant that other things had to give way, primarily personal life. The limits of twenty-four hours a day had become a problem in the late 1960s, and this became increasingly severe in the 1980s. There are, needless to say, very real compensations—personal, emotional, and intellectual.

DA: What were the decisive events that most influenced you?

NC: The escalation of the war in 1964 was, for me, the decisive factor, which made it impossible to avoid any longer a serious commitment to activism. As I began to do more intensive research on U.S. foreign policy and on specific areas of Southeast Asia, I, of course, learned a lot that I had not known, but I can't frankly say that my understanding of the nature and sources of policy has changed in any fundamental way.

Trying to identify specific events that influenced my perceptions and feelings is not easy. There were too many. One element was the great courage shown by many young resisters. Another was a trip to Indochina, which had a large emotional impact, particularly in Laos, where I learned a great deal, thanks primarily to Fred Branfman.[38]

DA: What are some of your present thoughts regarding the future of Indochina and of U.S. policies?

NC: With regard to Indochina, it is only possible to observe with continuing horror how U.S. elites have proceeded to "bleed Vietnam" to the extent possible, reveling in their successes in ravaging Indochina and leaving it in a state from which it may not recover for 100 years; and to watch as the very effective U.S. ideological system labored to refashion the history of those years so as to establish the basis for new atrocities, which were not long in coming.

As for the future, with all the horrors and tragedies of the past years, and the new ones that are yet to come, there is still a noticeable and very significant change in this country, a very healthy change, impelled by the dissidence and activism of the 1960s, which has helped stimulate a dissident culture of quite significant scale as well as a moral and intellectual revolution that I suspect cannot be reversed. It is simply a very different country than it was twenty-five years ago, elites excepted. The changes are much too slow, but nevertheless detectable, and they offer what hope there is for a decent future.

## THE YOUNG FACULTY MEMBER: MARK SELDEN

Mark Selden began his teaching career in history and Asian studies at Washington University, St. Louis, in 1967. He was one of the key members of the Committee of Concerned Asian Scholars and has been an editor of the *Bulletin of Concerned Asian Scholars* since its beginning. Although more of a China specialist, his scholarship and life have been deeply influenced by the Indochina War. Most recently, he was part of a scholarly delegation to Vietnam in the summer of 1990.

DOUG ALLEN: What were your first antiwar commitments after you began teaching?

MARK SELDEN: From the fall of 1967, I was active in CCAS and in the antiwar movement in St. Louis and in Japan. The original impetus for CCAS in the spring of 1968 came out of the graduate student group at Harvard. Together with Felicia Oldfather and a few other graduate students from Washington University, I attended the Philadelphia Association for Asian Studies meetings when CCAS was born.[39] Perhaps our scholarship and our politics could be brought into unity.

I was among those organizing a summer seminar at Harvard in 1968 and 1969 exploring issues of the U.S. in Asia and imperialism. This was one of the first CCAS activities directed toward rethinking issues of imperialism and revolution and eventually led to a book, *America's Asia: Dissenting Essays in Asian American Relations* (1971), coedited with Edward Friedman.

DA: How did this commitment develop in the early 1970s?

MS: I was working on, and attempting to connect, several fronts and issues: antiwar activism, particularly GI resistance support work and the McDonnell Project in St. Louis,[40] and efforts to develop and promote a critical scholarship, reconceptualizing perspectives on revolutionary change and imperialism, focusing on Indochina and China. This also meant finding ways to bring the fruits of our research to wider "mass" audiences and attempting to influence public policy and popular views on the war and on China. This is where, at the borders of intellectual work and political activism, I felt we could make a contribution.

So I became involved with the *BCAS*, serving as coeditor in the early 1970s. I also sought to promote the series of CCAS books that began with our *America's Asia*, continued through *The Indochina Story* (our most important scholarly contribution to the antiwar effort), and our most widely read effort, *Inside the People's Republic of China*. While the Indochina War seemed to me to be the central issue, I was also active in supporting recognition of China in the early 1970s.

I saw antiwar and anti-imperialist Asia scholars, through CCAS, as building alternative scholarship and an alternative institutional fabric transcending the irrelevance or worse of the Association for Asian Studies and sought to make our annual meetings (coinciding with AAS meetings) important forums for debate and challenge. This we did with some success in the years 1969–1972 or so before the Indochina-China divisions[41] and the withdrawal of U.S. forces eroded our unity and our strongest appeal to others in or entering the profession.

DA: As a young faculty member how did you relate to the more established Asian studies professors?

MS: The late 1960s context provided a fruitful climate for students and some young faculty to think critically about the Indochina War, imperialism and U.S. imperialism in particular, and revolutionary change in Asia. This was a wrenching experience for many of us. Just as we were attempting to "become professionals" as scholars of Asia, we found ourselves critically questioning and challenging the wisdom handed down by many of our most respected teachers.

Well, that was a dimension that included intergenerational conflict and combat. But that was only one dimension. Many of our teachers had also been critics of post–World War II U.S. policy in Asia and some had paid for it with destroyed or aborted careers during the McCarthy years. So it was important that liberals like John Fairbank, Mary Wright, and Owen Lattimore, for example, helped to open up some of the critical terrain, even though their students would in many cases rush beyond them and frequently enter into conflict on issues of both scholarship and politics.[42]

DA: What have been the major changes in your career?

MS: I taught in the departments of history and Asian studies at Washington University from 1967 until 1979. In the late 1960s, I redirected my principal research to issues of the Indochina War and the American empire. This involved collaborative works (*America's Asia, Open Secret: The Kissinger-Nixon Doctrine in Asia,* and *Remaking Asia: Essays on the American Use of Power*).

From the early/mid-1970s, while continuing antiwar work, much of my scholarship was redirected back toward the Chinese revolution. Indeed, from the early 1970s to the present, my principal research has centered on problems of Chinese development and socialist transitions, stimulated initially by the Cultural Revolution and subsequently by the post-Mao reform agenda.

From 1979, I joined the sociology department and the Fernand Braudel Center at SUNY Binghamton, working with a strong core of critical scholars, a variety of Marxist, radical and world-system perspectives, and many Third World students. The intellectual milieu has been supportive and stimulating. Yet the central strand of CCAS at its best, and of the antiwar movement, the ability to link our work in the classroom and our writing with ongoing popular movements challenging the political status quo, has been elusive, to say the least, for over fifteen years. This remains the central, and for me, quite unresolved dilemma, and the heart of my own auto-critique.

DA: What are some of your present thoughts and feelings about Asian studies?

MS: CCAS, in small ways, as a stream feeds a mighty river, made some praiseworthy contributions: to raising the costs and thereby helping to end the war against the Indochinese peoples; to opening a new page in U.S. relations with China; to undermining the hegemony of modernization theory and other dominant ideologies of U.S. postwar hegemony.

Yet the moments that tasted sweetest also spelled the end of CCAS as an organized movement, though not the end of some of our intellectual work, particularly through the *BCAS*. Above all, the beginning of the end of U.S. military intervention in Indochina also spelled our fragmentation as Indochina-China divisions sharpened and the earlier unity dissolved.

That unity also dissolved intellectually. We challenged, with some success, some of the dominant models for comprehending America and Asia. It became possible, for example, to discuss revolutionary change in sympathetic ways little known earlier in U.S. discourse of the postwar era. And as the issues of American imperialism were debated by Marxists, dependency and world-system theorists, and others, CCAS may be seen as a small part of that debate: less interesting theoretically to be sure, but drawing strengths of empirical research missing in much of the critical literature and thereby enriching it. Yet our organizational challenge to the establishment Association for Asian Studies was short-lived and in the end abortive; and our intellectual opening also tended to be absorbed in other debates even as it contributed to them.

## THE GRADUATE STUDENT: NINA ADAMS

Nina Adams was one of many bright young graduate students of the 1960s who were drawn to Indochina studies and had every reason to believe they would be among the next generation of leaders in Asian studies. While still a graduate student at Yale University, she and Alfred McCoy coedited *Laos: War and Revolution*. The Indochina War radically redefined her life and career.

DOUG ALLEN: What were your expectations and commitments in the 1960s?

NINA ADAMS: I had been part of the first demonstration against Mme. Nhu in spring 1963 at Cornell and had taken a seminar with P. J. Honey, who was a consultant to McNamara and knew the U.S. planned to get ever more heavily involved.

I visited Vietnam in the fall of 1966 and was most struck by the size of the U.S. military machine, the youth of the GIs, the crowding of Saigon with refugees, and the imperviousness of Americans to what Vietnam was as a culture and a political cauldron.

I believed that the Asian studies establishment was in bed with the CIA and the Pentagon, and that American policy was genocidal in impact if not in intent. I believed that the war was about keeping U.S. hegemony and about a racist indifference to Vietnamese deaths and wounds, and that those who made policy would use young Americans as cannon fodder in the most cynical way.

I believed that the Vietnamese had a right to choose their own socialist form of government, the National Liberation Front (NLF) was primarily a southern force, and the Third Force would be crushed by American intransigence.

DA: You were one of the most active antiwar scholars of Asia right from the beginning.

NA: Yes, in the fall of 1966, Leigh and Richard Kagan, Len Adams and I, Dave Denny, John Berninghausen, Ted Farmer, and one or two others sent a mailing from Taiwan (conveyed to Hong Kong for us) to 200 members of the Association for Asian Studies asking them to come out against the war. There was very little response. When we returned to the U.S. in the spring of 1967 (I as a graduate student at Yale), we were in touch with others who talked about setting up meetings to begin what became the Committee of Concerned Asian Scholars. The organizing of the Vietnam Caucus for the Philadephia AAS meeting in 1968 was done by others. (See Note 39.) What I remember was John King Fairbank trying desperately to be our leader and restrain us simultaneously.

DA: What have been the major changes in your life and career?

NA: In the late 1960s, most of us expected to be the major figures in Asian studies in the future. This did not occur. Those graduate students and young faculty who seemed never to have had an original idea found secure positions, while creative scholar-activists were most often driven from Asian studies.

For me, the career change came in 1973 when, after three years of expatriation, I took a teaching position at a working-class university (Sangamon State University) rather than a major research center. This meant I would not be an Asia scholar. I have no regrets. In retrospect, I'm sure that I would have been prevented from getting any other kind of academic job.

Had it not been for the war and the antiwar movement, I would have been working in the South; I had started political work in the civil rights movement, and Howard Zinn was my model. Had it not been for the antiwar movement, I would not have expatriated for three years and joined the women's liberation movement in London, worked with it in Paris and Hong Kong; I consider myself lucky to have been introduced to feminism in very socialist, analytical, and activist contexts somewhat different from those in the U.S. at that time.

DA: What were the decisive events in the U.S., Indochina, and Asian studies that most influenced you?

NA: Decisive events were the assassinations of John F. Kennedy and Ngo Dinh Diem; Lyndon Johnson's sending troops that ensured a long struggle; Association for Asian Studies indifference to the issues and constant complicity in the war; AAS calling in the Pinkertons at their annual meeting to protect their cozy arrangement; visiting Vietnam in 1966 and observing the election farce in September; meeting Vietnamese in France and discovering that I did not have to be 200 percent on their side or become Vietnamese, but that I had reached the right conclusions on the issues; finding out that the white male Left in which I had been raised was impervious to change in response to feminism; and working with Vietnam vets beginning in 1973 after working with deserters in Europe.

DA: What is your present situation?

NA: I'm a tenured associate professor of history and women's studies at an open admissions university, which had previously fired and punished me on several occasions. I consider myself primarily a women's studies person. Two of my six courses each year are on Asia. I use my Asia background in teaching contemporary history, feminist science fiction, feminist theory, and women and development. I think it's crucial for all area studies people to integrate their analysis and information into "mainstream" courses.

DA: What are your present thoughts and feelings regarding Indochina, U.S. policy, and Asian studies?

NA: I returned to Vietnam twenty years after my first visit, and what impressed me most was the combination of poverty and determination. I don't expect much in the way of material improvements, and I don't expect U.S. policy to change. I believe the U.S. is taking its revenge, and those who fought in Vietnam and were junior people are now upper management in the U.S. They have fought the Vietnamese to the last Cambodian. Just as Ollie North started his glorious career in Laos, so did many others now found under rocks in Central America and selling drugs all over the world.

I am not optimistic. I believe we underestimated the complexity and strength of imperialism, the naked economic power that the U.S. can use even as we were correctly analyzing the elements of neocolonialism. We underestimated the power of the covert warriors. And we seriously underestimated the extent and effectiveness of liberals and cold warriors and those feathering their nests in Asian studies. We never laid a glove on them, and the proof is in viewing who has been driven from the field, who has been marginalized, and who has been made successively redundant, the gypsy scholars and free lancers of whom there are fewer each year.

I've learned that the fierce independence of the Vietnamese has never let them take much advice from foreigners; that CCAS's track record for analyzing and predicting revolutionary movements is a good one; that our record in analyzing U.S. moves is good, but our success in countering them is negligible.

The Vietnam War occupied twelve years of my life, dominated my politics, delayed my dissertation, took me past my confused career goals into understanding where my commitments are. We are marked by the war years as an earlier generation was marked by the Depression, and like them, find our insights and passions often misunderstood or labeled foolish by the next generation, which is more obedient and acquisitive, more of what we would have been if we hadn't encountered issues of life and death at an early age. The war taught us that people our own age could waltz off in pretty uniforms and come home in boxes; that entire villages could cease to exist when someone like ourselves pushed a button in a high tech machine; that friends could be driven to drop out, drug out, suicide out, and sell out when the war went on and on and so did the government's opposition to our very existence. We are not who we started out to be in the prosperous years of the 1960s. Some of us have made our peace with who we are and who we might have been, and some of us have not.

**THE GRADUATE STUDENT: MARTHA WINNACKER**

Martha Winnacker, while a graduate student at Berkeley in the late 1960s, was typical of many young Asian studies scholars who would have devoted little if any attention to Indochina if it had not been for the war. The Indochina War became their central concern and in many cases led these young scholars in directions that precluded possibilities for an academic career.

DOUG ALLEN: How did you relate to Vietnam in the late 1960s while at Berkeley?

MARTHA WINNACKER: Although I had come from an extremely conservative background, I was horrified by the war in Vietnam and saw it first as a slaughter and second as an intervention against a struggle for self-determination. Academically, my interest was in China and its revolution, but the political project of the day seemed to me to be ending the war. Ultimately, the tension between political and academic commitments was more than I could handle, and I left graduate school in 1970, abandoning my fellowship and with an unfinished Ph.D.

DA: Describe some of the Asian studies activism at Berkeley.

MW: The Committee of Concerned Asian Scholars came to Berkeley in late spring of 1968. During the next two years, we drafted flyers, ran speakers' bureaus, formed a contingent in demonstrations, and talked about such things as activism versus professionalism. The front line of Berkeley activism shifted to Third World Studies[43] and People's Park.[44] We became a sort of "me-too" participant. The focus shifted to Asia in 1970 with the invasion of Cambodia, and CCAS became a dynamic center for information; I think this was our high point.

DA: Starting in 1971, the Indochina Resource Center (IRC), through its *Indochina Chronicle* and other projects, was one of the key sources of educational information for the antiwar movement.[45] How did you become part of the staff at the IRC?

MW: The Indochina Resource Center had a Berkeley office, and I began working there in 1976, traveling to Vietnam for the IRC in 1977. David Marr was leaving for Australia, John Spragens was moving to Texas, and David Barton was taking his first "real-world" job. They faced closing the center or finding a whole new staff to take it into the postwar era. They pieced together a group of part-timers, who were not Indochina specialists.

DA: This became the Southeast Asia Resource Center?

MW: Yes, thanks to a generous and unusual grant from the Christopher Reynolds Foundation, the renamed Southeast Asia Resource Center (SRC) was able to expand and stabilize for five years between late 1977 and 1982. We upgraded the *Southeast Asia Chronicle* and developed a growing network of scholars and activist writers. The *Chronicle* was widely used by activists and in some circles of the academy. I alternated between the Thailand and Indochina desks. Unfortunately, the SRC never had enough money to send staff on research trips, and, in any case, I was having babies and not free to travel. Eventually, I began to restrict my own writing in favor of editing the work of people with more firsthand or in-depth knowledge. In retrospect, I'm not sure this was necessary or wise, but it was dictated by a very academic kind of respect for sources and specialization.

DA: What were the major issues at the SRC regarding Vietnam and Indochina?

MW: SRC was very much affected by charges of human rights violations against Vietnam, by the Vietnam-Kampuchea war, and by the Vietnam-China split (which also led to splits between the Vietnamese and Thai and Filipino revolutionaries). I think we dealt with these issues with a critical honesty not always apparent in other circles.

I was particularly disturbed by the way a lot of progressive China specialists in academia seemed to swallow the Chinese versions of events whole and embraced the U.S. opening to China, which came quite explicitly at the expense of normalization with Vietnam at the end of 1977. Going to China was a good thing, of course, but the cost to the Vietnamese of continued U.S. hostility—expressed in the trade embargo, denial of desperately needed aid, and active support for the defeated Khmer Rouge—has been enormous.

We who first defined our professional lives in terms of ending the war owed it to the Vietnamese to push hard for postwar aid and reconciliation. (I think it is reasonable to argue that continuation of U.S. hostility helped consolidate the position of the most security-conscious hardliners in Hanoi.) I think it was and is possible to criticize anything we found wrong in Vietnam while simultaneously pushing for aid and normalization. This position was not fashionable.

DA: How did such positions on Vietnam and Indochina affect the SRC?

MW: We at SRC didn't agree with each other on the Vietnam-Kampuchea-China issue, and we published a *Chronicle* outlining our differences, but we continued working together and for normalization of relations with Indochina. We lost support, though, both because a fair number of people were so distressed by those events that they stopped working on Asia and because some people thought we should take an institutional stand. The critical blow came when the Reynolds Foundation decided to phase out support for the SRC, not over the Vietnam-China debacle but because (I think) they were uncomfortable with the amount of attention we were giving to the Philippines and other non-Indochina countries.

DA: How did the closing of the SRC affect your feelings about the antiwar scholars of Asia with whom you had identified?

MW: It took two years for the SRC to die, and that experience left me with a lot of unanswered questions about the whole idea of our alternative goals and commitments. In a nutshell, where was everybody? In essence, I think SRC embodied precisely the ideals CCAS was organized around: making scholarship on Asia usable beyond the academic context and in the interest of thwarting imperialism. Yet we got very little support from such scholars of Asia, particularly the academic ones, and I often sensed (perhaps I am hypersensitive?) a kind of academic snobbism toward what we did, the same kind of issue we used to debate in terms of activism versus professionalism. Did we not count for much because we functioned outside the university context?

For me personally, it turns out that spending eight years in a very low-paying, avowedly anti-imperialist institution was a very costly thing to do, since it left me with no "career" track, money, or security. I, of course, am not an isolated case. I've seen this kind of situation for people like Sandy Sturdevant, Joe Moore, and Cheryl Payer. I can't help thinking that many of us have paid an inordinate price for making a professional commitment to the kind of activist scholarship progressive Asia scholars once professed. Nobody in an "alternative" institution has much security, which is why there are so few of them, but the Asia network seemed particularly unable to spread a safety net or even a solidarity handshake.

I guess I'd like to pose a challenge to the idea of what progressive Asia scholars stood for by asserting that there has to be some communal sense of responsibility for maintaining and nurturing the institutions and the people who embody what we believe in. I don't think CCAS, for example, ever really exisited in that way, but there was a vague sense of a largely invisible community, and CCAS did pose the ideal.

DA: What are your present feelings about Asian studies?

MW: I'm not really sure. Asian studies gave me a framework for idealism and perhaps a rather impractical context within which to work. If nothing else, it taught me humility and the importance of developing my own political positions rather than anointing any movement or government as by definition correct. I've missed it since I've been out of the field, and part of my pondering now is whether I can find a way back in that builds on what I have done. At the same time, I'm trying to deal with such tough questions as whether one can jump on the Pacific Rim commercial bandwagon without serving the very forces we were committed to challenging, specifically multinational-driven "development."

**KEY ISSUES FOR ANTI-IMPERIALIST SCHOLARS OF ASIA**

In this concluding section, I shall formulate some of the issues that confronted antiwar scholars of Asia during the Indochina War and in many cases continue to confront those who have remained within Asian studies. Most of our focus will be on scholars of Asia who were members of the Committee of Concerned Asian Scholars, since that was the major grouping of U.S. anti-imperialist scholars, but these issues were also relevant to the concerns of other progressive Asian studies scholars.

**ACADEMIC COMPLICITY**

Some of the older scholars in Asian studies had known colleagues who had been purged, especially during the McCarthy era, or had themselves suffered from repressive political backlash. There was a desire by some to uphold an ideal of detached scholarly "objectivity," free from political influences, or at least to avoid being dragged into a potentially bloody, political controversy. A number of the older scholars were admired by the younger faculty and by their graduate students, and the ensuing battles often produced complex and ambivalent generational relations.

It was the war in Indochina that really forced the confrontation of issues of academic support for and, in some cases, direct involvement in U.S. Indochina policies. Most scholars had defined their scholarship as "nonpolitical," "value free," "objective," "avoiding extremes," and falling within the "gray" areas of the mainstream academic status quo. Much of their "nonpolitical" research and service was for the government, corporations, and the military, but this was rarely challenged as being shaped by definite value assumptions and commitments and as highly political. The Indochina War and reactions outside and within the field of Asian studies radically changed this situation. Contradictions were rendered explicit and intensified; the somewhat illusory but effective huge "gray," "nonpolitical," "middle" of the past rapidly deconstructed and collapsed, forcing most scholars to take sides.

Strong antiwar opposition led to the recognition of the "complicity of silence of our profession" with regard to U.S. policy, as the CCAS Statement of Purpose began. But this was often more than some well-intentioned, innocent, or unaware position of scholarly silence tacitly upholding U.S. policies. "Complicity" conveys the sense of participation or association with wrongdoing. When one analyzed the highly political funding sources, the well-paid and influential faculty consulting positions with governmental agencies and corporations, and the vital participation of some professors in technical assistance projects, it became apparent that many in Asian studies, as clearly revealed in the Indochina field, were actively participating in U.S. neocolonial policies. Many graduate students and faculty began to make the connections, as when they analyzed the interlocking structures of the military-industrial-academic complex.

Antiwar critics were often attacked for attempting to "politicize" the academic discipline of Asian studies. But anti-imperialist critics had found that the field of Asian studies was already highly politicized. Exposing and criticizing such academic complicity with the U.S. war effort became one of most important contributions made by progressive scholars of Asia.

## SCHOLARSHIP VERSUS ACTIVISM

Probably the major division within the Committee of Concerned Asian Scholars and within other anti-imperialist groups and caucuses in history, economics, sociology, and other disciplines was between those scholars who viewed their work as a source of alternative radical scholarship and those who saw themselves as part of an action-oriented "movement" deeply involved in contemporary struggles. As is clear from the Statement of Purpose and the histories of CCAS and the BCAS, there was an ideal of an activist scholar and a scholarly activist. Radical Asia scholars could bring their scholarly knowledge and skills to activism; and it was an activist commitment that helped to distinguish their approach and analysis from others in Asian studies. Unfortunately, this was easier said than done, and there existed and continues to exist a tension between scholarly and activist priorities, approaches, and goals.

For example, many anti-imperialist scholars have felt that they should strive to publish technical, specialized, scholarly articles meeting the highest standards of "establishment" journals. They could "beat the establishment scholars at their own game," critiquing their assumptions, hidden agendas, distortions, ethnocentrism, and false objectivity, while demonstrating that their alternative analysis was more objective, more rigorous, more scholarly. For some scholars, the Indochina experience had been a temporary aberration, forcing them into a mild activism; in their scholarship and basic temperament, they were not activists.

On the other hand, there were anti-imperialist scholars who included in their research projects an essential activist orientation. Some antiwar activists felt that at least part of their research should be accessible and of use to general readers and to other anti-imperialist activists who were not Asia scholars. They argued that when the BCAS and other "alternative" publications moved in the direction of nonactivist, "respectable," "legitimate" scholarship, it was more a sign of defeat than scholarly achievement.

The basic scholarship-activism tension continues within alternative publications and within the scholarly community relating to various anti-imperialist struggles. At its best, it becomes a creative tension, making real some of the ideals and challenges formulated in Asian studies in the late 1960s.

## UNREALIZED EXPECTATIONS AND CAREERS DESTROYED

Many young antiwar and anti-imperialist scholars correctly felt that they were "the best and the brightest" of their generation; these were the progressive and creative scholars who would become future leaders in Asian studies. Instead, the overwhelming majority of such activist scholars either never secured any academic position, voluntarily left or were forced out of Asian studies, have struggled through a series of temporary positions, or finally attained some university or other employment outside the specialized field of Asian studies. Among the major reasons that their academic hopes were dashed and their careers destroyed were the following developments.

First, and probably most important, were the consequences from the United States losing the war in Indochina, at least in terms of priorities involving funding of Asian studies. While Washington continued its efforts to undermine any stability in Cambodia and to devastate Vietnam, teaching the lesson that revolution does not pay, the kinds of cultural, educational, and technical assistance programs necessitating major university participation were no longer a priority. Funds for Indochinese studies were drastically cut, with positions eliminated and careers destroyed.

Second, at least partially related to the backlash resulting from the U.S. failure in Indochina, were the many political purges, firings, denials of tenure, and difficulties in securing research grants and other funding.[46] Those of us successful in challenging the firings and denials of tenure were a small and lucky minority. Meanwhile conservative scholars, U.S. veterans, Vietnamese refugees, and graduate students and young faculty who had been guilty of complicity or who had posed no challenge to the status quo were much more likely to be rewarded with the limited number of Indochina positions within Asian studies.

Third, some young faculty and graduate students may have miscalculated their own antiwar and anti-imperialist strengths as well as the potential weaknesses within the Asian studies establishment.[47] These progressive scholars raised a number of excellent issues, such as the antiwar opposition to U.S. policies in Indochina, the exposure of academic participation in that largely discredited war, and the need for U.S. recognition of China. These issues sometimes seemed to place activist-oriented scholars on the offensive, and the Asian studies establishment on the defensive. CCAS conferences, for example, with speakers such as Noam Chomsky, Howard Zinn, and Eqbal Ahmad, were dynamic, intense, challenging, and significant, attracting large, highly motivated audiences; sessions at the neighboring AAS meetings, by contrast, were often on highly specialized scholarly topics, which struck most Asia scholars, not to mention any larger general audience, as rather trivial and of interest to only a few. At the national meetings of many scholarly associations, activist scholars passed or came close to passing antiwar and anti-imperialist resolutions.

But all of this scholarly activism really created illusions of seriously challenging for power. As soon as the antiwar activism dissipated and the Indochina War ended, it became clear that the Asian studies establishment was firmly in control and could use its considerable financial, political, and academic connections and resources to shape the future direction of the field.

Fourth, a significant number of faculty, who might have defended and supported the victimized activist scholars more strongly, did not do so because their orientation during the late 1960s and early 1970s was somewhat misleading. They were not activists and had for many years during the 1960s resisted taking antiwar and anti-imperialist stands. The pressing Indochina and China issues, as well as pressure from their graduate students and young faculty, finally forced them to oppose the established policies. Even then, their opposition, when examined in retrospect, was usually very weak, only infrequently expressed as the ideological resistance of an anti-imperialist activist scholar. With the diplomatic recognition of China and the end of the Indochina War, they resumed their more comfortable academic orientation and were easily absorbed within the mainstream of Asian studies.

The withdrawal of many professors from even mild scholarly activism not only had consequences for the unrealized expectations and destroyed careers of young radical scholars but affected other issues we have considered: less research exposing academic complicity and the military-industrial-academic complex; less of an activist component in the scholarship-activism tension; greater difficulty in sustaining anti-imperialist organizations and publications.

## UNRECOGNIZED ACCOMPLISHMENTS

In light of these developments, in many respects resulting in the elimination or neutralization of a generation of scholars of Asia, there has been an understandable reaction of nostalgia, bitterness, and regret on the part of some radical scholar activists. But it's important to emphasize that this is only part of the story. Just as most people involved in the antiwar movement felt frustrated and powerless and never realized the profound effect they collectively had on restraining and changing U.S. policy toward Indochina, on the downfall of Lyndon Johnson, on the forced withdrawal of U.S. troops from Cambodia in 1970, and on the events leading to Watergate and the downfall of Nixon, many antiwar and anti-imperialist scholars of Asia minimized or overlooked their own accomplishments.

As indicated by Mark Selden, the legacy of CCAS—when combined with other scholarly developments largely rooted in the 1960s—profoundly changed the context within which many of us teach and write. Profoundly changed have been not only more academic contexts, but also the contexts within which many scholars reach out to the larger community.

For example, before a second national conference in October 1971 to expose and organize against the Vietnam Center at Southern Illinois University, local activists discussed the dangers of the title: "Imperialism: USA & SIU." True, we were struggling against U.S. imperialism in Indochina and SIU's eager complicity in such neocolonial objectives, but we had not studied Lenin, Nkrumah, and the other major theorists of imperialism. We felt somewhat apprehensive about our ability to formulate a rigorous analysis of imperialism. In addition, would the term "imperialism" confuse, or even offend, many in our audience? (It didn't.)

Today, many progressive scholars, without a second thought, quite naturally use such terms as imperialism at the heart of our teaching, writing, and public speaking. Many have had the same kinds of experiences as those shared by Noam Chomsky in his response: He can now present radical analysis to audiences throughout the United States in ways impossible even during the height of the anti–Vietnam War movement. Progressive scholars have found the same legacy in their Central America, Persian Gulf, antiapartheid, and other activism, often involving attempts to share and apply the lessons of Vietnam and Indochina to contemporary U.S. policies and anti-imperialist resistance.

## SWING TO THE RIGHT?

Before doing the survey for "Antiwar Asian Scholars and the Vietnam/ Indochina War" and speaking with many other scholars, it was my belief that there had been a definite swing to the right on the part of former antiwar and anti-imperialist scholars of Asia. There certainly seemed to be such evidence outside Asian studies, as in the well-publicized transformations of Tom Hayden renouncing his earlier radical positions; of Peter Collier and David Horowitz, formerly of *Ramparts*, defining themselves as neoconservatives and attacking the Left with a vengeance; of millions of former antiwar demonstrators becoming the self-centered, me-generation, career-oriented professionals of the 1980s.

There seemed to be at least a partial analogy with political shifts from the 1930s. A large number of Left intellectuals had romanticized and uncritically identified with the Soviet Union. The Stalinist revelations left most of them stunned and disillusioned. Many gave up on their former radical activism. A minority of these intellectuals from the "Old Left" swung sharply to the right and included some of the most vicious opponents of the antiwar, student power, black power, and feminist movements in the late 1960s, as well as some of the most prominent neoconservatives identified with *Commentary* and other liberal-turned-reactionary publications.

Similarly, it seemed that many of the young antiwar and anti-imperialist scholars of Asia had romanticized and placed Vietnam and China on a pedestal. With the revelations about the Cultural Revolution and the Gang of Four, the postwar reeducation camps in Vietnam and the fleeing Vietnamese "boat people," and the genocidal policies of Pol Pot and the Khmer Rouge in Cambodia, many former activist scholars also seemed stunned and disillusioned and some turned sharply to the Right.

It is now my position, on the basis of more evidence, that my earlier impression was largely inaccurate. What is remarkable is how deep and lasting were the formative influences of the 1960s on the antiwar and anti-imperialist scholars. An entire generation of activist scholars had their fundamental values, commitments, ideals, world views, and orientations shaped by the Vietnam/Indochina War.

While being extremely self-critical, often angry and bitter, and sometimes poking fun at their earlier romanticism and miscalculations, these scholars, much more often than not, speak proudly of their past antiwar and anti-imperialist commitments, struggles, and ideals. They have not renounced their opposition to class exploitation, monopoly capitalism, imperialism, racism, sexism, and academic complicity with unjust policies. What is truly remarkable is how few of the radical scholars, even when faced with the prospect of unemployment and being forced out of Asian studies, reversed their positions, took what they perceived to be tainted money, and sold out their own values for the sake of careerism.

## NOTES

For their helpful suggestions, constructive criticisms, and support, I express my appreciation to Ilze Petersons, Noam Chomsky, Ngo Vinh Long, John Kelly, Mark Selden, Martha Winnacker, Douglas Valentine, Howard Schonberger, Michael Howard, Susan McEachern, and Bill and Nancy Doub.

1. See George McT. Kahin, *Intervention: How America Became Involved in Vietnam* (New York: Anchor Press/Doubleday, 1986), pp. 78–92 and 456–460; Gabriel Kolko, *Anatomy of a War: Vietnam, the United States, and the Modern Historical Experience* (New York: Pantheon Books, 1985), pp. 82–96 and 567–568.

2. Although much of this research is classified, it is surprising how many revealing studies are in the public domain. For example, the RAND Corporation publishes documents such as *A Bibliography of Selected Rand Publications: Asia* (Santa Monica, CA: The RAND Corporation, Jan. 1985), which lists articles written for RAND, many by professors, under such headings as "counterinsurgency." Many of Noam Chomsky's books are full of such self-incriminating revelations. See Noam Chomsky, "Objectivity and Liberal Scholarship," in *American Power and the New Mandarins* (New York: Vintage Books, 1969), pp. 23–158; and Noam Chomsky, "Indochina: The Next Phase," in *For Reasons of State* (New York: Vintage Books, 1973), pp. 259–284.

3. See, for example, Senator J. William Fulbright's comments in the *Congressional Record* of 13 December 1967, in which he charged that universities, under the corrupting

influences of access to money and power, had "joined" the military-industrial complex, thus "betraying a public trust." In a speech at Denison University in 1969, Fulbright asserted that "tempted by lucrative government contracts, many universities—especially the big and famous ones—have become neglectful of their paramount responsibilities and have gone dangerously far toward becoming servants of the state. Because the major source by far of government contract funds is the military establishment, the universities have been drawn primarily into military, or militarily useful, research in physical and social sciences, becoming in the process card-carrying members of the military-industrial complex." Quoted in Jonathan Feldman, *Universities in the Business of Repression: The Academic-Military-Industrial Complex in Central America* (Boston: South End Press, 1989), p. v.

4. See Ellen W. Schrecker, *No Ivory Tower: McCarthyism and the Universities* (New York: Oxford University Press, 1986); Michael Paul Rogin, *The Intellectual and McCarthy: The Radical Specter* (Cambridge, MA: MIT Press, 1967); Richard Kagan, "McCarran's Legacy: The Association for Asian Studies," *Bulletin of Concerned Asian Scholars* 1, no. 4 (May 1969), pp. 18–22; O. Edmund Clubb, "McCarthyism and Our Asia Policy," *Bulletin of Concerned Asian Scholars* 1, no. 4 (May 1969), pp. 23–26; and Ross Y. Koen, *The China Lobby and American Politics*, edited by and with an introduction by Richard Kagan (New York: Harper & Row, 1974).

5. While fewer U.S. troops were fighting and dying during this period of Vietnamization, it is important to note that this was the stage of the heaviest U.S. bombing of Indochina. A key assumption of Vietnamization policy was that the U.S. public would be less concerned about the war and less resistant to Washington's policy, even if the devastation of Indochina continued and escalated, so long as the policy resulted in a "changing of the color of the corpses."

6. Michael T. Klare, *The University-Military Complex: A Directory and Related Documents* (New York: North American Congress on Latin America, 1969). There are many studies of the military-university relationship. See, for example, Sidney Lens, *The Military-Industrial Complex* (London: Kahn & Averill, 1971), pp. 123–138, in which Lens lists numerous universities engaged in military research on poison gas and germ warfare, defoliants and herbicides targeted for Indochina, and "anti-personnel" and incendiary weapons designed to counter guerrilla warfare in Vietnam; Sidney Lens, *Permanent War: The Militarization of America* (New York: Schocken Books, 1987), pp. 185–193; James Ridgeway, *The Closed Corporation: American Universities in Crisis* (New York: Random House, 1968); Seymour Melman, *Pentagon Capitalism: The Political Economy of War* (New York: McGraw Hill, 1970), pp. 97–106; Jonathan Feldman, "The Warfare State and the University," and "Growing Pentagon Hegemony over Universities," in *Universities in the Business of Repression*, pp. 139–223.

7. *Educational and Nonprofit Institutions Receiving Prime Contract Awards for RDT&E, Fiscal Year 1987* (Washington, DC: Directorate for Information, Operations and Reports, the Pentagon, 1988); Feldman, *Universities in the Business of Repression*, p. 160.

8. David Wise and Thomas B. Ross, *The Espionage Establishment* (New York: Random House, 1967), p. 153. "Langley" refers to the CIA headquarters in Langley, Virginia.

9. Ithiel de Sola Pool, "The Necessity for Social Scientists Doing Research for Governments," in Irving Louis Horowitz, *The Rise and Fall of Project Camelot* (Cambridge, MA: MIT Press, 1967), pp. 267–280; Pool, "Political Alternatives to the Viet Cong," *Asian Survey* 7, no. 8 (August 1967), pp. 555–566; Chomsky, *For Reasons of State*, pp. 316–317; Chomsky, *American Power and the New Mandarins*, pp. 49–50; Chomsky, *At War with Asia* (New York: Pantheon, 1970), pp. 60–62. Issues of Robert Scalapino's *Asian Survey* devoted to Indochina are often invaluable in revealing the ideological biases and value-laden research of Asia scholars in furthering U.S. political and corporate interests.

10. James Ridgeway, *The Closed Corporation: American Universities in Crisis*, p. 146.

11. *Ibid.*, pp. 6, 146–150.

12. Feldman, *Universities in the Business of Repression*, p. 164; see Appendix 2: Military Advisors and Their Academic Affiliations, pp. 295–299; see also Howard Ehrlich, "The University-Military Research Connection," *Thought and Action* 1, no. 1 (Fall 1984), pp. 119–120.

13. Marvin Harris, "Big Bust on Morningside Heights," in Mitchell Goodman, ed., *The Movement Toward a New America* (Philadelphia: Pilgrim Press; New York: Alfred A. Knopf; 1970), pp. 26–30; reprinted from *The Nation*, 10 June 1968.

14. Frank Baldwin, "The Jason Project: Academic Freedom and Moral Responsibilities," *Bulletin of Concerned Asian Scholars* 5, no. 3 (Nov. 1973), pp. 2–12; reprinted from *Christianity and Crisis*, 18 Sept. 1972 and 11 Dec. 1972.

15. Jonathan Goldstein, "Vietnam Research on Campus: The Summit/Spicerack Controversy at the University of Pennsylvania, 1965–67," *Bulletin of Concerned Asian Scholars* 15, no. 4 (Oct.–Dec. 1983), pp. 26–38. See also Seymour M. Hersh, *Chemical and Biological Warfare, America's Hidden Arsenal* (New York: Anchor Books, 1969), pp. 185–186; Sol Stern, "War Catalog of the University of Pennsylvania," *Ramparts* 5, no. 3 (August 1966), pp. 32–40.

16. Robert Scigliano and Guy H. Fox, *Technical Assistance in Vietnam: The Michigan State University Experience* (New York: Praeger, 1965), pp. v–vi, 1ff.; Warren Hinckle, with Sol Stern and Robert Scheer, "MSU: The University on the Make," *Ramparts* 4, no. 12 (April 1966), pp. 11–23.

17. For documentation and analysis of the MSUG, see Hinckle, with Stern and Scheer, "MSU: University on the Make"; Scigliano and Fox, *Technical Assistance in Vietnam*; Robert Scheer and Warren Hinckle, "The Vietnam Lobby," in Marcus G. Raskin and Bernard B. Fall, *The Viet-Nam Reader* (New York: Vintage Books, 1965), pp. 66–81 (reprinted from *Ramparts* 4, no. 3, July 1965, pp. 16–24); Robert Scheer, *How the United States Got Involved in Vietnam* (Santa Barbara, CA: Center for the Study of Democratic Institutions, 1966); Stanley K. Sheinbaum, "The Michigan State–CIA Experience," *Bulletin of Concerned Asian Scholars* 3, no. 2 (Winter 1970–1971), pp. 71–75; Douglas Valentine, *The Phoenix Program* (New York: William Morrow, 1990); Irving Louis Horowitz, *Professing Sociology* (Chicago: Aldine Publishing Co., 1969); Frances Fitzgerald, *Fire in the Lake* (New York: Vintage Books, 1973); Gloria Emerson, *Winners and Losers* (New York: Random House, 1976; HBJ paperback, 1978); Annual Reports of the United States Operations Mission (USOM) to Vietnam.

18. Douglas Valentine, *The Phoenix Program*, p. 31. In a dramatic claim, Sidney Lens (*Permanent War*, p. 188) asserts that in 1955 the "fifty-four professors from Michigan State University acted as cover for the U.S. to violate the Geneva accords (of 1954). . . . As a whole, this project was the most brazen interference by a university in the internal affairs of another nation, and undoubtedly contributed to the full-scale war that later ensued under President Johnson." See Scheer, *How the United States Got Involved in Vietnam*, pp. 33–38.

19. Valentine, *The Phoenix Program*, pp. 31–35.

20. Stanley K. Sheinbaum, "The Michigan State–CIA Experience," *Bulletin of Concerned Asian Scholars*, pp. 71–72.

21. For documentation and analysis of the SIU Vietnam Center, see the *Bulletin of Concerned Asian Scholars* 3, no. 2 (Feb. 1971). This special issue, devoted entirely to the Vietnam Center, contains a chronology, communications, letters of resignation, and documents; articles on the center by C. Harvey Gardiner, Robert G. Layer, Douglas Allen, David Marr, Nina Adams, Ngo Vinh Long, Huynh Kim Khanh, and Gabriel Kolko as well as articles on AID and on the university. See also the yearly *Annual*

*Report to the Agency for International Development on AID Institutional Development Grant CSD-2514 of June 29, 1969* submitted by SIU; Douglas Allen, "Universities and the Vietnam War: A Case Study of a Successful Struggle," *Bulletin of Concerned Asian Scholars* 8, no. 4 (Oct.–Dec. 1976), pp. 2–16 for an overview; John F. Kelly, *Center for Vietnamese Studies* (privately published; Rantoul, IL: Rantoul Press, 1971), especially for CIA and other governmental connections of center personnel; Jonathan Mirsky, "The Carbondale Caper," *Bulletin of Concerned Asian Scholars* 2, no. 4 (Fall 1970), pp. 71–73; Jim Morrell, "The Carbondale Caper: A Sequel," *Bulletin of Concerned Asian Scholars* 2, no. 4 (Fall 1970), pp. 74–79; *Police on the Homefront* (Philadelphia: American Friends Service Committee, 1971). For a presentation of the remarkable "Vietnamese Invasion of Carbondale" in April 1972, involving fifteen anticenter anti-imperialist Vietnamese, see Gloria Emerson, *Winners and Losers*, and the May 1972 issue of *Thoi-Bao Ga* (Cambridge, MA: Vietnam Resource Center).

22. As part of SIU's aggressive lobbying, Republican Senate leader Everett Dirkson was an influential backer of funding for the Vietnam Center. SIU's opportunism and pecuniary motivation was present from the beginning. SIU administrator Oliver Caldwell sent memoranda of 7 February and 27 March 1969 to Vice President Ralph W. Ruffner indicating that John Hannah's appointment to head USAID, with his emphasis on technical assistance funds, was good news and that SIU should take advantage of this opportunity for funding. The *Daily Egyptian,* the SIU student newspaper, of 15 August 1970, reported that Assistant to the Chancellor and Center backer "(Bruce) MacLachlan, asked why a Vietnam study center was sought by SIU, said the reason was opportunism. . . . First, there were gobs of money available for such a center . . ." In *International Curricula and Degree Programs in International and Area Studies* (a proposal to the United States Commissioner of Education, April–May 1969), SIU Dean John O. Anderson argued that SIU should be a major participant in U.S. postwar reconstruction policies in Vietnam, that the Vietnam Center operating budget for its sixth year (1974–1975) will be $2,500,000, and that the Center will "continue for a period of not less than ten years."

23. A memo of 10 January 1969 from SIU administrator Alfred J. Junz to Vice President Ruffner, while Junz was en route to Bangkok to see individuals about the proposed AID grant to establish the center, contains an itinerary with the names of key people involved in offshore oil and pacification programs in Indochina but with no indication of any interest in meeting with Asia scholars. (Junz had also presented General William Westmoreland with an SIU student petition supporting U.S. policy in Vietnam.) During the spring of 1969, SIU's initial proposal was rejected; SIU then successfully resubmitted the proposal to AID with a list of "scholars" known by Washington to be in favor of U.S. policy in Vietnam.

24. See *Education Projects in South Vietnam* (Saigon: USAID, 1966); *Education Projects in the Republic of Viet Nam* (Saigon: USAID, 1968); John F. Kelly, *Center for Vietnamese Studies.*

25. Clark Kerr, *The Uses of the University* (Cambridge, MA: Harvard University Press, 1963), p. 124. See Richard Lichtman, "The University: Mask for Privilege?" *The Center Magazine* 1, no. 2 (Santa Barbara, CA: Center for the Study of Democratic Institutions, 1968), pp. 2–19, for a strong attack on Kerr's view of the university and for rejoinders by Kerr and others.

26. Historically revealing is Wesley Fishel's article, "Vietnam's Democratic One-Man Rule," *The New Leader*, 2 Nov. 1959, in which he argues that although his friend Diem has the power of a dictator, he doesn't operate like one. This historical falsification, with the need to create a positive public-relations image of Diem (and future anti-Communist leaders in Saigon), was typical of the Vietnam Lobby (which included

Colonel and later General Edward Lansdale—the most influential CIA person in Vietnam, Cardinal Spellman of New York, ex-Austrian socialist Joseph Buttinger, Fishel, Supreme Court Justice William O. Douglas, Senators Mike Mansfield and John F. Kennedy, and other liberal anti-Communist Democrats) and the lobby group Friends of Vietnam, of which several generals and Fishel served as chairpersons.

27. Fishel quotes are from the (Vietnam Center's) Development Advisory Committee, 2 May 1969, and the Task Force on Sisterhood Relationships, 22 July 1969. See "letters of resignation," *Bulletin of Concerned Asian Scholars* 3, no. 2 (1971), pp. 5–12. For additional documentation on Fishel's background and CIA connections, see John F. Kelly, *Center for Vietnamese Studies*, pp. 85–88.

28. I. Milton Sacks, "Restructuring Government in South Vietnam," *Asian Survey* 7, no. 8 (August 1967), pp. 515–526; Chomsky, *American Power and the New Mandarins*, pp. 48–50; Kelly, *Center for Vietnamese Studies*, pp. 88–90.

29. The final Vietnam Center grant proposal (*AID Institutional Development Grant CSD-2514 of June 29, 1969*) submitted by SIU for AID funding appears in the *Bulletin of Concerned Asian Scholars* 3, no. 2 (Feb. 1971), pp. 89–96.

30. Cited in Douglas Allen, "Universities and the Vietnam War," *Bulletin of Concerned Asian Scholars* 8, no. 4 (Oct.–Dec. 1976), pp. 4–5.

31. See Allen, ibid., pp. 2–16, for an analysis of the success of those opposing SIU's Vietnam Center.

32. The anticipated period of Washington's policy of postwar economic and social reconstruction, in which U.S. university participation would have been most needed, never developed. The actual period for postwar reconstruction of Indochina, but without U.S. control and domination, did begin in May 1975. Quite understandably, neither Washington nor U.S. universities have shown much interest in economic and social assistance programs in which the Vietnamese and other Indochinese determine their own priorities and policies. On the contrary, Washington has used its military, economic, and political muscle to block and sabotage such reconstruction and assistance programs from other sources. This claim—that the United States has used its economic embargo and other pressure to punish Vietnam—has been developed in many chapters in this book. See especially Chapters 1, 2, 3, and 5. For some recent mainstream confirmation, see David Banker and others, *Vietnam: An Economic Report* (Washington, DC: World Bank, 1990); and Zamir Hafan and others, *Vietnam—Transforming a State Owned Financial System* (Washington, DC: International Monetary Fund, 1990).

33. As the "OFF-AID" struggle became increasingly effective, measures to punish and silence the center's critics became increasingly repressive. Nearly 400 SIU students were arrested during May 1970 demonstrations, and nearly 100 students were arrested one evening in May 1972. What distinguished SIU from most other antiwar university actions was that the Vietnam Center always presented a specific target as a local manifestation of U.S. intervention and imperialism toward Indochina. Key student activists in the anticenter struggle were not allowed to enroll in classes; some were informed that they were subject to arrest if they set foot on campus; students were teargassed and beaten by police; organizations and classes were infiltrated by informers. The few SIU faculty activist critics also did not escape this repression. For documentation, see the *Bulletin of Concerned Asian Scholars* 3, no. 2 (Feb. 1971); Douglas Allen, "Universities and the Vietnam War"; John F. Kelly, *Center for Vietnamese Studies*.

34. My article on "Antiwar Asian Scholars and the Vietnam/Indochina War" in the "Twentieth Anniversary Issue on Indochina and the War" for the *Bulletin of Concerned Asian Scholars* 21, nos. 2–4 (April–Dec. 1989), pp. 112–134, attempted to provide some sense of the history of the Committee of Concerned Asian Scholars and the *BCAS*. Most of this CCAS and *BCAS* history has been deleted from this article.

35. The Statement of Purpose was adopted at the national meeting of the Committee of Concerned Asian Scholars held in March 1969 in Boston. If one excludes the "Vietnam Caucus" at the March 1968 meeting of the Association for Asian Studies (AAS) in Philadelphia, the Boston conference was the first of a decade of CCAS annual meetings that took place at the same time and in the same cities as the annual meetings of the AAS. The CCAS Statement of Purpose was first published in the *Bulletin of Concerned Asian Scholars* 2, no. 1 (October 1969).

36. In addition to interviews with Noam Chomsky, Mark Selden, Nina Adams, and Martha Winnacker, my article in the special issue of the *BCAS* (see note 34) also included interviews with Ngo Vinh Long, Christine White, Gareth Porter, Edward Friedman, Sandy Sturdevant, Felicia Oldfather, Elaine Emling, James Morrell, and Kathleen Gough.

37. We have previously noted that by the late 1960s, especially after the Tet offensive, a clear majority of U.S. Asia scholars had taken an antiwar position. It is important to clarify that if universities gained an antiwar reputation, this was almost entirely because of students and, to a lesser extent, young faculty. If one examines the writings of the older, more established scholars, for the most part moderate liberals, their "antiwar" positions are surprisingly weak. Usually they came out against the war for rather narrow "pragmatic" and occasionally "moral" reasons (the costs are too great, the U.S. can't win, the war is too bloody, and so on), and only with rare exceptions for the kinds of anti-imperialist "ideological" reasons contained in the CCAS statement of purpose. For a survey of views on the war by the leading "intellectual elite," see Charles Kadushin, *The American Intellectual Elite* (Boston: Little Brown, 1974); Noam Chomsky, *Towards a New Cold War* (New York: Pantheon, 1982), pp. 60–85.

38. Fred Branfman, who observed U.S. destruction of Laos firsthand as a volunteer with the International Voluntary Services (IVS)/Laos, probably did more than anyone else to educate the public and Congress about the U.S. air war in Indochina. He was a founder of the Indochina Resource Center, Director of Project Air War in Washington, D.C., and wrote *Voices from the Plains of Jars: Life Under an Air War* (New York: Harper & Row, 1972).

39. Many respondents referred to the Philadelphia "Vietnam Caucus" held at the same time as the annual meetings of the Association for Asian Studies. In later years, many dated the beginning of CCAS to the Philadephia 1968 meeting. See, for example, the preface to Committee of Concerned Asian Scholars, *The Indochina Story* (New York: Bantam Books, 1970); Jim Peck, "Reflections on the Implications of the Vietnam Caucus," *Bulletin of Concerned Asian Scholars* (called *CCAS Newsletter* until vol. 2) 1, no. 1 (May 1968), pp. 2–4. John Fairbank's view of the Vietnam Caucus is presented in John King Fairbank, *Chinabound: A Fifty-Year Memoir* (New York: Harper & Row, 1982), p. 399, and in Paul M. Evans, *John Fairbank and the American Understanding of Modern China* (New York: Basil Blackwell, 1988), pp. 267–268.

40. McDonnell-Douglas was the largest industry in St. Louis and a producer of bombers for use in Vietnam. In the late 1960s and early 1970s, the McDonnell Project, locally organized with national support, targeted McDonnell-Douglas as a major contributor to the war effort.

41. In the late 1960s and early 1970s, Vietnam and China served for many scholars of Asia as two inspirational models, sometimes romanticized, of revolutionary struggle, perseverance, anti-imperialist resistance, and alternative economic, political, and cultural priorities and values. Washington's obsession with Indochina, the urgency felt by the antiwar movement to prevent the genocide and not become "good Germans," the need to expose and resist the complicity of some Asia scholars in the war effort, and the desire to express solidarity with the Indochinese peoples made the war a top

priority. At the same time, awareness of the emerging importance of China, of the earlier purges of Asia scholars in the China field, and especially the urgency felt in working for U.S. recognition of the People's Republic of China (PRC) made China a top priority. For a period of time, progressive Asia scholars assumed a special role in working for diplomatic and cultural openings with the PRC.

For a period in the early 1970s, an Indochina War–China division emerged in CCAS regarding the priorities of progressive Asia scholars. The China-Vietnam tension within Asian studies was certainly exacerbated in the years following the formal end of the Indochina War. Postwar economic and political developments in both China and Indochina, the Vietnamese invasion of Cambodia at the end of 1978, the Chinese invasion of Vietnam in February 1979, and Chinese support for the Khmer Rouge have resulted in disillusionment and disagreements among Asia scholars.

42. Of the influential mainstream liberal scholars of Asia, John King Fairbank of Harvard seemed most willing to take seriously the criticisms of his younger students and faculty and enter into debate with them. "An Exchange: The C.I.A. at Harvard," *Bulletin of Concerned Asian Scholars* 1, no. 2 (Oct. 1968), pp. 6–12, reproduced a heated exchange of letters between Jim Peck, Jon Livingston, Fairbank, and Ezra Vogel. Peck's "The Roots of Rhetoric: The Professional Ideology of America's China Watchers" appeared in the *Bulletin* 2, no. 1 (Oct. 1969), pp. 59–69 (reprinted in Edward Friedman and Mark Selden's *America's Asia,* Vintage Books, 1971), followed by "An Exchange" between Fairbank and Peck in the *Bulletin* 2, no. 3 (April–July 1970), pp. 51–70. Future issues of the *Bulletin* contained exchanges between Fairbank and his critics on Chinese studies and imperialism. See the *Bulletin* 3, nos. 3–4 (Summer–Fall 1971); 4, no. 4 (Dec. 1972); and 5, no. 2 (Sept. 1973). See Fairbank, *Chinabound,* pp. 399–400, and Evans, *John Fairbank and the American Understanding of Modern China,* pp. 268–81, 316–318.

43. This little-known, at times violent, struggle spread from San Francisco State College, where African-American students demanded a Black Studies program, to Berkeley, with the formation of the Third World Liberation Coalition in early 1969. This militant activist coalition of African-Americans, Chicanos, and Asian-Americans demanded a minority studies program, organized a strike, received considerable support from the community and a sometimes violent response from the authorities. See W. J. Rorabaugh, *Berkeley at War: The 1960s* (New York: Oxford University Press, 1989), pp. 85, 154, 219–220, and 248, for a brief account, not particularly sympathetic to the students, and a useful bibliography.

44. The efforts by a combination of hippie countercultural youth and New Left radical students and others to create a People's Park in Berkeley in the spring of 1969, along with the brutal, sometimes violent response from authorities, has been documented in many sources. Todd Gitlin's *The Sixties: Years of Hope, Days of Rage* (New York: Bantam Books, 1987), pp. 354–361 and 473–474, provides an excellent account. See also W. J. Rorabaugh, *Berkeley at War,* pp. 155–166 and 248–252; William J. McGill, *The Year of the Monkey: Revolt on Campus, 1968–69* (New York: McGraw-Hill, 1982), pp. 164–194; April and May 1969 issues of the radical, countercultural weekly, the *Berkeley Barb;* the August 1969 issue of *Ramparts;* and articles in Mitchell Goodman, *The Movement Toward a New America* (see Note 13).

45. The Indochina Resource Center was founded in Washington, D.C., in 1971 by codirectors Don Luce (its most influential person over the past twenty years), leading Vietnam historian David Marr, and Fred Branfman. The IRC, which opened a West Coast office at Berkeley in 1973, was a major source of information on Vietnam, Laos, Cambodia, and U.S. involvement in Indochina not reported in the mass media. The IRC published the *Indochina Chronicle* and played a key role in the successful campaign to cut off aid to Thieu. The IRC was later renamed the Southeast Asia Resource Center

(East and West Coast offices), and expanded to include Thailand, Malaysia, Indonesia, and the Philippines in addition to Vietnam, Cambodia, and Laos, and published the *Southeast Asia Chronicle*. The SRC continues as the Asia Resource Center, located in Washington, D.C., which since 1987 has taken over the publication of the *Indochina Newsletter* published in the Boston area. See Gloria Emerson, *Winners and Losers*, pp. 339–356.

46. A comprehensive study of the academic-political backlash, repression, and victimization of antiwar faculty in general and progressive scholars of Asia in particular remains to be written. Philip J. Meranto, Oneida J. Meranto, Matthew R. Lippman, *Guarding the Ivory Tower: Repression and Rebellion in Higher Education* (privately published; P.O. Box 12671, Denver, CO 80212: Lucha Publications, 1985) lists many purges and firings and considers several case studies in detail; many of the professors considered in this book had strong antiwar positions, but few were scholars of Asia.

47. There were exceptions to this miscalculation of power. Many of the most active anti-imperialist scholars entertained no illusions: They knew that their challenges to the Asian studies establishment, funding sources, and governmental agencies were very risky, and they had little expectation of some future, "normal" academic career. As Ngo Vinh Long stated in Allen, "Antiwar Asian Scholars," *Bulletin of Concerned Asian Scholars* 21, nos. 2–4 (April–Dec. 1989), p. 121: "I already knew that I was sacrificing my career as well as the security and well-being of my family when I took on various activities after Tet. And so all the things that happened to me from 1978 on were only to be expected."

# 8

# U.S. Veterans: The War and the Long Road Home

Kevin Bowen

> "Vietnam drifted in and out of human lives, taking them or sparing them like a headless, berserk taxi hack, without evident cause, a war fought for uncertain reasons."
> —Tim O'Brien, *If I Die in a Combat Zone*

In the iconography of the war, the short-timer's calendar, the grid penned on the soldier's helmet or pinned up on his wall, marking the number of days left in-country, delineates once and for all the world of the soldier in Vietnam. In this world, Vietnam is not a place or a people, it is an empty expanse of days separating two irreconcilable worlds. Only in retrospect does Vietnam acquire a face or become a place. Then typically Vietnam is a world where our own cultural myths turn back in on us, a monstrous insane place where forces like O'Brien's updated version of Irving's headless horseman run amok. It is no wonder then that veterans and the public, when they look for images of personal reconciliation with the past, feel thwarted and frustrated.

The senselessness and insanity of the Vietnam War was something every U.S. soldier had to come to terms with when he or she returned home. With great courage, against the seductive forces of forgetfulness and myth, many Vietnam veterans struggled toward an articulation of the complex experience of the war they fought in Vietnam and its impact on their lives. Unfortunately, that story has not been adequately recorded.[1] This chapter is an attempt to redress this state of affairs somewhat and is borne out of twenty-odd years of experience grappling with these issues personally and with other veterans, American and Vietnamese.

## REMEMBERING THE WAR

Amnesia about the war, both the amnesia of the individual soldier and society, can be immobilizing. The last few years have seen the publication of numerous novels and personal recollections about the war

250

as well as almanacs and fact books. In effect, some of the facts of the war have been so often quoted that they are inscribed on our consciousness: 2.5 million men and women served in the U.S. armed forces in Vietnam; over 58,000 were killed in combat; over 300,000 were wounded; over 30,000 paralyzed; over 2,500 remain missing in action; and over 100,000 have died of unnatural causes since returning from the war.

This litany of facts is sobering, but as Tim O'Brien points out, when it comes to the war such acts of memory provide a way "to remember and a way to forget, a way to remain a stranger."[2] It is difficult enough to contemplate the faces these figures represent, but further beneath them is buried a whole other layer of flesh: 1.9 million Vietnamese killed; 200,000 Cambodians; 100,000 Laotians; 3.2 million Indochinese wounded; 14 million made refugees.[3]

How can an individual or a society reconcile these figures? In the aftermath of the Vietnam War, this is a question that has for many years gone unposed as we have chosen to remember certain figures and forget others. Understandably, we have chosen to memorialize the pain and sacrifice of veterans, but too often at the expense of other facts.

Still, who were these men and women who went to Vietnam? This is something else we also tend to conveniently forget. The facts on this issue are sobering. During the Vietnam era 27 million men were draft eligible. Of that 27 million, 11 million served in the military and 2.5 million went to Vietnam.[4]

During the years 1964 through 1973, the one abiding concern for the majority of young healthy male Americans was the selective service system and the local draft board. As the years passed by and the war progressed, the power of this institution became quite literally the power of life and death. Consider the facts: in 1965, 16 percent of combat deaths were draftees; by 1967 that figure had climbed to 34 percent; in 1969, 40 percent; and 1970, 43 percent. By 1970, 88 percent of all riflemen and 70 percent of all combat troops were draftees. The casualty rate for draftees was 234 per 1,000; fatality 31 per 1,000.[5]

The numbers were not good and there was a genuine equation between the draft and the prospect of going to Vietnam. For many, the odds were better stacked in challenging, circumventing, or avoiding the draft than they were in accepting it. The odds were better for individual survival. In fact, of the 16 million who never served, over two-thirds claimed to have taken deliberate measures to avoid service. For some the option was the National Guard, for others Canada, for others the system of student deferments. Many enlisted, not for ideological reasons, but rather to avoid the prospect of being drafted and sent to Vietnam. Less than 5 percent of enlistees chose combat specialties as their training preference.

The brunt of the draft burden, as we know, fell on some more than others. It fell primarily on the poor, on working and lower middle-class families, and on minorities.[6] It fell on those who lacked access to higher education (high school graduates were four times more likely to be drafted than college graduates) and to draft counseling; to those who though not ideologically motivated still held trust in institutions and perceptions that we would be on the "good" side or at least that in a complicated moral balance the scales would be weighted toward us; and it fell on those for whom the military offered the hope of escape from a dead-end existence.

The draft sorted and dispensed its verdict along the same lines of class and race upon which the country as a whole stood divided. And it did it in ways that exacerbated the antagonisms along the fissures. For inductees, marching to cadence, the lines of "Jody's got your girl and gone" often conjured an image of a pampered and privileged group of more affluent male evaders, parasites at home. For those who managed to avoid conscription, James Fallows, a Harvard student who fasted down to beneath the weight regulations to beat the draft, fastened a lasting image on the inductees as "the thick-necked proles of Chelsea" in his often reprinted article "What Did You Do in the Class War, Daddy?"[7]

As a matter of experience, before even being sent to Vietnam, before combat duty, soldiers and civilians of the same generation looked across at each other with anger, mistrust, and gross misunderstanding. To accept the truth of what was happening, to acknowledge the overwhelming evidence of draftee casualties and where they came from, or simply put, to accept that meat was being ground out for a machine, would have meant acknowledging complicity in a morally unconscionable atrocity.

For blacks and for the underprivileged the draft and enlistment system worked perhaps too efficiently. Project 100,000, an initiative of the Great Society, by 1966 was inducting 100,000 men annually into the military who would not have met peacetime standards of enlistment. Emerging from Daniel Moynihan's 1965 report, the program sought to offer blacks and the under-privileged an opportunity to break out of poverty through training and careers in the military. Over 40 percent of the New Standard soldiers were from minorities. For blacks especially, Moynihan saw the program as a way of winning back self-respect through exposure to military male role models, discipline, and training. Curiously, Moynihan seemed blind to the fact that in the year of his report 23.5 percent of the men killed in action in Vietnam were black.[8]

Project 100,000 had precedents. On August 13, 1964, less than two weeks after the Gulf of Tonkin Resolution, the Defense Department announced a special training and enlistment program that would take in 11,000 rejected volunteers. This was not enough, however; in May of 1966 Selective Service began administering tests to college students and there was discussion of calling up the reserves. The August draft call of 46,200 was to be the largest since Korea. On 23 August 1966, implementation of Project 100,000 began.

In a speech endorsing Project 100,000, Secretary of Defense Robert Mc-Namara paternalistically spoke of its potential benefit to young blacks:

What these men badly need is a sense of personal achievement. . . . They have grown up in an atmosphere of drift and discouragement. . . . It is not simply the sometimes squalid ghettos of their external environment that has debilitated them—but an internal and more destructive ghetto of personal disillusionment and despair. . . .[9]

What McNamara did not mention was that for most of these young men there would be no special training because no funding for special training had been appropriated; that 47 percent of these new enlistees would be draftees, not eager volunteers; that 40 percent would receive combat-related assignments, 37 percent in the infantry in Vietnam; that 36,000 of them would be killed, wounded, or dishonorably discharged before serving their first eighteen months. For an inordinate number of these men, then, the socializing experience of the military that was to lift them from the "destructive ghetto of personal disillusionment and despair" was a combat assignment in Vietnam. These men would see no irony in Michael Casey's lines: "If you own a farm in Vietnam, and a house in hell / Sell the farm / And go home."[10]

Blacks bore more than their share of the fighting in Vietnam, and their casualty rate was 30 percent higher than whites in Vietnam. Few had the option of the reserves or National Guard; and in seven states, including Mississippi, Alabama, Louisiana, and South Carolina, there were no blacks on local draft boards. In fact, in 1966 only 1.3 percent of all local draft-board members in the country were black.

This is not intended to present an image of the veteran as victim, rather to point out that from the start inequities bred resentments and anger; and for perhaps the first time in our nation's history, military service in a time of conflict was considered a sort of negative privilege. In spite of Reagan's reformulation of the war as a "noble cause" in 1980, it is important to remember there was no public appeal to patriotic duty made in raising this army to fight in Vietnam. No ad campaigns or posters depicting heroism or the need to heed a national call, draftees and enlistees were merely offered a rite of passage into manhood, a chance to do the right thing, and an opportunity to earn a bit of respect that was in the end less than forthcoming. Support for the war was mostly couched in expressions of support for the troops in Vietnam, never in terms of support for the necessary massive mustering of men. In essence, the problem of the hostile and indifferent homecoming veterans received was already engendered in the going forth.

Men and women went to Vietnam, then too often bore a sense of isolation and difference from the society that sent them. They had little knowledge of the long history of conflict in Vietnam that preceded their arrival; no knowledge of the culture into which they were immersed to be both friend and foe to virtually the same people; and with little ideological conviction. In the countryside, in jungles, fire bases, casualty clearing stations, and in the cities they fought a war marked by incredible contradictions. In the midst of a war conducted with the assistance of the most sophisticated technology—people sniffers, B-52s dropping bombs from invisible heights, swift and incredible fire power and air mobility—the individual soldier still found himself slogging through an entrenched situation not much different from the trench warfare of World War I. Despite the exertion of often continuous deadly bombardments, troops in the cities found themselves vulnerable to terrorist attacks,

*An Khe, 1st Air Cavalry, 1968. (Photo by C. E. Queen, from "Nam and the Sixties: A Personal American View." Collection of the William Joiner Center for the Study of War and Social Consequences, University of Massachusetts Archives.)*

troops at firebases found themselves day and night under harassing mortar and rocket attacks, and troops in the field suffered through scenario after scenario where they were used as bait to draw out an enemy who knew that all he had to do was wait to bring the fight onto his own turf and under his own terms.

Much as in World War I, where the front began to be defined as a world unto itself, a world beyond simple physical descriptions or geographical coordinates, Vietnam came to take on a reality of its own: it became "the Nam," a way of life and a place having little relation to home and "the world." Back in the "world" there were the assassinations of Martin Luther King, Jr., and Bobby Kennedy, there were the presidential elections and secret peace plans; there were the Paris talks and discussions of what shape the table at the talks should be; on an eerie night in July 1969, there was even a man walking on the moon; but in Vietnam there was only one thing, the war.

In the midst of these events, soldiers passed day and night over the Pacific, traveling to and from the consuming reality of the war. As the years clicked by, the passage became more difficult; Vietnam had become a war that no one on either side of this transit had much good to say about. In 1969 came Vietnamization, the shifting of the burden of fighting from U.S. to Vietnamese troops, changing the color of the bodies some said. For U.S. soldiers, it meant the end might be in sight at last. The irony of the soldier's lot in Vietnam became palpable. Who would be the last U.S. soldier to be killed in this morass?

**COMING HOME** Many veterans could not reconcile or forget what they had seen and experienced in Vietnam. Their frustration when they began to speak out was vividly caught by David Rabe in his play *Sticks and Bones*. Here the veteran returns from Vietnam to his Ozzie-and-Harriet family who insist on rejecting his experience because it threatens their all-American sitcom family script. But he will not go away. At the end of the play, the family assists him in committing suicide. But it is not a real suicide, in the end his suicide means only his silence, a collective amnesia.

The homecoming was hard. It was also somewhat surreal. Most came home alone, leaving friends behind.[11] There were exceptions. There were even parades. But there was something surreal about them as well. In July 1969, there was a parade in Seattle for troops coming home as part of the first phase of withdrawal. The parade was authentic, but not its makeup. This was not a returning unit, but a grouping of men under the banner of a unit that was being officially withdrawn. Most of the troops marching did not come from this unit. What had happened was that men at the end of their tours were brought home a bit early; those in the unit with more time left in Vietnam had been transferred to other units. To make up the difference, other men at the end of their tours in other divisions had been transferred into the unit. Still the papers reported the men "had their sights fixed on Mom's cooking."[12] They did not report on what the men who had been surreptitiously transferred out of the unit and left in Vietnam had their sights still fixed on. The homecoming was to work according to script and be publicly wholesome no matter what the truth was behind the scenes.

Like Rabe's hero, veterans were to return quietly to pick up their lives where they had left them. This was a difficult task. In 1969, just as the first wave of 1 million veterans was returning, Nixon began to cut back on government spending and private borrowing. Veterans preference meant little when there were 5 percent cutbacks and personnel freezes in the government. A massive public-relations campaign ("Jobs for Veterans") didn't help much with few jobs available and no public funding. In Chicago in 1972, when only 88 out of 7,000 veterans attending a federal "job fair" found work, veterans responded by wrecking the interviewing stands. Their anger was understandable. By the end of 1971, there were more unemployed veterans at home (330,000) than there were soldiers in Vietnam. By the end of 1972, there were more former soldiers in U.S. prisons (300,000) than troops in Vietnam.

The Veterans Administration (VA), meanwhile, was both ill equipped and ill disposed to addressing the issues of returning Vietnam veterans. Over half its budget was dedicated to serving older veterans with nonservice-connected illnesses and disabilities. With little experience in treating soldiers just returned from battlefields, unable to respond to veterans demanding the immediate attention they expected, the VA itself soon became a battlefield.

Angry encounters became commonplace. In the spring of 1972, *Time* ran a piece entitled "The Violent Veterans." The "human time bomb" view of veterans passed into popular currency. Television programs like "Kojak" and "Hawaii Five O" seemed to feature a deranged vet once a week as their villain.[13] It was a strange time in America. It was as if Vietnam veterans had been suddenly beamed down from the planet Mars. They were no longer the sons and daughters everyone knew; they were aberrant, bizarre, and unruly. Some were even "un-American."

The role of veterans in the antiwar movement has been loosely documented, but the actual history of the emergence of antiwar veterans and their organizing into local as well as national groups is only now being studied.[14] One very important effort to organize Vietnam veterans against the war and to fight spreading amnesia occurred between 31 January and 2 February 1971, at the Howard Johnson Motor Lodge in Detroit, where the Vietnam Veterans Against the War (VVAW) held open testimony on the conduct of the war under the title "Winter Soldier Investigations." Across the river in Windsor, Ontario, Vietnamese students who had survived massacres or imprisonment for political offenses held similar hearings. Visas for students planning to attend the hearings from North Vietnam were denied. At the end of the three days a Peoples Peace Treaty was signed by the U.S. veterans and South Vietnamese student representatives.

The testimony was powerful and moving. Veterans spoke openly of the hard facts of standard operating procedures in Vietnam. Yet no one seemed to want to listen. The veterans were frustrated. Later, in Washington in April 1971, 1,500 VVAW members (Nixon claimed that less than 30 percent of them were veterans) camped out on the mall in Operation Dewey Canyon III, demanding an end to the war, amnesty for resisters, public hearings into the charges of war crimes against the peoples of Indochina, increased GI benefits, and proper care and treatment for all veterans, including psychological and drug counseling programs.

As the press sifted through these events for appropriate images, the substance of the veterans' grievances received short shrift. Yet, the veterans themselves came away with a strong sense of solidarity and empowerment. John Kerry, now a U.S. senator from Massachusetts, put the issue into the framework of a last mission in his testimony before the Senate Foreign Relations Committee, where he now serves:

> We are determined to undertake one last mission, to search out and destroy the last vestige of this barbaric war, to pacify our own hearts, to conquer the hate and fear that have driven this country these last ten years and more, and so when thirty years from now our brothers go down the street without a leg, without an arm, or a face, and small boys ask why, we will be able to say 'Vietnam' and not mean a desert, not a filthy obscene memory but a place where America finally turned and where soldiers like us helped it in turning.[15]

This "last mission," this "turning point," was to take on many faces in the years ahead. In March 1973, with the Peace accords signed and the prisoners of war (POWs) returned, the country entered a second period of selective and collective amnesia. After 1973, and especially after 1975, Vietnam veterans were more or less abandoned to confront their contradictory experiences and the contradictory responses these experiences evoked alone. For most Americans, Vietnam simply disappeared from the map.[16]

During the years of the Ford and Carter administrations, the issue of postwar reconciliation was a purely domestic issue. Clemency, amnesty, and pardons were the issues most publicly debated. Although, after much debate, sweeping measures were instituted to "pardon" resisters, the more difficult cases of 500,000 deserters and 400,000 veterans with less than honorable discharges were left to languish out of the public eye. For veterans the conditions for reconciliation were fairly straightforward: separate the issues of the warrior, the veteran, from the issues of the war. Issues such as Agent Orange, unemployment, psychological readjustment, and disability compensation replaced the issues of the war. For veterans to agree to this agenda meant better treatment, but it also meant the emergence of a pathology of the veteran, a reinforcement of the image of the marginalized, troubled, and "violent" veteran.

Silence on the subject of the war was enforced in many ways. Self-censorship operated to some extent as veterans learned that it was sometimes better to leave their record of military service off their job applications, especially where spin codes might offer employers a view into that record. The press seemed stuck on domestic atrocity stories—Viet vets gone amok. Commercial publishing houses seemed uninterested in pursuing understanding of veterans or the war.[17]

For many veterans, the answers lay in returning to school. In spite of inadequate federal benefits, many veterans were able to return to state universities and colleges. Unfortunately, the enrollment rate was highest for those who already had some college (55.7 percent). For those with a greater educational need, the rates were lower: 27 percent for high school graduates, 13 percent for high-school dropouts. This was a period of often quiet grass-roots organizing. In Massachusetts, for example, from a few campus veterans organizations in the mid-1970s, the numbers grew to over forty such organizations by the end of the 1970s. A common experience of frustration and exclusion brought veterans together to mobilize behind efforts to establish programs to address their needs.

Many states established their own special commissions to examine the issues veterans were raising. Over twenty-four states established Agent Orange commissions. In Congress, a Vietnam-era veterans' caucus was established. A national organization, Vietnam Veterans of America (VVA), was established under the leadership of former members of VVAW. With the dedication of the Vietnam Veterans Memorial in Washington, D.C., it seemed for a moment that the nation was at last recognizing and reconciling with those veterans.

Throughout this mobilization, there was one unwritten law: Don't talk about the war. Veterans stuck to domestic issues. The perception of an official government policy of neglect coupled with insinuations of government and chemical company collusion in the issue of Agent Orange transformed the image of the Vietnam veteran from social aberrant to social victim, a sort of populist hero victimized by big government and big business. Although there were substantive gains for veterans in terms of programs and recognition, the materials for the making of the Rambo myth were accumulating.

In the late 1970s and early 1980s, amnesia about the war was transformed into a recasting of the war in terms of cultural myths that found the Vietnam veteran at their center. Films like *Apocalypse Now* and *The Deer Hunter* resonated with images and references connecting the war in Vietnam with a cultural legacy that encompassed such disparate elements as authors James Fenimore Cooper and Joseph Conrad. The war in Vietnam was the continuation of the march of empire westward, the veteran protagonist a typical U.S. "isolato." Curiously, both films have military personnel missing in action (MIAs) at their centers, Kurtz and Michael, heroes whose silence is only broken by the moment that is at once both their deliverance and death.[18] The individual and collective repositories for the experience of this war, they both go insane and then die before they can tell us the truth.

With the release of the Rambo films the plot takes a strange twist as the fate of the Vietnam veteran is directly linked to the fate of the abandoned POWs. In the Rambo films both the veterans and the POWs have been abandoned and betrayed by their government. This is a powerful and arresting myth. Its power can actually be tracked in the emergence of the POW-MIA issue in the 1980s as an issue of paramount importance to veterans[19] and as the images of Vietnam in both film and television took on traditional heroic mantles.

For those who did wish to talk about the real war, there were problems because the myths were more comfortable to hold onto. As an example, in Boston when Sylvester Stallone came to Harvard to receive his Man-of-the-Year Award from the Hasty Pudding Club, a group of Vietnam veterans picketed outside. The veterans were less than amused when groups of teenagers told them to go "back where they came from," that Sylvester Stallone was a real vet, they weren't.

Veterans wishing to counter the powerful hold these myths exert over the young and the general public have done everything from picketing the films to giving out body bags at shopping malls where G.I. Joe and Rambo dolls are sold. As in the incident described above, these actions had, for the most part, mixed results.

For most veterans the domestic agenda remained the most vital. In spite of internal disagreements among groups, in the late 1970s and early 1980s there emerged a sense of a community of veterans with a distinct mission, a mission that was to be carried forward without the use of the traditional symbols appropriated by veterans' organizations. Action was itself taken to be healing if it was done in concert with other veterans. And there was much to be done. The particular issues of black, Hispanic, Asian, and women veterans remained largely unaddressed through the decade after the war. Only with the concerted

*Vietnam veterans Kevin Bowen (left) and Ralph Timperi (second from left) are introduced to a former North Vietnamese soldier (center) at a center for the disabled in Hanoi. All three had fought in Tay Ninh. (Photo by Leslie Bowen. Collection of the Joiner Foundation.)*

efforts of these groups did the Veterans Administration and traditional organizations begin to face them. Other issues such as homelessness (30 percent of the homeless are veterans), Agent Orange, post–traumatic stress disorder (PTSD) (40 percent of Vietnam veterans exhibit some symptoms), and bad discharges still require resolution. They remain the Vietnam veterans' calling card before the U.S. public.

## THE ROAD HOME: GOING BACK

But in the juggling of all these priorities, there is a sense for many veterans that some ultimate law of physics is being denied. Vietnam still remains the emotional nub, a point that pulls at us, an elastic memory that tugs, tenses, and releases at the oddest times, often making the most mundane and most critical moments in the lives of veterans reverberate with meanings, creating sometimes lost moments and sometimes saving graces.

Since 1986, for some veterans, reconciliation has begun to mean going back to Vietnam. The amnesia and denial of society regarding the consequences of the war, coupled with the creation of a new mythology about the past, perhaps pushed some veterans to seek a tangible connection with a pivotal part of their past, engaging again a landscape and people who helped shape them and who, in turn, were as surely shaped by the multiplicity of their actions.

Though proportionally the figures may seem small, veterans have been going back to Vietnam in increasing numbers. In fact, after refugees, Vietnam veterans represent the single largest group returning to Vietnam. The road back has not always been a smooth one. The first delegation of Vietnam veterans from VVA returning to Vietnam in 1982 were publicly chastised for placing a wreath on Ho Chi Minh's grave. Members of the delegation found themselves under close scrutiny: Again the question, were they really veterans? VVA was thrown into turmoil, finally voting to take no stands on foreign policy matters. By the end of the 1980s, however, even POW-MIA groups were returning. VVAW groups, VVA groups, POW-MIA organizations, Veterans for Peace, the Vietnam Veterans Motorcycle Club, doctors, nurses, carpenters, teachers, veterans in wheelchairs, and veterans from all parts of the country have gone back.

Increasingly, these veterans have taken a role in providing assistance to the Vietnamese in addressing the many consequences of the war. Like the Quakers, the Mennonites, Catholic Relief, Church World Services, and United Nations organs, veterans' groups now play an increasing role in building health clinics; providing medical supplies, textbooks, prosthetics, training, and food to orphanages and centers for the disabled; and in promoting cultural exchange.

In a sense, the veterans are undertaking their "last mission," and sometimes finding they have more in common with some of their opponents of twenty years ago than with some of their peers at home. The irony that the "homecoming" they receive in Vietnam is more receptive and conciliatory than the one afforded in the United States is not lost on them. In the enemy they respected, they have found a mutual respect and recognition returned.

This does not always go down easy at home. ARVN liberation groups in the United States see these efforts at reconciliation as a threat and betrayal. Others are not so ready to humanize the enemy, or as they say "to trade rice for bones." And in the press and the electronic media, these voyages of return are often played out as curious and sentimental nostalgia tours, soft stories, not genuine commitments.

These efforts, however, mark a historical "turning point," transforming the meaning of Vietnam for many veterans. These journeys provide a means of connecting the past with the present, a way of talking about the war that is palpable and meaningful, cutting through the amnesia and myths.

How much these efforts affect the general public is questionable. Ironically, veterans of Vietnam still seem more willing than the general public to look directly at the consequences of the war in Vietnam. Perhaps this sense of rejection spurs on further efforts. That would be one explanation for a growing body of literature, and poetry in particular, by veterans that is historically rivaled only by the literature of World War I.[20]

In June 1990, U.S. writers who are veterans were invited by their counterparts in Vietnam to attend a conference on this literature. In January 1991, at the invitation of U.S. artists who are veterans, a delegation of veteran-artists from Vietnam were to come to the United States for a joint exhibit of works by forty American and Vietnamese veteran-artists. These may seem small

*World War II veteran mourns his son lost in the Vietnam war, at Vietnam Veterans Memorial in Washington, D.C. (Copyright © 1990 David Zadig. Reprinted with permission.)*

steps, but they mark efforts to forge face-to-face encounters with the past, to reenter history at a fresh point. In the words of Israeli veteran and Peace Now activist, Amos Oz, they may be seen as "a covert struggle between two powerful impulses: the obsessive wish to relive the historical experience over and over again, and the desire to break out of the stocks of the past in order to try to shape the future as free men."[21]

As Vietnam seems to disappear deeper and deeper into the past for most, having only the reality of a bumper sticker encountered on the highway, a television program playing in the background, or a book jacket on the table, it becomes increasingly important for veterans to speak out.

At the close of the writers' conference the following poem, which had been taken from a North Vietnamese soldier killed twenty years previously, was read by one of the Americans.

Toi Buon (I Am Sad)

When I got back to base
I sensed something had happened.
They said you went to the hospital yesterday
And my heart was torn and sad.
I always think of you, Bui Huu Phai,
Your life runs like a red silk banner.
So many of your friends are waiting
anxiously for news about you.

*Shadows of onlookers reflect against the names of the U.S. Vietnam war dead, at Vietnam Veterans Memorial in Washington, D.C. (Copyright © 1990 David Zadig. Reprinted with permission.)*

Dear brother, my feelings well up
and I wish so much I could see you.
Stronger than vast oceans or blue mountains,
because mountains fall and seas dry up,
my feelings for you endure.
My feelings for you are unshakable.
You and I must keep safe
and march home in victory soon.
I came to Ha-Tay on the first ship
nurturing this dream and not losing heart.
Perhaps we mustn't dream about life.
Life is now too hard, dear brother,
and so many dreams float in the air.
The more I think, the sadder I get
—how can one find his way to the future?
I think of you and weep these long nights.
I think of us chatting in an immense dusk,
listening to poems sung in the evening
and drinking tea together.
Wouldn't that be a happy moment!
These images seem so real in this poem,
but right now they're hard to believe
even as I clutch a pen to write you.[22]

The dream of "chatting in an immense dusk, listening to poems sung in the evening, and drinking tea together" is alluring; it is a soldier's dream of final reconciliation of a time when it doesn't matter at last whether anyone else is listening. But then again, for the sake of this soldier, and all the soldiers, we know it does.

## NOTES

1. Gloria Emerson's *Winners and Losers* (New York: Random House, 1977) remains the most important work on this subject. More recently, issues of *Vietnam Generation* have focused on the experiences of minorities and antiwar soldiers and veterans, but very little work has been done on the origins, nature, or impact of activism among Vietnam veterans.

2. Tim O'Brien, *If I Die in a Combat Zone* (New York: Dell, 1969), p. 41.

3. These figures represent casualties between 1965 and 1973 only.

4. Sources in Paul Starr, *The Discarded Army—Veterans After Vietnam* (Washington, DC: Center for the Study of Responsive Law, 1973).

5. Ibid.

6. See Lawrence Baskir and William Strauss, *Chance and Circumstance: The Draft, the War, and the Vietnam Generation* (New York: Vintage, 1978).

7. James Fallows, "What Did You Do in the Class War, Daddy?" *The Wounded Generation: America After Vietnam*, ed. A.D. Horne (Englewood Cliffs, NJ: Prentice-Hall, Inc., 1981).

8. Sources in Starr, *The Discarded Army*, and Lisa Hsiao, "Project 100,000: The Great Society's Answer to Military Manpower Needs in Vietnam," *Vietnam Generation* 1, no. 2 (Spring 1989). Hsiao's article is rich in information and should be read beside the recent final government summary of the success of Project 100,000.

9. Quoted in Hsiao, *Vietnam Generation*, p. 14.

10. Michael Casey, "A Bummer," *Winning Hearts and Minds*, ed. Jan Barry, Basil Paquet, Larry Rottmann (Brooklyn: 1st Casualty Press, 1972), p. 7.

11. The POWs, the one group to genuinely return as a group after the war, managed to gain, in a sense, all the collective gratitude, sanctions, and rewards that their predecessors who returned home alone did not. In some ways this may explain the desire to discover more POWs, whose rescue and return will afford veterans who are now their advocates the respect and thanks that the veterans never got in their own homecoming. (During the war enlisted men in Vietnam showed little identification with POW pilots whose experience of the war was different.)

12. Cited in Jonathan Schell, *Observing the Nixon Years: Notes and Comment from* The New Yorker *on the Vietnam War and the Watergate Crisis* (New York: Pantheon, 1989), p. 7.

13. See Charles Figley and Seymour Leventman, *Strangers at Home* (New York: Praeger, 1980).

14. One would hope that recent efforts to document the history of the Vietnam veterans' movement on both local and national levels will result in works that will throw fresh light on lives after the war.

15. John Kerry, statement before the Senate Foreign Relations Committee, 22 April 1971, quoted in *The New Soldier*, John Kerry and Vietnam Veterans Against the War (New York: Macmillan, 1971).

16. Talk of reconciliation with Vietnam disappeared with the return of the POWs. "Operation Homecoming" in which over eighty military public-relations personnel

participated, effectively killed chances for reconciliation as former prisoners became agents of recrimination against antiwar activists and the Vietnamese.

17. *Winning Hearts and Minds*, a collection of poetry by Vietnam veterans, was peddled to over forty commercial publishers for two years with no success. It was finally printed in the spring of 1972 through donations. Yet, the interest of veterans was there. When the call went out over a few short months, 10,000 pages of material were submitted. Veterans had something to say, but few places to say it. But perhaps this all made sense given the nature of the war and the fact that, as Bill Ehrhart pointed out, the war was fought by a population traditionally without a voice. But with the end of the war, other veteran publications such as Jan Barry and W. D. Erhart, eds., *Demilitarized Zones* (Perkasie, PA: East River Anthology, 1976) failed to fare as well.

18. There has been much searching discussion of the significance of these films. Most recently see Linda Dittmar and Gene Michaud, eds., *From Hanoi to Hollywood: The Vietnam War Film in American Film* (New Brunswick, NJ: Rutgers University Press, 1991).

19. In a survey of 20,000 Vietnam veterans in the Commonwealth of Massachusetts the POW-MIA was ranked the number one issue on the agenda, above education, AIDS, Agent Orange, and other issues.

20. Another dimension largely unexplored is the emergence of Vietnam veterans as teachers and scholars in the past few years.

21. Amos Oz, "The Hypnosis of the Past," in *The Slopes of Lebanon* (New York: Harcourt Brace Jovanovich, 1987), trans. Maurie Goldberg-Bartura, pp. 120–121.

22. This poem appears in microfilm copy in the CDEC collection, a microfilm collection of enemy documents seized during the war. The poem's author was a soldier in the 9th Battalion, 101st Regiment of the North Vietnamese Army fighting in Tay Ninh province along the Cambodian border. Translation by John Balaban and T. L. Nguyen.

# PART THREE

# Films and Scholarly Literature on Vietnam

# 9

## Jenefer Shute | Framing Vietnam

Sometime around 1985, after a decade of resolutely avoiding this political hot potato, Hollywood decided that it was safe—and profitable—to address Vietnam. Historical amnesia and Rambo-style revisionism (see Chapter 10) had apparently done their work, and the "national trauma" was now fit to be recycled as action-adventure for a generation too young to remember or too upwardly mobile to care. The result—typified by the Robin Williams's vehicle *Good Morning, Vietnam* (1987)—was a devolution of public discourse about the war, from deep shame to near shamelessness.

Apart from the 1980s wave of exploitation "quickies," the four big, ambitious Vietnam films—Michael Cimino's *The Deer Hunter* (1978), Francis Ford Coppola's *Apocalypse Now* (1979), Oliver Stone's *Platoon* (1985), and Stanley Kubrick's *Full Metal Jacket* (1987)—had foundered in their quest for a cinematic vocabulary adequate to the task. The war movie as a genre, predicated as it was on unambiguous heroism, had become obsolete almost overnight. By the end of the decade, in *Born on the Fourth of July* (1989), Oliver Stone would attempt to rehabilitate the notion of heroism—ironically, in the figure of an antiwar veteran.

Though there are profound differences among these films—most obviously, those of the 1970s seek an American myth grandiose enough for the subject, while those of the 1980s share the ostensible project of demystification—what they have in common is a profound avoidance of political inquiry. Instead, the war is cast as a moral and psychological crisis, a rite of passage for the individual and a deep wound to America's self-image—which it was, but not that only and not that first.

Granted, all films about Vietnam face a representational problem hitherto unique: that of portraying a war whose repertoire of images is already numbingly familiar from the nightly news. This may partly explain the swerve

Revised and excerpted with permission from *Tikkun* magazine, vol. 4, no. 2 (March–April 1989), a bimonthly Jewish critique of politics, culture, and society, based in Oakland, California.

toward mythic inflation, especially in those films made shortly after the war (*Apocalypse Now* and *The Deer Hunter*). But even *Platoon*, hailed for its you-are-here, war-is-hell realism, resolves itself into the tidy dichotomies of the morality play. And, though *Full Metal Jacket* directs its cool, corrosive irony at precisely those myths that make war and war movies possible, Kubrick remains too removed to commit himself to political questions. His film vanishes finally into its own distance, leaving, like a cinematic Cheshire cat, only a smirk behind.

Cimino's much-hailed and much-derided *The Deer Hunter* is, in about equal measures, a paean to the holy rites of male bonding (which, despite death and mutilation, seem to make war almost worthwhile), and a self-important deployment of genre conventions. Like the Western, Cimino's epic establishes the dual poles of "nature" (realm of male comradeship and the noble "one-shot" ethos of the hunt) and "civilization" (the female domain of domestic entrapment). Like the Western hero, Cimino's protagonist, Michael (Robert de Niro), lives by a stoic code that sets him apart and helps him survive. But *The Deer Hunter* fails, ultimately, to make a political connection between its Western iconography and the Vietnam War. Its imagery gestures vaguely toward history, announcing portentous intentions, but producing, finally, mere bombast.

Though Cimino shows the dark satanic mills of his characters' working lives, and their ritual affirmations of community, he establishes no continuity between the society they inhabit and the society that sends them to Vietnam. Vietnam is something that simply happens to them, somewhere they just have to go—and this powerlessness is not deemed problematic, as it might have been. Their propulsion into the war is as arbitrary as the sudden, audacious cut Cimino uses to jolt the viewer from cosy Clairton, Pennsylvania, to the hell of Vietnam. For Michael and his buddies, the war is simply a given—to be seized, certainly, as a test of manhood—but as uncontrollable as a roll of the dice or a spin of the gun chambers in Russian roulette.

Russian roulette is, of course, Cimino's governing metaphor for the war, and a perverse one at that. Not only does the fantasy of sadistic Vietcong forcing U.S. prisoners to play Russian roulette have no historical basis whatsoever, but as an image of the individual's relation to the war, it suggests only chance, accident, fate. Wars have about as little causal logic as Russian roulette, *The Deer Hunter* suggests, and can only be out-toughed, not understood, prevented, or resisted. As a metaphor for the war, Russian roulette may be dramatically powerful, but it's determinedly ahistorical.

Coppola's vision in *Apocalypse Now* cannot be called ahistorical—if anything, its historical reach exceeds its grasp—but the film incorporates so many mythic strains that it collapses into incoherence, a triumph of spectacle over sense. Over the murky, something-evil-at-the-heart-of-man moral vision of Conrad's *Heart of Darkness*, Coppola has imposed at least two incompatible narrative modes: a jaded voice-over, derived from the hardboiled tradition, that turns Willard's mission into a culpable quest through the jungle's mean streams; and a hyperbolic, hallucinatory visual style that presents war as a bad acid-trip (or as a nightmare Disneyland, or, simply, as spectacle).

Through his imagery, heightened by an acid-rock soundtrack, Coppola explores the continuity between Vietnam and the sixties culture back home. Coppola's preferred transition here is the dissolve, with its psychedelic associations, and his imagery aspires toward hallucinatory absurdity (the soldiers surf during a firefight—a firefight engaged to secure precisely that wave) and apocalyptic beauty (sunsets and infernos). The "grunts," described as "rock-and-rollers with one foot in the grave," read about Charles Manson as they were en route to mass murders of their own. Music by Wagner blasts out during a helicopter attack, suggesting an entire cultural heritage gone beserk. But what, exactly, is the diagnosis?

The diagnosis, it seems, is offered by the briefing officer at the beginning of the film. By way of explaining Kurtz, he tells Willard: "There's a conflict in every human heart between the rational and irrational, between good and evil, and good does *not* always triumph. Sometimes the dark side overcomes. . . ." That's it? All the ponderous cultural references, all the evocations of Disneyland and Manson and Playboy Bunnies, all the images of a society swung crazily out of control, to blame, finally, Essential Evil. (Kurtz, someone tells Willard, is "worse than crazy, he's evil.") Coppola, following Conrad (but why Conrad, for *this* war?) presents the issue as ultimately a psychological one, something to do with the "human heart" and its wiring. This may conceivably be a way to explain wars of imperialist aggression, but somewhere along the way, despite a few references to "their" lies, a whole category of analysis—the political—has been sidestepped.

*Platoon*, the only one of these movies made by an ex-grunt, has an even more schematic moral vision than *Apocalypse Now*, though its mythic trappings are humbler, tending more toward genre film and morality play than *Götterdämmerung*. Unlike Coppola, Stone does not present war as spectacle: His skillfully staged firefight scenes work on the nerves and suggest that war is not pretty, perhaps not even fun. But the movie's much-touted "realism"— belied in any case by improbable jungle lighting—turns out to be a thin stylistic veneer covering a conventional, not to say melodramatic, coming-of-age story. From the opening shots of a plane's metallic maw disgorging raw recruits into Vietnam to the final image of their return trip "bagged and tagged," *Platoon* focuses on the spiritual development of its blank-slate grunt.

Unlike other Vietnam protagonists, Chris (Charlie Sheen) knows why he's there: he volunteered. He doesn't see why only poor kids should go to war, and, besides, he wants to do what his dad did in World War II and his grandad did in World War I. This qualifies him, in the film's terms, as "a crusader." Fighting for the soul of this bemused "crusader" and presiding over his initiation into the twin mysteries of killing and comradeship are the platoon's two sergeants: Barnes, who embodies the spirit of My Lai, and Elias, a tortured Christ figure. Between them they create what Chris calls "a civil war in the platoon—fighting each other when we should be fighting them."

What's interesting about this "civil war," however, is that it never mirrors the "civil war" that rent the United States during Vietnam. What divides Barnes from Elias is not the political question of their presence or purpose in

*Oliver Stone's* Platoon *does not romanticize or idealize the Vietnam War. Focusing on U.S. soldiers, as in dramatic firefight scenes, the film suggests that war is not pretty and is internalized into personal moral crises. Left to right: actors Charlie Sheen, Corey Glover, Chris Pedersen, Willem Dafoe, Forrest Whittaker, and Keith David. (Photo by Ricky Francisco. Copyright © 1986 Orion Pictures Corporation. All rights reserved.)*

Vietnam, but the ethical one of how to conduct their killing once they're there. Elias wants to play by the rules, Barnes doesn't, but the rules themselves remain fundamentally unchallenged. In the film's moral universe, Barnes and Elias become Good and Evil personified, fighting for Chris's soul, turning him into "the child born of these two fathers." Once again, the conflict is internalized, translated into a personal moral crisis. Though the voice-over preaches that "in Vietnam we fought ourselves and the enemy is in us," this enemy is conceived apolitically, as Pure Evil, rearing its ugly head when Barnes turns to strike Chris down, meat-cleaver-style, his eyes demonically aglow.

Kubrick's *Full Metal Jacket*, the most complex and analytical of these Vietnam films, is of course much too cerebral to entertain any image of pure evil: Kubrick is concerned to dismantle myths rather than rehabilitate them. Instead of placing the viewer in a voyeuristic position relative to war as spectacle, Kubrick subjects him (and, more problematically, her) to a prolonged brutalization analogous to basic training. Just as the grunts are violated, dehumanized, and infantilized by their drill sergeant, so the viewer is assaulted by a relentlessly distasteful experience. In the second half of the film, the messy, nerve-jangling confusion of urban warfare takes over, leaving the viewer, like the grunts, rudderless amidst random carnage.

*Stanley Kubrick's complex film* Full Metal Jacket *portrays an all-pervasive irony, as seen in this juxtaposition of "born to kill" with a "peace button." (Copyright © 1987 Warner Bros., Inc. All rights reserved.)*

If Cimino's governing metaphor for the Vietnam War is Russian roulette, Coppola's is bad acid trip, and Stone's is morality play, Kubrick's is garbage dump or refuse heap. His green-and-gray urban dreamscapes under a pale, drained sky suggest the detritus of a civilization rather than (as in Coppola and Stone) the rank undergrowth of the unconscious. Stylistically, too, his cool irony picks over the fragments, turning up what's left of once functional myths and fables. In the film's most self-reflective moment, the grunts, interviewed for "Vietnam—the movie," produce a series of live-TV clichés and glib, Jean-Luc Godardesque allusions to George Custer and John Wayne. But such knowing evocations, like all the film's potentially political moments, dissolve in Kubrick's all-pervasive irony, which affords the viewer no reference point or point of emotional purchase. As if to ensure this effect, Kubrick has sealed off his protagonist, Private Joker, behind a smirking mask, where the only emotion one can impute to him is cynicism.

In *Good Morning, Vietnam*, Robin Williams, as Adrian Cronauer, professional smart aleck, offers the final and most unnerving vision of the war: the war as big joke. Cronauer, we are to believe, is heroic because, as a DJ on the military radio station, he resists his immediate superiors to tell the grunts

*In this scene from* Full Metal Jacket, *actor Lee Ermey portrays a brutal drill sergeant inspecting the recruits he's toughening for their combat duty in Vietnam. Director Stanley Kubrick subjects viewers to a prolonged brutalization analogous to the dehumanization of basic training.* (Copyright © 1987 Warner Bros., Inc. All rights reserved.)

the "truth" about the war. Having established these minimal political credentials for its protagonist, the film feels free to turn everything else into fodder for its peculiarly juvenile, scatological humor (presented here as somehow "liberating," like rock and roll). In this context, harassing Vietnamese women on the street is boyish high spirits; teaching uncomprehending Vietnamese adults in an English class to parrot obscenities is "relating" to them; and showering dollar bills on the family of a Vietnamese woman, who chaperone her on a date, is merely endearing. The smug condescension implicit throughout is epitomized in Cronauer's tone when he discovers that a Vietnamese friend is a "terrorist," implicated in blowing up a bar frequented by Americans: "I fought to let you into that bar and now you blow the place up," he reproaches him, a picture of paternalism betrayed.

If it had used the Vietnam war merely as a setting for tasteless, if xenophobic, jokes, *Good Morning, Vietnam* might be negligible, only another exploitation movie (albeit based loosely on "fact," the life of the real Adrian Cronauer). But through its comic structure, *Good Morning, Vietnam* does implicitly offer an interpretation, which is finally an exculpation, of the U.S. role in Vietnam. Cronauer's conflict is always with his immediate superior, the humorless, venal, chronically uptight Sergeant-Major Dickerson. Above Dickerson, however, is the benevolent and basically fair General Taylor, who thinks Cronauer is one hell of a guy and ensures that justice prevails by transferring Dickerson to Guam. The power structure, in other words, is fundamentally benign: a just, generous Big Daddy presides over the military, keeping a twinkling eye on things and guaranteeing that decency reigns. Sure, Cronauer ultimately gets shipped out—hobnobbing with "terrorists" is not part of Taylor's benevolent scheme—but not before he teaches the happy, smiling Vietnamese to play baseball (with melons, *faute de mieux*) in an orgy of good will that cancels all conflict.

Even with this rosy resolution, it's hard to make a movie set in Saigon in 1965 without showing a little violence. So director Barry Levinson does provide a few hints that, in addition to a constant comedy act over Armed Forces Radio, there's a war going on. A bar is blown up—but we see only American casualties. Cronauer gets a nasty surprise when his jeep drives over a land mine—but this encounter derives directly from the personal animosity of his superior officer, who has knowingly sent him into danger. And then there is an ironic montage sequence, to Louis Armstrong's "What a Wonderful World," that shows a series of war images, some brutal, emphasizing the victimization of the Vietnamese. But this brief string of decontextualized images, sealed off from the rest of the film and proffered with the cheap irony of the Armstrong accompaniment, serves mainly as a siphon, allowing the narrative to return, unaffected, to its anodyne task. Never mind, *Good Morning, Vietnam* tells its audience, the war was a big joke, and anyway, decent people were running it.

It's hard to imagine a more cynical take on the war; at the time, it suggested that, in mass culture at least, any serious attempt to grapple with Vietnam—with the war in the past and the war in the present—had tacitly been abandoned. But then Oliver Stone capped the decade, and to some extent redeemed it, with *Born on the Fourth of July*.

Based on the autobiography of veteran and war-resister Ron Kovic (played by Tom Cruise) and touted as Hollywood's ultimate antiwar statement, the film provides the viewer with a powerful—perhaps overpowering—emotional experience. Stone has never shown much penchant for subtlety, and here he pumps his style up to a hyperkinetic, overblown high: Most of the images are close-ups or so tightly framed that the screen can hardly contain them.

Matching its over-the-top style, *Born on the Fourth of July* has an epic trajectory, charting Kovic's transformation from gung-ho marine to wheelchair-bound war-resister. Its opening scenes of main-street parades, boyish war games, and high-school wrestling serve to delineate the institutions (family, community, church, school) that socialize young Ronnie until his highest aspiration is to "waste" fellow humans in the name of patriotism. The scenes of Kovic's Vietnam wounding and torment in a hellish veterans' hospital are compelling, as is the Grand Guignol of dueling wheelchairs when he hits bottom among a community of the mutilated in Mexico. Thereafter, the narrative swells to successive climaxes in tracing Kovic's gradual, apparently autonomous but inexorable elevation into an antiwar hero.

Yes, a hero—and there's the rub. For all its apparent irony, for all its demystification, *Born on the Fourth of July* ends by embracing the notion of heroism Kovic ostensibly outgrows—that of the lone, impassioned, patriotic leader. At the film's climax, as Kovic wheels toward the podium to address the 1976 Democratic National Convention, the soundtrack reiterates his mother's dream for him: that one day he would speak stirringly to a great crowd. Little Ronnie has fulfilled that dream, with a twist; its content may differ but the model of heroism remains the same. Even militarism hasn't been expunged from it: when Vietnam Veterans Against the War disrupt the Republican National Convention, Kovic puts his marine training to good use, seizing command with the cry to "retake the hall." And, like his childhood heroes, he appears to achieve his goal single-handedly because the film's focus never expands beyond Kovic the individual to encompass the antiwar movement.

Speaking on behalf of Vietnam veterans at the film's close, Kovic announces that they've finally "come home." Sure, Uncle Sam needed to be shown the error of his ways, but "America" is still home, still family; home and family are still absolute values; patriotism is still the highest good. Those small-town communities glowing with golden autumnal light embody values to be embraced in the end, not—as Kovic's career might suggest—to be resisted.

Although Oliver Stone doesn't encourage such an equation, it's tempting to see the figure of Ron Kovic as symbolizing the United States—crippled and castrated after its long, horrible nightmare of Vietnam. So far, U.S. filmmakers have shown themselves unwilling or unable to confront this nightmare without the scrim of myth. Perhaps a truer, more unflinching vision of the war will be offered only by those who suffered its worst horrors—not Americans, but the people of Vietnam.

# 10

Gaylyn
Studlar
&
David
Desser

# *Rambo*'s Rewriting of the Vietnam War

"History is what hurts," writes Fredric Jameson in *The Political Unconscious*, "It is what refuses desire and sets inexorable limits to individual as well as collective praxis."[1] The pain of history, its delimiting effect on action, is often seen as a political, a cultural, a national liability. Therefore, contemporary history has been the subject of an ideological battle which seeks to rewrite, to rehabilitate, controversial and ambiguous events through the use of symbols. One arena of ongoing cultural concern in the United States is our involvement in Vietnam. It seems clear that reconstituting an image—a "memory"—of Vietnam under the impetus of Reaganism appears to fulfill a specific ideological mission. Yet the complexity of this reconstitution or rewriting has not been fully realized, either in film studies or in political discourse. The manner in which the Reaganite right co-opted often contradictory and competing discourses surrounding the rehabilitation of Vietnam has also not been adequately addressed. A string of "right-wing" Vietnam films has been much discussed, but their reliance on the specific mechanism of *displacement* to achieve a symbolic or mythic reworking of the war has not been recognized. Also insufficiently acknowledged is the fact that, far from being a unique occurrence, the current attempt to rewrite Vietnam, and the era of the 1960s more broadly, follows a well-established pattern of reworking the past in postwar

This article (originally titled "Never Having to Say You're Sorry: *Rambo*'s Rewriting of the Vietnam War") is reprinted from *Film Quarterly*, vol. 42, no. 1 (Fall 1988), pp. 9–16. © 1988 by the Regents of the University of California, reprinted by permission.

Japan and Germany. Although it would be naive to advance a simple parallelist conception of history that foregrounds obvious analogies at the expense of important historical differences, the rewriting of the Vietnam War evidences a real, if complicated, link to previous situations where nations have moved beyond revising history to rewriting it through specific cultural processes.

That America's "rewriting" of the Vietnam War is ideological in nature, of a particular political postwar moment, is clear a priori. But the site at which it is occurring is perhaps less clear and therefore more significant. For what is being rewritten might justifiably be called a "trauma," a shock to the cultural system. Commonly used phrases such as "healing the wounds of Vietnam" are quite revelatory of this idea, but do not grasp the difficulty of any cultural recuperation from shock. In reality, the attempt to cope with the national trauma of Vietnam confronts less a physical than a psychic trauma. The mechanisms through which healing can occur, therefore, are more devious, more in need, if you will, of "analysis."

The central question of the problem of the Vietnam War in history is: How can the United States deal with not only its defeat in Vietnam, but with the fact that it never should have been there in the first place? By answering this question, the United States would confront the potentially painful revelations of its involvement in Vietnam, which is reminiscent of those questions faced by other nations: How can Japan cope with its role in the Pacific aggression of World War II? How can the West Germans resolve the Nazi era? These questions are virtually unanswerable without admission of guilt. But if, as Freud maintained, individuals find guilt intolerable and attempt to repress it, why should cultures be any different?[2] And if guilt, in spite of repression, always finds an unconscious avenue of expression in the individual's life, we must similarly mark a return of the repressed in cultural discourse as well.

In one respect, the return of the repressed explains the number of Vietnam films appearing simultaneously, or at least in waves of films during the 1980s. Given the nature of film production, the box-office success of any individual film cannot account for so many Vietnam films appearing within a short period of time. Nor can the popularity of such films, left and right, automatically be taken as an indicator of psychic healing. On the contrary, their coexistence might be read as a register of the nation's ambivalent feelings over the war, and ambivalence, Freud tells us, is one of the necessary ingredients in the creation of guilt feelings.[3]

Psychoanalytic therapy maintains that to be healed one must recall the memory of the trauma which has been repressed by a sense of guilt. Otherwise, a "faulty" memory or outright amnesia covers the truth, which lies somewhere deep in the unconscious. The more recent the trauma, the more quickly the memory can be recalled; the more severe the original trauma, the more deeply the memory is buried, the more completely it is repressed. In this respect, cultures can be said to act like individuals—they simply cannot live with overwhelming guilt. Like individual trauma, cultural trauma must be "forgotten," but the guilt of such traumas continues to grow. However, as

Freud notes, the mechanism of repression is inevitably flawed: the obstinately repressed material ultimately breaks through and manifests itself in unwelcome symptoms.[4] In 1959 Theodor Adorno, calling upon the psychoanalytic explanation of psychic trauma in his discussion of postwar Germany, observed that the psychological damage of a repressed collective past often emerges through dangerous political gestures: defensive overreaction to situations that do not really constitute attacks, "lack of affect" in response to serious issues, and repression of "what was known or half-known."[5] Popular discourse often equates forgetting the past with mastering it, says Adorno, but an unmastered past cannot remain safely buried: the mechanisms of repression will bring it into the present in a form which may very well lead to "the politics of catastrophe."[6]

One example of the politics of catastrophe was Germany's own unmastered response to World War I. Although Hitler's rise to power was complex (as is America's rewriting of the Vietnam War), there was a crucial element of psychic trauma that enabled Hitler to step in and "heal" the nation. In *The Weimar Chronicle*, Alex de Jonge offers a telling account of an element of this trauma. At the end of the war, the Germans were unable to comprehend that their army, which proudly marched through the Brandenburg gate, had been defeated. Instead of blaming the enemy, or the imperial regime's failed policy of militarism, the Germans embraced the myth of the "stab in the back." Defeat was explained as a conspiracy concocted by those Germans who signed the surrender.[7] William Shirer has noted that the widespread "fanatical" belief in this postwar myth was maintained even though "the facts which exposed its deceit lay all around."[8] This act of "scapegoating" evidences both the desire to rewrite history and to repress collective cultural guilt and responsibility. Resistance to the truth meant that, for Nazi Germany, ideology functioned as "memory," fantasy substituted for historical discourse, and the welcome simplicity of myth replaced the ambiguity of past experience. While World War I should have logically signalled an end to German militarist impulses, it served as merely a prelude and a "founding myth" for its most virulent expression.[9]

This example, replayed in many more contemporary realms, including the current discourse surrounding Vietnam, allows us to posit a "will to myth"— a communal need, a cultural drive—for a reconstruction of the national past in light of the present, a present which is, by definition of necessity, better. Claude Lévi-Strauss has suggested that primitive cultures which have no past (i.e., do not conceive of or distinguish between a past and present) use myth as the primary means of dealing with cultural contradictions. Modern societies, of course, are cognizant of a past, but frequently find it filled with unpleasant truths and half-known facts, so they set about rewriting it. The mass media, including cinema and television, have proven to be important mechanisms whereby this rewriting—this reimaging—of the past can occur. Indeed, it was Hitler's far-reaching use of the media that allowed him to solidify the National Socialist state and set his nation on its monstrous course in a carefully orchestrated exploitation of the will to myth.[10]

A common strategy by which "the will to myth" asserts itself is through the substitution of one question for another. This mechanism is invoked by Lévi-Strauss as he notes how frequently one question, or problem, mythically substitutes for another concept by the narrative patterns of the myths. In dream interpretation, psychoanalysis calls this strategy "displacement." If we allow the notion that cultures are like individuals (and recall the commonplace analogy that films are "like" dreams), we should not be surprised to find displacement occurring in popular discourse. Displacement accounts for the phenomenon of "scapegoating," for instance, on both individual and cultural levels. But there are more devious examples, more complex situations in which the displacement goes almost unrecognized, as has been the case thus far with the current wave of Vietnam films and the project of rewriting the image of the war.

In the case of the recent right-wing Vietnam War films, the fundamental textual mechanism of displacement that has not been recognized is that the question "Were we right to fight in Vietnam?" has been replaced (displaced) by the question "What is our obligation to the veterans of the war?" Responsibility to and validation of the veterans is not the same as validating our participation in the conflict in the first place. Yet answering the second question "mythically" rewrites the answer to the first.

One of the key strategies in this displacement of the crucial question of America's Vietnam involvement is that of "victimization." The Japanese have used this method of coping with their role as aggressor in World War II, just as the Nazis used it to rewrite World War I. The Japanese soldiers who fought in the war now are regarded as victims of a military government that betrayed the soldiers and the populace. The Japanese do not try to justify their actions in the war nor even deal with the fact that their policies started the war in the first place. Rather, they try to shift (displace) blame for the war onto wartime leaders who are no longer alive. Contemporary Germany, too, relies on this strategy in an attempt now to rehabilitate West Germany's Nazi past. Strangely enough, its appropriation was given public sanction by President Reagan in his visit to the Bitburg cemetery.

That America's problem of/with the Vietnam War might be related to Germany's Nazi past and the controversy over Reagan's visit to Bitburg is addressed in an interesting, if disturbing way, in a letter quoted by Alvin Rosenfeld. The letter writer claimed that Reagan's trip to Bitburg signified "that we are beginning to forgive the German people for their past sins, in much the same way that America has begun to seek forgiveness for Vietnam."[11] But is America (or, for that matter, West Germany) actually seeking "forgiveness" for the past? Reagan told the Germans at Bitburg what they wanted to hear, that the German soldiers buried in the military cemetery were themselves victims of the Nazis "just as surely as the victims of the concentration camps."[12] The American resistance to admitting culpability for Vietnam, like the Bitburg affair, revolves around a collective cultural drama of memory and forgetting. In essence, what we find in Japan's revision of its wartime history, Reagan's Bitburg speech, and many of the Vietnam films of the 1980s, is that the appeal to victimization via "the will to myth" is a powerful rhetorical tool to apply to the problem of guilt. To be a victim means never having to say you're sorry.

**MIAs; OR I AM A FUGITIVE FROM BUREAUCRACY**

As of this writing, two waves of Vietnam War films in the 1980s have been claimed: the right-wing revisionism of *Uncommon Valor* (1983), *Missing in Action* (1984), and *Rambo: First Blood II* (1985); and the ostensibly more realistic strain of Vietnam films emerging with *Platoon* (1986), *Hamburger Hill* (1987), and *Full Metal Jacket* (1987). At first glance, the comic-book heroics of the earlier films seem antithetical to the "realism" of the later ones, but in spite of such differences the films are actually very much alike in their dependence on the strategy of victimization. The films all work to evoke sympathy for the American GI (today's veteran) and pay tribute to the act of remembering the war as private hell. While the right-wing films, especially *Rambo*, justify a private war of national retribution for the personal sacrifice of vets, the realist films demonstrate the process of victimization of the draftee or enlisted man. *Platoon* even goes so far as to transpose its conflict from the specificity of Vietnam into the realm of the transcendental: the two sergeants, Barnes and Elias, become mythic figures, warrior archetypes, battling for the soul of Chris (Christ?). The crucifixion image as Barnes kills Elias is too clear to miss, while Chris becomes the sacrificial victim who survives.

The right-wing films, especially *Rambo*, most clearly demonstrate the strategy of mythic substitution or displacement in the use of an oft-repeated rumor: that American MIAs (military personnel missing in action) are still being held captive in Southeast Asia. That *Rambo* was not only the most commercially successful of all the Vietnam films thus far, but also became culturally ubiquitous (a television cartoon series, formidable tie-in merchandise sales, and, like *Star Wars*, becoming part of political discourse) speaks to the power of the will to myth. The need to believe in the MIAs gives credence to the view that the Vietnamese are now and *therefore have always been* an inhuman and cruel enemy. Vietnam's alleged actions in *presently* holding American prisoners serves as an index of our essential rightness in fighting such an enemy *in the past*. Moreover, our alleged unwillingness to confront Vietnam on the MIAs issue is taken to be an index of the government's cowardice in its Vietnam policy: Confrontation would mean confirmation. The American bureaucracy remains spineless: They didn't let us win then, and they won't let us win again.

Consequently, while it appears to embrace the militaristic ideology of the radical right, *Rambo* simultaneously delegitimizes governmental authority and questions the ideological norms of many other Vietnam films. Within its formula of militaristic zeal, *Rambo* sustains an atmosphere of post-Watergate distrust of government. The MIAs, John Rambo's captive comrades, are regarded only as "a couple of ghosts" by the cynical official representative of

*Actor Sylvester Stallone plays Rambo in the film* Rambo: First Blood Part II. *(Copyright ©
1985 Tri-Star Pictures. All rights reserved.)*

*Another scene from the film* Rambo: First Blood Part II. *(Copyright © 1985 Tri-Star Pictures. All rights reserved.)*

the government, Murdock, who lies about his service in Vietnam. He is willing to sacrifice the MIAs to maintain the status quo of international relations. President Reagan's portrait graces the wall behind Murdock's desk, but Murdock is a "committee" member, aligned, it seems, with Congress, not with the avowed conservatism of the executive branch. Colonel Trauptman, Rambo's Special Forces commander and surrogate father-figure, reminds Murdock that the United States reneged on reparations to the Vietnamese, who retaliated by keeping the unransomed captive Americans. Failure to rescue the MIAs is the direct result of their economic expendability. Murdock says the situation has not changed; Congress will not appropriate billions to rescue these "ghosts."

Abandoned once by their country (or rather, "government"), the MIAs/POWs (prisoners of war) are abandoned yet again in a highly symbolic scene: airdropped into Vietnam to find and photograph any living MIAs/POWs, Rambo locates an American; the rescue helicopter hovers above them as Vietnamese soldiers close in. Murdock abruptly aborts the mission. Rambo is captured and submitted to shocking (literally) tortures. His Russian interrogators taunt him with the intercepted radio message in which he was ordered abandoned. Rambo escapes, but not before he swears revenge against Murdock.

The mythical MIA prisoners may represent the ultimate *American* victims of the war, but *Rambo: First Blood II* also draws on the victimization strategy on yet another level, through the continued exploitation of its vet hero, John

*Veterans protest outside Harvard University's Hasty Pudding Club where Sylvester Stallone received the annual award. (Photo by Leslie Bowen.)*

Rambo. The film opens with an explosion of rock at a quarry. A tilt down reveals inmates at forced labor. Colonel Trauptman arrives to recruit Rambo for a special mission. Separated by an imposing prison yard fence, Rambo tells Trauptman that he would rather stay in prison than be released because "at least in here I know where I stand." The Vietnam vet is the 1980s version of the World War I vet, the "forgotten man" of the Depression era. Like James Allen in Warner Brothers' most famous social consciousness film, *I Am a Fugitive from a Chain Gang* (1932), Rambo is a Congressional Medal of Honor winner who feels "out of step" with a society that has used and discarded him. Condemned as a common criminal, Rambo is released from military prison and promised a pardon because his unique combat skills are again required by the government. He does not realize that he is also needed for political purposes. He will provide the gloss of a veteran's testimonial to the mission's findings, which have been predetermined: no Americans will be found.

As far removed from an appeal to victimization as Rambo's aggressive received myth-image might appear to be, his personal mission of victory and vengeance crucially hinges on his status as present and past victim, as neglected, misunderstood, and exploited veteran. Ironically, in a film that has no memory of the historical complexities of the Vietnam War, Rambo's personal obsession with the traumatic past of Vietnam is cited as the truest measure of his unswerving patriotism. Even Colonel Trauptman feels compelled to tell him to forget the war. Rambo replies: ". . . as long as I'm alive—it's still alive."

Stallone explained the film in an interview: "I stand for ordinary Americans, losers a lot of them. They don't understand big, international politics. Their country tells them to fight in Vietnam? They fight."[13] Rambo and the captive MIAs are the innocent victims of wartime and postwar government machinations that preclude victories. By implicating American policy and government bureaucracy in past defeat and current inaction, the film exonerates the regular soldier from culpability in American defeat as it pointedly criticizes a technologically obsessed, mercenary American military establishment. This echoes both the Japanese strategy of blaming dead leaders for World War II and Reagan's declaration at Bitburg that the Holocaust was not the responsibility of a nation or an electorate, but an "awful evil started by one man."[14] Similarly, in his statements on Vietnam, Reagan had employed a strategy of blaming Vietnam defeat on those who cannot be named: "We are just beginning to realize how we were led astray when it came to Vietnam."[15]

"Are they going to let us win this time?" Rambo first asks Trauptman when the colonel comes to pull Rambo out of the stockade rock pile for sins committed in the presequel. Trauptman says that it is up to Rambo, but the colonel is unaware that Murdock is merely using Rambo to prove to the American public that there are no POWs. As the film's ad proclaims: "They sent him on a mission and set him up to fail." Rambo, setting the ideological precedent for Ollie North, is the fall guy forced into extraordinary "moral" action by the ordinary immoral inaction of bureaucrats. According to official standards, Rambo is an aberration, the loose cannon on the deck who subverts the official system, but in doing so he affirms the long-cherished American cult of the individual who goes outside the law to get the job done. He ignores the "artificial" restraints of the law to uphold a higher moral law, but (unlike Ollie) Rambo manages to avoid the final irony of conspiracy making.

**CONFRONTING THE OTHERNESS OF FRONTIER ASIA**

In rewriting the Vietnam defeat, *Rambo* attempts to solve the contradiction posed by its portrayal of the Vietnam vet as powerless victim *and* supremacist warrior by reviving the powerful American mythos of a "regeneration through violence." Identified by Richard Slotkin as the basis of many frontier tales, this intertext illuminates the way in which *Rambo*'s narrative structure resembles that of the archetypal captivity narrative described by Timothy Flint, whose *Indian Wars of the West, Biographical Memoir of Daniel Boone (1828–1833)* typified this form of early frontier story. In this formula, a lone frontier adventurer is ambushed and held captive by Indians. They recognize his superior abilities and wish to adopt him, but he escapes, reaches an outpost, and with the help of a handful of other settlers wins a gruesome siege against hundreds of his former captors.[16] Sanctified by the trial of captivity, the hunter confronts an Otherness, represented by the wilderness and the Indians, that threatens to assimilate him into barbarism. Through vengeance, he finds his identity—as a white, civilized, Christian male.

Rambo's war of selective extermination inverts the wartime situation of Vietnam into a hallucinated frontier revenge fantasy that literalizes Marx's description of ideology: "circumstances appear upside down. . . ."[17] Rambo is an imperialist guerrilla, an agent of technocrats, who rejects computer-age technology to obliterate truckloads of the enemy with bow and arrow. Emerging from the mud of the jungle, from the trees, rivers, and waterfalls, Rambo displays a privileged, magical relationship to the Third World wilderness not evidenced even by the Vietnamese. As Trauptman remarks: "What others call hell, he calls home."

Charmed against nature and enemy weapons, Rambo retaliates in Indian-style warfare for the captivity of the POWs, the death of his Vietnamese love interest, and his own wartime trauma. He stands against a waterfall, magically immune to a barrage of gunfire. His detonator-tipped arrows literally blow apart the enemy—who is subhuman, the propagandist's variation of the Hun, the Nip, the Nazi. Held in contempt even by their Russian advisors, the Vietnamese are weak, sweating, repulsive in their gratuitous cruelty and sexual lasciviousness. Rambo annihilates an enemy whose evil makes American culpability in any wartime atrocities a moot point. In *The Searchers*, Ethan Edwards says: "There are humans and then there are comanch [sic]." In *Rambo*, there are humans and then there are gooks who populate a jungle which is not a wilderness to be transformed into a garden, but an unredeemable hell which automatically refutes any accusation of America's imperialist designs.

With regard to the captivity narrative, it is also significant that Rambo is described as a half-breed, half German and half American Indian, a "hell of a combination," says Murdock. The Vietnam vet's otherness of class and race is displaced solely onto race. The Indianness of costume signifiers: long hair, bare chest, headband, and necklace/pendant ironically reverse the appropriation of the iconography of Native Americans by the sixties counterculture as symbolic of a radical alternative to oppressive cultural norms.[18] Ironically, the film's appropriation of the iconography of the Noble Savage also permits Rambo to symbolically evoke the Indian as the romanticized victim of past government deceitfulness disguised as progress (i.e., genocide). These invocations of Indianness should not overshadow the fact that Rambo is a white male, as are most of the men he rescues. Thus the film elides the other question of color—the fact that "half the average combat rifle company . . . consisted of blacks and Hispanics."[19] American racism, and the class bias of the culture found the U.S. armed services in Vietnam consisting of a majority of poor whites and blacks, especially among the combat soldiers, the "grunts." The captivity narrative overshadows the historical narrative of rebellion in the ranks of the grunts (fragging—the killing of officers) and the feeling of solidarity that soldiers of color felt for their Vietnamese opponents.

The reliance on the captivity narrative and Indian iconography evidences a desperate impulse to disarticulate a sign—the Vietnam veteran—from one meaning (psychopathic misfit, murderer of women and children) to another, the Noble Savage. Stallone admitted in an interview that the rushes of the film made Rambo look "nihilistic, almost psychopathic."[20] The film cannot repress an ambivalence toward the Vietnam veteran in spite of the Noble Savage iconography. By emphasizing the efficiency of Rambo as a "killing machine" created by Trauptman, Stallone's protagonist becomes an American version of Frankenstein's monster. He begins to evoke figures from genre films such as *The Terminator*, or Jason in *Friday the 13th*, in his sheer implacability and indestructibility. One critic has written that Michael, the hero of *The Deer Hunter*, confronts the perversity of Vietnam's violence "with grace."[21] Rambo, as the embodiment of the return of the repressed, can only confront perversity with perversity.

Through the castrated/castrating dialectic of sacrifice and sadistic violence, Rambo redeems the MIAs and American manhood, but in spite of his triumph of revenge, he has not been freed of his victim status at the end of the film. Trauptman tells him: "Don't hate your country. . . ." Rambo's impassioned final plea states that all he wants is for his country to love the vets as much as they have loved their country. Trauptman asks, "How will you live, John?" Rambo replies, "Day by day." The ending suggests that the screenwriters absorbed much from Warner Brothers' *I Am a Fugitive from a Chain Gang* in which veteran Allen, duped by bureaucrats, is returned to prison and denied his promised pardon. He escapes a second time to tell his fiancée, "I hate everything but you. . . ." She asks, "How do you live?" Allen: "I steal." While Allen disappears into darkness, Rambo's walk into the Thai sunset also serves to recall the ending of numerous Westerns in which the hero's ambivalence toward civilization and the community's ambivalence toward the hero's violence precludes their reconciliation. Like Ethan Edwards, Rambo is doomed to wander between the two winds, but to a 1980s audience, no doubt, the ending does not signal the awareness of the tragic consequences of unreasoning violence and racial hatred as in Ford's film, but the exhilarating possibility of yet another Stallone sequel.

**LUXURIATING IN THEIR PATRIOTIC SYMPTOMS**

Like populist discourses such as Bruce Springsteen's "Born in the USA," *Rambo* plays upon a profound ambivalence toward the Vietnam vet, the war, and the U.S. government, but like Springsteen's song, *Rambo* has been incorporated into the popular discourse as a celebration of Americanism. In its obvious preferred reading, the film is decoded by its predominantly post-Vietnam, male audience as a unified, noncontradictory system.[22] This kind of integration into the cultural discourse is possible because the will to myth overrides the ideological tensions that threaten the coherence of the film's textual system. The film does not require a belief in history, only a belief in the history, conventions, and myth-making capacity of the movies.

In a challenging essay in *Postmodernism and Politics*, Dana Polan speaks of cinema's "will-to-spectacle," the banishment of background, the assertion that "a world of foreground is the only world that matters or is the only world that *is*."[23] If one eliminates the past as background, events can be transformed into satisfying spectacle, hurtful history into pleasurable myth. Drawing on this will-to-spectacle, the mythogenesis of *Rambo* lies, not in history, but in the *ur-texts* of fiction that provide its mythic resonance as a genre film and its vocabulary for exercising the will to myth.

In fact, virtually all background is eliminated in *Rambo*, and the spectacle becomes the half-clad, muscle-bound body of Sylvester Stallone: the inflated body of the male as the castrated and castrating monster. John Rambo is the body politic offered up as the anatomically incorrect action doll—John Ellis describes an ad for the film showing Rambo holding "his machine gun where his penis ought to be."[24] Rambo declares that "the mind is the best weapon," but Stallone's glistening hypermasculinity, emphasized in the kind of languid camera movements and fetishizing close-up usually reserved for female "flash-dancers," visually insists otherwise.

*Rambo*'s narcissistic cult of the fetishized male body redresses a perceived loss of personal and political power at a most primitive level, at the site of the body, which often defined the division of labor between male and female in pretechnological, patriarchal societies. The male body as weapon functions as a bulwark against feelings of powerlessness engendered by technology, minority rights, feminism—this helps explain the film's popularity not only in the U.S. but overseas as well, where it similarly appealed to working-class, male audiences.[25] Most of all, however, the film speaks to post-Vietnam/post-Watergate America's devastating loss of confidence in its status as the world's most powerful, most respected, most moral nation. Our judgement and ability to fight the "good" war as a total war of commitment without guilt has been eroded by our involvement in Vietnam, as surely as a sense of personal power has been eroded by a society increasingly bewildering in its technological complexity.

Attempting to deliver its audience from the anxiety of the present, *Rambo* would seek to restore an unreflective lost Eden of primitive masculine power. Yet Rambo must supplement his physical prowess with high-tech weapons adapted to the use of the lone warrior-hero. A contradictory distinction is maintained between his more "primitive" use of technology and that of the bureaucracy. Rambo's most hysterical, uncontrollable act of revenge is against Murdock and Murdock's technology. He machine-guns the computers and sophisticated equipment in operations headquarters. Uttering a primal scream, he then turns his weapon to the ceiling in a last outburst of uncontrollable rage. Such an outburst is the predictable result of the dynamics of repression, for the film cannot reconstitute institutional norms except through the mythological presence of the superfetishized superman, who functions as the mediator between the threatened patriarchal ideology and the viewer/subject desperately seeking to identify with a powerful figure. As a reaction formation against feelings of powerlessness too painful to be admitted or articulated, Rambo's violent reprisals, dependent on the power of the overfetishized male body, may be read as a symptomatic expression, a psychosomatic signifier of the return of the repressed, suggesting profound ideological crisis in the patriarchy.

Freud warned that within the context of repression and unconscious acting out, the young and childish tend to "luxuriate in their symptoms."[26] *Rambo* demonstrates a cultural parallel, a luxuriating in the symptoms of a desperate ideological repression manifested in the inability to speak of or remember the painful past, a cultural hysteria in which violence must substitute for understanding, victimization for responsibility, the personal for the political. While *Rambo* reflects ambiguous and often inchoate drives to rewrite the Vietnam War, it also shows how in the will to myth the original traumatic experience is compulsively acted out in a contradictory form that leaves the origins of ideological anxiety untouched: the need to reconcile repressed material remains.

## NOTES

1. Fredric Jameson, *The Political Unconscious: Narrative as a Socially Symbolic Act* (Ithaca, NY: Cornell University Press, 1981), p. 102.

2. Sigmund Freud, "Repression," *General Psychological Theory*, ed. Philip Rieff (New York: Macmillan-Collier, 1963), p. 112.

3. Ibid., pp. 114–115.

4. Ibid., pp. 112–113.

5. Theodor W. Adorno, "What Does Coming to Terms with the Past Mean?" *Bitburg in Moral and Political Perspective*, ed. Geoffrey H. Hartman (Bloomington, IN: Indiana University Press, 1986), p. 116.

6. Ibid., p. 128.

7. Alex de Jonge, *The Weimar Chronicle* (London: Paddington Press, 1978), p. 32.

8. William Shirer, *The Rise and Fall of the Third Reich* (Greenwich, CT: Fawcett, 1960), pp. 55–56.

9. de Jonge, *Weimar Chronicle*, p. 32.

10. Robert Edwin Herstein, *The War that Hitler Won: The Most Infamous Propaganda Campaign in History* (New York: Putnam, 1978).

11. Alvin H. Rosenfeld, "Another Revisionism: Popular Culture and the Changing Image of the Holocaust," in Hartman, *Bitburg*, p. 96.

12. Ibid., p. 94.

13. Richard Grenier, "Stallone on Patriotism and 'Rambo'," *New York Times*, 6 June 1985, p. C21.

14. Ronald Reagan, "Never Again . . ." in *Bitburg and Beyond*, ed. Ilya Levkov (New York: Shapolsky, 1987), p. 131.

15. Francis X. Clines, "Tribute to Vietnam Dead: Words, a Wall," *New York Times*, 11 November 1982, p. B15.

16. Richard Slotkin, *Regeneration Through Violence: The Mythology of the American Frontier, 1600–1860* (Middletown, CT: Wesleyan University Press, 1973), p. 421.

17. Karl Marx and Friedrich Engels, *The German Ideology* (London: Lawrence & Wishart, 1965), pp. 37–38.

18. Slotkin, *Regeneration*, p. 558.

19. Gabriel Kolko, *Anatomy of a War: Vietnam, the United States, and the Modern Historical Experience* (New York: Pantheon, 1985), p. 360.

20. Grenier, "Stallone."

21. Judy S. Kinney, "The Mythical Method: Fictionalizing the Vietnam War," *Wide Angle*, vol. 7, no. 4 (1985), p. 40.

22. John Ellis, " 'Rambollocks' is the Order of the Day," *New Statesman* 8 (November 1985), p. 15.

23. Dana Polan, " 'Above All Else to Make You See': Cinema and the Ideology of Spectacle," *Postmodernism and Politics*, ed. Jonathan Arac (Minneapolis: University of Minnesota Press, 1986), p. 60. Emphasis in original.

24. Ellis, " 'Rambollocks'," p. 15.

25. Ellis, " 'Rambollocks'."

26. Sigmund Freud, "Remembering, Repeating, and Working-Through," *The Standard Edition of the Complete Psychological Works*, 23 vols., ed. and trans. James Strachey, vol. 12 (London: Hogarth Press, 1953–1966), p. 152.

# 11

# Against Cartesianism: Three Generations of Vietnam Scholarship

## Marvin E. Gettleman

*The reader may properly ask why I have not come forth with my story [of the OSS and Vietnam's August 1945 Revolution] until now [1980]. In 1946 I drafted a much shorter account . . . but other commitments prevented me from completing that manuscript. After the French collapse at Dien Bien Phu, my manuscript was ready for publication, but it was too late. Our nation was embroiled in the era of McCarthyism. Sensitive to adverse criticism of American foreign policy by members of the military establishment, the Department of the Army decreed that any public disclosure of information or opinion by me on the question of American involvement in Viet Nam would be regarded with official displeasure and I would be subject to disciplinary action. Under protest I acceded to the Department's injunction.*

Former officer in the OSS (Office of Strategic Services)
Archimedes L.A. Patti, in the preface to his
*Why Viet Nam? Prelude to America's Albatross*
(Berkeley: University of California Press, 1980)

Southeast Asia scholarship, more than most areas of scholarly work, was and is the extension of war by ideological means. Therefore this highly selective bibliographical survey must begin by identifying one of the main war-linked ideological problems—one that interacts with and intensifies the

I acknowledge with gratitude the comradely advice and support of Ellen Schrecker, Doug Allen, Ngo Vinh Long, and Marilyn Young, not all of whom agree with the assessments of this survey. This chapter is © 1989 by Marvin E. Gettleman and is reprinted with permission from Marvin E. Gettleman, "Against Cartesianism: Preliminary Notes on Three Generations of English-Language Political Discourse on Vietnam," *Bulletin of Concerned Asian Scholars* 21, nos. 2–4 (April–Dec. 1989), pp. 136–143.

McCarthyist distortion mentioned by Archimedes Patti and also obscures in other ways any clear view of the recent struggles in Southeast Asia (not to speak of those more remote in time). I call it Cartesian imperialism,[1] which in Latin would be something like: *vici ergo estes,* I invade you, therefore you exist. Among other connotations it contains the linguistic chauvinism inherent in the use of the word "Vietnam" to mean the open war the U.S. government waged against Vietnam from at least 1950 to 1975 (as distinguished from the covert war waged since, to punish Vietnam for humbling the American giant). This usage reduces a country with a rich and complicated historical tradition stretching back centuries to a mere episode in U.S. foreign policy.

Versions of this Cartesianism—especially in its ethnocentric form—permeate not only Western scholarship on Vietnam but popular attitudes as well. Unable to perceive the Vietnamese nationalists as significant agents in their own victory, American Cartesians conceive only of an American defeat. Clinging to notions of American military omnipotence, these Cartesians thus (as French militarists did after Dien Bien Phu)[2] blame the outcome on backstabbers on the home front, either the media or the antiwar movement or both—anyone but themselves.

A few Western scholars, however, despite their focus on the American side of the war in Vietnam and their lack of mastery of indigenous languages, have avoided some of the more debilitating results of Cartesianism. Perhaps the best example is University of Kentucky historian George C. Herring, who himself strongly criticized the ethnocentric biases in American reports in "Vietnam Remembered," *Journal of American History,* vol. 80 (June 1986), and contributed what is arguably the best textbook on the U.S.-Vietnam conflict, *America's Longest War: The United States and Vietnam, 1950–1975,* 2d ed. (New York: Knopf, 1987 [first published 1979]).

Aside from mentioning Herring's exemplary work, I will leave a full survey of materials within the Cartesian consensus to some future team of Southeast Asia specialists. Instead, I offer here a tentative road map of the terrain, outlining the main contributions of what I call three generations of Western scholars of Indochina.

The concept of "generations" is a loose one and does not imply rigid sequence. Often the work of and polemics between the three generations go on simultaneously. Yet they are, as I shall try to demonstrate, distinct in method, in conclusions, and in the social and political milieu that gave rise to each.

**THE FIRST GENERATION: CIRCUMSCRIBED POLITICAL DIVERSITY**

Having defined and attacked the particular form of Cartesian imperialism that has infected the Western discourse on Indochina, I retreat a bit to concede the elements of truth that do lurk even in this Cartesian fallacy. In Third World areas, modern nationalist and revolutionary movements do develop partially in response to imperialism, as L. S. Stavrianos shows in his massive, immensely useful synthesis, *Global Rift: The Third World Comes of Age* (New York: Morrow, 1981). But Cartesianism usually comes into lethal play when those movements challenge the power of the imperialists and the local comprador elites, who then respond by upping the ante, calling in those self-proclaimed global gendarmes, the Yankee militarists, who have been all too eager to respond, whether in Greece, Central America, or Southeast Asia. At this point American troops arrive and Third World "trouble spots" move predictably onto newspaper front pages and into public attention. *Only then does the historical clock start running for Western audiences.* Thus, this practical Cartesianism introduces an insistent presentism that, backed by American power, becomes something of a self-fulfilling prophecy. On the level not only of scholarship, but also of the internal conceptualizations entertained by the Washington policymakers (which we are now able to penetrate, partially thanks to the *Pentagon Papers* and other source materials), the Cartesian construct has often substituted for reality itself. Thus, even when they are accorded pro forma recognition, the histories of indigenous resistance movements and their relationships to later national liberation struggles and other aspects of "native" culture functionally disappear, and scholarship flattens out. The all-too-familiar cold war dichotomies then come into play, obscuring far more than they illuminate.

In one form or another "first generation" writers espoused the prevailing Cartesian fallacy, sometimes disguising it with an overlay of scholarship. Joseph Buttinger is a case in point. An old Indochina hand, a wealthy ex-Austrian Social Democrat, Buttinger (1906–   ) became involved in Indochina through "rescue" of refugees from the northern zone of Vietnam after the 1954 Geneva Conference. He composed *The Smaller Dragon: A Political History of Vietnam* (New York: Praeger, 1958) while under the spell of what he called a "conversion" (p. 4) to the questionable cause of Ngo Dinh Diem. Immensely learned (but only in Western source materials, many drawn from his own vast private library of Indochinese materials, which he generously made available to some other scholars), Buttinger was nothing if not an activist-scholar, a charge that was later used selectively against antiwar scholars. He was dedicated to discovery or manufacture of the legitimate Vietnamese anteced-ents of a "third force" (neither communist nor obvious puppet of imperialism) that had to be identified and supported by the West. Not content merely to urge such a policy, Buttinger helped found the American Friends of Vietnam— Ngo Dinh Diem's lobby in the United States.[3]

Although Buttinger belatedly repudiated Ngo Dinh Diem and his unsavory regime, his anticommunist successors in this first generation of Vietnam scholars continued to write and act as if there were some legitimate revolu-tionary forces in Vietnam other than the one dominated since 1930 by the communists. As it turned out, and as some recognized early,[4] they were searching for a phantom, and their books now serve mainly as ideological curiosities of the cold war.[5]

One of the most effective, or at least determined, advocates of this cold war line on Vietnam was—and continues to be—the ubiquitous U.S. government–connected Douglas Pike. His books, especially *Vietcong: The Organiza-tion and Techniques of the National Liberation Front of South Vietnam* (Cambridge: Massachusetts Institute of Technology Press, 1966) and *History of Vietnamese Communism, 1925–1976* (Stanford: Hoover Institution Press, 1978), express a sophisticated version of the standard Cartesian view: namely, that the victo-rious insurgents who defeated imperialism in Indochina were, because of their espousal of communism, ipso facto aliens and outsiders in the very country they were instrumental in liberating. His version of the history of Vietnamese communism, especially in *Vietcong*, which was a veritable manual for coun-terinsurgency, feeds so well into the widespread Western ahistorical distor-tions that it is hard to resist the conclusion that it was intended for the purpose. Pike's work, now amplified at an academic base at the University of California at Berkeley, is emblematic of an entire corpus of first-generation, U.S. govern-ment–linked studies that attempt to lift the movement for national liberation led by the Vietnamese Communists out of history and recast it as demonology, so as to buttress the policies of Washington cold war hard-liners.

This first generation's Vietnam scholarship did not fade away when its findings were superseded; its original practitioners and their student-disciples purvey their tawdry wares, often from privileged academic sanctuaries in California and Virginia, to the present day (even with some of the linguistic equipment characteristically deployed by the third generation). An example of unreconstructed Cartesianism is the recent work of another old Indochina hand, Ellen Hammer, whose 1954 classic *Struggle for Indochina* was required reading in those parched days of the early antiwar movement when the second generation of Vietnam scholars was just becoming active. Her new book, *Death in November: America in Vietnam, 1963* (New York: Dutton/Oxford, 1987) upholds the old myths that Ngo Dinh Diem and his relatives and cronies constituted a viable alternative to a Communist Vietnam.

Also keeping alive (but barely) the cherished first generation right-wing verities, including particularly vulgar notions of Cartesian imperialism, are a group of American military writers whose special mission is to explain away the U.S. defeat in Vietnam. The major spokesperson of this we-would-have-won-if-only school is Colonel Harry G. Summers, Jr., whose *On Strategy: A Critical Analysis of the Vietnam War* (New York: Dell, 1982) is a classic of the genre. The writings of Summers & Co. must be seen as post facto rationales bearing marked similarities to the post–Dien Bien Phu posturing of French militarists, with Central America playing for the Americans the role Algeria played for the Gallic *revanchistes*. Summers's own view was that in Vietnam the Americans could have triumphed in an all-out conventional war, including an invasion of the northern zone of Vietnam. The most generous comment that can be made on Summers's unproved and unprovable thesis is that it presents a marvelously transparent view of military Cartesianism at work: a war in which the nature of the "enemy" is *on principle* left out of the calculations!

But not all old—or new—Indochina hands were anticommunist. The left wing of this first generation of Vietnam scholars who wrote in English was represented almost singlehandedly by the Australian Wilfred Burchett (1911–1983). Burchett's books, informed by long, unparalleled journalistic experience in Southeast Asia, portrayed the Indochinese Communist revolutionaries not only as the wave of the future, but also (especially in perhaps his most valuable book, *Mekong Upstream* [Hanoi: Red River Publishing House, 1957]) the direct descendants of early nationalistic movements in this region. But Burchett's books, published abroad or by left-wing outfits in the United States, were scorned or ignored by conventional "experts." For example, Pike (*Vietcong*, p. xi) dismissed Burchett's *Vietnam: Inside Story of the Guerrilla War* (New York: International, 1965) as untrustworthy and, with a revealing ethnocentric twist, as being of no "value to the American reader." An objective observer might conclude just the contrary; that because of their revolutionary perspectives, Burchett's work might have had its greatest value for American readers! Lest the treatment of Burchett's work be downplayed as a remnant of a now-vanished McCarthyism, the similar response now accorded Noam Chomsky's political writings shows how dissenting work of great significance can still be dismissed from mainstream discourse.

Another serious problem with the Cartesian fallacy was (and is) that it fits only too well with, even feeds, the historical amnesia that is endemic in the United States, on and off college campuses. Nourished on the ideology of "putting it behind us," and "getting on with the business at hand," Yankees consider themselves outside history. So what one generation bequeaths to another is systematically undervalued. They are a strange breed indeed: these modern anti-Burkean conservatives. No wonder so many of them were blind to the historical reality of a Vietnam whose patriots harkened back to the Trung sisters, to the futile Can Vuong mandarin-patriots, to Phan Boi Chau, and to the many-generational struggles encapsuled in the life of Nguyen Ai Quoc/Ho Chi Minh. It became the task of later generations of Western scholars to redress the balance.

## THE SECOND GENERATION: COMPENSATORY SCHOLARSHIP

Except for the work of Bernard Fall (more French than American, whose contributions will be examined below), there was little Indochina scholarship going on in the United States on the eve of the 1965 escalation in Vietnam. There was no bureau or agency in America equivalent to the French l'Ecole d'Extrême-Orient. The Institute of Pacific Relations, the one group that conceivably could have fulfilled such a role, was smashed in the McCarthyist furor over the "loss" of China.[6] As a result, the U.S. imperial enterprise was carried out with multiple forms of deception, including a self-deception partially rooted in sheer ignorance.

The second generation of Vietnam scholars thus arose in a veritable intellectual vacuum, and its tasks were historically defined—to counter the lies and distortions of those who defended U.S. policy in Vietnam and the rest of Indochina with the threadbare and increasingly bizarre doctrines of

Cartesian imperialism. The scholarship produced was politically motivated in the broadest sense; its practitioners sought to enlighten and mobilize an American citizenry to action against an unjust struggle being carried out by Washington geopoliticians and militarists. Antiwar academics and journalists did quick studies to counter the transparent lies being issued by Washington, and the supporting rationalizations formulated by such conservative and mainstream pundits as Berkeley professor Robert Scalapino. Scalapino and like-minded academics went around to campuses to debate antiwar scholars, invoking bizarre notions of double and even triple manipulation at a distance. With breezy confidence not justified by later disputes among Communist countries in Southeast Asia, they maintained that the Vietnamese revolutionaries in the southern zone were mere puppets of Hanoi, while Ho Chi Minh and his fellow Vietnamese revolutionaries in the North were considered agents of the Chinese Communists.[7] Some went so far as to label the Chinese Communists as creatures of the ultimate masterminds of the international Communist conspiracy sitting at the controls in Moscow, pushing buttons that miraculously caused guerrillas to spring up from the ground in the southern zones of Vietnam (or from the villages of Central America or the dusty plains of Lebanon, etc.). Or so many Americans, apparently including some in power in Washington, thought and still think. The unacknowledgeable existence of wholly owned *U.S.* puppets was a powerful deterrent to honest discourse.

For those of us who served in the second generation's intellectual demolition efforts, and who were not trained Asianists, it would be hard to overestimate the combined influence of Noam Chomsky and the late I. F. Stone. It was Izzy Stone (1907–1989) with his brilliant dissection of the 1965 *Aggression from the North* "White Paper"[8] and other exemplary exercises in investigative journalism, who emboldened many of us to question official rationales. Perhaps the most powerful document produced in the honorable shadow of Stone was Robert Scheer's pathbreaking and still useful pamphlet, *How the United States Got Involved in Vietnam,* issued by Robert Hutchins's Center for the Study of Democratic Institutions.

Noam Chomsky's eloquent essay "The Responsibility of Intellectuals"[9] introduced many of us who were not linguists to his writing. Aside from the manifest content of the essay (intellectuals should tell the truth, not lie, as so many were doing in defense of Washington's goals in Vietnam), it served, especially for those of us who lacked Ivy League credentials, to demystify the esoteric discourse of the academic mandarins at such august institutions as Chomsky's own Massachusetts Institute of Technology. Once revealed by Chomsky as puffed-up worshippers of power, these mandarins and their intellectual productions were fair game for all of us in the second generation. But since the mandarins controlled many of the respectable publishing outlets, we had to found our own journals, including *Viet-Report* (New York, 1965–67) and the *Bulletin of Concerned Asian Scholars* (begun at Cambridge, MA, in 1968 as the *CCAS Newsletter*).

The trained Asianists in the second generation, many of whom had studied with John Fairbank at Harvard, George McT. Kahin at Cornell, or Franz

Schurmann at the University of California at Berkeley, did not need Stone or Chomsky to prompt them to question the pervasive distortions of the Cartesian and other fallacies.[10] The simplistic McCarthyist myths of how China "was handed" to the Communists gave these Asianists a proximate professional example of how cold war dogmas could warp understanding of an indigenous revolutionary movement.[11] It was a short step to the realization that official Washington's argument that the Vietnamese revolutionaries were outside aggressors in their own country was a replay of the China lobby's distortions of the defeat of Chiang Kai-shek by 1949.[12]

Bernard Fall (1926–1967), who in the absence of much competition was for a time the leading U.S.-based expert on Indochina, was clearly a special case. Vienna-born and raised in France where he joined the anti-Nazi resistance as a teenager, he came to the United States in the 1950s and earned graduate degrees at Syracuse. From his earliest work on the Viet Minh to his posthumous *Last Reflections on a War* (New York: Doubleday, 1967), Fall's central preoccupation was with "revolutionary warfare," how insurgents can be defeated, and at what cost. At times this put Fall on the side of the French imperialists and their American successors, and a good case can be made for including him in the first generation. His *Street Without Joy: Indochina at War, 1946–1954* (Harrisburg, PA: Stackpole, 1961) ambiguously concluded that the French effort to hold on to Indochina before Dien Bien Phu "bought freedom" for 20 million people. In a similar vein, an essay attributed to Fall, "Street Without Joy Revisited," included in *Last Reflections*, concluded that the "first step in the making of a better life" for the people of Indochina was the American-assisted effort of "eliminating the insurgent[s]."[13]

Yet even such a cold warrior as Fall came to develop a vivid sense of the futility of U.S. counterinsurgency, and some of his most powerful journalistic pieces (especially "This Isn't Munich, It's Spain," which appeared in the leftist magazine *Ramparts* in 1965 and is reprinted in *Last Reflections*) demonstrated that the lethal U.S. escalation in Vietnam had been undertaken without ample calculation of the political costs. The U.S. effort had become fanatical in the technical sense—ardent pursuit of means that actually undermined American goals and interests. Thus Fall belatedly joined the second generation's demolition project, the precondition (as will be suggested below) for the third generation's reconstruction of a reliable and useful Vietnamese national history.

Much of the second generation's scholarly effort to clear the record of the detritus of Washington's (and other parties') distortions eventually saw print. Belatedly, this included Archimedes Patti's awkwardly subtitled but valuable memoir of the creation of the Democratic Republic of Vietnam in 1945 (an excerpt from which is cited as an epigraph to this essay). Patti's honest chronicle makes clear that the McCarthyist fantasy of communism originally being "installed" in Vietnam by some outside force was, and is, absurd. Similar but more comprehensive efforts of the Committee of Concerned Asian Scholars warrant mention here. CCAS produced the popular volume *The Indochina Story* (New York: Bantam, 1970) that competed with prowar paperbacks on drugstore and airport book racks, and kept churning out issues of its invaluable *Bulletin*.

The work of second-generation Indochina scholars was often developed in the intellectual gladiatorial contests that were institutionalized (unfortunately, temporarily) in the teach-in movement of the 1960s.[14] A participant in that movement, I vividly remember our opponents' intellectual weakness—their inability to defend Washington's policies convincingly on either moral or geopolitical grounds. And sadly their intellectual weakness was unmatched by institutional weakness—the U.S. government was on their side. On teach-in platforms the State Department spokespersons we debated (for a brief period when Foggy Bottom permitted its employees to attend), or the inter-locking directorates of the American Friends of Vietnam and Freedom House, or assorted old Indochina hands, often were forced to fall back on a particular form of ad hominem argument. It went something like: "Sonny" (we were already "Mister" or even "Professor" to a yet younger generation, and hated the term "Sonny"), "if you knew what we knew, if you were privy to the inside data revealed to those of us with security clearance, you would join the team." It was hard to counter this position, based as it was on evidence that by its very nature could not be revealed. This of course illustrates how important the *Pentagon Papers* were to the public discourse on Vietnam. While the revelations handed down by Daniel Ellsberg and Tony Russo surprised few of us of the second generation of Vietnam scholars who had studied Vietnam in the 1960s, they made it impossible for our antagonists to use the "Sonny, if you knew . . . " routine with any credibility. But it was already almost too late; the casualties of the U.S.-Vietnam War were well on their way to the final grim totals—2,282,000 dead and over 3 million wounded.[15]

The task thrust upon the scholar/activists of the second generation, both credentialed Asianists and self-taught types, was "compensatory scholarship" (to borrow a term derived from an early stage in feminist studies). In certain ways it was too easy to counter the official line, and in some of the ephemeral discourse of the teach-in era, pundits occasionally mounted podiums to point up the idiocies of U.S. policy with the muted implication that if *they* guided policy, the Viet Cong could be finished off in short order. (There is no evidence that anyone got the call from the Pentagon.)

The second generation's more substantial arguments, now accepted by the mainstream, were that there were *not* two Vietnams, that the Geneva Accords did *not* create an independent political entity in southern Vietnam, that modern Vietnamese history was *continuous* and the Viet Minh struggle against the French was an earlier stage of the revolutionary resistance to the Ameri-cans, that the southern insurgents had substantial popular support, and that Ngo Dinh Diem's and all the later American-backed regimes were *tainted in one way or another with collaborationism.* Because of all of the official lies, these truths announced in teach-in talks, in essays and books, were brought forth as if their blinding veracity would of itself instantly halt the Vietnam War.[16] There was a touching naiveté in the operative principle of the era: speak truth to power. However, recognizing early the futility of convincing our Washing-ton antagonists,[17] some either abandoned the fray or recklessly assayed revolutionary tactics in the United States in supposed imitation of the Viet-namese themselves.

But for those who stayed with scholarship (usually with accompanying political activity), and who lacked the tools that the next (third) generation would deploy, the study of the American/Vietnam encounter resolved itself into an examination of the Washington policy apparatus itself. Space limitations do not permit here the careful review of common and diverse themes in the important and deserving work of such scholars as Paul Joseph, Hugh Higgins, James P. Harrison, Peter Dale Scott, and Loren Baritz.[18]

However, Frances Fitzgerald's *Fire in the Lake: The Vietnamese and the Americans in Vietnam* (Boston: Atlantic/Little Brown, 1972) demands separate attention, partly because of its fame (it won the Pulitzer Prize in 1973), and partly because Vintage Books has kept the paperbound version in print for a remarkable decade and a half. Fitzgerald's twofold project was meritorious: to look at the Vietnamese-American encounter in its deepest cultural terms, and to penetrate the pseudoreality of public-relations hype that obscured the American war effort. But she failed at both. Her understanding of Vietnamese culture was limited by the pervasive second-generation inability to read the *quoc ngu*, by her unwillingness to compensate by tapping what by the late 1960s was a rich body of Vietnamese documents, historical narratives, and tales in translation, and by relying excessively on Otare Mannoni's model of indigenous attitudes toward the West based on the inapplicable example of Madagascar (*Prospero and Caliban* [New York: Praeger, 1964]). Also, as Ngo Vinh Long correctly charged in his review of *Fire in the Lake* (*Ramparts*, 27 October 1972), Fitzgerald's reduction of Vietnamese culture to Confucianism, and her stated belief that the ancient Chinese *Book of Changes*, the *I Ching*, contained "all the clues to the basic design" of the Vietnamese world view was an inexcusable distortion. In her view, Marxism's appeal to the Vietnamese was merely the reaction of an unsophisticated peasantry still sunk in traditional Confucian values. Fitzgerald's view of the American side of the conflict was almost as shallow, as she could not bring herself to use the "i" word—imperialism—and hence missed the geopolitical imperatives to consolidate and extend capitalism. No wonder her book has been such a success in an America that wants its failure in Vietnam explained—but not too harshly.[19]

Far more successful attempts to decipher the American side in the Vietnam War were made by George McT. Kahin, whose *Intervention: How America Became Involved in Vietnam* (New York: Knopf, 1986; and [paperback] Garden City, NY: Anchor/Doubleday, 1987) reflected three decades of careful study and experience, and by James Wilson Gibson, who in *The Perfect War* (Boston: Atlantic Monthly Press, 1986; and New York: Vintage Books/Random House, 1988) skillfully used the arcane techniques of deconstruction to uncover layer after layer of deception in the American effort to defeat the Vietnamese revolutionaries. Neil Sheehan provided a unique and enlightening perspective on American military operations in his Pulitzer Prize–winning *A Bright Shining Lie: John Paul Vann and America in Vietnam* (New York and Toronto: Random House, 1988), which traces two phases—both unsuccessful—of a model U.S. soldier's search for a winning strategy.

With these books by Kahin, Gibson, and Sheehan, as well as with Herring's earlier-mentioned exemplary textbook, the Cartesian project of attempting to understand what happened in Vietnam reached its outer limits. How and why America *lost* was analyzed and reanalyzed, but no successful explanation could be attained until the other side of the equation was explored: *how and why the Vietnamese won*. But this called for a different approach by a new generation of Vietnam scholars.

**THE THIRD GENERATION: CARTESIANISM PARTIALLY VANQUISHED**

As Gabriel Kolko's *Anatomy of a War: Vietnam, the United States and the Modern Historical Experience* (New York: Pantheon, 1985) revealed, reading knowledge of the *quoc ngu* was not absolutely essential. Making the finest use yet of the JPRS (U.S. Joint Publications Research Service) translations of Vietnamese materials, of American government sources, and of a basic "plain Marxist" outlook, Kolko produced the best all-around Western book on the Vietnam-American encounter. Particularly valuable in *Anatomy of a War* is its recognition of time as a semi-independent variable that worked in favor of the Vietnamese revolutionaries, who recognized it as a counterweight to the vast, technologically superior American war machine.

Kolko's achievement was something of a tour de force since by the early 1970s a third generation of Indochina scholars who knew the indigenous languages and had broken free from ethnocentric Western blinders had emerged. Five main publications mark their debut, one of which, Truong Buu Lam's *Pattern of Vietnamese Response to Foreign Intervention, 1858–1900* (New Haven, CT: Yale University Press, 1967), actually appeared a half-decade earlier. But David G. Marr's *Vietnamese Anticolonialism, 1885–1925* (Berkeley: University of California Press, 1971), written by a former U.S. Marine Corps intelligence officer who studied Vietnamese at the military language center in Monterey, California,[20] with its sympathetic treatment of patriotic resistance in French Indochina, represented the coming of age of serious Vietnamese scholarship in the United States. The next year the University of California also published Jeffrey Race's *War Comes to Long An: Revolutionary Conflict in a Vietnamese Province*, based on clear-sighted field work. Ngo Vinh Long's *Before the Revolution: The Vietnamese Peasants under the French* (Cambridge, MA: MIT Press, 1973) was not only a distinguished historical work based on sources in indigenous and European languages, but also helped dispel some of the romantic haze that had settled over French imperialism, which in retrospect had mistakenly begun to be seen as less oppressive than its American successor. Lastly, the translation into English of Nguyen Khac Vien's *Tradition and Revolution in Vietnam* (Berkeley, CA: Indochina Resource Center, 1974), edited and with a preface by David Marr and Jayne Werner and translated by Linda Yarr, Jayne Werner, and Tran Tuong Nhu, was in part an act of homage to and respect for the Vietnamese perspective and to a distinguished patriotic Vietnamese scholar. These five works heralded the birth of a new generation of Vietnamese scholarship, one based on greatly enhanced knowledge of sources, with the promise (not always fulfilled, however) of overcoming the besetting Cartesianism by admitting the Vietnamese into their own history.

At its best the third generation has produced a rich body of work, including further publications of Marr and Werner, along with books and essays by Gareth Porter, Huynh Kim Khanh, Christine White, David Elliot, Edwin Moise, Ben Kiernan, and Michael Vickery.[21] Although space limitations prevent giving the attention here that this work deserves, Doug Allen's insightful essays elsewhere in this book (Chapter 7) and in the *Bulletin of Concerned Asian Scholars* 21 (April–Dec. 1989) describe the often adverse conditions, including enforced migration, under which this work has been produced. Meanwhile, a diverse group of centrist and right-wing scholars, whose command of indigenous sources, if not their political acumen, admits them to the third generation, have mounted a kind of intellectual counterrevolution of Cartesianism. Their corpus ranges from the unrestrained reactionary publications of Nguyen Van Canh and Nguyen Ngoc Huy,[22] to the subtly hostile books of William J. Duiker, and the middle-of-the-road works by William Turley and Alexander Woodside.[23] The existing structures of academic power and authority, including lavishly funded research centers at Stanford University and at George Mason University in Fairfax, Virginia, under the control of unreconstructed first generationers, prolong the destructive effects of Cartesianism on Indochina scholarship. But theirs is surely a doomed rear-guard effort, a belated attempt to salvage from the ruins of Western imperialism in Southeast Asia a few crumbs of post-facto justification.

So, the struggle continues.

## NOTES

1. I here try to call things by their names, ignoring the trendy, sanitized academic vocabulary that has become au courant in "advanced" university circles in the United States and elsewhere (where the terms "core" and "periphery" are used in place of what I believe is the still-useful, blunt term "imperialism"). I have been recently emboldened in this effort by the hard-hitting essay by James Petras in *In These Times* (Chicago), 4–10 November 1987.

2. For an example of the self-serving French militarist exculpatory views, see Henri Navarre, *Les temps des Vérités* (Paris: Plon, 1979), esp. pp. 280–282.

3. On the Vietnam lobby, see Robert Scheer, *How the United States Got Involved in Vietnam* (Santa Barbara, CA: Center for the Study of Democratic Institutions, 1965), available in M. Gettleman, Jane and Bruce Franklin, and Marilyn Young, eds., *Vietnam and America: A Documented History* (New York: Grove, 1985), reading 24. Journalist Stanley Karnow's *Vietnam: A History* (New York: Viking, 1983) has been widely and unjustifiably touted as definitive, but it omits any mention of the American Friends of Vietnam. (See Noam Chomsky's highly critical review of it in *The Boston Review*, February 1984.) Karnow's more recent book on the Philippines, *In Our Image* (New York: Random House, 1989) is similarly sanitized. Both Karnow works were (and are) companions to TV shows on Vietnam and the Philippines. The Karnow *Vietnam* had an excellent companion book of readings, far superior to the "parent" text: Steven Cohen, *Vietnam: Anthology and Guide to a Television History* (New York: Knopf, 1983). The thirteen-part U.S. Public Broadcasting System (PBS) TV series "Vietnam: A Television History" should be widely known to Asia scholars.

4. While the official U.S. line remained that the Vietnamese Communists were somehow interlopers in their own country, even the earliest Vietnam scholars, including those with the most impeccably conservative credentials (for example, Roy Jumper and Marjorie Weiner Normand, who contributed the "Vietnam" portion to George McT. Kahin's authoritative *Government and Politics in Southeast Asia,* 2d ed. [Ithaca, NY: Cornell University Press, 1964]), acknowledged that by the outbreak of World War II, the Communists had established the greatest "claims to historic leadership of the Vietnamese Nationalist movement" (p. 390).

5. In addition to Karnow's *Vietnam,* one classic work deservedly consigned to the rubbish heap of Vietnam War "scholarship" (where it still merits careful attention for its sophisticated justification of the U.S. role in Vietnam) is Gunther Lewey's *America in Vietnam* (New York: Oxford, 1978).

6. On the IPR and its fate in the McCarthyist era, see Ellen Schrecker, *No Ivory Tower: McCarthyism and the Universities* (New York: Oxford, 1986), chap. 6 and passim.

7. For Robert Scalapino's cocksure remarks on the inevitability of Chinese domination of Indochina, see his statements at the Washington, D.C., National Teach-In, 15 May 1965, in Marvin Gettleman, ed., *Vietnam: History, Documents and Opinions,* 1st ed. (New York: Fawcett, 1965, Penguin, 1966, and New American Library, 1971), pp. 398–403, 405–407. On the teach-in movement itself, see Louis Menashe and Ronald Radosh, eds., *Teach-Ins USA* (New York: Praeger, 1966).

8. I. F. Stone's rebuttal of the 1965 "White Paper" appeared in his *Weekly* (Washington, D.C.), 8 March 1965, and is reprinted, along with the document it refuted, in Gettleman/Franklin/Young, *Vietnam and America,* readings 37–38. Scheer's work is presented in readings 25, 26.

9. Noam Chomsky's great essay appeared in *The New York Review of Books,* 23 February 1967, and was reprinted in Chomsky's essay collection, *American Power and the New Mandarins* (New York: Pantheon, 1969). My criticism of Cartesianism in this essay has no bearing whatsoever on the linguistic Cartesianism espoused by Chomsky.

10. John King Fairbank's reflections on the building of Harvard's East Asia Institute appear in his *Chinabound: A Fifty-Year Memoir* (New York: Harper, 1982). In chapter 29 he recounts the development of dissenting views on the Vietnam War among the members and graduates of the East Asia Institute, including the founding of the Committee of Concerned Asian Scholars (for which Fairbank claims credit), many of whose members then attacked him (which he claims to accept with philosophical resignation).

11. On McCarthyism and Asian studies, see Fairbank, *Chinabound,* chap. 25, supplemented by Schrecker, *No Ivory Tower.*

12. On the China lobby, see the Committee of Concerned Asian Scholars edition of Ross Y. Koen's *The China Lobby in American Politics* (New York: Harper & Row, 1974). Its chilling preface by Richard C. Kagan describes the suppression of the 1960 edition of Koen's book.

13. Startlingly revealing of the limitations of Fall's work is the essay "Street Without Joy Revisited," which Dorothy Fall, his widow, thinking it was by her late husband, printed in *Last Reflections* along with Fall's other essays. The article turned out to have been written by Major Edward Laurance for *Armor* magazine, published by the U.S. Armor Association! (See *Publisher's Weekly,* 8 April 1968, p. 36:3.)

14. For the teach-ins, see the Menashe/Radosh book mentioned in note 7, above.

15. I rely on the judicious presentation of these grim statistics in the *Indochina Newsletter* (Dorchester, MA), November/December 1982.

16. Historically speaking, here is where my own 1965 anthology, *Vietnam,* comes in. The book was in part motivated by the belief that when policymakers became aware

of what was so easily discoverable in the historical record they would have no alternative but to make peace in Vietnam. It is doubtful if the simultaneously produced anthology (Bernard Fall and Marcus Raskin, *The Viet-Nam Reader* [Vintage, 1965]) was prompted by quite the same naiveté, but the Fall/Raskin *Reader*, far more than my *Vietnam*, was explicitly addressed to Washington policymakers. A third Vietnam anthology of note, far more scholarly than either my collection or Fall/Raskin's (but unsuitable for that same reason for undergraduate classroom use), is Gareth Porter, ed., *Vietnam: The Definitive History of Human Decisions* (2 vols.) (Crugers, NY: Earl M. Coleman Enterprises, Inc., Publishers, 1979), abridged as *Vietnam: A History in Documents* (New York: New American Library, 1981). There was also another Indochina anthology that I coedited with Susan Gettleman, Lawrence and Carol Kaplan, *Conflict in Indochina: A Reader on the Widening War in Laos and Cambodia* (New York: Random House/Vintage, 1970). This book, though now out of print, and of course out of date, may still be found in libraries, and contains a few useful items. The right-wing competition was Wesley Fishel's pathetic *Vietnam: Anatomy of a Conflict* (Greenwich, CT: Peacock Press, 1968).

17. In addition to the sober satisfaction that the *Pentagon Papers* gave in its verification of second-generation conclusions, there was another, less satisfying conclusion to be drawn from the same body of source material. That was: if U.S. government officials knew everything we did (and more) about the Vietnam War, *and persisted*, then it was not merely the policymakers' lack of relevant and reliable data that permitted the war to go on, and on, and on. . . .

18. See Paul Joseph, *Cracks in the Empire*, 2d ed. (New York: Columbia University Press, 1987); Hugh Higgins, *Vietnam*, 2d ed. (London: Heinemann, 1982); James P. Harrison, *The Endless War: Vietnam's Struggle for Independence* (New York: McGraw Hill, 1982); Peter Dale Scott, *The War Conspiracy* (New York: Harper & Row, 1972); Jonathan Schell's books combined into *The Real War: The Classic Reporting on the Vietnam War with a New Essay* (New York: Pantheon, 1987); and Loren Baritz, *Backfire: A History of How American Culture Led Us into Vietnam and Made Us Fight the Way We Did* (New York: Morrow/Ballantine, 1985), etc.

19. Some of these critical remarks on *Fire in the Lake* appeared earlier in *Science & Society*, Spring 1974.

20. See Marr's "The Rise and Fall of 'Counterinsurgency,' 1961–1964," in *The Pentagon Papers* (Gravel ed., Boston: Beacon, 1971), vol. 5, pp. 202–210.

21. See David G. Marr, *The Vietnamese Tradition on Trial, 1920–1945* (Berkeley: University of California Press, 1981); Jayne Werner, *Peasant Politics and Religious Sectarianism* (New Haven, CT: Yale University Press, 1981); Gareth Porter, *A Peace Denied: The United States, Vietnam and the Paris Agreements* (Bloomington, IN: Indiana University Press, 1975); Huynh Kim Khanh, *Vietnamese Communism, 1925–1945* (Ithaca, NY: Cornell University Press, 1982); Christine P. White, "Socialist Transformation of Agriculture and Gender Relations: The Vietnamese Case," in Sussex University *Institute of Development Studies Bulletin*, vol. 13 (1982); White, "Agricultural Planning . . . in Vietnam," *World Development*, vol. 13 (1985); White, ". . . The Socialist Transformation of Agriculture in Postwar Vietnam," in Marr and White, eds., *Postwar Vietnam: Dilemmas of Socialist Development* (Ithaca, NY: Cornell Southeast Asia *Publications*, 1988); David Elliot, "Institutionalizing the Revolution," in Turley, *The Second Indochina War* (see n. 23 below); Edwin Moise, "Land Reform and Land Reform Errors in North Vietnam," *Pacific Affairs* (Spring 1976); Moise, "Classism in North Vietnam, 1953–56," in Turley, ed., *Vietnamese Communism in Historical Perspective* (Boulder, CO: Westview Press, 1980); Ben Kiernan and Chanthou Boua, eds., *Peasants and Politics in Kampuchea, 1941–1981* (London: Zed Books, 1982); Michael Vickery, *Cambodia, 1975–1982* (Boston, MA: South End Press, and Hempstead, UK: Allen and Unwin, 1984).

22. Nguyen Van Canh, *Vietnam Under Communism, 1975–1982* (Stanford, CA: Hoover Institute Press, 1983); Nguyen Ngoc Huy, "Vietnam Under Communist Rule," George Mason University, *Vietnamese Studies Papers*, no. 1 (May 1982).

23. William J. Duiker, *The Rise of Nationalism in Vietnam, 1900–41* (Ithaca, NY: Cornell University Press, 1976); Duiker, *The Communist Road to Power in Vietnam* (Boulder, CO: Westview Press, 1981); William Turley, ed., *Vietnamese Communism*; Turley, *The Second Indochina War* (Boulder, CO: Westview Press, 1986); Turley, "The Military Construction of Socialism: Postwar Roles of the Peoples' Army of Vietnam," in Marr and White, eds., *Postwar Vietnam*; Alexander Woodside, *Community and Revolution in Modern Vietnam* (Boston, MA: Houghton Mifflin, 1976); Woodside, "Nationalism and Poverty in the Breakdown of Sino-Vietnamese Relations," *Pacific Affairs* (Fall 1979).

# Chronology

**1858–1884**

Beginning with the French invasion of Da Nang (1858), France spreads its colonial rule throughout Indochina.

**1890**

May 19: Birth of Nguyen Tat Thanh (Ho Chi Minh).

**1920**

Dec. 25–30: Ho Chi Minh, calling himself Nguyen Ai Quoc, becomes a founding member of the French Communist Party at the Tours Congress.

**1927**

Nov.: Foundation of the Viet Nam Quoc Dan Dang (Vietnam Nationalist Party), which was almost totally destroyed by the French in 1930.

**1930**

Feb. 3: Delegates from the three Communist parties of Tonkin, Annam, and Cochin China, along with representatives from anticolonial movements in Cambodia and Laos, meet at Kowloon (Hong Kong) at invitation of Ho Chi Minh and form the Indochinese Communist Party (Vietnamese name, Dang Cong San Dong Duong).

**1940**

Sept.: Japanese troops, with French cooperation, occupy Indochina.

**1941**

May 10–19: At Pac Bo, the Viet Nam Doc Lap Dong Minh (Vietnam Independence League or Viet Minh) is founded. U.S. Office of Strategic Services (OSS) works with Viet Minh against the Japanese in Vietnam.

**1945**

March 11: Emperor Bao Dai proclaims independence and cooperation with Japan.

Aug.: The August Revolution in which the Viet Minh seize power throughout Vietnam, defeating the French and Japanese, forcing Bao Dai to abdicate, and creating the first postcolonial independent state in Asia.

Sept. 2: Ho Chi Minh proclaims the founding of the Democratic Republic of Vietnam. In coming months, the United States supports French efforts to reimpose colonialism in Vietnam.

**1946**

Nov. 23: French warships bombard Haiphong killing 6,000, provoking Vietnamese response, and starting First Indochina War (1946–1954).

Dec. 19: Viet Minh and Cambodian and Laotian allies throughout Indochina attack French forces.

**1949**

March 8: Bao Dai and France sign the Élysée Agreement making Vietnam an "associated state" within the French Union. Bao Dai arrives in Saigon as head of state (13 June). His State of Vietnam is an alternative to the Democratic Republic of Vietnam.

**1950**

Feb. 7: The United States and Britain recognize Bao Dai's government. The United States begins giving large amounts of military aid to the French, eventually funding 80 percent of the French war effort by 1954.

**1951**

March 3: The Vietnam Workers Party (Dang Lao Dong Viet Nam or Lao Dong) created as a substitute for the Indochinese Communist Party.

**1954**

May 7: Defeat of French at Dien Bien Phu.

July 7: Ngo Dinh Diem, appointed premier of the State of Vietnam by Bao Dai, arrives in Saigon.

July 21: Geneva Accords signed. Agreements call for cessation of hostilities in Indochina and withdrawal of French and Viet Minh to either side of a provisional demarcation zone (DMZ) in Vietnam pending reunification elections to be held by 20 July 1956.

Sept. 8: In reaction to the Geneva Accords, interpreted by Washington as a setback, Secretary of State Dulles orchestrates creation of the Southeast Asia Treaty Organization (SEATO) through the Manila Pact. A protocol extends the security arrangement over Laos, Cambodia, and southern Vietnam.

Oct. 24: President Eisenhower writes to Ngo Dinh Diem pledging U.S. support and military aid, thus reaffirming U.S. commitment to maintaining a non-Communist government in Saigon.

**1955**

United States steps up direct aid to Saigon government and training of Saigon army.

Oct. 26: Ngo Dinh Diem defeats Bao Dai in rigged election, proclaims the Republic of Vietnam and becomes its first president. The United States immediately recognizes his government.

**1956**

July 20: Deadline for Vietnam reunification elections provided by Geneva Accords passes.

**1958**

Guerrilla activities spread in southern Vietnam.

**1959**

April 4: Eisenhower speech linking U.S. vital interests to survival of a non-Communist state in South Vietnam.

**1960**

Nov. 11–13: Saigon military coup against Diem fails.

Dec. 20: Formation of National Front for the Liberation of South Vietnam (NLF), usually called the "Viet Cong" by Saigon and Washington.

**1961**

Jan.: President John F. Kennedy approves secret military plans for Vietnam and Laos, sends Vice-President Lyndon Johnson (May) and General Maxwell Taylor (Oct.) to Saigon, and pledges increased aid to Saigon (Dec.).

May: Kennedy discloses sending Special Forces to southern Vietnam and approves clandestine warfare against the North and a secret war in Laos.

Dec. 31: Total U.S. military personnel in Vietnam reaches 3,200.

**1962**

Feb. 8: U.S. sets up the Military Assistance Command, Vietnam (MACV) under General Paul D. Harkins.

Dec. 31: U.S. strength in Vietnam reaches 11,300.

Saigon and Washington promote strategic hamlet program started in Sept. 1961.

**1963**

Jan. 2: NLF forces defeat much larger and better equipped Saigon (ARVN) troops at Ap Bac in the Mekong Delta.

June 11: Buddhist monk (Thich Quang Duc) commits suicide by self-immolation in Saigon to dramatize opposition to Diem regime. Part of growing Buddhist opposition.

Nov. 1: Ngo Dinh Diem and his brother, Ngo Dinh Nhu, assassinated in military coup led by General Tran Van Don and General Duong Van Minh with knowledge and approval of Kennedy administration.

Nov. 22: John F. Kennedy assassinated. Lyndon Johnson becomes president and assures Saigon of continued U.S. support (23 Nov.).

Dec. 31: U.S. military strength in Vietnam at 15,000. During 1963, $500 million in U.S. aid given to Saigon and 489 Americans killed or wounded.

**1964**

Jan. 30: General Nguyen Khanh seizes power in military coup in Saigon with prior U.S. approval. Khanh appoints self as premier and deposes General Duong Van Minh as chief of state (8 Feb.).

Aug. 2: In a largely exaggerated and fabricated report, the United States claims North Vietnamese torpedo boats attacked U.S. destroyers in Gulf of Tonkin.

Aug. 7: Congress passes Gulf of Tonkin Resolution allowing President Johnson to escalate U.S. involvement without declaring war. Senate vote: 88–2; House vote: 416–0.

Dec. 19: First U.S. nationwide protests against the war.

Dec. 31: About 23,000 U.S. troops in a full-scale undeclared war in southern Vietnam.

**1965**

Jan. 1, Feb. 7: NLF inflicts heavy casualties on ARVN and U.S. installations at Binh Gia and Pleiku.

Feb.: In retaliation, Johnson orders sustained bombing campaign against North Vietnam. Operation Rolling Thunder will continue from 2 March 1965 until 31 Oct. 1968.

April 17: Students for a Democratic Society (SDS) organize first national antiwar demonstration in Washington, D.C.

June: After a series of coups and countercoups, Air Vice Marshal Nguyen Cao Ky becomes premier with General Nguyen Van Thieu as head of state of the eighth Saigon government since Diem was overthrown.

Dec. 31: U.S. military strength in Vietnam at 184,300.

**1966**

Escalation of U.S. bombing and military buildup throughout year.

March: 50,000 in antiwar march in Central Park. Demonstrations organized throughout the year.

Sept. 1: President Charles de Gaulle of France, speaking in Cambodia, urges U.S. withdrawal of its forces from Vietnam before settlement possible.

Dec. 31: U.S. troops in southern Vietnam at 389,000, plus 60,000 offshore and 33,000 in Thailand. During the year 5,008 Americans were killed and 30,093 wounded. The war has become the dominant event in world affairs.

**1967**

April 4: Martin Luther King, Jr., delivers his "Beyond Vietnam" speech at Riverside Church, New York.

April 15: Hundreds of thousands march in New York and San Francisco in largest peace demonstrations so far in U.S. history. Draft cards are burned by 175 men.

July 30: A Gallup poll shows that 52 percent of Americans disapprove of the Vietnam war policy of the United States.

Sept. 3: In rigged election, Nguyen Van Thieu is elected president and Nguyen Cao Ky vice-president in South Vietnam.

Oct. 16–21: Antidraft demonstrations throughout United States, with largest at the Army Induction Center in Oakland, California.

Oct. 21–22: About 100,000 war protesters march on Pentagon.

Dec. 31: U.S. military strength in Vietnam reaches 475,000. U.S. costs for the year: about $21 billion; 9,353 dead; 99,742 wounded.

**1968**

Jan. 31: Tet offensive begins as NLF and Northern forces launch major attacks on southern cities and towns.

Feb.–March: General William Westmoreland requests additional 206,000 troops. Clark Clifford, succeeding Robert McNamara as secretary of defense, and other "wise men" advise Johnson against further escalation.

March 16: Massacre of hundreds of villagers in the hamlet of My Lai-4.

Aug.: Antiwar demonstrations during Democratic National Convention in Chicago.

Oct. 31: Johnson orders halt to bombing of North Vietnam.

Nov. 5: Richard M. Nixon elected president.

Dec. 31: The United States has 540,000 troops in Vietnam. Largest and costliest year of U.S. war: $30 billion; 14,314 killed; 150,000 wounded.

**1969**

Jan. 25: First substantial session of Paris peace talks with representatives of the DRV ("North Vietnam"), the RVN ("South Vietnam"), the southern NLF, and the United States.

March 6: U.S. forces reach peak of 541,000 troops in Vietnam.

May 14: Richard Nixon announces Vietnam peace offer of simultaneous withdrawal of U.S. and northern forces from the South and in June announces the beginning of withdrawal of 25,000 U.S. troops.

July 23: Nixon in Guam presents the "Nixon Doctrine" of economic and military aid rather than direct involvement of U.S. combat ground forces.

June 25: NLF forms Provisional Revolutionary Government.

Sept. 3: President Ho Chi Minh, 79, dies; collective leadership chosen in Hanoi.

Oct. 15: Millions of people participate throughout the United States in the largest antiwar demonstrations in U.S. history.

Nov. 15: In largest single antiwar demonstrations, approximately 1,000,000 people participate in Washington and San Francisco demonstrations protesting Nixon's Vietnamization.

Dec. 31: U.S. troop strength down to 479,500.

**1970**

April 30: Nixon announces sending U.S. combat troops into Cambodia, setting off hundreds of antiwar demonstrations.

May 4: Four students killed at Kent State University (Ohio) by National Guard and on 14 May two students killed at Jackson State College (Mississippi). Demonstrations and strikes at most campuses in the United States.

June 24: Senate repeals Gulf of Tonkin Resolution.

Dec.: U.S. troop strength in Vietnam is 339,200. Paris peace talks end second year without progress.

Nixon's Vietnamization policy and air war during 1969 and 1970 caused the most death and destruction of the entire war.

## 1971

March: Saigon forces, with U.S. air support, invade Laos to interdict supply routes down Ho Chi Minh Trail, but suffer major defeat.

March 29: Lieutenant William Calley convicted of premeditated murder of civilians at My Lai.

June 13: *New York Times* begins publication of the *Pentagon Papers*.

Oct. 3: Thieu reelected president of South Vietnam in one-candidate election.

Dec.: U.S. troop strength in Vietnam at 160,000. Vietnamization is not working and Paris talks remain stalled.

## 1972

March 30: Northern troops (PAVN) cross DMZ in coordination with major NLF offensive throughout the South. This is their first major ground offensive since 1968.

April 15: Nixon authorizes heavy bombing in vicinity of Hanoi and Haiphong. Air war carried out all over Vietnam.

May 1: Northern forces capture Quang Tri.

May 8: Nixon orders mining of Haiphong and other northern ports and blockade of supplies for the North.

Aug. 11: U.S. withdraws last combat unit from Vietnam, but 44,000 U.S. troops remain in the South.

Oct. 8: Peace talks between Le Duc Tho and Henry Kissinger continue in Paris throughout the year and finally produce a tentative settlement of the war, but Thieu rejects the proposed settlement (22 Oct.).

Dec. 18–31: Nixon orders "Christmas bombing," including B-52 raids in Hanoi-Haiphong area; 30,000 tons of bombs dropped on North Vietnam, the most concentrated single air offensive of the war.

## 1973

Jan. 8–18: Kissinger and Le Duc Tho reach an agreement similar to the one previously rejected by Thieu.

Jan. 27: Representatives of Hanoi, Saigon, the PRG, and Washington sign peace accords in Paris, providing hope that longest war in U.S. history has ended, but warfare continues until 1975.

Feb.–March: U.S. draft ended; 590 American POWs released by North Vietnam; last U.S. troops leave Vietnam (March 29).

## 1974

Jan.–May: Cease-fire of Jan. 1973 breaks down. Saigon's ARVN conducts offensive operations. Intense fighting in Central Highlands and west of Saigon.

Aug.: NLF decides to launch major counterattack against Saigon's military aggression.

Aug. 9: President Nixon resigns; replaced by Gerald Ford, who pardons Nixon (8 Sept.).

Dec.: Hanoi authorizes its armed forces (PAVN) to join revolutionary NLF forces in the South in launching a major offensive against Thieu's forces in 1975.

**1975**

Jan.–April: Through a combination of attacks by the PAVN and internal uprisings, Saigon loses control over all key cities and towns.

April 21: Thieu resigns, turns government over to Tran Van Huong, who transfers power to General Duong Van Minh (28 April).

April 30: Evacuation of remaining 1,000 Americans from Saigon and beginning of evacuation of 130,000 Vietnamese, many to settle in the United States.

April 30: Liberation of Saigon, marking end of war. President Minh surrenders unconditionally as PAVN/PRG victoriously enter and occupy Saigon. Three million Vietnamese have been killed and 10 million made refugees.

May 4: Khmer Rouge attack Vietnamese islands.

May 16: U.S. imposes embargo against Vietnam.

June 12: Vietnam occupies Cambodian island.

**1976**

July 2: National unification as the Socialist Republic of Vietnam (SRV) with its capital at Hanoi.

Sept.: International Monetary Fund and Asian Development Bank recognize SRV as a new member.

Dec. 14–20: Fourth National Congress of the Communist Party of Vietnam (CPV), previously known as the Vietnam Workers Party. Premier Pham Van Dong outlines Second Five-Year Plan (1976–1980). Le Duan elected secretary-general of the CPV.

**1977**

Jan.–Dec.: Border disputes escalate between Democratic Kampuchea (Cambodia) and the SRV. Khmer Rouge launches attack on Vietnamese villages (30 April); attacks Vietnamese village, killing hundreds of civilians (24 Sept.). Vietnam launches attack on Cambodia (25 Dec.).

Jan. 21: President Jimmy Carter pardons most of the 10,000 draft resisters.

Feb. 24: Peking tells Vietnam it is unable to give new aid.

May 3: U.S.-Vietnam normalization talks begin in Paris.

July: Decision on collectivization of agriculture in the South.

July 18: "Friendship and Cooperation Treaty" signed between Vietnam and Laos.

Sept. 20: SRV becomes the 149th member of the United Nations.

Dec. 31: Cambodia severs diplomatic relations with Vietnam.

**1978**

March 24: Vietnam begins its campaign to clamp down on "compradors," the majority of whom are ethnic Chinese.

June 29: SRV joins the Council for Mutual Economic Assistance (CMEA or Comecon), the Soviet economic bloc.

July: SRV relations with China deteriorate. Termination of all Chinese economic aid (3 July).

Oct. 11: President Carter decides to shelve plans to normalize relations with Vietnam pending establishment of full-scale diplomatic relations with China (15 Dec.).

Nov. 3: Treaty of Friendship and Cooperation signed between Vietnam and USSR. Friendship pact attacked by China.

Dec. 25: Vietnam launches invasion of Cambodia.

**1979**

Jan. 7: Phnom Penh falls to the Vietnamese with the overthrow of the regime of Democratic Kampuchea (Pol Pot).

Jan. 28: Deng Xiaoping arrives in Washington; plans to teach a "lesson" to Vietnam.

Feb. 17–March 19: Chinese invasion of Vietnamese provinces bordering China.

Feb. 18: Peace, Friendship and Cooperation Treaty signed between SRV and People's Republic of Kampuchea.

**1980**
Dec. 18: New constitution adopted by Vietnam's National Assembly.

**1982**
Vietnam begins a gradual pull-out of its troops from Cambodia.
March: National Congress of the Communist Party decides to streamline the government and further decentralize and liberalize the economy.
Nov. 11: Vietnam Veterans Memorial unveiled in Washington, D.C.

**1985**
New census shows that Vietnam has population of 59.8 million; 26 percent are salaried workers, half of whom are government employees.
Sept: Price, wage, and currency reform. Food subsidies abolished, state sector wages raised, inflation results.

**1986**
July 10: Death of Le Duan, 79, the Communist Party's secretary general since 1960.
Dec. 15–18: Sixth Party Congress in Hanoi. Three Politburo leaders (Truong Chinh, Pham Van Dong, and Le Duc Tho) step down but retain advisory positions. Nguyen Van Linh elected general secretary.

**1987**
April 19: Election of 496 persons for Eighth National Assembly.
Sept. 2: National Day amnesty for 6,685 prisoners.
Dec. 23–29: Second session of Eighth National Assembly passes important laws on land use, foreign investment, and import-export taxes as well as a draft criminal code. Foreign companies allowed to establish wholly owned enterprises in Vietnam.

**1988**
April 5: Politburo resolution on renovation of economic management in agriculture.
Vietnam withdraws half of its remaining 100,000 troops from Cambodia.

**1989**
Sept.: Remaining Vietnamese troops withdrawn from Cambodia.
Inflation is reduced to 35 percent compared with 700 percent in 1988.
Staple production increases to 21 million metric tons in rice equivalent. Vietnam exports 1.5 million metric tons of rice, making it the third largest rice exporter in the world.

**1990**
April: Demonstrations in Ho Chi Minh City by overseas Vietnamese, most of whom return from United States posing as tourists. Nguyen Van Thieu, now living in United States, announces that he is ready to lead a liberation movement against Vietnam.
May: A number of former members of the NLF and Saigon's antiwar movement, such as Father Chan Tin, Father Nguyen Ngoc Lan, and student leader Huynh Tan Mam, are detained by Vietnamese government for advocating a multiparty system.
Sept.: Secretary General Nguyen Van Linh, Prime Minister Do Muoi, and former Prime Minister Pham Van Dong travel to Beijing to work on improving relations with China.
Oct. 17: In first such meeting since 1975, Foreign Minister and Deputy Prime Minister Nguyen Co Thach meets with Secretary of State James Baker 3rd in Washington, D.C., to discuss major stumbling blocks to normalization of relations.
Oct. 22: The European Community (EC) decides to establish full diplomatic relations with Vietnam, the most important diplomatic step between the two since 1975.

Nov. 22–25: Prime Minister Do Muoi and Thailand's Prime Minister Choonhavan Chatichai sign treaties on trade protection and taxes, an important step in development of relations between Vietnam and ASEAN.

**1991**

Jan. 2: The Council of Government issues corporate and commercial laws, including right of citizens to establish or participate in private companies enjoying the same rights as economic operations in other sectors.

Jan. 7: Abu Hassam Omar, foreign minister of Malaysia, speaking before a meeting of ASEAN representatives in Kuala Lumpur, urges that Vietnam be admitted to the organization.

## CAMBODIA

**1863**

A French protectorate is established over Cambodia. Siam (Thailand) takes control of the northwestern provinces of Battambang and Siem Reap.

**1884**

French troops are sent to Phnom Penh, forcing King Norodom to sign a convention making Cambodia a colony of France.

**1887**

Cambodia becomes part of the French Indochinese Union, which includes Laos and the three so-called "countries" of Tonkin, Annam, and Cochin China.

**1940**

The French colonial government agrees to Japanese occupation of Indochina.

**1941**

King Monivong dies. The French pass over his son and choose nineteen-year-old Sihanouk of the Norodom branch of the royal family as next king because they thought he was more pliable and cute. "Qu'il est mignon, ce petit!" the wife of the French Governor Jean Decoux had exclaimed, looking at Sihanouk when he was invited to lunch at the governor's palace in Saigon.

Thailand annexes Battambang and Siem Reap provinces with Japanese assistance.

**1945**

Japanese forces surrender. Collaborationist Son Ngoc Thanh leads a coup, arrests all pro-French ministers, and declares himself premier. Subsequently Thanh is arrested. His supporters flee to Thailand and form the Khmer Issarak (Khmer Independence) movement.

**1946**

France grants Cambodia autonomous state status within the French union.

Thailand returns Battambang and Siem Reap provinces to Cambodia by terms of the Washington Conference of 1946.

**1950**

The United States establishes diplomatic relations with Cambodia. Sihanouk takes a stronger stance against the activities of the Indochinese Communist Party in Cambodia.

**1951**

The Indochinese Communist Party breaks up into three separate revolutionary national parties for Cambodia, Laos, and Vietnam, respectively, partly in order to counter the propaganda that the Vietnamese revolutionaries are seeking to dominate all of Indochina.

Sept.: The Khmer People's Revolutionary Party (KPRP) is set up. Its provisional executive committee is composed of 1,800 locally born Vietnamese and 150 Khmers.

**1952**

Antigovernment activity from both Communists and non-Communists increases; Sihanouk takes emergency powers.

**1953**

Jan.: The twenty-five-year-old Saloth Sar, later known by his *nom de guerre* of Pol Pot, returns after three years in Paris. He asks to join the KPRP, showing a membership card of the French Communist Party, which he obtained as a student at the École de Radio-Électricité in Paris.

France agrees to Sihanouk's call for independence in order to free their hands in dealing with the Vietnamese revolutionaries. Sihanouk begins efforts to oust Viet Minh forces. The United States offers him aid.

**1954**

Under pressure from the Chinese and Soviet delegates to the Geneva Conference on Indochina, the Vietnamese revolutionaries are forced to accept temporary partition of Vietnam and give up the claims of the Khmer Issarak–liberated areas to the Royal Government of Cambodia led by Sihanouk. The Khmer Issarak is ordered to disband. Some two thousand Khmer resistance fighters withdraw to northern Vietnam. Ultranationalistic French-educated Communists such as Pol Pot, Ieng Sary, and Son Sen, accuse the Vietnamese of sacrificing the gains made by Khmers during the anti-French resistance as they attempt to gain control of the Khmer revolutionary movement.

**1955**

Sihanouk abdicates throne, competes in national elections, wins overwhelming victory. Sihanouk and China reach understanding for peaceful coexistence and no foreign bases.

**1956**

Thailand and Saigon impose blockade of Cambodia in retaliation for Sihanouk signature of aid agreement with China. The United States suspends aid.

**1958**

Khmer Serei (Free Cambodia) movement organized, principally by Son Ngoc Thanh and Sam Sary, with CIA, Thai, and Saigon aid.

Sihanouk announces a neutralist policy.

**1959**

Bangkok Plot exposed, calling for anti-Sihanouk invasion from Thailand by Khmer Serei forces and creation of new opposition political party. United States, Thailand, and Saigon implicated in plot.

**1960**

Sihanouk made chief of state for life as a result of a national referendum.

Sept.: Samouth, a monk-turned-Communist who had close ties with the Vietnamese revolutionaries, is named party secretary of the KPRP. Pol Pot, then a schoolteacher in Phnom Penh, is elected to be the deputy secretary in 1961.

**1961**

Thailand accuses Cambodia of giving sanctuary to Communist elements that seek to subvert the rest of Southeast Asia. Saigon persecutes Cambodian minority, resulting in stream of refugees fleeing to Cambodia.

**1962**

July: Samouth mysteriously disappears, and Pol Pot takes over the responsibilities of secretary of the clandestine KPRP. Soon after, Pol Pot, his brother-in-law Ieng Sary, and others flee to the jungle to reorganize the party. They are not heard of again until 1970.

Aug.: Sihanouk asks President Kennedy for guarantee of Cambodia neutrality or he will turn to China if the United States refuses.

**1963**

Cambodia protests continued Saigon discrimination against Cambodian ethnic minority in Vietnam and repression of Vietnamese Buddhists; diplomatic relations broken. Khmer Serei increases activity against Sihanouk with help from Saigon, Thailand, and the CIA. Sihanouk cancels U.S. aid agreements; Pentagon reacts by calling for intervention in Cambodia.

**1964**

USSR and France ask U.S. support for declaration of Cambodian neutrality. U.S. refuses unless Cambodia first resolves its differences with its neighbors.

**1965**

May: U.S. planes attack two Cambodian border villages, prompting Sihanouk to break ties with Washington; in June, Sihanouk expresses his support for the South Vietnam National Liberation Front with a gift of medical aid.

The Vietnamese are grateful for Sihanouk's support, and in the summer when Pol Pot pays a secret visit to Hanoi on his way to China—where he stays for five months during the height of the Cultural Revolution—the Vietnamese advise him to support Sihanouk's anti-imperialist foreign policy.

Oct.: U.S. planes destroy another Cambodian village.

Nov.: Sihanouk announces conditions for renewed relations with the United States: cessation of military incursions, recognition of Cambodian territorial integrity, indemnity for losses caused to life and property.

**1966**

Vietnamese revolutionaries organize a unit designated as P-36 to support the Cambodian Communist Party and train their fighters. Pol Pot's *Black Book* later claims, however, that by 1966 "there was a fundamental contradiction between the Cambodian revolution and the Vietnamese revolution. The Vietnamese wanted to put the Cambodian revolution under their thumb."

**1967**

The United States hires members of the Khmer Serei for covert missions in Cambodia.

April: Pol Pot decides to found a revolutionary army to fight against the Sihanouk regime, which he considers feudal.

Sihanouk sends army against the Communist rebels, which he terms the Khmer Rouge (Red Khmer) and continues his military action to counter Khmer Serei attacks still being mounted from Thailand and South Vietnam.

June: Cambodia establishes diplomatic relations with Hanoi and offers to renew relations with Thailand if borders are recognized.

Sept.–Oct.: Sihanouk accuses China of imperialism and internal interference in Cambodia and threatens to seek aid from the United States.

Nov.–Dec.: The United States continues to refuse to recognize existing borders and upholds border incursions by U.S. army "in hot pursuit."

**1968**

Jan.: Khmer Rouge guerrillas begin a sporadic campaign of ambushing, kidnapping, and executing government forces and government officials. The Vietnamese party is embarrassed and annoyed by this development. But Sihanouk is not aware of rift between the two parties and so he blames Hanoi and Peking for fomenting the conflict.

**1969**

April: Cambodia offers to reestablish diplomatic relations with the United States in exchange for recognition of its territorial integrity. The United States states that it recognizes and respects the sovereignty, neutrality, and territorial integrity of Cambodia, but its planes continue to bomb border regions with Sihanouk's blessings.

Aug.: U.S. embassy reopens in Phnom Penh. New cabinet formed under General Lon Nol.

**1970**

March: While Sihanouk is in Europe, Premier and Defense Minister Lon Nol sanctions the sacking of the embassies of Hanoi and the NLF purportedly to protest the presence of Vietnamese troops in Cambodia. Sihanouk is blamed for allowing the Vietnamese sanctuaries and is deposed in a coup led by Lon Nol and Prince Sirik Matak, the leading right-wing leaders in Cambodia. The United States recognizes and supports the Lon Nol regime.

Sihanouk arrives in Peking but neither Zhou Enlai nor Pol Pot, who is in Peking at the time, takes any initiative to win Sihanouk to the side of the resistance. Three days after the coup Vietnam Prime Minister Pham Van Dong leads a secret high-level delegation to Peking to persuade Zhou and Pol Pot to welcome Sihanouk. After meeting with Dong, Sihanouk launches an appeal for resistance. By the end of March hundreds of Cambodians are trained and armed by Vietnamese, forming a Sihanoukist army known as Khmer Rumdo (Liberation Khmers.)

April: During negotiations in Hanoi, Pol Pot turns down a Vietnamese suggestion that a mixed military command be set up.

May: With the blessing of Lon Nol, the United States launches military assaults into Cambodia purportedly to wipe out the Viet Cong and North Vietnamese sanctuaries. More than 50,000 "allied" forces are involved and massive B-52 bombardment destroys most of the villages in the border areas.

July 30: Senate passes Cooper-Church Amendment barring further U.S. military operations in Cambodia and aid to Lon Nol without congressional approval.

Sept.: According to a CIA report in September, Khmer Rouge troops fire on Vietnamese Communist forces from behind while the latter are attacking a Lon Nol unit in Kompong Thom.

**1971**

Jan. 1: U.S. Congress bars use of U.S. combat troops, but not air power, in Laos and Cambodia.

**1972**

The simmering tension between the Vietnamese and the Khmer Rouge reaches a crisis in late 1972 when, during the final stage of the Vietnamese-U.S. peace talks in Paris, the Vietnamese relay Henry Kissinger's demand that the Khmer Rouge negotiate with Lon Nol. Pol Pot rejects the idea scornfully, saying that the Lon Nol regime is on its last legs and a quick victory could come easily. Vietnam warns the Khmer Rouge that their refusal would bring heavy punishment from the United States, but Pol Pot sees this warning as a blackmail attempt.

**1973**

Feb.–Aug.: U.S. bombers drop 257,500 tons of bombs on Cambodia—50 percent more than the total tonnage dropped on Japan during World War II.

After the Paris Agreement the Khmer Rouge attack Vietnamese arms depots, hospitals, and base camps in Cambodia on a regular basis. The attacks are explained away by the Pol Pot group as stemming from misunderstanding and unruly behavior by lower-level soldiers.

July 16: U.S. Senate Armed Services Committee begins hearings on secret bombing of Cambodia, and the United States stops bombing Cambodia (14 Aug.).

By the end of the year reports of armed clashes between the Khmer Rumdo and the Khmer Rouge come out more frequently.

**1974**

Aug.: Ten Hanoi-trained cadres in eastern Cambodia are eliminated by Pol Pot.

Sept.: Ninety of one hundred cadres returned from Hanoi are executed in southwestern Cambodia.

**1975**

April 17: Phnom Penh falls to the Khmer Rouge.

May 4: Khmer Rouge attack Vietnamese islands.

June 12: Vietnam occupies Cambodian island in retaliation.

Aug. 18: China pledges massive economic aid to visiting Cambodian delegation.

**1976**

Feb. 6: China signs secret military aid agreement totaling over one billion in U.S. dollars with Cambodia.

April 14: Democratic Kampuchea, a new government headed by Pol Pot, is announced.

**1977**

April 30: Khmer Rouge launches an attack on Vietnamese villages.

Sept. 24: Khmer Rouge attacks Vietnamese village, killing hundreds of civilians.

Sept. 28: Pol Pot begins triumphant tour of China.

Nov. 21: Vietnam Communist Party chief Le Duan visits Beijing in effort to disengage China from Khmer Rouge.

Dec. 3: Chinese vice-premier Chen Yonggui visits Cambodia.

Dec. 25: Vietnam attacks Cambodian border area.

Dec. 31: Cambodia severs diplomatic relations with Vietnam.

**1978**

Feb. 5: Hanoi proposes cease-fire and negotiation with Cambodia.

Nov. 5: Chinese delegation visits Cambodia.

Dec. 15: U.S.-Chinese normalization is announced; agreement with Vietnam on normalization is scuttled.

Dec. 25: Vietnam launches invasion of Cambodia.

**1979**

Jan. 7: Phnom Penh falls to the Vietnamese. A new Cambodian government is formed with Heng Samrin as president and, subsequently, with Hun Sen as prime minister.

Jan. 14: Secret Thai-Chinese meeting to support guerrilla war against the Vietnamese in Cambodia.

**1982**

Under pressure by ASEAN and the United States, the Coalition Government of Democratic Kampuchea is formed. It includes three parties: the Democratic Kampuchea group led by Pol Pot, Ieng Sary, and Khieu Samphan; the Khmer People's National Liberation Front led by Son Sann; and the Sihanouk group.

Vietnam begins a gradual phaseout of its troops.

**1988**

Vietnam pulls out half of its remaining troops in an effort to start a peace process, but leaves behind about 50,000 in Cambodia.

**1989**

Sept.: All Vietnamese troops are withdrawn. But peace negotiation in Paris breaks down over U.S., Chinese, and Sihanouk's insistence that the Phnom Penh government should disband itself before elections to form a quadripartite coalition government that includes the Khmer Rouge.

**1990**

July 18: Secretary of State James A. Baker III announces that the United States would no longer support the Khmer Coalition seat at the United Nations and asks Vietnam to put pressure on the Phnom Penh government to accept neutrally conducted elections to decide the political future of Cambodia.

Aug. 6: Officials from the United States and Vietnam meet in New York to discuss settlement of the conflict.

Aug. 12: Prime Minister Hun Sen of Cambodia expresses hope that the United States will talk directly to his government on ending the long war in his country.

Oct. 23: U.S. House and Senate vote to end all covert assistance to the noncommunist resistance in Cambodia, while approving a $20 million aid package to benefit citizens of Cambodia.

Dec. 23: Cambodia's four warring factions approve most proposals of a United Nations peace plan, including provisions for a cease-fire and free elections. Approval becomes snagged over proposal to demobilize and disarm Cambodian national army and three oppositional guerrilla groups.

**1991**

Jan. 17–20: The Central Committee of the Kampuchean People's Revolutionary Party, at its twelfth plenary session, expresses desire to normalize relations with Thailand and other ASEAN countries and improve relations with China.

## LAOS

**1893**

Franco-Siamese treaty establishing French control over Laos is signed.

**1899**

In northern Laos a revolt breaks out and is only brought under control with the death of the Tai Lu chieftain in 1910.

**1900**

The French choose Vientiane as their administrative capital. From 1901 to 1919 there are many revolts against French rule.

**1935**

The Indochinese Communist Party in Laos, which came into being in 1930, is reorganized. Its executive committee includes mostly ethnic Vietnamese and only one ethnic Lao. Due to French policy, the majority of the population in the urban centers of Laos is now ethnic Vietnamese.

**1941**

Japan forces France to cede all Laotian territories west of the Mekong to Thailand.

**1945**

March: After Japan seizes all administrative power from the French, Crown Prince Savang Vatthana responds by calling on the name of King Sisavang Vong for a popular uprising against the Japanese.

After Japan is defeated, Prince Phetsarath, as prime minister, declares Laos independence. French agents arrive in Luang Prabang and the king responds by reaffirming the French protectorate and dismissing his prime minister. A Provisional People's

Assembly meeting in Vientiane votes to depose the king and establish a government known as the Lao Issara (Free Laos). A defense force is established under the command of Phetsarath's younger half-brother Souphanouvong, with the assistance of the Vietnamese government of Ho Chi Minh.

**1946**

All negotiations with the French fail although the king is reinstated as a constitutional monarch.

March: French forces begin their attacks from southern Laos. By May, Laos is in French hands, and the Lao Issara government goes into exile in Thailand.

**1947**

Jan.: Thailand officially restores to Laos those territories on the west bank of the Mekong that it had annexed with Japan's support in 1941.

In southern Laos, the Committee of Lao Resistance in the East, which is a coalition of various groups, is formed to carry on anti-French resistance. One of the main leaders is Kaysone Phomvihane.

**1949**

Jan.: Kaysone founds the first regular unit in the Army of Free Laos, forerunner of the Lao People's Liberation Army (LPLA).

Because the majority of the Lao leaders in Lao Issara decide to accommodate the French, the provisional government of Laos in Bangkok is dissolved.

Aug.: Souphanouvong announces the formation of the Lao Liberation Committee dedicated to continuing anti-French resistance.

**1950**

Jan.: The United States and the United Kingdom recognize the Lao government.

Aug.: First Congress of People's Representatives of the Lao Resistance Front appoints a Lao resistance government of the "Land of the Lao"—or *Pathet Lao* (PL)—with Souphanouvong as prime minister and minister of foreign affairs and Kaysone Phomvihan as minister of defense.

**1951**

Nov.: Souvana Phouma, elder half-brother of Souphanouvong, forms his first government in Vientiane with the avowed aim of working toward national reconciliation.

**1954**

May 7: French defeated in Vietnam. The following day the Geneva conference on Indochina opens.

Agreement is reached among the various Lao parties to negotiate for a coalition government.

**1955**

The clandestine Lao People's Party (LPP) and its broad political front organization, the Lao Patriotic Front (LPF) (Neo Lao Hak Sat), are formed. The LPF operates as a political party with its statutes submitted and approved by the Royal Lao Government (RLG).

**1956**

Souvana is again prime minister of the RLG.

**1957**

Nov.: First coalition government is established with Souphanouvong as minister of planning, reconstruction, and urbanization. The United States is the only major power that expresses dissatisfaction over formation of the new government.

**1958**

May: Supplementary elections are held for twenty-one new seats in the National Assembly. LPF candidates win nine seats and their allies in the Santiphap (Peace) Party another four. Right-wing parties suffer a severe defeat.

Right-wing groups with U.S. backing oust Prime Minister Souvana Phouma and replace him with the staunchly anticommunist government of Phoui Sananikone. Phoui removes all LPF ministers, denies LPF deputies any further political role, and allies his government closely with the United States and SEATO.

**1959**

Royal Lao Army–directed repression against LPF is stepped up. LPF deputies imprisoned.

July: Guerrilla warfare resumed throughout the country.

U.S. military aid and personnel, including Special Forces troops, pour into Laos.

**1960**

In a blatantly rigged election, the U.S. CIA installs its own people in a newly formed government of the extreme right, thus foreclosing all possibility of compromise with the Pathet Lao and opening the way for civil war.

Aug.: A young paratroop captain named Kong Le stages a coup and makes Souvanna Phouma prime minister again.

Dec.: With U.S. dollars, material, and training, Phoumi Nosavan builds up his military and political forces and begins to move against Vientiane. Kong Le, Souvanna, and members of his government move north to the Plain of Jars. Laos henceforth has two governments.

**1961**

Jan.–March: Kong Le and Souvanna Phouma forces, in alliance with the Pathet Lao, seize the offensive and threaten the Phoumi Nosavan government.

April: United States accepts reconvening of Geneva Conference, after opposing it for months, as a means of avoiding total collapse of Phoumi Nosavan regime.

**1962**

July: Geneva Accords signed, by which Laos is to be neutralized. A tripartite coalition government with "neutralist" Souvanna Phouma as prime minister is to be established. Foreign forces are to be withdrawn. Pending integration of the army and police, a de facto partition is to be in effect in Laos.

Anti-Communists retain control of government, army, police, and finances. "Neutralist" Souvanna Phouma decides to cooperate with Americans and right wing while Vang Pao's Meo mercenaries, trained by the CIA behind the de facto partition, continue to receive U.S. support and training in direct violation of the Geneva Accords.

**1963**

Outbreak of conflict between pro-Souvanna/Kong Le "neutralists" and dissident "neutralists" who disagree with Phouma's cooperation with the Americans.

**1964**

May: The United States begins air raids against Pathet Lao forces on the Plain of Jars. The PL takes control of the Plain of Jars.

**1965**

Conflict among right-wing factions in Vientiane for control of government.

**1966**

Jan.: Thai infantry and artillery, backed by the United States, are engaged in Laos against the Pathet Lao and dissident neutralists.

Nov.: Kong Le resigns and leaves Laos in protest against integration of "neutralists" and right-wing forces.

**1968**

U.S. air raids increase tenfold in PL-populated areas.

**1969**

Aug.: CIA-backed Meo tribesmen take Plain of Jars from PL.

**1970**

Feb.: PL takes back Plain of Jars. Effectiveness of the Meo army is virtually destroyed. The United States then evacuates 20,000 progovernment civilians and Meo mercenaries and begins to bomb systematically the Plain of Jars and PL territory, resulting in about 600,000 refugees or about a quarter of the country's population.

June: Pathet Lao announces the capture of the last government-fortified town, Mong-Bua, in the crucial Saravane area of Laos.

**1971**

Attempt by the United States and Saigon forces to cut the Ho Chi Minh Trail at Highway 9 in southern Laos ends in a total rout.

**1972**

The PL steps up pressure for a political settlement by offering to engage in negotiations with the RLG without preconditions. The offer is accepted by Souvanna and negotiations begin in Vientiane in October.

**1973**

Feb. 21: The Agreement on the Restoration of Peace and Reconciliation in Laos is signed.

Sept. 14: The protocol establishing the third coalition government is signed.

**1974**

April 5: New Provisional Government of National Union (PGNU) and policymaking National Political Consultative Council (NPCC) are sworn in. Prince Souvanna heads the PGNU and Prince Souphanouvong presides over the NPCC.

May 22: Thailand withdraws the last of its troops from Laos.

May 24: NPCC unanimously adopts a far-ranging eighteen-point political program specifically calling for the United States to pay reparations for damages from the war.

June 3: United States pulls its last military personnel out of Laos, one day before the deadline for the exit of all foreign military personnel.

**1975**

Jan.: Souvanna Phouma bans all demonstrations nationwide.

May 1: Twenty-one Organizations for Peace demonstrate in Vientiane and demand the ouster of Sisouk Na Champassasak, the defense minister, and other rightist cabinet members.

May 9: Resignations of the leading rightists announced. Five leading Force Armée Royale generals also leave for Thailand.

Aug.: PL revolutionary committees take power in Vientiane on thirtieth anniversary of the uprising at the end of World War II. Two hundred thousand reportedly celebrate.

Dec.: Proclamation of the Lao People's Democratic Republic (LPDR) in Vientiane.

**1976**

Almost 20,000 lowland Lao flee the country because of the new harsh economic conditions. Consumer prices rise at rate of 400 percent.

**1977**

July 18: Twenty-five-year Treaty of Friendship and Cooperation between Laos and Vietnam is formalized, accompanied by a three-year economic assistance agreement.

Economic situation improves; inflation now rises less than 50 percent toward end of year.

July–Nov.: Thailand imposes de facto blockade on transshipment of goods to Laos.

**1978**

A total of about 500–600 Soviet personnel are estimated to be in Laos.

China continues road construction in the northern areas and reportedly keeps 15,000 laborers on hand for such work.

May: Political decision made to press ahead with rapid cooperativization of agriculture. Economic effects of this decison are disastrous. Cooperativization is not preceded by land reform. Opposition to cooperativization is widespread.

A total of about 50,000 lowland Lao flee to Thailand, more than twice the total number in 1977; many of them are peasants mainly from southern Laos.

**1979**

Mid-July: The cooperativization program is terminated on the advice of Premier Alexei Kosygin and high-ranking Vietnamese leaders.

Nov.: Central Committee of the Party decides to carry out an economic reform in the direction of "market socialism." This reform document is known as the Seventh Resolution.

**1980**

It is evident by the end of the year that the reforms are having the desired effects. Food and consumer goods are freely available in markets. Rice production reaches 1 million metric tons of paddy.

**1981**

An ambitious first Five-Year Plan is adopted.

**1982**

The government is reorganized on three levels in the efforts to liberalize the economy and decentralize the administrative decisionmaking process.

**1983**

Corruption is on the rise, perhaps as a result of more opportunities. A number of vice-ministers are arrested and tried.

The Supreme Court is established.

**1984**

Laos protests continuing incursions by Thai military.

**1985**

Feb.: Remains of thirteen U.S. MIAs are recovered at a crash site and identified in a joint mission.

Aug.: According to an interview with the president of the Lao United Buddhist Association, Maha Thongkhoune Annantasounthope, there are now 6,897 monks and 9,415 novices in Laos living in 2,812 *wats*.

**1986**

Jan.: A high-ranking United States delegation, jointly led by assistant secretaries of the state and defense departments, visits Vientiane.

Nov.: Fourth Party Congress of the Communist Party of Laos convenes and authorizes more economic liberalization.

**1987**

A small war breaks out along the southern border with Thailand.

**1988**

A liberal investment code is promulgated, allowing for continued existence of various forms of economic activities and particularly encouraging development of joint ventures and capitalist organizations.

Jan.: Relations with China are normalized and ambassadors exchanged.

**1989**

March: In the first national election since 1975, voters elect 79 members to the Lao Supreme People's Assembly from a field of 121 candidates.

May: Meeting of the Lao Supreme People's Assembly, the country's first elected national legislative body since 1975.

**1990**

May: Following approval by the Lao People's Revolutionary Party in April, a draft constitution is promulgated for nationwide discussion. Various freedoms are protected, but opposition parties and political activity against the government are not.

Oct. 23: U.S. Congress allocates funds for Laos and Cambodia for humanitarian assistance, the first time since 1975 in Laos and 1979 in Cambodia that the United States has provided aid money.

Dec. 2: Huge public meeting held in Vientiane to celebrate fifteenth anniversary of the establishment of the People's Democratic Republic of Laos.

**NOTES**

Major sources for this chronology are Archimedes L. A. Patti, *Why Viet Nam: Prelude to America's Albatross* (Berkeley: University of California Press, 1980); Stanley Karnow, *Vietnam: A History* (New York: Viking Press, 1983); Nayan Chanda, *Brother Enemy: The War After the War* (New York: Harcourt Brace Jovanovich, 1986); David G. Marr and Christine P. White, eds., *Postwar Vietnam: Dilemmas in Socialist Development* (Ithaca, NY: Southeast Asia Program, Cornell University, 1988); George Donelson Moss, *Vietnam: An American Ordeal* (Englewood Cliffs, NJ: Prentice-Hall, 1990).

# Selected Bibliography

**VIETNAM**

Beresford, Melanie. *Vietnam: Politics, Economics and Society.* London: Pinter, 1988.

Brender, Joel Osler, and Erwin Randolph Parsons. *Vietnam Veterans: The Road to Recovery.* New York: Plenum Press, 1986.

Burchett, Wilfred. *Catapult to Freedom: The Survival of the Vietnamese People.* London: Quartet Books, 1978.

———. *Vietnam Will Win.* New York: International Publishers, 1969.

———. *Vietnam North.* New York: International Publishers, 1966.

———. *Vietnam: Inside Story of the Guerrilla War.* New York: International Publishers, 1965.

Buttinger, Joseph. *Vietnam: The Unforgettable Tragedy.* New York: Horizon, 1977.

———. *A Dragon Defiant: A Short History of Vietnam.* New York: Praeger, 1972.

Chanda, Nayan. *Brother Enemy: The War After the War, A History of Indochina Since the Fall of Saigon.* New York: Macmillan, Collier Books, 1986.

Dacy, Douglas C. *Foreign Aid, War, and Economic Development: South Vietnam, 1955–1975.* London: Cambridge University Press, 1986.

Davidson, Phillip. *Vietnam at War: The History, 1946–1975.* Novato, CA: Presidio Press, 1988.

Dittmar, Linda, and Gene Michaud, eds. *From Hanoi to Hollywood: The Vietnam War in American Film.* New Brunswick, NJ: Rutgers University Press, 1991.

Duiker, William. *Vietnam: Nation in Revolution.* Boulder, CO: Westview Press, 1983.

———. *Vietnam Since the Fall of Saigon.* Athens: Ohio University, Center for International Studies, 1980.

Ehrhart, W. D., ed. *Carrying the Darkness: American Indo-China—The Poetry of the Vietnam War.* New York: Avon, 1985.

Emerson, Gloria. *Winners and Losers.* New York: Random House, 1977.

Fforde, Adam. *The Agrarian Question in North Vietnam, 1974–1979.* New York: M. E. Sharpe, 1989.

Fforde, Adam, and Stefan de Vylder. *Vietnam—An Economy in Transition.* Stockholm: Swedish International Development Authority, 1988.

FitzGerald, Frances. *Fire in the Lake: The Vietnamese and the Americans in Vietnam.* New York: Random House, 1972.

---

This selected bibliography on Indochina contains only books in English. We would like to thank Michael Vickery and Carol and Randall Ireson for suggesting Cambodia and Laos items. Under the Vietnam bibliography, we have listed several books by U.S. Vietnam veterans and have excluded Vietnam anthologies and the many works of fiction about the war.

Gibson, James William. *The Perfect War: The War We Couldn't Lose and How We Did.* New York: Vintage Books/Random House, 1988.

Hammer, Ellen J. *A Death in November: America in Vietnam, 1963.* New York: E. P. Dutton, 1987.

_____ . *The Struggle for Indochina, 1940–1955.* Palo Alto, CA: Stanford University Press, 1966.

Hammer, Richard. *One Morning in the War: The Tragedy at Son My.* New York: Coward-McCann, 1970.

Harrison, James Pinckney. *The Endless War: Fifty Years of Struggle in Vietnam.* New York: Free Press, 1982.

Herring, George C. *America's Longest War: The United States and Vietnam, 1950–1975.* New York: Alfred A. Knopf, 1986.

Hersh, Seymour M. *Cover-up: The Army's Secret Investigation of the Massacre at My Lai 4.* New York: Random House, 1972.

Hosmer, Stephen, et al. *The Fall of South Vietnam: Statements by Vietnamese Military and Civilian Leaders.* Santa Monica, CA: Rand Corporation, 1978.

Huynh Kim Khanh. *Vietnamese Communism, 1925–1945.* Ithaca, NY: Cornell University Press, 1986.

Issacs, Arnold R. *Without Honor: Defeat in Vietnam and Cambodia.* Baltimore: Johns Hopkins University Press, 1983.

Kahin, George McT. *Intervention: How America Became Involved in Vietnam.* New York: Alfred A. Knopf, 1986; Anchor Books, 1987.

Karnow, Stanley. *Vietnam: A History.* New York: Viking Press, 1983.

Kerry, John, and Vietnam Veterans Against the War. *The New Soldier.* Edited by David Thorne and George Butler. New York: Macmillan, 1971.

Kimura, Tetsusabureo. *Vietnam: International Relations and Economic Development.* Tokyo: Institute of Developing Economies, 1986.

_____ . *The Vietnamese Economy, 1975–86.* Tokyo: Institute of Developing Economies, 1989.

Kolko, Gabriel. *Anatomy of a War: Vietnam, the United States, and the Modern Historical Experience.* New York: Pantheon, 1985.

Lewy, Guenther. *America in Vietnam.* New York: Oxford University Press, 1978.

Marr, David G. *Vietnamese Anti-Colonialism, 1885–1925.* Berkeley: University of California Press, 1971.

Marr, David G., and Christine P. White, eds. *Postwar Vietnam: Dilemmas in Socialist Development.* Ithaca, NY: Cornell University Southeast Asia Program, 1988.

Melling, Philip H. *Vietnam in American Literature.* Boston: Twayne Publisher, 1990.

Moise, Edwin E. *Land Reform in China and North Vietnam.* Chapel Hill: University of North Carolina Press, 1983.

Moss, George Donelson. *Vietnam: An American Ordeal.* Englewood Cliffs, NJ: Prentice Hall, 1990.

Murray, Martin J. *The Development of Capitalism in Colonial Indochina (1870–1940).* Berkeley: University of California Press, 1980.

Ngo Vinh Long. *Before the Revolution: The Vietnamese Peasants Under the French.* Cambridge, MA: MIT Press, 1973.

Ngo Vinh Long and Nguyen Hoi-Chan. *Vietnamese Women in Society and Revolution.* Cambridge, MA: Vietnam Resource Center, 1974.

Nguyen Khac Vien. *Tradition and Revolution in Vietnam.* Berkeley, CA: Indochina Resource Center, 1974.

Nguyen Thi Dinh. *No Other Road to Take.* Ithaca, NY: Cornell University Southeast Asia Project, 1976.

Norman, Michael. *These Good Men: Friendships Forged from War*. New York: Crown Publishers, 1990.

Patti, Archimedes L.A. *Why Viet Nam? Prelude to America's Albatross*. Berkeley: University of California Press, 1980.

*The Pentagon Papers. New York Times* edition, 1 vol. New York, 1971.

*The Pentagon Papers*. Senator Gravel edition, 5 vols. Boston: Beacon Press, 1971.

Pike, Douglas. *PAVN: People's Army of Vietnam*. Novato, CA: Presidio, 1986.

———. *War, Peace and the Viet Cong*. Cambridge, MA: MIT Press, 1969.

Porter, Gareth. *The Myth of the Bloodbath: North Vietnam's Land Reform Program Reconsidered*. Ithaca, NY: Cornell University Press, 1975.

———. *A Peace Denied: The United States, Vietnam, and the Paris Agreements*. Bloomington: Indiana University Press, 1975.

Race, Jeffrey. *War Comes to Long An: Revolutionary Conflict in a Vietnamese Province*. Berkeley: University of California Press, 1972.

Schell, Jonathan. *The Real War*. New York: Pantheon, 1988. This is the republication of Schell's *The Village of Ben Suc* (Random House, 1967) and *The Military Half: An Account of Destruction in Quang Ngai and Quang Tin* (Alfred A. Knopf, 1968) with a new introductory essay.

Severo, Richard, and Lewis Milford. *The Wages of War: When America's Soldiers Come Home—From Valley Forge to Vietnam*. New York: Simon and Schuster, 1989.

Sheehan, Neil. *A Bright Shining Lie: John Paul Vann and America in Vietnam*. New York: Random House, 1989.

Snepp, Frank. *Decent Interval*. New York: Random House, 1977.

Starr, Paul. *The Discarded Army: The Veterans After Vietnam. The Nader Report on Vietnam Veterans and the Veterans Administration*. New York: Charterhouse, 1973.

Tran Van Tra. *Vietnam: History of the Bulwark B-2 Theater, Vol. 5: Concluding the 30-Years' War*. Ho Chi Minh City: Van Nghe Publishing House, 1982. Trans. into English and published in the U.S. in *Southeast Asia Report*, No. 1247, JPRS 82783, 2 February 1983, by Foreign Broadcast Information Service.

Trullinger, James W. *Village at War*. New York: Longman's, 1981.

Truong Nhu Tang. *A Viet Cong Memoir: An Inside Account of the Vietnam War and Its Aftermath*. New York: Vintage Books, 1986.

Turley, William S. *The Second Indochina War: A Short Political and Military History, 1954–1975*. Boulder, CO: Westview Press, 1986.

———, ed. *Vietnamese Communism in Comparative Perspective*. Boulder, CO: Westview Press, 1980.

Van Tien Dung. *Our Great Spring Victory: An Account of the Liberation of South Vietnam*. New York: Monthly Review Press, 1977.

Vickerman, Andrew. *The Fate of the Peasantry: Premature "Transition to Socialism" in the Democratic Republic of Vietnam*. New Haven: Yale University Southeast Asia Series, 1980.

Vo Nhan Tri. *Vietnam's Economic Policy Since 1975*. Singapore: Institute of Southeast Asian Studies, 1990.

Warner, Denis. *Certain Victory: How Hanoi Won the War*. Kansas City: Sheed Andres and McMeed, 1977.

Weigersma, Nancy. *Vietnam, Peasant Land, Peasant Revolution*. New York: St. Martin's Press, 1988.

Woodside, Alexander B. *Community and Revolution in Vietnam*. Boston: Houghton Mifflin, 1976.

Young, Marilyn. *The Vietnam Wars, 1945–1990*. New York: Harper/Collins, 1991.

## CAMBODIA

Ablin, David A., and Marlowe Hood, eds. *The Cambodian Agony*. Armonk, NY: M. E. Sharpe, Inc., 1987.

Becker, Elizabeth. *When the War Was Over*. New York: Simon and Schuster, 1986.

Briggs, Lawrence Palmer. *The Ancient Khmer Empire*. Transactions of the American Philosophical Society, New Series, vol. 41, part 1. Philadelphia: The American Philosophical Society, 1951.

Burchett, Wilfred. *Mekong Upstream*. Berlin: Seven Seas Publishers, 1959.

Burgler, R. A. *The Eyes of the Pineapple*. Nijmegen Studies in Development and Cultural Change 3. Saarbrucken–Fort Lauderdale: Verlag Breitenbach Publishers, 1990.

Carney, Timothy. *Communist Party Power in Kampuchea (Cambodia): Documents and Discussion*. Ithaca, NY: Cornell University Press, 1977.

Chandler, David P. *A History of Cambodia*. Boulder, CO: Westview Press, 1983; 2nd ed. forthcoming.

———. *Pol Pot: A Political Biography*. Boulder, CO: Westview Press, 1991.

———. *The Tragedy of Cambodian History: Politics, War and Revolution Since 1945*. New Haven: Yale University Press, 1991.

Chandler, David P., and Ben Kiernan, eds. *Revolution and Its Aftermath in Kampuchea: Eight Essays*. New Haven: Yale University Southeast Asia Studies, 1983.

Chandler, David P., Ben Kiernan, and Chanthou Boua, eds. *Pol Pot Plans the Future*. New Haven: Yale University Southeast Asia Studies, 1988.

Ebihara, May Mayko. "Svay, a Khmer Village in Cambodia." Ph.D. diss., Columbia University, 1968.

Evans, Grant, and Kelvin Rowley. *Red Brotherhood at War*. London: Verso, 1984.

Kiernan, Ben. *How Pol Pot Came to Power*. London: Verso, 1984.

———. *The Samlaut Rebellion and Its Aftermath, 1967–70: The Origins of Cambodia's Liberation Movement*, Parts I-II, in Monash University, Center of Southeast Asian Studies, Working Papers, Nos. 4 and 5, n.d. (1975–1976).

Kiernan, Ben, and Chanthou Boua. *Peasants and Politics in Kampuchea, 1941–1981*. London: Zed Press, 1982.

Jackson, Karl, ed. *Cambodia, 1975–1978: Rendez-vous with Death*. Princeton: Princeton University Press, 1989.

Khieu Samphan. *Cambodia's Economy and Industrial Development*. Translated by Laura Summers. Ithaca, NY: Cornell University Southeast Asia Program Data Paper No. 111, 1979.

Lanchester, Donald. *Emancipation of French Indo-China*. New York: Oxford University Press, 1961.

Osborne, Milton E. *Before Cambodia*. London: Allen and Unwin, 1979.

———. *Politics and Power in Cambodia*. Hawthorn, Australia, 1973.

———. *The French Presence in Cochinchina and Cambodia: Rule and Response (1859–1905)*. Ithaca, NY: Cornell University Press, 1969.

Ponchaud, Francois. *Cambodia Year Zero*. New York: Holt, Rinehart and Winston, 1978.

Reddi, V. M. *A History of the Cambodian Independence Movement, 1863–1955*. Tirupatti, India, 1971.

Shawcross, William. *Sideshow: Nixon, Kissinger and the Destruction of Cambodia*. New York: Simon and Schuster, 1979. Touchstone Books, 1987.

———. *The Quality of Mercy*. New York: Simon and Schuster, 1984.

Someth May. *Cambodian Witness*. New York: Random House, 1987.

Vickery, Michael. *Kampuchea: Politics, Economics and Society*. London: Frances Pinter, and Boulder, CO: Lynne Rienner Publishers, 1986.

_____ . *Cambodia: 1975–1982*. Boston: South End Press, 1984.

## LAOS

Adams, Nina S., and Alfred W. McCoy, eds. *Laos: War and Revolution*. New York: Harper & Row, 1970.

Barber, Martin John Philip. "Migrants and Modernisation: A Study of Change in Lao Society." Ph.D. diss., University of Hull, 1979.

Brown, MacAlister, and Joseph J. Zasloff. *Apprentice Revolutionaries: The Communist Movement in Laos, 1930–1985*. Stanford, CA: Hoover Institution Press, 1986.

De Berval, Rene, ed. *Kingdom of Laos*. Saigon: France-Asie, 1959.

Dommen, Arthur J. *Laos: Keystone of Indochina*. Boulder, CO: Westview Press, 1985.

_____ . *Conflict in Laos: The Politics of Neutralization*, rev. ed. New York: Praeger, 1971.

Evans, Grant. *Lao Peasants Under Socialism*. New Haven: Yale University Press, 1990.

Goldstein, Martin E. *American Policy Toward Laos*. Teaneck, NJ: Fairleigh Dickinson University Press, 1973.

Gunn, Geoffrey C. *Political Struggles in Laos (1930–1954)*. Bangkok: Editions Duang Kamol, 1988.

Hannah, Norman B. *The Key to Failure: Laos and the Vietnam War*. New York: Madison Books, 1988.

Kaysone Phomvihane. *Revolution in Laos*. Moscow: Progress Publishers, 1981.

Langer, Paul F., and Joseph J. Zasloff. *North Vietnam and the Pathet Lao*. Cambridge, MA: Harvard University Press, 1970.

Schell, Jonathan. *The Time of Illusion*. New York: Vintage, 1975.

Stuart-Fox, Martin, ed. *Contemporary Laos: Studies in the Politics and Society of the Lao People's Democratic Republic*. St. Lucia, Australia: University of Queensland Press, and New York: St. Martin's Press, 1982.

_____ . *Laos: Politics, Economics and Society*. London: Frances Pinter, and Boulder, CO: Lynne Rienner Publishers, 1986.

Thee Marak. *Notes of a Witness: Laos and the Second Indochinese War*. New York: Random House, 1973.

Toye, Hugh. *Laos: Buffer State or Battleground*. New York: Oxford University Press, 1968.

Viravong, Maha Sila. *History of Laos*. Trans. from Lao by U.S. Joint Publications Research Service. New York: Paragon Book Reprint Co., 1964.

Wyatt, David K., ed. *Iron Man of Laos: Prince Phetsarath Ratanavongsa*. Trans. by John B. Murdoch. Ithaca, NY: Cornell Southeast Asia Program Data Paper no. 110, 1978.

_____ , ed. *Lao Issara: The Memoirs of Oun Sananikone*. Trans. by John B. Murdoch. Ithaca, NY: Cornell Southeast Asia Program Data Paper no. 100, 1975.

Zasloff, Joseph J. *The Pathet Lao*. Lexington, MA: D.C. Heath and Co., 1973.

# About the
# Book & Editors

Despite the plethora of works on the Vietnam War, this is the first book to present an accessible overview from both the Indochinese and antiwar perspectives. The authors trace the prewar history, war years, and postwar experiences of Vietnam, Cambodia, and Laos before turning to the U.S. experience, where they focus on government policies, the antiwar movement, veterans, and films and literature on Vietnam. Those who experienced the war era will find their memories vividly rekindled; those who wish to learn more about Indochina, the war, and its aftermath will find these issues provocatively discussed and analyzed.

**Douglas Allen,** professor of philosophy at the University of Maine, is an editor of *Bulletin of Concerned Asian Scholars* and specializes in the phenomenology of religion (myth, symbolism, interpreting meaning), Hinduism and Buddhism, and political philosophy (especially Marxism). He is the author of *Structure and Creativity in Religion, Mircea Eliade: An Annotated Bibliography* (coauthored with Dennis Doeing), *Mircea Eliade et le phénomène religieux,* and the forthcoming *Religion and Political Conflict in South Asia* and *Mircea Eliade on Myth.* **Ngo Vinh Long,** assistant professor of history at the University of Maine, is also an editor of *Bulletin of Concerned Asian Scholars* and teaches Chinese, Japanese, and Southeast Asian history, with specializations in peasant studies and agricultural development. He is author of *Before the Revolution: The Vietnamese Peasants under the French* (reissued with a new introduction in 1991). Recent publications include "Communal Property and Peasant Revolutionary Struggles in Vietnam," *Peasant Studies* 17 (Winter 1990).

# Index